Video Verification in the Fake News Era

Vasileios Mezaris · Lyndon Nixon ·
Symeon Papadopoulos · Denis Teyssou
Editors

Video Verification in the Fake News Era

 Springer

Editors
Vasileios Mezaris
Centre for Research and Technology Hellas
Information Technologies Institute
Thermi, Thessaloniki, Greece

Lyndon Nixon
MODUL Technology GmbH
MODUL University Vienna
Vienna, Austria

Symeon Papadopoulos
Centre for Research and Technology Hellas
Information Technologies Institute
Thermi, Thessaloniki, Greece

Denis Teyssou
Agence France-Presse
Paris, France

ISBN 978-3-030-26754-4   ISBN 978-3-030-26752-0   (eBook)
https://doi.org/10.1007/978-3-030-26752-0

This Springer imprint is published by the registered company Springer Nature Switzerland AG
The registered company address is: Gewerbestrasse 11, 6330 Cham, Switzerland

Preface

The digital media revolution is bringing breaking news to online video platforms, and news organizations often rely on user-generated recordings of breaking and developing events shared in social media to illustrate the story. However, in video there is also deception. In today's 'fake news' era, access to increasingly sophisticated editing and content management tools and the ease in which fake information spreads in electronic networks require the entire news and media industries to carefully verify third-party content before publishing it. This book presents the latest technological advances and practical tools for discovering, verifying and visualizing social media video content, and managing related rights. These are expected to be of interest to computer scientists and researchers, news and media professionals, and even policymakers and data-savvy media consumers.

The book is organized in four main parts. Part I presents the necessary Problem Statement, Part II covers the various Technologies that can contribute to video verification, Part III introduces three complete Applications that integrate several verification technologies and Part IV presents some Concluding Remarks.

Part I Problem Statement

The first step in addressing the problem of 'fake news', or disinformation, is to understand the problem. Chapter 1, 'Video Verification: Motivation and Requirements', attempts to introduce us to the peculiarities of the video verification problem by initially presenting the motivations of those involved in video verification, showcasing the respective requirements and highlighting the importance and relevance of tackling disinformation on social networks. Then, this chapter provides an overview of the state of the art of techniques and technologies for video verification. It also highlights the emergence of new threats, such as the so-called 'deep fakes'. Finally, the chapter concludes by formulating an empirical typology of false videos spreading online.

Part II Technologies

In this part of the book, Chaps. 2 through 8 present in-depth analyses of different technologies that contribute to video verification. Chapter 2, 'Real-Time Story Detection and Video Retrieval from Social Media Streams', starts one step before coming to verifying a specific video: it discusses how a journalist can detect emerging news stories online and find videos around that story, which may then require verification. The chapter starts by reviewing the prior research in the area of topic detection, and then presents a keyword-graph-based method for news story discovery out of Twitter streams. Subsequently, it presents a technique for the selection of online videos that are candidates for news stories, by using the detected stories to form a query against social networks. This enables relevant information retrieval at web scale for news-story-associated videos. These techniques are evaluated by observation of the detected stories and of the news videos that are presented for those stories, demonstrating how journalists can quickly identify videos for verification and reuse.

Chapter 3 focuses on 'Video Fragmentation and Reverse Search on the Web'. Such search is a first and simple, yet often very valuable, means for checking if a video under examination, or a slightly modified version of it, has appeared in previous times in the web and social sphere. Video reuse is in fact the 'easy fake': it does not take elaborate editing tools and effort to fake an event in this way; it suffices to fetch some older footage of, e.g. a terrorist attack or a plane crash from the web, and repost it claiming that this is happening right now, right before your eyes. Chapter 3 presents technologies for the fragmentation of a video into visually and temporally coherent parts and the extraction of a representative keyframe for each defined fragment that enables the provision of a complete and concise keyframe-based summary of the video; these keyframes can then be used for performing a fragment-level search for the video on the web. Following a literature survey on the topic, the chapter describes two state-of-the-art methods for video subshot fragmentation—one relying on the assessment of the visual coherence over sequences of frames, and another one that is based on the identification of camera activity during the video recording. It then goes on to present a web application that enables the fine-grained (at the fragment-level) reverse search for near-duplicates of a given video on the web, and evaluation results and conclusions about the effectiveness of these technologies as well as some thoughts on future developments.

Chapter 4, 'Finding Near-Duplicate Videos in Large-Scale Collections', sticks to the topic of detecting video reuse for combating the 'easy fakes' that we started to deal with in Chap. 3, but views this from a different—and complementary—perspective. In Chap. 3, we discussed web-scale search, which inevitably relies on the reverse image search functionalities that are offered by popular web search engines. The latter provide excellent coverage of the whole web, but on the other hand only allow us to deal with reverse video search in a 'quick and dirty' way: by searching for and matching just isolated keyframes. In Chap. 4, we deal with finding duplicate or near-duplicate videos (Near-Duplicate Video Retrieval—NDVR) in our own, closed collections of videos. This means that the coverage of the search is more limited (since we cannot index the whole web in the way that major web search engines do), but on the other hand we can do a much more elaborate and accurate search, because we have full control of the indexing and searching process. Thus, having indexed, for instance, a large number of web videos that show previous terrorist attacks and related content, if we want to check the possible prior use of an (allegedly) new terrorist attack video we can complement the web-scale search of Chap. 3 with a more accurate search in our own collection of such videos. As the main objective of a typical NDVR approach is, given a query video, to retrieve all near-duplicate videos in a video repository and rank them based on their similarity to the query, the chapter starts by reviewing the literature on this topic, and then goes on to present two methods for video-level matching. Extensive evaluation on publicly available benchmark datasets documents the merits of these approaches, and their complementarity to keyframe-based web-scale search.

Chapter 5, 'Finding Semantically-Related Videos in Closed Collections', takes the search for similar video content one step further. When trying to verify a video, and an associated news story, important cues can come from looking at the greater picture: what other videos out there (and thus also in our closed collection of videos, as long as we keep collecting videos related to specific, potentially news-worthy events, such as terrorist attacks) can support (or disprove) the claims made with the help of the specific video in question? For this, besides any near-duplicate videos (as discussed in Chaps. 3 and 4), we would like to detect semantically similar videos. That is, videos showing the same event/actors/activities from a different viewpoint or videos coming from the same source ('channel'—in the broad sense). In other words, we need to be able to organize any content that we collect from the web and social media sources. For this, we discuss two classes of techniques in this chapter: the detection of semantic concepts in video (a.k.a. the annotation of the video with semantic labels) and the detection of logos that are visible in videos and can help us to identify their provenance. Both classes of techniques rely on deep learning (deep neural networks), which is a learning paradigm that is considered to be a key element of Artificial Intelligence (AI). The chapter discusses the state of the art in these two sub-problems of video under-standing and presents two techniques developed by the authors of the chapter and their experimental results.

Chapter 6, 'Detecting Manipulations in Video', discusses another fundamental problem related to video verification: can we trust what we see? If an event really unfolded before our eyes, the answer would be yes. But if it is shown on video, how can we assess if the video is an accurate depiction of (some) reality or an alternate 'reality' whose capture in video was only made possible with the help of digital video editing tools? To answer this question, this chapter presents the techniques researched and developed within InVID for the forensic analysis of videos, and the detection and localization of forgeries. Following an overview of state-of-the-art video tampering detection techniques, the chapter documents that the bulk of current research is mainly dedicated to frame-based tampering analysis or encoding-based inconsistency characterization. The authors built upon this existing research, by designing forensics filters aimed to highlight any traces left behind by video tampering, with a focus on identifying disruptions in the temporal aspects of a video. Subsequently, they proceeded to develop a deep learning approach aimed to analyse the outputs of these forensics filters and automatically detect tampered videos. Experimental results on benchmark and real-world data, and analyses of the results, show that the proposed deep-learning-based method yields promising results compared to the state of the art, especially with respect to the algorithm's ability to generalize to unknown data taken from the real world. On the other hand, the same analyses also show that this problem is far from being resolved, and further research on it is in order.

Chapter 7, 'Verification of Web Videos Through Analysis of Their Online Context', continues in the direction of previous chapters, most notably Chap. 5, of looking at the greater picture for verifying a specific video. Contrary (and complementarily) to Chap. 5, though, we are not examining here other related videos that can help debunk the video under examination; instead, we are looking at the online 'context' of this video. The goal is to extract clues that can help us with the video verification process. As video context, we refer to information surrounding the video in the web and/or the social media platforms where it resides, i.e. information about the video itself, user comments below the video, information about the video publisher and any dissemination of the same video through other video platforms or social media. As a starting point, the authors present the Fake Video Corpus, a dataset of debunked and verified UGVs that aim at serving as reference for qualitative and quantitative analysis and evaluation. Next, they present a web-based service, called Context Aggregation and Analysis, which supports the collection, filtering and mining of contextual pieces of information that can serve as verification signals.

Chapter 8, 'Copyright Management of User Generated Video for Journalistic Reuse', concludes this part of the book on technologies, by considering what comes after a newsworthy piece of user-generated video is verified: how can the journalist use it in a legal way? For this, i.e. for reviewing the copyright scope of reuse of user-generated videos usually found in social media, for journalistic purposes, the starting point of this chapter is the analysis of current practices in the news industry. Based on this analysis, the authors provide a set of recommendations for social media reuse under copyright law and social networks terms of use. Moreover, they describe how these recommendations have been used to guide the development of the InVID Rights Management module, focusing on EU copyright law given the context of the InVID EU project.

Part III Applications

Chapter 9, 'Applying Design Thinking Methodology: The InVID Verification Plugin', kick-starts the presentation of integrated, complete tools for journalists who what to verify user-generated videos. It describes the methodology used to develop and release a browser extension which has become one of the major tools to debunk disinformation and verify videos and images, in a period of less than 18 months. This is a tool that combines several of the technologies discussed in Chaps. 2 through 8 in a free, easy-to-use package, which has attracted more than 12,000 users worldwide from media newsrooms, fact-checkers, the media literacy community, human rights defenders and emergency response workers dealing with false rumours and content.

Chapter 10, 'Multimodal Analytics Dashboard for Story Detection and Visualization', is the second tool presented in this part of the book. The InVID Multimodal Analytics Dashboard is a visual content exploration and retrieval system to analyse user-generated video content from social media platforms including YouTube, Twitter, Facebook, Reddit, Vimeo and Dailymotion. That is, it is not a tool for video verification, but rather a tool for discovering emerging newsworthy stories and related video content, which then may be verified (either using the InVID Verification plugin, presented in the previous chapter; or by directly transferring the video in question, with a click of a button, to the InVID Verification Application that will be discussed in the following chapter). The InVID Multimodal Analytics Dashboard uses automated knowledge extraction methods to analyse each of the collected postings and stores the extracted metadata for later analyses. The real-time synchronization mechanisms of the dashboard help to track information flows within the resulting information space. Cluster analysis is used to group related postings and detect evolving stories, which can be analysed along multiple semantic dimensions— e.g. sentiment, geographic location, opinion leaders (persons or organizations) as well as the relations among these opinion leaders. The result can be used by data journalists to analyse and visualize online developments within and across news stories.

Chapter 11, 'Video Verification in the Newsroom', comes as a natural extension of both Chap. 9 (which presented a first tool for the exact same problem: video verification) and Chap. 10, whose Multimodal Analytics Dashboard provides a direct, one-click link for importing newsworthy videos detected with the latter tool into the newsroom's video verification pipeline. The chapter starts by describing the integration of a video verification process into newsrooms of TV broadcasters or news agencies. The authors discuss the organizational integration concerning the workflow, responsibility and preparations as well as the inclusion of innovative verification tools and services into an existing IT environment. Then the authors present the InVID Video Verification Application or Verification App for short. This can be considered to be an 'InVID Verification plugin on steroids', i.e. a more complete and professional application for video verification, which can serve as a blueprint for introducing video verification processes in professional newsroom systems. This verification application, similarly to the InVID Verification plugin, combines several of the technologies discussed in Chaps. 2 through 8.

Part IV Concluding Remarks

The book concludes with Chap. 12, 'Disinformation: the Force of Falsity', which departs a bit from the primarily technology-oriented presentation in previous chapters, to engage in a more forward-looking discussion on how can we avoid the proliferation of fake videos, and stop them from spreading over and over again. This final chapter borrows the concept of force of falsity from the famous Italian semiotician and novelist Umberto Eco, to describe how manipulated information remains visible and accessible despite efforts to debunk it. It illustrates, with the help of real-life examples, how search engine indexes are getting confused by disinformation and they too often fail to retrieve the authentic pieces of content, the ones which are neither manipulated nor decontextualized. The chapter concludes with some further thoughts on how to address this problem.

Thessaloniki, Greece   Vasileios Mezaris
Vienna, Austria   Lyndon Nixon
Thessaloniki, Greece   Symeon Papadopoulos
Paris, France   Denis Teyssou
May 2019

Acknowledgements Most of the work reported throughout this book was supported by the European Unions Horizon 2020 research and innovation programme under grant agreement No 687786 'InVID: In Video Veritas—Verification of Social Media Video Content for the News Industry', 2016–2018.

Contents

Contributors

Evlampios Apostolidis Centre for Research and Technology Hellas, Information Technologies Institute, Thessaloniki, Greece;
School of Electronic Engineering and Computer Science, Queen Mary University, London, UK

Konstantinos Apostolidis Centre for Research and Technology Hellas, Information Technologies Institute, Thessaloniki, Greece

Albert Berga Universitat de Lleida, Lleida, Spain

Roger Cozien eXo maKina, Paris, France

Paloma de Barrón Private Law Department, Universitat de Lleida, Lleida, Spain

Daniel Fischl MODUL Technology GmbH, Vienna, Austria

Rolf Fricke Condat AG, Berlin, Germany

Roberto García Computer Science and Engineering Department, Universitat de Lleida, Lleida, Spain

Rosa Gil Computer Science and Engineering Department, Universitat de Lleida, Lleida, Spain

Max Göbel webLyzard technology gmbh, Vienna, Austria

Alexander Hubmann-Haidvogel webLyzard technology gmbh, Vienna, Austria

Ioannis Kompatsiaris Centre for Research and Technology Hellas, Information Technologies Institute, Thessaloniki, Greece

Giorgos Kordopatis-Zilos Centre for Research and Technology Hellas, Information Technologies Institute, Thessaloniki, Greece;
School of Electronic Engineering and Computer Science, Queen Mary University, London, UK

Foteini Markatopoulou Centre for Research and Technology Hellas, Information Technologies Institute, Thessaloniki, Greece

Grégoire Mercier eXo maKina, Paris, France

Alexandros I. Metsai Centre for Research and Technology Hellas, Information Technologies Institute, Thessaloniki, Greece

Vasileios Mezaris Centre for Research and Technology Hellas, Information Technologies Institute, Thessaloniki, Greece

Lyndon Nixon MODUL Technology GmbH, Vienna, Austria

Symeon Papadopoulos Centre for Research and Technology Hellas, Information Technologies Institute, Thessaloniki, Greece

Olga Papadopoulou Centre for Research and Technology Hellas, Information Technologies Institute, Thessaloniki, Greece

Ioannis Patras School of Electronic Engineering and Computer Science, Queen Mary University, London, UK

Gerard Rovira Universitat de Lleida, Lleida, Spain

Tobi Schäfer webLyzard technology gmbh, Vienna, Austria

Arno Scharl webLyzard technology gmbh, Vienna, Austria

Jochen Spangenberg Deutsche Welle, Berlin, Germany

Maria Teixidor Universitat de Lleida, Lleida, Spain

Denis Teyssou Agence France-Presse, Paris, France

Jan Thomsen Condat AG, Berlin, Germany

Markos Zampoglou Centre for Research and Technology Hellas, Information Technologies Institute, Thessaloniki, Greece

Part I
Problem Statement

Chapter 1
Video Verification: Motivation and Requirements

Denis Teyssou and Jochen Spangenberg

Abstract The production and spreading of manipulated videos have been on the rise over the past years, and is expected to continue and increase further. Manipulating videos have become easier from a technological perspective, and can be done with freely available tools that require less expert knowledge and fewer resources than in the past. All this poses new challenges for those who aim to tackle the spreading of false, manipulated or misleading video content. This chapter covers many of the aspects raised above. It deals with the motivations of those involved in video verification, showcases respective requirements and highlights the importance and relevance of tackling disinformation on social networks. Furthermore, an overview of the state of the art of available techniques and technologies is provided. The chapter then describes the emergence of new threats like so-called 'deep fakes' created with the help of artificial intelligence. Finally, we formulate an empirical typology of false videos spreading online.

1.1 Introduction

The rise of the smartphone and the convergence of affordable devices, powerful camera technology, ubiquitous mobile Internet access and social media platforms have enabled a massive growth of citizen and eyewitness-powered news coverage. As Malachy Browne, Senior Story Producer at the New York Times stated some years ago: 'one byproduct of this is an enormous amount of video being uploaded and shared every minute, every hour' [1].

Indeed, although Facebook has been facing criticism and regular complaints from advertisers for allegedly failing to disclose errors in its video viewership metrics [2], there is no doubt that video consumption, especially on mobile devices, is steadily

D. Teyssou (✉)
Agence France-Presse, Paris, France
e-mail: denis.teyssou@afp.com

J. Spangenberg
Deutsche Welle, Berlin, Germany
e-mail: jochen.spangenberg@dw.com

© Springer Nature Switzerland AG 2019
V. Mezaris et al. (eds.), *Video Verification in the Fake News Era*,
https://doi.org/10.1007/978-3-030-26752-0_1

on the rise. YouTube statistics of October 2018 reports more than one billion users of its video platform, with one billion hours watched daily, 70% of them on mobile devices.[1]

'The revolution in information technology is not over, and the volume of newsworthy user-generated content will only grow. Journalists have a new responsibility—to quickly gather, verify and ascertain the usage rights of UGC.[2] Traditional values of investigation apply, but a new skillset is required for media such as video', predicted Malachy Browne in the above-mentioned Verification Handbook, edited by Craig Silverman and published by the European Journalism Centre in 2014. He was right!

In journalism, the verification of information has been a commonplace activity for decades. It is part of the craft of journalism for everyone who takes the profession seriously. What is relatively new, however, for both newsrooms and journalists alike, is the rather systematic verification of third-party eyewitnesses digital information such as images or videos that are being shared and distributed via social platforms.

For media organisations, this meant 'crossing a Rubicon', as stated by the former Director of BBC News—now Professor of Journalism at Cardiff University—Richard Sambrook [3] during the London bombings of July 2005. 'Trapped in the London Underground, witnesses used their mobile phones to take pictures and make video recordings of the events as they unfolded. Unable to deploy journalists to the bombing sites, the BBC relied on eye-witness accounts and survivors' stories', as media scholar Valerie Belair-Gagnon pointed out [4].

Speaking on the same matter Helen Boaden, Director of BBC News from 2004 until 2013, said that during the London bombings, the scope and reach of user-generated content was greater than ever before. She stated that within 24 h, the Corporation received more than 1,000 pictures and videos, 3,000 text messages and 20,000 e-mails [5]. The amount of user-generated content in news stories was unprecedented: 'Twenty-four hour television was sustained as never before by contributions from the audience', explained Belair-Gagnon [4].

As hinted above: the digitisation of information, and especially the emergence of social networks, has resulted in fundamental changes when it comes to the gathering and spreading of information. Nowadays, it is possible (at least technically) for anyone to publish and distribute digital content with ease and speed to a potentially worldwide audience, and reach, potentially, millions of people. In turn, the so-called 'legacy media' (news agencies, traditional newspapers, magazines, broadcasters, etc.) are no longer the exclusive gatekeepers who decide what is being circulated to a wider audience, and what is not.

All this poses new challenges and brings up numerous issues that need to be addressed both by established and emerging media organisations as well as newsrooms, independent journalists and fact-checkers. The challenges are not an exclusive domain of the journalistic profession though: for example, human rights workers and emergency response personnel are also confronted with related tasks when it comes to assessing whether material that is being circulated digitally is right or wrong.

---

[1] https://www.youtube.com/intl/en/yt/about/press/.

[2] User-generated content.

To start with, let us outline some of the challenges that exist when it comes to the verification of digital content, focusing on video. According to sources such as the Verification Handbook [6] or the First Draft Visual Verification Guide for Video [7], issues include the following:

1. Identifying the video provenance (is it the original version of the video? Who captured the video?).
2. Verifying the source (who is the producer/uploader, and what can we find out about him/her?).
3. Locating the video (where was the video captured?).
4. Verifying the date (when was the video captured?).
5. Identifying what the video shows (why was the video captured?).

The above list provides a selection of aspects that need to be considered and addressed in the context of verification of digital content. In this introductory chapter, we will focus on a variety of aspects regarding the verification of digital video content. In particular, we will look at incentives for video verification, and look at corresponding needs and requirements, as well as solutions. Furthermore, we will portray some of the actions and activities that are being undertaken in the sphere. All this is to lay some foundations for what is to come in subsequent chapters, while we approach the issue from a broader perspective in this introductory chapter.

1.1.1 Who Verifies Video, Which Groups Are We Dealing With and Why Is This Important?

While anybody with an interest in video content is a potential verifier of such content, here we are limiting ourselves to a list of five groups of professionals (excluding the military, intelligence, law and enforcement sectors), namely:

1. Journalists (working in media organisations or on their own);
2. Fact-checkers (from media organisations, associations and fact-checking groups, e.g. from civil society, NGOs, etc.);
3. People working in the human rights sector (e.g. to document war crimes, crimes against humanity and such like);
4. People working in the emergency response sector (e.g. people working for relief agencies after natural disasters, accidents or catastrophes);
5. Media education scholars (people working on media literacy projects and respectively research, teach and lecture on the subject).

For all the above stakeholder communities, the verification of video content and dealing with related consequences are becoming more and more important for a variety of reasons. As also indicated above in the introduction, the consumption and popularity of online video content with consumers, in general, have been steadily on the rise, and is expected to grow further.

Next, most people these days are equipped with smartphones that can record, capture and share video content in steadily increasing quality. Then, data tariffs for uploading/sharing as well consuming online video content have gone down steadily as well, and are likely to go down even further ('flat fees', new networks from LTE to 5G, etc.).

All this means that what has happened in the text and image sector before will increasingly apply to video, too. And it has huge potential due to the attractiveness of video content. In other words, we will see more and more (high quality) video content being shared as well as consumed by ordinary citizens in the years to come. All this material, obviously, also has the potential to play an increasing role for

1. the newsgathering and reporting process (in the field of journalism);
2. the documenting of human rights abuses (in the human rights sector);
3. other sectors like the emergency response field.

1.1.2   The Value of Video Analysis

Having at your disposal (verified) video material can have tremendous value: it is a great asset for newsgathering and reporting, it can detect human rights abuses and violations, while it can also play a life-saving role in guiding emergency response operations.

Video material captured on any device and shared via social networks or by direct communication has thus opened up new avenues for all the above sectors and domains.

As stated previously, being able to verify and authenticate digital material that is being circulated (e.g. on social networks) is of paramount importance in order to avoid the spreading of false information and judgements or assessments based on the wrong foundations.

The availability of so-called 'Open Source Intelligence' (OSINT)[3] tools have particularly changed the verification sphere and respective possibilities profoundly.

The example below[4] is just one of many examples in which OSINT tools and meticulous desk research have exposed the truth behind a crime and human rights violation, which made headline news in numerous media outlets.

In the above case of the murder of two women and two young children in Cameroon, researchers/journalists of the BBC, Bellingcat and Amnesty International

---

[3] By OSINT we mean information and data that is gathered from public (or open) sources. OSINT tools are digital tools (software, platforms) that are freely available and facilitate research and investigations, such as satellite imagery to identify or cross-check a particular geographic location.

[4] ATTENTION: the video that is linked here includes graphic imagery that some people may find disturbing and/or painful to watch. Do not view unless you are prepared accordingly. In case of viewing the video (this also applies to other disturbing/traumatic imagery) and this having negative effects on you, do not hesitate to seek professional help.

Fig. 1.1 Screenshot of a BBC Africa Eye documentary in Cameroon; 24 Sep. 2018. Video available on YouTube: https://www.youtube.com/watch?v=XbnLkc6r3yc

supported by others were able to identify where exactly the crime took place, when this happened, and who was involved (and largely responsible) (Fig. 1.1).

Doing all the research using OSINT tools like satellite imagery, geo-tools or software that calculates the level of the sun at a given time anywhere in the world (here: suncalc), and other aids took considerable time and effort, as reporters dealing with the case have repeatedly pointed out.[5]

This is one use case in which technology significantly supports (and helps enable) the work of journalists as well as human rights personnel.

1.1.3 Tools/Platforms 'Made for Video Verification'

To date (in the first half of 2019, at the time of writing) there are not many tools available on the market that have been designed and developed with the specific purpose of verifying videos. Rather, people who are trying to determine the veracity of digital online videos (especially user-generated video) use a variety of different tools and platforms in combination, such as satellite imagery (e.g. Wikimapia, Google Earth Pro, Terra Server), reverse image search (e.g. Google Images, Tineye,

---

[5] See, for example, an interview with one of the reporters of the story, Aliaume Leroy, on CBC Radio Canada. The site includes a link to an 8-minute audio interview with Leroy about the team's work on the case: https://www.cbc.ca/radio/asithappens/as-it-happens-Monday-edition-1.4836241/how-bbc-africa-uncovered-the-story-behind-an-execution-video-of-women-and-children-1.4836248.

Yandex), geo-based search that helps in finding out more about particular locations (e.g. Echosec, Liveuamap, GeoNames), tools that provide more information about people/sources (e.g. Pipl, various directories), image forensic tools (e.g. FotoForensics and Forensically), metadata /Exif data viewers (e.g. Jeffrey's Exif Viewer) and so on.

A very comprehensive list of tools, called online investigation toolkit is maintained by investigative platform Bellingcat[6] and Christiaan Triebert[7] as a shared document[8] that is frequently updated by the user community.

One exception, i.e. a (basic) platform that has been built specifically for video analysis and verification, is Amnesty International's YouTube Data Viewer, launched in mid-2014. In a nutshell, it enables users to key in the URL of a YouTube video, and then let it automatically extract the correct upload time and all thumbnails associated with the video. The thumbnails can then be used to perform a reverse image search to see if identical images exist elsewhere online, especially with earlier upload times.

According to Christoph Koettl, Amnesty International's main architect behind the YouTube Data Viewer,[9] 'Many videos are scraped, and popular videos are re-uploaded to YouTube several times on the same day, so having the exact upload time helps to distinguish these videos ... and a reverse image search is a powerful way of finding other/older versions of the same video'.[10]

The YouTube Data Viewer thus became part of the standard kit of online verification experts and investigators dealing with assessing the credibility of online videos. It is however limited to the YouTube platform, and the thumbnails provided by this platform can be changed by the uploaders.

Then came InVID with its Verification Plugin. Obviously, the authors of this chapter are biased, as we have been involved in its development (with one of the authors, Denis Teyssou of AFP, being the main driver behind its development). Nevertheless, based on feedback obtained from the verification community,[11] it can be stated that the InVID Verification Plugin with its added features and functionalities nowadays provides journalists and human rights investigators with a very powerful and useful tool for video analysis. How it looks like exactly, and what functionalities are included, will be portrayed in Chap. 9 of this book.

---

[6]https://www.bellingcat.com/.

[7]https://twitter.com/trbrtc.

[8]https://docs.google.com/document/d/1BfLPJpRtyq4RFtHJoNpvWQjmGnyVkfE2HYoICKO GguA/edit.

[9]See https://citizenevidence.amnestyusa.org/.

[10]Christoph Koettl, quoted on Poynter in the article Amnesty International launches video verification tool, website, by Craig Silverman, 8 July 2014. https://www.poynter.org/news/amnesty-international-launches-video-verification-tool-website.

[11]Some user feedback has been collected in Twitter Moments here: https://twitter.com/i/moments/888495915610275840.

Fig. 1.2 Screenshot of a deep fake video by BuzzFeedVideo, 17 April 2018. Video available on YouTube: https://www.youtube.com/watch?v=cQ54GDm1eL0

1.1.4 A New Challenge: 'Deep Fakes'

Sadly, methods and ways to manipulate digital content (including video) and mislead audiences are becoming more and more sophisticated. A relatively new concept of faking (or manipulating) video is called 'deep fakes'.

Deep fakes involve the use of algorithms and artificial intelligence for face re-enactment, face swapping, lip-syncing and the synthetic mimicking of voices. In other words, movements of the mouth are transferred from one person (e.g. an actor) to the face and facial expressions of another person (in most cases, a celebrity). The same goes for voice. To fully understand this, it helps a lot to see deep fakes in action (as in the video example below, in which the words and lip movements of actor Jordan Peele are 'transported' to the face of Barack Obama) (Fig. 1.2).[12,13]

Researchers from the University of Erlangen-Nuremberg and the Max-Planck-Institute for Informatics in Europe, from Washington and Stanford University in the USA, in turn, demonstrated how comparatively easy it is to make a person say something convincingly—that is difficult to detect—that he or she never uttered in

---

[12]Deep fakes are particularly popular on Reddit. Apps (such as FakeApp) exist that allow users with little to no technical knowledge to create video manipulations—some of it amusing and rather creative. Inserting the actor Nicolas Cage into deep fake videos, in turn, has almost become its own sub-genre. Other usage 'scenarios'—besides celebrity manipulations—are (child) pornography, revenge porn, extortion and mis-/disinformation of various types.

[13]In the referenced video, Barrack Obama's mouth is lip-synced automatically. The words that seem to be spoken by Obama come from actor and film-maker Jordan Peele, who does an impression of the former US President. Obama (aka Peele) says things like 'This is a dangerous time. Moving forward, we need to be more vigilant with what we trust from the internet. This is a time when we need to rely on trusted news sources'. https://www.youtube.com/watch?v=cQ54GDm1eL0.

Fig. 1.3 Real-time facial re-enactment. Demonstrated by the University of Erlangen-Nuremberg, Max-Planck-Institute for Informatics, presented at CVPR 2016. Video available on YouTube: https://www.youtube.com/watch?v=ohmajJTcpNk

real life. All it takes is enough original video footage of that person (which exists in abundance with, e.g. prominent politicians or celebrities), train the respective algorithms accordingly, and set up the system and actors/speakers/'modellers' as required. How this is done is demonstrated in the video (Fig. 1.3).

Obviously, if manipulated videos like the ones showcased above do the rounds, and technology to alter them becomes even more sophisticated (and easily available), this will create even more suspicion with everything we watch. The dangers are obvious, especially as many would say that 'if something has been caught on (video) tape, it must be real'. To put it differently, sophistically manipulated videos will create a new kind of suspicion about everything we watch. Politicians as well as others with vested interests are likely to exploit this. At its worst, deep fakes can damage brands and careers, manipulate and impact the political process, and go as far as destroy people's lives or even cause wars.

This raises a whole set of questions, such as: will technical advances that allow for the fabrication of videos with ease destroy one of our remaining beliefs that we cannot even trust our eyes and ears any longer? Is there a need for (and chance of) a coordinated international effort to agree on norms of behaviour when it comes to this kind of manipulation technology?

On the other hand, it becomes obvious that what has been outlined above makes the need to develop and supply tools and technologies that allow for the detection of manipulations more important than ever.

Furthermore, it is not only technology that should be at the centre of attention here: what about regulation, ethics and a sort of—at least to some extent—common agreement about what we label and commonly refer to as 'reality'?

Sam Dubberley, Special Advisor to Amnesty International's Evidence Lab, adds another dimension. Asked about what worries him when it comes to verifying and analysing information, chasing the truth and what keeps him awake at night, Dubberley stated in an interview with one of the authors of this paper that it is 'the people who build these [deep fake] tools are doing so without an ethical framework'.[14] So apart from developing tools and services that help in detecting fakes and manipulations (as we do in InVID), it may be time to also bring this to the highest levels of the political agenda. Whether agreements on a supra-national level can be reached remains doubtful. It is nevertheless vital that everything possible is done in the fight against manipulations and distortion. Nothing less than democracy is at stake!

Although deep fakes were not part of the scope of the InVID project, we applied some of the technologies (especially fragmentation and reverse image search to be discussed in Chap. 3) to tackle this specific problem. We showed, for instance, that a deep fake video of Donald Trump allegedly asking Belgian people to withdraw from the Paris climate agreement (made by the Flemish Socialist Party in a campaign to mobilise citizens for the environment) was made by manipulating a previous video of Mr. Trump announcing strikes against Syria in retaliation for the use of chemical weapons against civilians by the Syrian regime, in a public address from the White House, on the 13 April 2018.[15]

1.1.5 Typology of Fake Videos

There are a variety of ways in which videos can be manipulated, or—in other (better) words—ways in which the audience can be deceived with video content.

To start with, a video can be actively manipulated. For example, video frames can be added or deleted, components can be inserted (e.g. via an overlay/insert) or even created by a computer as we just saw above. Examples abound,[16] from the Pope apparently performing a 'magic table cloth trick' (Fig. 1.4) during a visit to the US[17]

---

[14]Sam Dubberley, Special Advisor to Amnesty International's Evidence Lab (and an InVID project reviewer), interviewed by Jochen Spangenberg on 27 September 2018.

[15]https://www.slideshare.net/InVID_EU/invid-at-ifcn-global-fact-v.

[16]Here is a selection: https://youtu.be/ccENfRThXOk.

[17]Watch the (fabricated) video sequence here: https://youtu.be/1KFj6b1Xfe8?t=14. It was created for the US-based 'The Ellen Show'. Here https://youtu.be/ABy_1sL-R3s you can see the original video footage next to the manipulated version.

Fig. 1.4 Screenshot of manipulated video from the satirical 'The Ellen Show', showing Pope Francis miraculously 'pulling the cloth'

to an eagle apparently snatching a baby from a pram and 'taking it up high'[18] or a snowboarder being chased by a bear while going down a slope in Japan.[19]

Another way of deceiving audiences is by taking a video out of context, and distributing it with misleading captions. In such cases, the video is not actively manipulated, but instead presented as being something that it is not. For example, whenever there is a plane crash, videos (and images) from previous plane crashes very quickly make the rounds on social networks or certain websites. As video footage of plane crashes is still relatively rare, it is usually the same footage that appears again and again, whenever there is such an accident.[20]

Polarising topics like migration are often used for disinformation campaigns against migrants: a Russian news item about a drunk man assaulting nurses in a

---

[18]See the video here: https://youtu.be/Xb0P5t5NQWM. The video is the product of three students studying animation and digital design at Montreal's Centre NAD, as part of a digitised class project, not a real snatching. See also NPR update: 'Eagle Snatches Kid' Video Makers Admit Hoax, by Mark Memmott, 19 December 2012. https://www.npr.org/sections/thetwo-way/2012/12/19/167610327/eagle-snatches-kid-video-the-debunking-begins?t=1537977241104.

[19]See https://youtu.be/vT_PNKg3v7s for the video. Debunks here: https://youtu.be/lXmk-Bx XXhY, https://www.nationalgeographic.com/adventure/adventure-blog/2016/04/12/bears-really-do-chase-skiers-but-this-video-is-fake/ and https://www.snopes.com/fact-check/snowboarder-girl-chased-by-bear/.

[20]This video https://youtu.be/A-8Ig67O3ck of a plane crash of a US cargo Boeing 747 near Bagram Airfield, Afghanistan, in May 2013 is one such video. Whenever there is a new plane crash, this video (and others that capture previous plane crashes—of which there are not that many) are being shared and distributed pretending to be of the current plane crash. WARNING: some people may find watching the video distressing or disturbing, as it portrays a real plane crash that resulted in the loss of lives.

Novgorod hospital in February 2017 started to circulate 1 month later in various countries (France, Italy, Spain, Belgium, Turkey), copied and widely distributed on Facebook and Twitter, as allegedly being an assault perpetrated by a migrant in those respective countries.[21] More recently, an amateur video taken by a Czech tourist in Crete (Greece) was at the origin of a conspiracy theory accusing mainstream media of staging migrant arrivals on European beaches, while the scene was actually the making of a film about the 1922 Greek exodus from Asia Minor.[22]

The challenges for those working with video are thus to

1. detect fakes and manipulations as quickly and accurately as possible;
2. do so using traditional verification techniques (from direct contact with eyewitnesses to counterchecks and such like);
3. have tools at their disposal to assist in the process of digital content/video verification;
4. familiarise themselves with tools and techniques;
5. integrate the required activities into respective workflows;
6. have available the respective infrastructure as well as (organisational) support mechanisms;
7. be clear about and aware of possible effects on mental well-being (having psychological support is vital, and learning about respective coping mechanisms something that everyone dealing with user-generated video should be familiar with).[23]

Our work in InVID helped us to draw up the following typology of fake video content:

1. Decontextualised videos (unchanged or almost unchanged with high level of similarity, including low-quality copies for clickbait purposes);
2. Decontextualised videos altered (cut in length to one or several fragments of the original video, or cropped to remove, e.g. a timestamp in a CCTV camera footage);
3. Staged videos (e.g. produced on purpose by a video production company);
4. Tampered videos (through editing software to remove, hide, duplicate or add some visual or audio content);
5. Computer-Generated Imagery (CGI) including deep fakes (false images generated by artificial intelligence) made entirely from a computer or mixed with a blend of previous footage.

---

[21] https://observers.france24.com/en/20170323-no-internet-man-hitting-nurse-not-migrant.

[22] https://factcheck.afp.com/no-not-video-journalists-staging-migrants-drowning.

[23] Dealing with traumatic imagery and gruesome material is not the focus of this chapter. Nevertheless, it is of vital importance in this context and deserves utmost attention in order to avoid trauma. Equally important: to learn and develop respective coping mechanisms. For more on the dealings with digital material and its possible psychological effects see, for example, the work of Eyewitness Media Hub (now incorporated into First Draft News) and the Dart Center. A very useful read is the study [8].

In the chapters that follow, we will review the technologies mobilised to discover newsworthy user-generated videos and to verify them. These include video fragmentation and reverse image search on the Web, an approach giving good practical results to tackle decontextualised videos, techniques for finding duplicate or near-duplicate videos in closed collections, techniques for detecting digital manipulations within the videos and methods for the contextual analysis of the videos' surrounding metadata. Then, we will focus on the current state of user-generated video copyright management. These technology-oriented chapters will be followed by a detailed presentation of the complete applications developed within the InVID project: the Verification Plugin, the multimodal analytics dashboard and the InVID Verification Application tailored for newsrooms. We will conclude with some findings on the current state of disinformation spreading on social networks and some directions for future research to increase the efficiency of dealing with it.

References

1. Browne M (2014) Verifying video. European Journalism Center, EJC
2. Vranica S (2018) Advertisers allege Facebook failed to disclose key metric error for more than a year. Wall Street J. https://www.wsj.com/articles/advertisers-allege-facebook-failed-to-disclose-key-metric-error-for-more-than-a-year-1539720524
3. Sambrook R (2005) Citizen journalism and the BBC. Verification handbook. https://niemanreports.org/articles/citizen-journalism-and-the-bbc/
4. Belair-Gagnon V (2015) Social media at BBC news: the re-making of crisis reporting. Routledge
5. Boaden H (2008) The role of citizen journalism in modern democracy. http://www.bbc.co.uk/blogs/theeditors/2008/11/the_role_of_citizen_journalism.html
6. Silverman C et al (2014) Verification handbook. European Journalism Center, EJC
7. First Draft News. Visual verification guide for video. https://firstdraftnews.org/wp-content/uploads/2017/03/FDN_verificationguide_videos.pdf
8. Dubberley S, Griffin E, Mert Bal H Making secondary trauma a primary issue: a study of eyewitness media and vicarious trauma on the digital frontline. https://eyewitnessmediahub.com/research/vicarious-trauma

Part II
Technologies

Chapter 2
Real-Time Story Detection and Video Retrieval from Social Media Streams

Lyndon Nixon, Daniel Fischl and Arno Scharl

Abstract This chapter introduces two key tools for journalists. Before being able to initiate the process of verification of an online video, they need to be able to determine the news story that is the subject of online video, and they need to be able to find candidate online videos around that story. To do this, we have assessed prior research in the area of topic detection and developed a keyword graph-based method for news story discovery out of Twitter streams. Then we have developed a technique for selection of online videos which are candidates for news stories by using the detected stories to form a query against social networks. This enables relevant information retrieval at Web scale for news story-associated videos. We present these techniques and results of their evaluations by observation of the detected stories and of the news videos which are presented for those stories, demonstrating state-of-the-art precision and recall for journalists to quickly identify videos for verification and re-use.

2.1 Introduction

The starting point for any journalist before any content verification will be to find online content that purports to show events that are in relationship with the news story. In this age of 24 h news channels and online breaking news, sometimes the starting point is actually asking what are the current news stories and choosing which one would be relevant for reporting, necessitating the identification and verification of potentially relevant online media. The InVID solution has therefore also considered

L. Nixon (✉) · D. Fischl
MODUL Technology GmbH, Vienna, Austria
e-mail: nixon@modultech.eu

D. Fischl
e-mail: daniel.fischl@modul.ac.at

A. Scharl
webLyzard technology gmbh, Vienna, Austria
e-mail: scharl@weblyzard.com

© Springer Nature Switzerland AG 2019
V. Mezaris et al. (eds.), *Video Verification in the Fake News Era*,
https://doi.org/10.1007/978-3-030-26752-0_2

17

the pre-verification step, since no-one can easily verify online video purporting to show a news story without being first able to find suitable candidate videos.

A Web dashboard (see Chap. 10) will provide the results of the pre-verification analysis to the user: the automatic identification of news stories out of social media streams and the ranked listing of relevant online video postings associated to that news story. In this chapter, we will explain how this has been implemented.

Traditionally, newswires have been responsible for identifying and spreading the news of a new event or story to the global news institutions—newspapers and radio/TV stations. The speed in which a newswire would pick up on and report breaking news was directly related to the presence of their journalists at the news event, since media professionalism dictated that there was an independent, trustworthy source for news reporting. The Web, and especially social media, has rapidly changed how news is reported in the few decades it has existed, as it has given a globally accessible voice to any person who wants to announce something as breaking news. Journalists at professional news organizations are now faced with a much broader range of sources of potential news, much quicker in reaction than the traditional newswires but potentially uncorroborated.

Identifying a news story in social media is advantageous to journalists as it can point them to previously unknown information, indicate eyewitnesses who could potentially be interviewed and corroborate events, and link to eyewitness media, i.e., photos or videos taken as the news story took place. Since the journalists themselves cannot be present at every news event, especially when they happen in a previously unannounced fashion, nor arrive in a timely manner when they have been informed of an event, eyewitness media is becoming ever more significant in news reporting. However, they first must identify the stories that are happening and could be relevant for their news reporting cycle. While eyewitness reporting on social media means a news story can be announced there very shortly after its occurrence, the bulk and variety of social media content means such emerging news stories can be easily lost in the noise. Furthermore, the lack of secure controls regarding who is posting social media about a news story or why (e.g., political motivation) leads to the growing problem of "fake news"—both "misinformation" (possibly unintended false or inaccurate information) and "disinformation" (deliberately published false or inaccurate information, specifically intended to deceive). Hence, the discovery of social media from non-professional news sources is intricately linked to the task of content verification.

The SNOW 2014 Data Challenge [1] was the first challenge to tackle newsworthy topic detection. It confirmed that it is a challenging task: the top F-score of the competing solutions was only 0.4 (precision: 0.56, recall: 0.36). To develop an effective tool for news story detection in InVID, we had to consider:

1. Data acquisition through a real-time news monitor: we chose the Twitter Streaming API.
2. Data selection and preprocessing mechanism including spam/noise filtering.
3. Content modeling (e.g., from the state of the art: bag-of-words model, n-grams, TF-IDF) including semantic enrichment and (cross-lingual) linking/disambiguation via a knowledge base.

4. Clustering into distinct news stories.
5. Burst detection (identification of rapidly emerging or growing clusters in real time).
6. Ranking the clusters' newsworthiness (based on, e.g., content relevance, content popularity, credibility measures).

In this chapter, we introduce the InVID approach to news story detection and news video retrieval from social media streams. The next section looks at related work and the state of the art in news story detection. Then we present the InVID approach, its implementation, and an evaluation of the results. Based on the news story detection, we present how we automate news video retrieval from social media streams. A further section explains the implementation and evaluation of this video retrieval approach. We close with a summary of what we have achieved and acknowledgments.

2.2 News Story Detection: Related Work/State of the Art

Extracting new and continuing news stories in social media requires textual and statistical-analytical approaches to both find news stories due to their density (i.e., a growing number of posts reporting the same event) but also their distinctiveness (i.e., postings that are different from the previous discussion may indicate an emerging new story).

Contemporary journalistic workflows require that the journalist constructs queries over Web data to find news stories (or, naturally, waits for the story to be communicated to their organization by one of the news wires). The majority of journalists turn to Facebook and Twitter to source their news stories, whereas 26% reported searching YouTube.[1]

Standard tools or applications include TweetDeck from Twitter (https://tweetdeck. twitter.com), a social media dashboard application that allows the journalist to set up multiple Twitter searches and follow the multiple timelines of tweets in a single interface. Facebook provided newsrooms with a tool called Signal which displayed topics which are trending on the platform (including Facebook-owned Instagram) and related public content to any selected topic. Signal is now replaced by an equivalent tool developed by CrowdTangle (https://www.facebook.com/facebookmedia/ solutions/crowdtangle). However, it seems the primary starting point for journalistic discovery is the "advanced search" forms directly on the social media platforms (e.g., the InVID Verification Plugin also includes a tab for simplified access to the Twitter advanced search fields).

The starting point is one or more keywords, meaning that the journalist needs to have some idea of what they want to find even before finding anything, so often those initial keywords are as general as possible to capture any potential lead, e.g., the REVEAL project investigated typical searches which journalists use to initiate

---

[1] https://www.mynewsdesk.com/blog/how-journalists-use-social-media.

news discovery[2] and found they use very general terms at the outset and still need to spend quite some time sorting the newsworthy content out from the noise.

What is a news story? News is usually tied to specific events that occur within a period of time, and a temporal connection of related events over a longer period of time is a natural way to group them into "Stories". The threshold between different stories would be a subjective decision by a news organization but the extent of similarity between two events would be the usual decisive factor. For example, two different criminals being sentenced for their crimes would be seen as two distinct stories; however, if they were both part of the same crime, it may be more likely to consider the two cases of sentencing as part of the same news story. Likewise, the reporting of the crime, the arrest of the suspect, their court case, the sentencing, and their entrance into prison would potentially be seen as one news story with a longer temporal extent. Hence, one can also consider news detection from two perspectives: the identification of a set of news stories which are occurring at a single time point, or the identification of news stories as a set of temporally connected events over a longer time period.

News discovery begins with the automated extraction of potential news stories from a large, temporally ordered collection of data. Initial work in this area focused on crawling and indexing Web documents, and several online services provide news discovery based on indexing of online news articles ordered by time of publication:

- European Media Monitor [2]—a fully automatic system that gathers and aggregates about 300 000 news articles daily. The NewsBrief interface[3] groups related items, classifies them, and presents them as news story clusters, updated every 10 min;
- The Global Database of Events, Language and Tone (GDELT) [3]—an academic effort to analyze online content for events and thus create a real-time, open-source index of the world's news[4] provided as an open data stream reporting current world news every 15 min;
- Event Registry [4, 5]—an online system continually crawling and analyzing multilingual news articles online to identify mentioned world events and provide a Web interface to browse news grouped by event and find related events.[5]

The growth in the volume of content being published on social networks and the timeliness of the content which is shared on them (in terms of time between the occurrence of an event and the publication of content related to that event) has made them a primary source of data for news discovery algorithms over the past decade of research. In particular, Twitter is considered for its "rising potential in news reporting" that can "fundamentally change the way we produce, spread and consume news" [6]. The analysis showed that "the people who broke the news were able to convince many Twitter users before confirmation came from mass media"

---

[2]https://revealproject.eu/how-to-find-breaking-news-on-twitter.
[3]http://emm.newsbrief.eu/NewsBrief/clusteredition/en/24hrs.html.
[4]http://www.gdeltproject.org.
[5]http://eventregistry.org.

using Bin Laden's death as a case study. Thus, there is an evident motivation for conducting real-time news detection in the Twitter data stream.

The challenges in this work include the density of content about a subject on social media which can be used to determine a "trending topic" but we need additionally to restrict our trends to those which are newsworthy; the velocity of content on social media means a high throughput of data to analyze, even though APIs only provide smaller samples of all the posts (the Twitter Streaming API may deliver up to 3000 tweets per minute); the variety in posted content with multiple languages and linguistic formulations (in particular tweets have developed their own form of shorthand) including the use of hashtags; and the imbalance in coverage of content with posts being generated by bots as well as artificially spread by sharing accounts.

Topic modeling is a common approach that can be applied to detect breaking news on Twitter [7–9]. Topic detection (modeling) algorithms, such as Latent Semantic Analysis (LSA) [10, 11] or Latent Dirichlet Allocation (LDA) [12], provide means to organize a collection of electronic documents into semantically coherent groups (topics) based on the frequent word co-occurrence matrix (e.g., TF-IDF metrics). Topic detection approaches often involve topic clustering, ranking, and labeling stages [13–18]. A few approaches to extract open-domain events from tweets have been proposed [19–21]. Lendvai and Declerck [22] use the Longest Common Subsequence (LCS) method to extract events and also link tweets to Web documents.

First Story Detection (FSD) was proposed to identify the first story about a certain event from a document stream [23]. The state-of-the-art FSD approaches use similarity metrics over documents, such as TF-IDF vectors or Locality Sensitive Hashing (LSH) [23, 24], to determine if candidate documents are close to existing documents or could constitute a new event. These approaches have been improved by combination with external data sources, such as WordNet to build lexical chains [25] or Wikipedia to rank and filter the produced stories [26]. However, FSD focuses on the retrospective correct identification of stories (and hence the first document in a story thread) rather than the timely detection of the emergence of a new story in the document stream.

The SNOW 2014 Data Challenge [1] stipulated further research in mining Twitter streams to extract and summarize newsworthy topics [13–15, 17, 27]. The notion of "newsworthiness" was further defined as a set of topics for a given time slot "covered in mainstream news sites" [1], thereby setting the mainstream news sites as a reference point for the gold standard data on "important" news stories. Later, Martín-Dancausa et al. [16] utilized the same definition of newsworthiness to evaluate their method for topic detection on Twitter data, but additionally decomposed the notion into "the combination of novelty and significance". One method to find novel (emerging or recent trending) topics from a data stream is looking for bursts in frequent occurrences of keywords and phrases (n-grams) [7, 8, 14, 16, 28].

Only a few studies focused on other data sources than Twitter streams, in particular Wikipedia [26, 29]. Steiner et al. [29] implemented the Wikipedia Live Monitor application[6] for the task of breaking news detection. They defined a set of criteria for

---

[6]http://wikipedia-live-monitor.herokuapp.com, last checked and operational on 20 March 2019.

the news to be considered as breaking based on monitoring of the recent changes, such as speed and number of concurrent edits on Wikipedia articles. However, we note that comparative reviews of topic detection using different sources have demonstrated that Twitter is the most suitable data source, i.e., better results could not be acquired using news articles, Wikipedia or any other sources. Other recent publications have shown that the topic of event detection (particularly from Twitter) remains very relevant and a subject of ongoing research. A problem with this research area is the lack of consistency in how work is evaluated, with different datasets being used in publications for evaluation (or often created in an ad hoc manner for each publication). This makes it very difficult to draw direct comparisons, especially as the purpose of event detection may differ (e.g., in InVID we consider also how the detected stories may be used to also precisely collect related media content from social networks. Information retrieval is usually not a considered purpose of other event detection publications). We consider latest research related to news detection.

Twitter hashtags have been used with text and geolocation features [30] to both determine if a hashtag was associated with an event and which group of hashtags was associated with the same event. They demonstrate computational efficiency in the event detection and tweet clustering but do not address the newsworthiness of the events they detect nor evaluate the accuracy of the identification of (news) events.

Burst detection has been tested with Arabic language Twitter. Hammad and El-Beltagy [31] used tf/idf and entropy measures over sequential time frames. Evaluation was restricted by the lack of gold standards for the Arabic language. However, they looked only for detection of up to three significant events in 12–23 h periods, which is much less detailed than InVID (with topics, up to 100 distinct stories in a 24 h period).

Previous work of the PHEME project on story detection from Twitter was extended to "sub-story" detection [32]. For this, they make use of annotated datasets restricted in each case to one "main" story, e.g., Ferguson riots. Sub-stories are definitely an area of future interest in story detection for InVID; however, it can be noted that the Story Flow visualization already provides users with a means to identify and track larger stories over time (and while the story is connected across time frames, one can still see changes in the associated keywords as the story develops) whereas the reported "automated" results reflect the challenge of sub-story disambiguation (highly variable evaluation scores from 0.11 to 0.7).

"Disruptive event" detection in Twitter was the focus of [33] through text-based Naive Bayes classification and cosine similarity-based clustering. A temporal tf/idf approach determines the top terms for each cluster. Precision@K results of event detection return values of 0.7–0.85. They then restrict this further to the "disruptive events". There is no event labeling, particularly for information retrieval, as in InVID—rather event summarization is done using centroid tweets in the clusters, an approach we initially experimented with before developing a more effective labeling by keywords.

A frame-based approach to event detection was presented in [34] as opposed to clustering. Frames can capture triples with relations between two arguments, thus modeling an event in a more structured manner than a cluster of keywords or tweets.

A more structured modeling of stories is something we have added through the use of a Semantic Knowledge Base for typing and disambiguating the keywords to allow determination of agency and relations between participants. Reported precision is 0.65–0.71; this is lower than what we found for InVID and other state-of-the-art systems but is attempting to detect events with a more structured representation of those events which understandably adds new complexity to the task.

Event detection was performed by using topic mining, named entity recognition and burst analysis in [35]. They evaluated this approach using news articles rather than tweets and reported an average precision of the event clusters of 0.93. Interestingly they reported similar errors to those we will report on later in the chapter, e.g., cluster merges where there are shared keywords among two distinct stories. We have been able to show significant removal of these false merges in our final story detection implementation.

A "semantic" tweet analysis for event detection was proposed in [36]. It models the tweet text in a structured manner using NLP then links to entities in Knowledge Graphs such as DBPedia. As such, it improves keyword search for events in Twitter. The work is thus distinct from ours as it is looking at improved "pull" of events (by search) whereas we seek to automatically "push" events (by detection). However, the extension of event detection with additional semantics for the terms being discussed is also for us very relevant; the keywords update with the Semantic Knowledge Base provided us too with this additional semantic layer for event understanding.

The most similar approach to ours for event detection was probably followed by [37]. Their paper focuses however on whether additional sources further improve results rather than whether Twitter alone works well. Reported F-score for event detection with Twitter alone is 0.85 and reaches 0.9 with the addition of one more source. As stated, this work entitled "Event Detection at Onset (EDO)" appears closest to what has been done in InVID, where we are reporting evaluation figures over 0.9 and providing shortened, accurate labels (EDO identifies events by their full set of keywords) which also serve for precise information retrieval.

We can also mention other tools or services that claim to offer the same functionality, i.e., automatic detection of news stories in a timely manner from a given dataset. Based on the tools and services known to us as used by or pitched to journalists for online social media content discovery, we can refer to the following with a brief statement on their reported "news story detection" support (at the time of writing):

- Banjo—claims to offer near real-time detection of news stories based on big data analysis over social network postings.
- Dataminr for News—offers story detection by clustering tweets and geo-locating the occurrence of the event.
- Echosec—does not automatically detect news stories.
- Nunki—developing a tool with news story detection from the Twitter stream.
- Spike by Newswhip—does not automatically detect news stories.

Some of the contemporary tools for journalists require an active search for content and do not automatically provide "stories" in their interface. However, it can be acknowledged that just as in the research, also in commercial tools there is a trend toward using big data analysis to add the functionality of story detection. The general outcome is to analyze and cluster the documents (social media posts) and present each cluster as if it were a separate story. Identification is typically through the presentation of a representative document from the cluster, which we also initially experimented with in taking the centroid in a cluster of tweets [38]. However, a single document selected from the cluster may not capture all aspects of the news story, and we modeled stories more richly with keyword labels (cf. Sect. 2.3.4). Furthermore, it should be noted that we tie story detection to content retrieval (and specifically video), whereas these tools directly cluster the data they are collecting and use them purely to support user browsing for news events. We find that the video retrieval based on stories helped us achieve a greater recall of newsworthy video than the contemporary tools (cf. Sect. 2.6).

2.3 InVID Approach to News Story Detection

To provide an initial relevance control on the Twitter stream we have configured the Streaming API with a news term filter so that we accept only a part of the entire tweet collection—depending on how tight we make the filter we can collect from around 200 tweets/hour (during the normal news cycle) up to 2 000 tweets/hour.

Data preprocessing aims to remove at the outset non-relevant tweets from the content collected from the Twitter Streaming API. Since the queries on the content from other sources will be determined by the analysis of the tweets we collect, our focus will be on ensuring satisfactory relevance (newsworthiness) of the Twitter content. A number of preprocessing steps will support this:

- **Length check**: tweets under 30 characters are filtered out since tweets with too little text cannot be adequately classified and annotated for further processing.
- **Blacklisted terms**: tweets which make reference to sexual language or are potentially offensive (considering blasphemy, racism, sexism, and other profanity) do not contribute to a store of newsworthy content and are filtered out according to a manually drawn up blacklist of terms.

Each tweet is then passed through a Natural Language Processing (NLP)/Named Entity Recognition (NER) pipeline to be annotated and those annotations are used in a clustering step to form document clusters where each cluster may be assumed to be one news story.

2.3.1 Content Annotation

Every tweet's text is analyzed by a Natural Language Processing (NLP) component to perform keyword extraction—keywords are n-grams, i.e., they may be single words, parts of words or word combinations. We use the Baeza-Yates algorithm for indexing large text corpora by statistically significant n-grams [39]. Each tweet is annotated with a set of these keywords, usually capped at 3 keywords/tweet for efficiency. Since the subsequent clustering will use the keywords extracted in this modeling step, we found that certain keywords would be extracted from news tweets that led to unintended associations between documents and thus the formation of clusters which mixed news stories. An example of this was news agencies which tweet with their organizational name in the tweet—we use keyword blacklisting to avoid creating news stories purely based on the common reference to this organization through the repeated presence of the organizational name as a keyword on multiple documents which are all about very different news stories.

To provide for multilinguality in the content, there are NLP pipelines for English, French, and German. This can be extended to other languages, while ad hoc association of keywords in multiple languages (beyond those supported by a full NLP pipeline) is also possible to a broader extent by capturing synonymy between keywords in different natural languages. Since the correct clustering requires the accurate content modeling in the document space, we utilize available external semantic resources which contain background cross-domain and cross-lingual knowledge, in order to be able to semantically enrich, interlink, and disambiguate social media content. This approach will enable us to adequately process and unify multilingual content, which is prevalent on social media, e.g., the tweets reporting on an earthquake should be grouped even when they mention "quake", "Erdbeben", "séisme", etc. We build an RDF graph for keywords, their alignment to one another (across languages and within languages) and to Named Entities (NEs) [40], and term this our Semantic Knowledge Base (SKB).

To determine the basis for the graph representation of keywords, we follow the principles of Word Sense Disambiguation (WSD) which is common in NLP applications. WSD indexes language according not to the written forms of words but according to the distinct "word senses" (or meanings) that exist and may be communicated by different written forms. So we would not index terms with an entry like the English word "mouse" but with the word senses "mouse_1" (for the rodent) and "mouse_2" (for the computer interaction device), where both of which happen to share the same written form in English "mouse" (in linguistics, this is known as homonymy). After all, different word senses—despite homonymy—still differ in grammatical inflections, synonymy, and translation (e.g., in Italian, the small rodent is "topo" and the device is "mouse"). The best known online resource for word senses is WordNet (for English) [41] which has since been extended into other languages [42].

Our Semantic Knowledge Base (SKB) therefore models every different word sense as a distinct entity (in RDF known as a "resource" each with its own unique local identifier) and associates it with multiple keyword n-grams (or labels) annotated with their respective natural language. It can be then used for machine translation of natural language and for supporting keyword annotation. The central piece of the SKB is a lexical model based on the Lemon model[7] (see Fig. 2.1). The Lemon model has at its core these types:

---

[7] https://lemon-model.net.

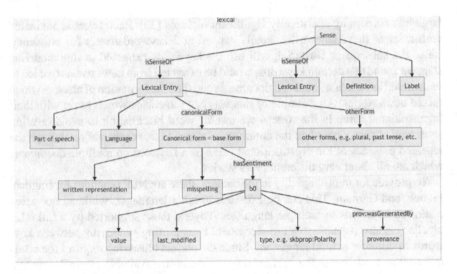

Fig. 2.1 The Lemon lexical model

- Lexical sense: A certain meaning.
- Lexical entry: A word that evokes the lexical sense. A lexical entry usually has a part of speech (i.e., one entry can be a verb evoking the meaning, another can be a noun evoking the same meaning) and a language.
- Lexical form: An entry can have several forms. A distinction is made between canonical forms (the lemma of a word) and other forms, e.g., tenses, plural, male/female forms, etc.
- Written representation: Each form has one or more written representations. This can, e.g., account for regional differences in spelling (UK/US) or maybe frequent misspellings.

An additional connection can be that a sense references an entity according to a Knowledge Graph, e.g., in DBPedia or WikiData. To seed the initial SKB, we took a dump of the English language OmegaWiki from the lemonUby project and translations into German, French, Spanish, Portuguese, Czech, Russian, and Chinese were included, where available. Since OmegaWiki only contains base forms, we collected (for English and German) frequencies of terms and the part of speech tags they got assigned by our NLP pipeline when processing textual documents. Together with a lemmatizer, we tried to attach non-lemmas to the correct base form. Additionally, we attached adverbs to the senses where the corresponding adjective got attached and similarly adjectives to where the verb got attached (if the lemmatizer reduced them to an adjective or verb, e.g., killed is the adjective to kill) (Fig. 2.2).

To use the SKB in improving keyword results, we experimented with the use of two services driven by the SKB in the first step of story detection: the creation of the keyword graph.

- A synonym service (REST endpoint) provides for a given term and language a list of sense definitions and base forms of the lexical entries, such that two or

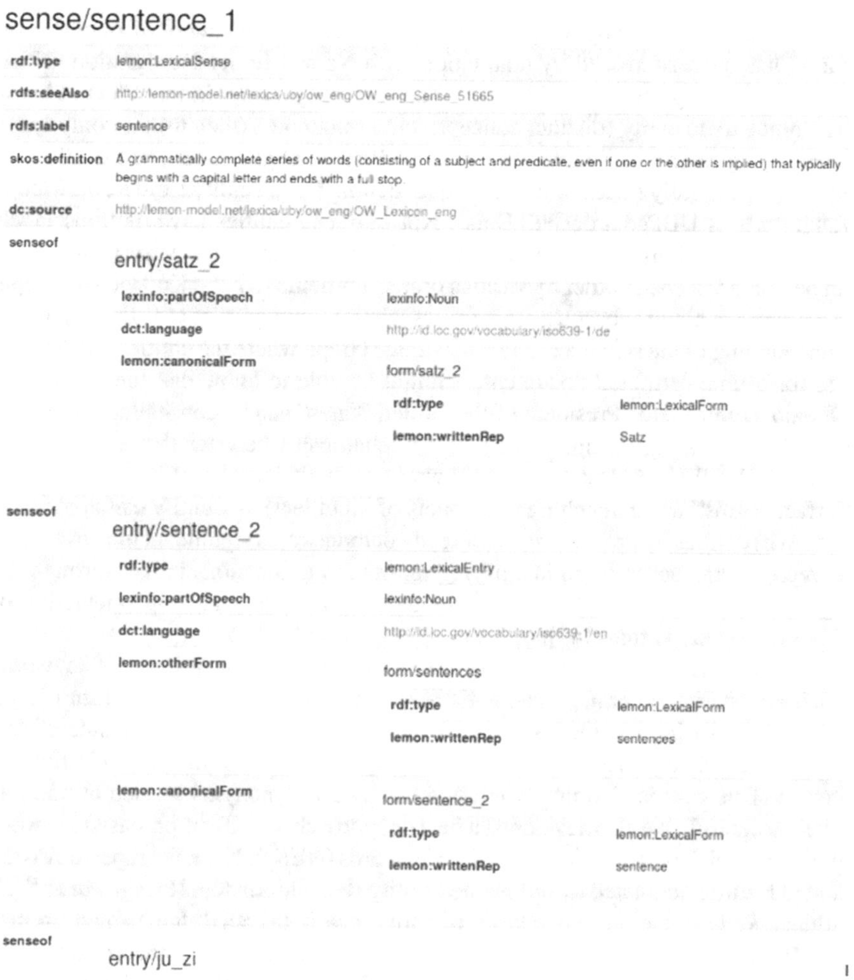

sense/sentence_1

rdf:type	lemon:LexicalSense
rdfs:seeAlso	http://lemon-model.net/lexica/uby/ow_eng/OW_eng_Sense_51665
rdfs:label	sentence
skos:definition	A grammatically complete series of words (consisting of a subject and predicate, even if one or the other is implied) that typically begins with a capital letter and ends with a full stop
dc:source	http://lemon-model.net/lexica/uby/ow_eng/OW_Lexicon_eng
senseof	

entry/satz_2

lexinfo:partOfSpeech	lexinfo:Noun
dct:language	http://id.loc.gov/vocabulary/iso639-1/de
lemon:canonicalForm	

form/satz_2

rdf:type	lemon:LexicalForm
lemon:writtenRep	Satz

senseof

entry/sentence_2

rdf:type	lemon:LexicalEntry
lexinfo:partOfSpeech	lexinfo:Noun
dct:language	http://id.loc.gov/vocabulary/iso639-1/en
lemon:otherForm	

form/sentences

rdf:type	lemon:LexicalForm
lemon:writtenRep	sentences

lemon:canonicalForm	

form/sentence_2

rdf:type	lemon:LexicalForm
lemon:writtenRep	sentence

senseof

entry/ju_zi

Fig. 2.2 Screenshot of a Lemon lexical sense in the SKB

more keywords that carry the same lexical sense can be merged in the graph. For example, "murder" as input would output, among others, "assassinate, kill, homicide, polish off, slay, bump off".

- A variants index (serialized into ElasticSearch) provides for one lexical form a set of variants of that form (plural/singular, tenses of verbs, declinations of nouns/adjectives, common misspellings) and a set of lexical senses that can be represented by that form. The idea is that in the story detection we can query for the variants of any given keyword and get candidate senses. Based on the other keywords in the story cluster, it may be possible to choose the correct sense, providing for a better keyword disambiguation. Cluster merging may also be improved since currently distinct keywords (lexical form) can be disambiguated and mapped to the same lexical sense.

We note that classically the problem of alignment in meaning of distinct text (n-grams) has been addressed by annotation with Named Entity Recognition (NER) and Named Entity Linking (NEL) [43]. These identify strings in input text as being a reference to an entity (distinct concept), either unknown (then usually only typed as belonging to an identifiable class such as Person, Organisation, or Location) or known (then usually matched to the unique identifier of an entity from a Knowledge Graph such as DBPedia or WikiData). Not only can entities have multiple labels (i.e., different strings can be annotated as references to the same entity) but entities can be related to one another by various properties defined in the Knowledge Graph. So a processor could subsequently infer associations or equivalences allowing for its understanding of the schema of the Knowledge Graph where the entities are defined, e.g., for a time-restricted document, it might be able to know that the entities for "Donald Trump" and "President of the United States" can be considered equivalent where the Knowledge Graph defines such a relationship between them.[8]

Our NER/NEL tool Recognyze [44] works with dictionaries of labels (known as "surface forms" when matching to snippets of input text) to identify candidate (still unknown) entities in the text, and has already demonstrated significant improvements in precision and accuracy in identifying references to locations in text through the expansion of the content of those dictionaries combined with implementation of additional syntactic rules [45].

We found that clustering by keywords also tends toward the grouping of keywords which are sharing a common semantic (e.g., "president" and "donald trump"), yet will not be associated in the SKB via Word Senses (the meaning of "president" as a political title is very distinct from the meaning of "donald trump" as an individual person). This case is also not covered either by the Synonyms service or variants index. As a result, we also developed a further approach to SKB graph-based keyword alignment which we term Named Entity Keywords (NEKs). Here, we capture also the Named Entities annotated by our Named Entity Recognition tool Recognyze as SKB entities. We have therefore two types of entity now in the SKB: the Named Entities from Recognyze NER/NEL annotation of the text and the other keywords extracted by NLP which were not identified as Named Entities. Relationships between both types of SKB entity captured by properties in the Knowledge Graphs can be used to align them in meaning beyond the case of word senses ("donald trump" holding the title of "president" for instance).

2.3.2 Clustering

Clustering is based on the sets of keywords annotated to each tweet since this provides already a more efficient means to similarity-cluster a large document set as it reduces the dimensionality of the clustering problem.

---

[8]https://www.wikidata.org/wiki/Q11696 at the time of writing has the property "officeholder" and its value is the entity for "Donald Trump". Of course by the time you read this, the value may have changed.

The initial baseline approach clusters candidate events from a chosen sample of documents, e.g., the last 1, 3 or 24 h of breaking news tweets. Dividing the observed time span into regular, smaller intervals and calculating the top 10 occurring keywords by frequency in the document set per time interval provided us with a very crude initial set of stories per time interval. A subsequent aggregation of the top 3 associations (co-occurring keywords) for each of these keywords was performed to get related keywords which are used to model the news story (as keyword quads) per time interval.

Since the documents (the tweets with their keyword annotations) are indexed in an Elastic Search index, Elastic Search aggregations were effective for this co-occurrence calculation.

2.3.2.1   Building the Keyword Graph

The list of keywords and their associations per time interval can be used to model an initial keyword graph. Each unique keyword per time interval became a single node within the graph and the aggregated frequency was considered as its weight. The identified co-occurring keywords were naturally used to create the edges of the graph, linking nodes together and again using the number of co-occurrences as a weighting function. This provides a starting point for story detection within a single time interval. However, a news story forms and persists over longer periods of time. Building up connectivity between each of the time intervals was then handled by comparing the keywords of consecutive time intervals with each other and connecting the same keywords with each other by creating edges between them, using the keyword counts as weights or adding them to the weights of already existing edges. The final result of finding relevant connections between all time intervals yielded the final weighted graph used as an initial input for detecting relevant stories over time.

The next step and significant improvement to this approach was the introduction of the Louvain Modularity algorithm [46]. The algorithm is more commonly used to detect communities within social networks—but in our case was used to detect "communities" of closely related keywords within the graph. We chose this algorithm as the graph of keywords is specifically structured in the same way as a community of social network contacts and it proved to be much more efficient than k-means clustering.

The effect of the algorithm is to partition the keyword graph into sub-graphs with optimized modularity, which is a scale value that measures connectivity of nodes inside communities compared to those of outside communities. Each sub-graph was considered as one news story and was then converted from a graph view to our data structure representing a story by merging equal nodes within the sub-graph together and labeling the story with the keywords in the sub-graph with the strongest weights.

2.3.2.2   Early Stories Evaluations

Observation of the story results led us to assess story quality and identify errors. Improving keywords has been discussed in the previous subsection. Besides this, we found we could classify errors in three types:

- disambiguation of the stories (meaning: each cluster should represent one distinct news story, and every distinct news story should be represented by one cluster);
- irrelevant keywords in the story label (meaning: the description of the cluster should clearly identify the news story represented by that cluster and not contain any parts irrelevant to that story);
- relevance of documents provided for the stories (meaning: since association of documents with a story is determined by document and story keywords overlap, the keywords within a cluster which is identified as a particular news story should be related to the keywords used by documents about the same news story).

To find solutions to the above issues, we looked at aspects of our clustering implementation which could help us to improve.

2.3.2.3   Keyword Postprocessing

When aggregating the top keywords (+ their associations) for building the graph which serves as input for the community detection algorithm, we generate a simple list of all aggregated keywords and initial relations. To compensate for possible differences in notations of annotated keywords, we found it beneficial with regard to the final outcome of the community detection algorithm, to check for component matches with already existing nodes in the graph when linking new keywords into it. This was done by always storing the shortest matching component as preferred name for each node for comparisons, e.g., "trump" is a component term of "Donald Trump" and "President Trump" and we store "Trump" (always the shortest common component) to both terms as preferred name. This heuristical assumption when building the graph to merge "donald trump" and "president trump" to simply "trump", although introducing a possible source for errors (e.g., by merging "melania trump" into the same node), made it possible to establish links which were previously missed, having a positive impact on the outcome of the clustering.

2.3.2.4   Cluster Merging by Description

The Louvain algorithm still exhibited mixed stories appearing within one cluster or several clusters belonging to the same story. Since the community detection algorithm is carried out on graph topology, and hence is blind of semantic context, it is necessary to do a refinement of the results.

As shown in Fig. 2.3, the same stories are partitioned into different clusters/subgraphs by the algorithm when the optimized modularity calculated by the algorithm

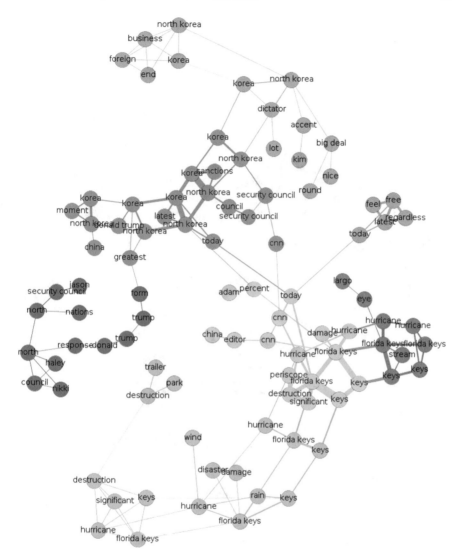

Fig. 2.3 Initial outcome of the Louvain community detection algorithm depicting nodes within the same community with the same color

wasn't accurate enough to merge them into the same sub-graph (i.e., the connections between the two sub-graphs that we consider the same story weren't dense enough), or when there were no connections between two sub-graphs because the same story appeared in different time ranges (e.g., a new report about a same event across several days). Those stories need to be merged retrospectively; therefore, we performed multiple subsequent postprocessing steps to achieve these merge and splitting operations.

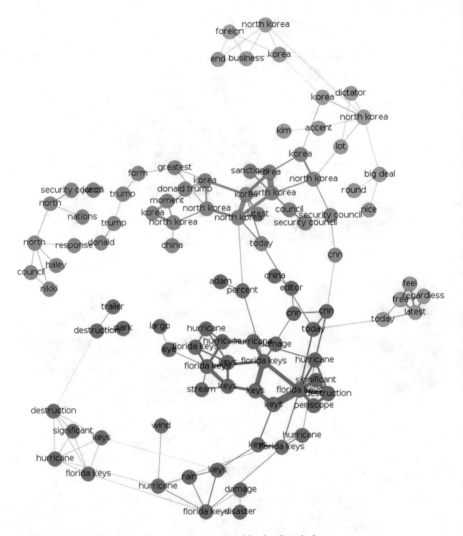

Fig. 2.4 Community graph after merging communities by description

For the initial merging, we found the descriptions of clusters to be sufficient. Our chosen initial description of a cluster is the top three unique keywords with the highest frequency within this cluster, which are representative for the cluster content. Figure 2.4 shows the result.

2.3.2.5   Cluster Splitting Based on Pairwise Keyword Co-occurrence

The resulting graph will still contain possibly mixed stories from the initial community detection algorithm, as well as additional errors introduced by the previous

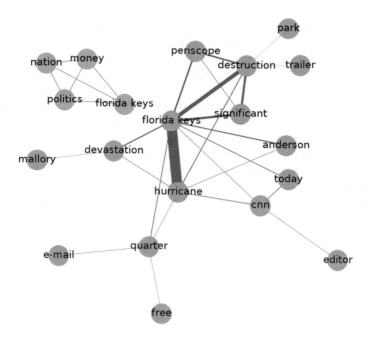

Fig. 2.5 Sub-graph of one community after splitting by triads. Detected triads are depicted via red edges

simple merge by description. Hence, we use "triads" for the splitting of clusters which merge two or more distinct news stories. Triads are ternary keywords that are pairwise connected. Any nodes which are not part of a triad are denoted as leaf nodes. We group triads together when each triad has at least one common link with another triad in the group. Figure 2.5 depicts a community split into two groups which were loosely connected by the jointly occurring keyword "florida keys".

After the triad groups are detected, they are split, keeping the leaf nodes directly connected to the triad nodes. Those leaf nodes which are connected to the joint keywords are abandoned, because it is hard to determine which group they might belong to.

2.3.2.6   Cluster Merging by Keyword Overlaps

As the splitting by triads would often over-perform and yield very similar stories, we decided to introduce one final merging rule for two clusters, based on seeing keywords as a bag of words (so n-grams become multiple unigrams) and calculating an overlap rate:

overlap rate = number of overlapped terms/number of total unique terms of both descriptions.

We tested varying the threshold set for the merging of clusters in the graph. This merge threshold was set at 0.5 in the initial implementation, meaning that there needs to be a 50% overlap in the unigrams which form the set of keywords in the cluster (i.e., overlap rate $\geq 50\%$) for both clusters to be merged. Testing showed that some duplicate stories could be merged by reducing the merge threshold but of course at the same time, this increased the chances of merging two stories which were actually distinct (e.g., keywords like "trump" and "usa" could co-occur for multiple, different stories). We found that the larger the document set from which the keyword graph was constructed, the more effective a lower merge threshold was in correctly merging two clusters about the same news story while not merging two clusters about different news stories. As a result, while we have retained the default of 0.5 for story detection in the InVID dashboard, in our evaluations we applied the lower merge threshold of 0.25 for the TOP stories (the stories being generated from ALL documents, which were in the thousands) whereas the original threshold of 0.5 was retained for the stories filtered to individual TOPICS (which were in the hundreds).

2.3.3 Ranking

Detected stories may be ranked according to their aggregated weight (sum of weights of each keyword in their sub-graph) or number of associated documents.

Another aspect of the story detection, which became much clearer through the story graph visualization, was the dominance in the ranking of our approach of news stories which are the subject of more tweets over more time. This is a natural result of clustering which determines its clusters based on all documents input to the clustering algorithm. In our case, those documents also have a time component (the date-time the document was published) but the temporal distribution of the documents has a limited role in the results of the clustering (we do look at the keyword co-occurrences within time splits, when clustering with a time span of 24 h of documents this time split is one hour, but we then connect the clusters per time split together to form larger clusters within the overall time span). So, for example, if at the end of the current time span a new story appears, it may be highly relevant for the journalist, and indeed, it may have the most related tweets within the final time split. However, for the Story View earlier stories have already been the subject of tweets over many previous time splits and thus (from volume of documents) are ranked higher, dominating the list of results. To address this, we decided to consider the area of "burst detection" as a means to better highlight quickly emerging news stories from those which are continually present in the news coverage.

This requires that we rank clusters based on giving a greater weight to those which have grown more rapidly in a brief past time. Burst detection has particular significance for highlighting the most recently emerging stories, since they should have a higher comparative weight for their clusters compared to stories which have been present in the Twitter stream since a longer time. This means in the classical episodic view those stories take some time to be visible, but in the burst detection view, they are more immediately highlighted. This is a contribution to the area of research which is called First Story Detection, i.e., the ability of an algorithm to identify a story from a stream in as early a time as possible after that story first appears.

While a story is any distinct news event within the selected time period, we consider a news story (**episode**) to be a set of temporally linear and semantically connected news events over multiple time periods whereas we consider an emerging news story (**burst**) to be a single news story which appears suddenly in the timeline.

Burst detection is a widely applied approach in research of event detection [33, 47, 48]. However, the abovementioned papers focus on the term level detection, i.e., aiming to detect those "bursty terms" from the whole collection of words in all documents, which is not designed for real-time applications.

It has also become a common method to find novel (emerging or recent trending) stories from a data stream by looking for bursts in frequent occurrences of keywords and phrases (n-grams) [8, 14, 16].

Our approach is to break the keyword clusters detected by the community algorithm into smaller keyword clusters based on their document timestamps. Thus, we both obtain **episodes** (keyword clusters across several time intervals) and **bursts** (keyword clusters located in a single time interval).

A sampling of results comparing episodes and bursts indicated that sharply emerging stories in a time span were indeed highlighted better in the burst results. We visualized this in the dashboard by representing each story as a single node (possibly connected across time), where in each time interval the comparative size of the node reflected the extent to which the story "emerged" at that time (burst). As can be seen in Fig. 2.6 in the time period March 13–18, 2019 while there were several top news stories, there was a "burst" (sharply emerging news story) on March 15 for the story "mosque, christchurch, mass shooting".

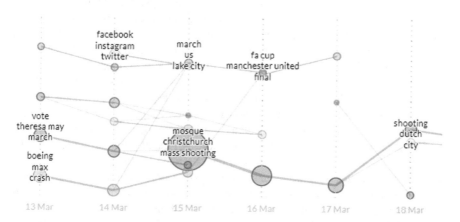

Fig. 2.6 Visualization of burst detection, where a story which "emerges" more strongly in the story stream is highlighted by a larger node in the graph

2.3.4 Labeling

Once the stories are detected, they are created in the sense that the set of keywords within the cluster are ranked by weight (i.e., cumulative sum of frequency of occurrences of initial aggregation and postprocessing merges, etc.) and used in (i) creating a label for the story from the three highest ranked keywords and (ii) collecting documents for the story based on an ElasticSearch weighted search over all documents using the (highest ranked) keywords.

Due to the fact that the story detection only happens through clustering annotated keywords per document and not directly on the documents itself (an approximation necessary due to the real-time requirement of the algorithm as well as being able to run it on any given subset of documents) we needed to find a way to revert the process and get from the detected keyword clusters back to a set of documents. Since keywords are only an abstraction of the underlying documents, keyword quality as well as the choosing the most relevant keywords for labeling a story were a big focus and major factors influencing the quality of the stories.

As stated previously, the initial description consists of the top three weighted and sorted keywords. Due to the aforementioned abstraction layer, it is possible that the top keywords were put into one cluster, although never appearing together within documents, hence corrective measures had to be taken to make the labels for stories more relevant. Multiple iterations were needed and several aspects were considered for choosing suitable labels used for descriptions as well as document retrieval for stories.

The initial top three keywords are used to retrieve an initial set of documents by requiring a minimum of two keywords to appear in each of the documents and an aggregation is performed on this set of documents to retrieve the top keywords on this set in order to improve label relevance to the document set. The so acquired set of keywords then undergoes several postprocessing steps, like the aforementioned merging of component term keywords into a single one if difference in frequency is within a certain percentage, as well as filtering out keywords that match the actual search terms defining the total subset of documents on which the clustering algorithm was performed. Then we iterate through the list in order of frequency and determine a new, more relevant story label made up of the new top three keywords, applying a combination of rules, such as requiring at least one keyword to be a named entity, such as person, organization or location and generally preferring named entities over regular detected keywords, as well as putting less emphasis on locations which haven't been identified as key. This procedure is repeated for all stories and the new labels set to each story. An effect of the corrected labeling procedure was the appearance of stories with the same label as separate stories in the dashboard, hence another merging step based on keyword overlap is performed to match similar stories and updated document counts and document sets for each story are retrieved based on combining the newly identified keywords in pairs. This leads to a second set of documents, more relevant to the new descriptive keywords.

2.4 Story Detection: Implementation and Evaluation

We set up two different Twitter streams to compare results: one using a list of trusted news accounts to monitor news stories in real time and one using a list of breaking news trigger terms to find user-generated media for news events.

The breaking news accounts stream will use as source a list of Twitter accounts known to trustworthily post breaking news. We drew up an initial list of 61 accounts[9] producing ca. 200 tweets/hour (normal news cycle), with a focus on a wide geographical distribution of the news sources for global news monitoring in English, French, and German yet also a core of news sources from France, Germany, and Austria to capture national news stories from those countries given our use case partners being AFP, Deutsche Welle, and APA. The initial list of international press accounts which tweet breaking news was generated based on Web search collecting several online articles about Twitter accounts to follow for breaking news. The partners AFP and Deutsche Welle added French and German language news accounts they trust and we used the APA Twitterlist[10] to select top Austrian news sources.

The breaking news terms stream will use as source a list of terms thought to indicate tweets which refer to breaking news. The foreseen "trigger" terms involve phrases with words such as live, breaking, just now, just saw, witness, footage. We will use specific term combinations (e.g., breaking + news) to try to keep spam and irrelevant content at a minimum. A list of circa 80 trigger terms was activated to collect approximately 500 000 tweets a day. These were drawn up based on a combination of REVEAL project work on the terms journalists should search in Twitter for to find breaking news[11] and own Twitter searches analyzing the presence of newsworthy media in the responses. Since this produced too many irrelevant tweets, we analyzed the number of occurrences of our terms in two datasets which captured tweets from an ongoing breaking news event: a dataset of 107 450 tweets from the terrorist attacks in Paris and a dataset of over 2.6 million tweets referring to the Germanwings flight 9525 crash. This resulted in a refined list of 12 search terms which represent typically the most occurring term combinations in breaking news tweets and should match with approximately 40–60 000 tweets daily from the Streaming API with much higher relevance. These terms are used in English, French, and German (Table 2.1)

We expect our stories to be news, i.e., they represent events or actions which are valid for reporting through journalists and news organizations. This can be reduced to a metric of "newsworthiness". It is defined as a set of stories for a given time slot "covered in mainstream news sites" [1]. However, every news site will have its own criteria for determining what is "news", and the validity of the news chosen by one site may be questioned by another site. Experts can be used to assess what is news based on positive and negative examples [1]. This then leads to a set of reference stories for a dataset for which a story detection algorithm can be evaluated based

---

[9]https://twitter.com/lyndonjbnixon/lists/breaking-news/members.

[10]http://twitterlist.ots.at.

[11]Published at http://revealproject.eu/how-to-find-breaking-news-on-twitter.

Table 2.1 Breaking news trigger terms

English	French	German
Watch live	regardez en direct	livebericht
Happening now	se passe maintenant	passiert gerade jetzt
Just saw	viens de regarder	gerade gesehen
Just witnessed	viens de témoigner	gerade miterlebt
Eyewitness news	témoin oculaire	augenzeug
Breaking news	flash info	eilmeldung
Video footage	enrégistrement vidéo	videoaufnahme
cctv footage	caméra de surveillance	überwachungskamera
Amateur footage		
Surveillance footage		
Cam footage		
Captured footage		

on recall, as is the case with the SNOW 2014 dataset. Wikipedia's Current Events portal can be seen as a crowdsourced version of this, where the crowd decides what is news. It can be observed how this leads to a more diverse set of stories as in expert-based definition, since the latter also relies on agreement between the experts to accept any story to the reference list. The result of either approach is that the story detection is evaluated as successful if it can detect the stories CHOSEN by the experts or the crowd. If it detects other stories, it is penalized even if these may also be arguably newsworthy. Another issue is how to compare the stories output by the tool to the stories defined as references in the evaluation dataset, unless the tool has been developed specifically to use the same story model. SNOW 2014, for example, provided a timestamp, descriptive sentence of the story, a set of top keywords, and a set of reference documents. It expected tools to produce up to 10 stories per 15-minute time slot. The final evaluation required a set of experts, and given the size of the data to be compared, a sampling approach was taken. Five time slots were chosen and for the up to 50 detected stories, each expert looked for detected stories which matched a part of the set of 59 reference stories. While difficult to scale this up, this means only 5% of the story detection output is actually checked and our implementation works with larger time slots than these (hourly for the bursts, 24 h is the default time span for the stories in the dashboard).

SNOW 2014 did confirm newsworthy story detection to be a challenging task: F-score: 0.4 Precision: 0.56 Recall: 0.36 [17]. For our evaluation, we want to use the tweets being collected by us in InVID as opposed to a ground truth evaluation dataset such as SNOW 2014. This of course raises the question of how we will get our ground truth and a measure for how to compare the results of our algorithm with the ground truth. We choose to evaluate two metrics of our story detection: quality and correctness, yet we choose not to create our own ground truth of reference stories for the evaluation. This is because we believe there cannot be an absolute ground truth in news detection (just as two different news sources will likely differ in the news stories they cover). Instead, manual observation of the story results in the dashboard, something we have been doing throughout the InVID project, will be formalized to produce quantitative measures for these metrics through observation over a consistent time period.

Correctness of the stories can be measured as a factor of whether a cluster can be unambiguously identified as representing a distinct story (action or event which may be newsworthy). Hence, the observer must not decide on the newsworthiness of the story, but simply that the cluster can be seen as representing a potential story. While this needs to be reflected by the (top) documents in the cluster, since we will look at cluster quality below, we will use the story label in this case as the determinant of the story of the cluster. Since different labels (which determines the separation between clusters) may, in fact, be referring to the same news story we add a complementary measure for distinctiveness, i.e., how many of the clusters identifiable as stories actually represent distinct news stories.

Clustering quality can be measured in terms of completeness and homogeneity. Two structural observations can be made on a list of clusters: whether a cluster actually merges two or more stories or whether a story is represented by two or more different clusters. This requires that every document in a cluster is individually marked as belonging in its cluster, in a different cluster, or in no cluster. In other words, completeness is the measure of the extent to which documents for the same story are in the same cluster. Whereas homogeneity is the measure of the extent to which clusters only contain documents from the same story.

Hence our methodology for the story evaluation is as follows. We will conduct a "live" evaluation, i.e., in real time using the story results visible in the InVID dashboard. It will be a manual exercise, as the human evaluator will make the assessment about the quality of the stories. Values will be drawn through a daily assessment of the stories detected from our Twitter Accounts stream (we will use the same process to compare stories from this stream with the stories from the Twitter News stream, which draws from user-generated tweets claiming to report breaking news). Detected stories will be assessed in terms of the "universal" stories (drawn from the entire Twitter stream) as well as the stories for the top 5 topics in that time period (measured in terms of topic size, i.e., the number of documents currently matching the defined topic). Topics are defined according to the IPTC NewsCodes (http://show.newscodes. org/index.html?newscodes=subj) as sets of keywords associated with news regarding that topic, so stories are classified within topics according to the keywords in their cluster. We take only the "top" topics as we observed already that topics with a small number of matching stories are less accurate for story detection, which is a factor of topic size and not related to the correctness of the topic definition. Our focus will be on English results in this evaluation. In each daily observation, the evaluator will determine the values of the following metrics, based on the (up to) ten stories given in the dashboard:

- **Correctness**—number of clusters identifiable by their labels as a distinct story/total number of clusters.

- **Distinctiveness**—number of distinct stories among the correct clusters/total number of correct clusters.
- **Homogeneity**—average of the individual homogeneity score for each distinct story, which is the sum of documents relevant to the story divided by the total number of documents (in our case, max 10 sorted by relevance).
- **Completeness**—one minus the average of the individual completeness score for each distinct story, which is the sum of documents relevant to some other distinct story divided by the total number of documents relevant to any story.

We provide evaluations of our story detection algorithm from two milestones in the InVID project, June 2017 and June 2018. The difference in results (for the same data) indicates the improvements in quality achieved by the various corrective approaches described previously in Sect. 2.2.

We also perform an additional evaluation for the final version of the algorithm against state-of-the-art story detection tools. This latter evaluation is restricted by what access we could gain to those tools, some of whom are commercial products and did not agree to provide us trial log-ins to compare their results with ours. This was the case with Banjo, Dataminr, and Facebook Signal. On the other hand, Echosec, Nunki, and Spike require an initial keyword-based search so only EventRegistry could be used to compare pre-detected news stories with InVID; Nunki gave us access to their beta event detection service Signal; however, it only provides reverse chronological tweets matching a "newsworthy" template similar to our "Twitter News" data feed and no clustering into distinct news stories.

The benchmark for the evaluation is based on the news stories detected for the period June 19–23, 2017 (top stories from the Twitter Accounts feed). The results are shown in Table 2.2. Previously we had noted (in the 2017 run) that a major issue of concern was the distinctiveness, which penalizes both merged and split stories in the results. It can be seen that we improved the values in both correctness and, significantly, distinctiveness, in the 2018 run. We had now three non-stories compared to five from the previous run and had noted already that these all were the result of the tweets of a single news organization, which we subsequently removed from our data feed. The results still include this news organization so the improved correctness value indicates that we more successfully rank more newsworthy stories more highly and can in cases remove unnewsworthy clusters from the results. However, the greatest improvement can be seen in the value of distinctiveness jumping from 0.597 to 0.96 over the exact same data. This is a clear demonstration that our efforts to improve the correct splitting and merging of clusters into a set of distinct news stories have been significantly effective. Finally, the values for homogeneity and completeness had already been good in the previous year, yet we could still show an increase in both—97% correctness and an almost perfect 99% in homogeneity, i.e., that the documents provided for each story are almost always relevant to that story.

We also want to look at more current news detection. Here, since we do not wish to take any single news source as a "ground truth" for the task, we can compare current news detected by our algorithm with the news stories provided via the interfaces of other story detection platforms. Here we can consider precision/recall in the sense

Table 2.2 InVID story detection benchmark (2017 run) and final results (2018 run)

2017 run	Cluster measures		Document relevance measures	
	Correctness	Distinctiveness	Homogeneity	Completeness
June 19, 2017	1	0.5	0.87	0.84
June 20, 2017	0.9	0.44	0.94	1
June 21, 2017	0.7	0.71	1	1
June 22, 2017	1	0.625	0.92	0.95
June 23, 2017	0.875	0.71	0.91	0.87
Avg over 5 day	**0.895**	**0.597**	**0.93**	**0.93**
2018 run				
June 19, 2017	1	1	1	0.97
June 20, 2017	0.9	0.89	1	1
June 21, 2017	0.9	1	1	1
June 22, 2017	0.9	1	1	1
June 23, 2017	1	0.9	0.94	0.86
Avg over 5 day	**0.94**	**0.96**	**0.99**	**0.97**

of whether we detect newsworthy stories that they do not or they detect newsworthy stories that we do not. As explained above, there is only one story detection platform available for us to compare to: EventRegistry. Over a period of three days (May 28–30, 2018) we took the top 10 stories from the InVID dashboard and the top 10 "recent events" from EventRegistry. We considered for each story list whether all stories are newsworthy (correctness) and distinct (distinctiveness); we also looked at the top 10 documents from every story (just as InVID sorts documents by "relevance", EventRegistry offers a sorting of documents by "story centrality"). We also looked at overlap between the top 10 stories each day, with the caveat that both systems of course detect many more stories so the absence of a story detected by one system in the list of the other does not mean the story was not detected. Thus, the overlap can only be a measure of the similarity of the story ranking of both systems, rather than an evaluation of story detection per se.

In Table 2.3, we show the evaluation of the InVID stories for three days in 2018. The almost perfect values demonstrate that the results indicated by the evaluation run on 2017 data are also consistent with more recent story detection quality in the InVID dashboard. Comparing it to EventRegistry, it can be said that they also perform almost perfectly on providing newsworthy events and separating them distinctly; sharing a 100% correctness score they scored 97% in distinctiveness due to one story duplication on the third day (where the story label was once in English and once in Russian, suggesting they may be issues in the cross-lingual translation). In terms of story coverage, the top stories between the platforms did vary with only between two and five stories being shared in the top 10 on both on the same day. EventRegistry ranked sports stories with US sports (basketball, baseball) higher, appearing three times whereas InVID had cricket twice; InVID had a single football

Table 2.3 Story detection run on data from May 2018

InVID story detection	Correctness	Distinctiveness	Homogeneity	Completeness
May 28, 2018	1	1	0.94	0.9
May 29, 2018	1	1	0.95	0.95
May 30, 2018	1	0.8	0.98	0.98
Three day average	**1**	**0.93**	**0.96**	**0.94**

(soccer) story in the top 10 while EventRegistry had five. EventRegistry also included a story on the Star Wars film Solo twice. InVID might also detect such stories but they tend to not reach the top 10 when there is other significant news and should be findable using the topics (sports, arts, and entertainment). It was our feeling that InVID highlighted more stories of news significance in its top 10, for example, on the first day this included the Storm Alberto in Florida and former President George Bush Sr.'s hospitalization, both of which were not shown by EventRegistry. Likewise, on May 29 InVID detected the memorial day celebrations at the Arlington Cemetery and on May 30 the Supreme Court rejecting a challenge to abortion law in Arkansas. We have already acknowledged that every news platform may have its own focus in the news it provides and thus it is not possible to say one list of news stories is "better" than another. Hence, InVID can be said to perform just as well as if not better than any other story detection tool—while we were unable to test other competitors, scores of 93–100% already indicate little more that can be perfected.

2.5 Video Retrieval from Social Media Streams

There are billions of posts on social media daily, and the rate of growth in the volume of video content has been particularly steep in this past decade. YouTube reported 400 h of video being uploaded to the platform every minute in 2017. Twitter began with separate apps for short videos (Vine) and live streaming (Periscope) but since 2015 has been actively integrating video natively within its own platform. Significantly a Pew Research survey in 2017 indicated that 74% of its (US-based) users say they use it to get news.[12] In the same survey, Facebook was the primary source of news from social media for the US population. Facebook Video launched in 2014, quickly replacing the sharing of videos on Facebook via third-party sites (principally YouTube) with videos natively hosted by Facebook. In 2018, Facebook Video acquired an average of 8 billion daily views and 100 million hours of watch time. Facebook followed this with Watch in 2017, a dedicated tab for its native video content. With more unique monthly users than Google's YouTube, some think Facebook will eventually overtake YouTube in terms of public video uploads and views.

---

[12]https://www.journalism.org/2017/09/07/news-use-across-social-media-platforms-2017.

One of the subjects of video uploaded to these platforms is news events. Before professional news sources create their own reports on those events and share them in social media, a process which takes some time due to the necessity of checking (verifying) the content and creating the report, the immediate reaction to a news event is that of social media users' uploading of their own video content. This may be the user sitting in front of the camera and offering some personal commentary about the event, for example, and a key characteristic of such UGC (user-generated content) is that claims can easily be made and spread that are not properly corroborated. For example, as reports emerged of shooting at a shopping center in Munich, Germany on July 22, 2016 first UGC videos uploaded to YouTube spoke about terrorism, or suggested there were multiple shooters or multiple attack locations. Only later, alongside police appeals to desist spreading uncorroborated information, was it established that the perpetrator was a single person, a German teenager who acted alone. Story detection over the video material can indicate how news stories are being communicated on the video platforms, e.g., the Munich events would likely emerge with a label such as "munich, terrorist, shooting", but cannot make any judgment on the veracity of that communication. Rather, by aiming to maximize the precision and recall of videos posted on social networks related to a news story, InVID aims to offer the user an optimal means to explore the video content for a news story (which can include eyewitness video of the event itself), understand the public discourse about it and uncover both the dominant themes as well as those which vary from the mainstream of the discussion.

2.5.1 Video Information Retrieval: Related Work/State of the Art

Looking for recent scientific publications on news video retrieval from social networks, our own paper [49] is returned. Indeed, the scientific literature seems to tend to consider video retrieval as a research subject when it, for example, researches query by visual input (and thus a visual similarity matching problem). The precision of keyword-based queries on social network APIs has not been a recent topic, and the domain of news has its own specifics since news stories tend to relate to world events with agents (those involved in the story), a location and a temporal aspect. Our own research suggested keyword pairs or triples, with a focus on using entity keywords (those which refer to persons, organizations, and locations), would be the most effective to query social networks for content related to news.

Some of the tools considered previously for comparison with our story detection approach also exhibited the functionality of collecting online media about the stories. Some were, as it turned out, lacking any automatic detection of news stories but acted as content discovery platforms for news where the user initiated the search. They could then, potentially, be subjects of a comparative evaluation with our social media extraction approach, whether based on detected stories or text searches. The state-of-the-art tools that we could compare in terms of news story-based online social media content discovery (and, for InVID, with a focus on retrieval of video content) are Echosec, Newswhip, and Nunki. Neither Banjo, Dataminr nor Facebook Signal gave us access to their platforms. EventRegistry, considered in the story detection, only collects news articles and not social media of any type. We compare the videos provided for news stories by the InVID dashboard with those for the same story from the three competitors in the Evaluation section below.

2.5.2   Video API Querying

We propose to construct queries for news-related video on the basis of the keywords aggregated per story in the story detection step. The label of a story (Sect. 2.3.4) provides a set of keywords which can be used in a social network API query. Stories themselves are reflections of what is currently being discussed as newsworthy in social media. We have assessed the value of the extracted keywords as descriptors of newsworthy content in video platforms. The results indicated that bi- or tri-grams of keywords were optimal to maximize on both precision and recall. Single keywords had high recall at the cost of too much loss of precision. Larger combinations of keywords had high precision at the cost of too much loss of recall, in fact often sharply reducing the number of videos retrieved to zero as the constructed query is too specific. Single keywords which can be associated with entities—agents such as persons and organizations, locations of events, and names for types of events—were more effective than non-entities, although generally we found that the combination of words derived from the labels of the stories, even when they were all non-entities, was still very effective as they reflected well the combinations of words being used at that precise time to describe the news story on social media.

2.5.3   Relevance Filtering and Ranking

Monitoring the videos returned for our dynamically generated queries, we noted that there was some noise generated from certain query terms when they could be more generally interpreted. While the YouTube API itself does a good job in relevance sorting query results, in those cases certain other irrelevant videos were being returned as relevant, probably because the videos themselves are popular on the YouTube platform and hence "gain" in relevance for Google's algorithm. Two examples for this are "audiobook" (which, for example, appears together with political topics) and "live concert" (which appears together with a concert location, which may match a news story location being searched for). We implemented a filter after the video API responses to remove videos whose title matched these and similar terms as they were constantly irrelevant to the newsworthy video collection task.

As already introduced in the content modeling section (Sect. 2.3.1), every document is subject to keyword extraction from its textual content. Just as tweets could be associated to a news story using the keywords that label the detected story in the keyword graph as a weighted query over the index of tweets which are all individually annotated with keywords, we can also associate videos to a news story in the same manner. The retrieved videos from the API queries are indexed in the same way, with keywords extracted from their textual metadata. Among the set of videos associated with a story, there is still a challenge to organize them in a meaningful order for a user. Our default ranking is a relevance measure 0–1, where relevance refers to the extent to which the video (as a document with keywords) matches to the story description (the keywords ordered by weight from the sub-graph representing that story).

2.6   Social Video Retrieval: Implementation and Evaluation

Social media APIs vary with respect to public access, content limits, and query support.

In particular, our interest is to be able to filter content responses to only video material. Another aspect is whether a posting on social media natively contains a video or makes a hyperlink reference to a video hosted on another platform. In recent years, the major platforms—Facebook and Twitter—have shifted to supporting native video content, reducing the need for video hyperlink resolution. Tables 2.4 and 2.5 summarize the query support of the different platforms. Plus (+) indicates support for a query function (Temporal = time restriction, Geo = location restriction, and Lang = language restriction) and minus (−) for lack of support.

Based on our analysis of social media APIs, we have selected the following platforms for social video retrieval: YouTube, Twitter, Vimeo, DailyMotion, Reddit. Instagram has restricted access to its API for third-party data requests as of April 2018. Facebook Video cannot be queried by search terms—one can only request the metadata for a known video (by URL).

Table 2.4 "Video-oriented APIs", designed (or may be configured) to return video content specifically

Platform	Endpoint	Query with	Temporal	Geo	Lang	Other parameters	Sort by
YouTube	Search	String	+	+	+	Safesearch, topic-id, license, caption, dimension, duration	Date, rating, views, relevance, title
Daily Motion	Data	String, tags	+	+	+	Channel, featured, genre, live, shorter than	Date, relevance, visited, commented, random, ranking, trending, live
Vimeo	Search	String	−	−	−	License	Date, alphabet, relevant, likes

Table 2.5 "Filter-dependent APIs", may contain video content among their results

Platform	Endpoint	Query with	Temporal	Geo	Lang	Other parameters	Sort by
Twitter	Search API	String, hashtags, users	+	+	+	include_entities	Recent, popular, mix
Twitter	Streaming API	String, hashtags, users	−	+	−		
Reddit	Search	String	+	−	−	Links	
Instagram	Search	Geo	−	+	−		
Instagram	Recent	Tag	−	−	−		

A queries list is generated out of the story detection in the Twitter Accounts stream and we perform conjunctive queries over each API at a 6 hourly interval. Currently, this results in the collection of 700–1100 videos daily, as queries are time-restricted (to only videos uploaded in the previous 24 h) we maximize the precision of the video retrieval to videos related to the current stories. YouTube has tended to be more effective in matching queries with videos (and the retrieved videos are more relevant), whereas retrieval from Vimeo and DailyMotion has tended to provide a lower volume of documents.

In Web retrieval, it is difficult to apply classical information retrieval measures which assume knowledge of the entire collection from which retrieval is done (i.e., both how many correct responses exist in the collection for a query as well as how many incorrect). Precision and recall are calculated according to knowledge of how many documents exist in the collection and, for one retrieval task, how many documents would actually be a correct response. In Web IR, we calculate "Precision at N" where N is the number of documents in the response where we cut off the set of documents to be considered in evaluation. So precision becomes "the percentage of the results which are relevant, where the number of results are capped at a certain number". Recall is not possible in the classical definition of the term since it is "the percentage of total relevant results correctly returned in the retrieval task". In an open Web scenario, e.g., a YouTube query, we cannot say what is the number of total relevant results on the YouTube platform for any query.

It happens that we cut off the number of documents returned by the video APIs in any case since the size of the response to each query is a factor in how many queries we can execute within the given API limits. Our default has been $n = 20$ which reflects the standard number of videos shown in the first page of YouTube search results.

We will evaluate the news video retrieval using metrics for precision (at n), accuracy and F-score. It has been noted that the classical IR metric of recall cannot be applied in Web IR; we consider in its place a metric of accuracy which is the proportion of videos in the query response which are considered newsworthy, even if not directly related to the news story queried for. This is an acknowledgment that our video retrieval seeks to collect fundamentally newsworthy video postings in social

Table 2.6 Newsworthy video retrieval evaluation

Metric	Avg value 2017 test	May 28, 2018 value	May 29, 2018 value	May 30, 2018 value	Avg value 2018 test
Precision	**0.54**	0.79	0.7	0.79	**0.76**
Accuracy	**0.82**	0.85	0.74	0.84	**0.81**
F-score	**0.65**	0.82	0.72	0.81	**0.78**

media, and that by querying in a general enough sense to prevent the exclusion of relevant videos from a query response (maximize the precision) we permit the possibility of videos from similar news stories to be included too (also maximize the accuracy).

Finally, to acquire a final metric to measure the overall accuracy of the information retrieval we calculate an F1-measure, classically seen as the harmonic mean of precision and recall. In our case we use the harmonic mean of precision and accuracy, capturing the overall relevance of the retrieved videos to the task of newsworthy video collection.

We will use the story labels from the top 10 stories from Twitter Accounts in the InVID dashboard for the time period May 28–30, 2018 as conjunctive query inputs. We will test results relevance by querying the YouTube API, using the default result sort by relevance. Since Web-based information retrieval excludes the possibility of knowing the total number of correct documents, recall in its classical form is no longer a meaningful metric and therefore "precision at n" is commonly used where n provides the cutoff point for the set of documents to evaluate for relevance. In line with the first page of search results, a standard choice in Web Search evaluation, we chose $n = 20$. In Table 2.6, we compare the average of the results of the evaluation in 2017 and the results for the dates May 28–30, 2018 with their average. It can be seen that our precision value has increased considerably, meaning that when we make a query for a newsworthy story we are more likely to only get videos that are precisely relevant to that story than video of any newsworthy story. This reflects the improvements in the specificity of the story labels to describe the news story, which in turn enables more precise API queries for videos related to that story. On the other hand, accuracy is more or less constant (the proportion of newsworthy video being collected into the InVID platform is probably still around 80% for YouTube), reflecting that we construct our queries specifically enough to avoid significant retrieval of unnewsworthy content.

We also evaluate the relevance of the social media video retrieval for news stories in the InVID Dashboard in comparison to other state-of-the-art tools for journalists. We gained trial access to a number of other commercial platforms which also provide functionality to find online social media video for news stories. Both platforms available to us (Echosec, Newswhip) work with keyword-based search and provide content filters to type and social network, so that results can be filtered to videos. Just as the default in the InVID dashboard, we set the time range to the last 24 h and

Table 2.7 Comparison of tools for news video discovery

Metric	Tool for video discovery	May 28, 2018 value	May 29, 2018 value	May 30, 2018 value	2018 avg value
Relevance	**InVID**	0.91	1	0.8	**0.9**
Volume	**InVID**	1060	728	548	
Relevance	**Echosec**	1	0.81	0.85	**0.89**
Volume	**Echosec**	609	328	309	
Relevance	**Newswhip**	1	0.94	1	**0.98**
Volume	**Newswhip**	52	44	114	

considered for each story detected by InVID the relevance of the video results on each platform. Note the differences in the social networks from which videos were retrieved:

• Echosec: Reddit, Vimeo, YouTube.
• InVID: DailyMotion, Twitter, Vimeo, YouTube.
• Newswhip: Facebook, Twitter, YouTube.

We compared the volume of search results and percentages of relevant video across the same stories on the InVID dashboard, Echosec, and Newswhip. For relevance, we look at precision at $n = 10$, and note that whereas InVID can sort story results by relevancy, Echosec only supports sort by recency, whereas Newswhip uses various sort options where we chose "highest velocity" which means video being currently spread (shared) at a higher frequency. We add volume since it may also be significant HOW MANY videos each platform can return for the current top news stories. We take absolute totals for search results based on the time restriction of the last 24 h. Table 2.7 shows the direct comparison of relevance and volume for all three platforms over all three days and their average. Looking at InVID compared to Echosec, which can be considered a state-of-the-art tool for journalistic discovery of news video on social media, the results are very similar for relevance. While both tend to provide a significant number of videos for each news story in the past 24 h, it can be seen that InVID offers more content on average, which is not only due to the additional sources (particularly Twitter) but also due to more matching video from YouTube. Comparing to Newswhip, the relevance value for them is almost perfect but this must be seen in the context of returning far fewer video results. To take an example from the 30th of May, ABORTION LAW + ARKANSAS + SUPREME COURT was a story with 21 videos in the InVID dashboard and 25 videos in Echosec, but Newswhip returned just 6. With apparently between 5 and 20% of the video coverage of the other two platforms, it must be acknowledged that a platform with 1 000 videos, of which 90% are relevant to the current news, compared to a platform with perfect relevance but just 100 videos, still means the former has nine times the amount of video material for a journalist to browse. InVID video discovery around news stories on social media therefore works very well and balances relevance with volume of retrieved video. While competing platforms can report similar or better relevance metrics, it must also be considered that the video discovery required a specific keyword-based search on selected news stories (and it seems that the keywords used to label the automatically detected stories by InVID work very well to find the relevant video).

2.7 Conclusions

In this chapter, we addressed the needs of journalists in a content verification workflow to first identify current news stories and then to find relevant video posted to social networks regarding a selected story. News story detection over Twitter has been able to identify current clusters of newsworthy content within both the professional news media and in user-generated content, label those clusters to express to the user which news story is in focus, and present the most relevant content (posts) related to the news story. Content retrieval for news stories has been focused on the APIs of social networks with video posts so that the user may browse video material being posted online about a selected news story, with a view to facilitate journalists discovering and verifying apparent eyewitness videos. Both the story detection and the social media retrieval contribute to content discovery in the InVID Dashboard (see Chap. 10).

Acknowledgements The work described in this chapter would not have been possible without the efforts and ideas of many other colleagues over the years. In particular, we acknowledge Walter Rafelsberger who initiated the story clustering implementation; Svitlana Vakulenko who first experimented with story detection on Twitter streams; Shu Zhu who contributed to the cluster merging, splitting, and burst detection; as well as Roland Pajuste who cleaned up the resulting code and worked on quality improvements and optimizations to make it more efficient.

References

1. Papadopoulos S, Corney D, Aiello LM (2014) Snow 2014 data challenge: assessing the performance of news topic detection methods in social media. In: SNOW-DC@ WWW, pp 1–8
2. Pouliquen B, Steinberger R, Deguernel O (2008) Story tracking: linking similar news over time and across languages. In: Proceedings of the workshop on multi-source multilingual information extraction and summarization. Association for Computational Linguistics, pp 49–56
3. Leetaru K, Schrodt PA (2013) Gdelt: global data on events, location, and tone, 1979–2012. In: ISA annual convention, vol 2, p 4
4. Leban G, Fortuna B, Brank J, Grobelnik M (2014) Cross-lingual detection of world events from news articles. In: Proceedings of the ISWC 2014 posters & demonstrations track a track within the 13th international semantic web conference, ISWC 2014, Riva del Garda, Italy, 21 October 2014, pp 21–24. http://ceur-ws.org/Vol-1272/paper_19.pdf
5. Rupnik J, Muhic A, Leban G, Skraba P, Fortuna B, Grobelnik M (2015) News across languages-cross-lingual document similarity and event tracking. arXiv:1512.07046
6. Hu M, Liu S, Wei F, Wu Y, Stasko J, Ma KL (2012) Breaking news on Twitter. In: Proceedings of the SIGCHI conference on human factors in computing systems. ACM, pp 2751–2754

7. Cataldi M, Di Caro L, Schifanella C (2010) Emerging topic detection on Twitter based on temporal and social terms evaluation. In: Proceedings of the tenth international workshop on multimedia data mining, MDMKDD '10. ACM, New York, NY, USA, pp 4:1–4:10. https://doi.org/10.1145/1814245.1814249
8. Aiello L, Petkos G, Martin C, Corney D, Papadopoulos S, Skraba R, Goker A, Kompatsiaris I, Jaimes A (2013) Sensing trending topics in Twitter. IEEE Trans Multim 15(6):1268–1282. https://doi.org/10.1109/TMM.2013.2265080
9. Wold HM, Vikre LC (2015) Online news detection on Twitter
10. Deerwester SC, Dumais ST, Landauer TK, Furnas GW, Harshman RA (1990) Indexing by latent semantic analysis. JAsIs 41(6):391–407
11. Landauer TK, Foltz PW, Laham D (1998) An introduction to latent semantic analysis. Discourse Process 25(2–3):259–284. https://doi.org/10.1080/01638539809545028
12. Blei DM, Ng AY, Jordan MI (2003) Latent Dirichlet allocation. J Mach Learn Res 3:993–1022. http://dl.acm.org/citation.cfm?id=944919.944937
13. Petkos G, Papadopoulos S, Kompatsiaris Y (2014) Two-level message clustering for topic detection in Twitter. In: SNOW-DC@ WWW, pp 49–56
14. Martín-Dancausa C, Göker A (2014) Real-time topic detection with bursty n-grams: RGU's submission to the 2014 SNOW challenge
15. Van Canneyt S, Feys M, Schockaert S, Demeester T, Develder C, Dhoedt B (2014) Detecting newsworthy topics in Twitter. In: Data challenge. Proceedings, Seoul, Korea, pp 1–8
16. Martín-Dancausa C, Corney D, Göker A (2015) Mining newsworthy topics from social media. In: Gaber MM, Cocea M, Wiratunga N, Goker A (eds) Advances in social media analysis. Studies in computational intelligence, vol 602. Springer International Publishing, pp 21–43. https://doi.org/10.1007/978-3-319-18458-6_2
17. Ifrim G, Shi B, Brigadir I (2014) Event detection in Twitter using aggressive filtering and hierarchical tweet clustering. In: SNOW-DC@ WWW, pp 33–40
18. Elbagoury A, Ibrahim R, Farahat A, Kamel M, Karray F (2015) Exemplar-based topic detection in Twitter streams. In: Ninth international AAAI conference on web and social media. http://www.aaai.org/ocs/index.php/ICWSM/ICWSM15/paper/view/10533
19. Popescu AM, Pennacchiotti M, Paranjpe D (2011) Extracting events and event descriptions from Twitter. In: Proceedings of the 20th international conference companion on world wide web. ACM, pp 105–106
20. Ritter A, Etzioni O, Clark S et al (2012) Open domain event extraction from Twitter. In: Proceedings of the 18th ACM SIGKDD international conference on knowledge discovery and data mining. ACM, pp 1104–1112
21. Katsios G, Vakulenko S, Krithara A, Paliouras G (2015) Towards open domain event extraction from twitter: revealing entity relations. In: Proceedings of the 4th DeRiVE workshop co-located with the 12th extended semantic web conference (ESWC 2015), Protoroz, Slovenia, May 2015, pp 35–46
22. Lendvai P, Declerck T (2015) Similarity-based cross-media retrieval for events. In: Bergmann R, Görg S, Müller G (eds) Proceedings of the LWA 2015 workshops: KDML, FGWM, IR, and FGDB. CEURS
23. Petrovic S, Osborne M, Lavrenko V (2012) Using paraphrases for improving first story detection in news and Twitter. In: Proceedings of the 2012 conference of the North American chapter of the Association for Computational Linguistics: human language technologies. Association for Computational Linguistics, pp 338–346
24. Phuvipadawat S, Murata T (2010) Breaking news detection and tracking in Twitter. In: 2010 IEEE/WIC/ACM international conference on web intelligence and intelligent agent technology (WI-IAT), vol 3, pp 120–123. https://doi.org/10.1109/WI-IAT.2010.205
25. Stokes N, Carthy J (2001) Combining semantic and syntactic document classifiers to improve first story detection. In: SIGIR 2001: Proceedings of the 24th ACM SIGIR conference, New Orleans, Louisiana, USA, 9–13 September 2001, pp 424–425. https://doi.org/10.1145/383952.384068

26. Osborne M, Petrovic S, McCreadie R, Macdonald C, Ounis I (2012) Bieber no more: first story detection using Twitter and Wikipedia. In: Proceedings of the workshop on time-aware information access. TAIA, vol 12
27. Burnside G, Milioris D, Jacquet P (2014) One day in Twitter: topic detection via joint complexity. https://hal-polytechnique.archives-ouvertes.fr/hal-00967776
28. Fujiki T, Nanno T, Suzuki Y, Okumura M (2004) Identification of bursts in a document stream. In: First international workshop on knowledge discovery in data streams (in conjunction with ECML/PKDD 2004). Citeseer, pp 55–64
29. Steiner T, van Hooland S, Summers E (2013) MJ no more: using concurrent Wikipedia edit spikes with social network plausibility checks for breaking news detection. In: Proceedings of the 22nd international conference on world wide web, WWW '13 Companion, Geneva, Switzerland, pp 791–794. http://dl.acm.org/citation.cfm?id=2487788.2488049
30. Yılmaz Y, Hero AO (2018) Multimodal event detection in Twitter hashtag networks. J Signal Process Syst 90(2):185–200
31. Hammad M, El-Beltagy SR (2017) Towards efficient online topic detection through automated bursty feature detection from Arabic Twitter streams. Procedia Comput Sci 117:248–255
32. Srijith P, Hepple M, Bontcheva K, Preotiuc-Pietro D (2017) Sub-story detection in twitter with hierarchical Dirichlet processes. Inf Process Manag 53(4):989–1003
33. Alsaedi N, Burnap P, Rana O (2017) Can we predict a riot? Disruptive event detection using Twitter. ACM Trans Internet Technol (TOIT) 17(2):18
34. Qin Y, Zhang Y, Zhang M, Zheng D (2018) Frame-based representation for event detection on Twitter. IEICE Trans Inf Syst 101(4):1180–1188
35. Mele I, Crestani F (2017) Event detection for heterogeneous news streams. In: International conference on applications of natural language to information systems. Springer, pp 110–123
36. Tonon A, Cudré-Mauroux P, Blarer A, Lenders V, Motik B (2017) Armatweet: detecting events by semantic tweet analysis. In: European semantic web conference. Springer, pp 138–153
37. Katragadda S, Benton R, Raghavan V (2017) Framework for real-time event detection using multiple social media sources
38. Vakulenko S, Nixon L, Lupu M (2017) Character-based neural embeddings for tweet clustering. In: Proceedings of the fifth international workshop on natural language processing for social media. Association for Computational Linguistics, Valencia, Spain, pp 36–44. https://doi.org/10.18653/v1/W17-1105
39. Baeza-Yates RA (1989) Improved string searching. Softw Pract Exp. 19(3):257–271. https://doi.org/10.1002/spe.4380190305
40. Nadeau D, Sekine S (2007) A survey of named entity recognition and classification. Lingvist Investig 30(1):3–26
41. Miller GA (1995) Wordnet: a lexical database for english. Commun ACM 38(11):39–41
42. Arcan M, McCrae JP, Buitelaar P (2016) Expanding wordnets to new languages with multilingual sense disambiguation. In: Proceedings of COLING 2016, the 26th international conference on computational linguistics: technical papers, pp 97–108
43. Ji H, Pan X, Zhang B, Nothman J, Mayfield J, McNamee P, Costello C (2017) Overview of tac-kbp2017 13 languages entity discovery and linking. In: TAC
44. Weichselbraun A, Kuntschik P, Brașoveanu AM (2018) Mining and leveraging background knowledge for improving named entity linking. In: Proceedings of the 8th international conference on web intelligence, mining and semantics, WIMS '18. ACM, New York, NY, USA, pp 27:1–27:11. https://doi.org/10.1145/3227609.3227670.
45. Weichselbraun A, Kuntschik P, Brasoveanu AMP (2019) Name variants for improving entity discovery and linking. In: Language, data and knowledge (LDK)
46. Blondel VD, Guillaume JL, Lambiotte R, Lefebvre E (2008) Fast unfolding of communities in large networks. J Stat Mech: Theory Exp 2008(10):P10008. http://stacks.iop.org/1742-5468/2008/i=10/a=P10008
47. Hasan M, Orgun MA, Schwitter R (2018) A survey on real-time event detection from the twitter data stream. J Inf Sci 44(4):443–463. https://doi.org/10.1177/0165551517698564

48. Zimmermann A (2014) On the cutting edge of event detection from social streams a non-exhaustive survey
49. Nixon LJ, Zhu S, Fischer F, Rafelsberger W, Göbel M, Scharl A (2017) Video retrieval for multimedia verification of breaking news on social networks. In: Proceedings of the first international workshop on multimedia verification, MuVer '17. ACM, New York, NY, USA, pp 13–21. https://doi.org/10.1145/3132384.3132386.

Chapter 3
Video Fragmentation and Reverse Search on the Web

Evlampios Apostolidis, Konstantinos Apostolidis, Ioannis Patras and Vasileios Mezaris

Abstract This chapter is focused on methods and tools for video fragmentation and reverse search on the web. These technologies can assist journalists when they are dealing with fake news—which nowadays are being rapidly spread via social media platforms—that rely on the reuse of a previously posted video from a past event with the intention to mislead the viewers about a contemporary event. The fragmentation of a video into visually and temporally coherent parts and the extraction of a representative keyframe for each defined fragment enables the provision of a complete and concise keyframe-based summary of the video. Contrary to straightforward approaches that sample video frames with a constant step, the generated summary through video fragmentation and keyframe extraction is considerably more effective for discovering the video content and performing a fragment-level search for the video on the web. This chapter starts by explaining the nature and characteristics of this type of reuse-based fake news in its introductory part, and continues with an overview of existing approaches for temporal fragmentation of single-shot videos into sub-shots (the most appropriate level of temporal granularity when dealing with user-generated videos) and tools for performing reverse search of a video on the web. Subsequently, it describes two state-of-the-art methods for video sub-shot fragmentation—one relying on the assessment of the visual coherence over sequences of frames, and another one that is based on the identification of camera activity during the video recording—and presents the InVID web application that enables the fine-grained (at the fragment-level) reverse search for near-duplicates

E. Apostolidis (✉) · K. Apostolidis · V. Mezaris
Information Technologies Institute, Centre for Research and Technology Hellas,
Thessaloniki, Greece
e-mail: apostolid@iti.gr

K. Apostolidis
e-mail: kapost@iti.gr

V. Mezaris
e-mail: bmezaris@iti.gr

E. Apostolidis · I. Patras
School of Electronic Engineering and Computer Science, Queen Mary University,
London, UK
e-mail: i.patras@qmul.ac.uk

© Springer Nature Switzerland AG 2019
V. Mezaris et al. (eds.), *Video Verification in the Fake News Era*,
https://doi.org/10.1007/978-3-030-26752-0_3

53

of a given video on the web. In the sequel, the chapter reports the findings of a series of experimental evaluations regarding the efficiency of the above-mentioned technologies, which indicate their competence to generate a concise and complete keyframe-based summary of the video content, and the use of this fragment-level representation for fine-grained reverse video search on the web. Finally, it draws conclusions about the effectiveness of the presented technologies and outlines our future plans for further advancing them.

3.1   Introduction

The recent advances in video capturing technology made possible the embedding of powerful, high-resolution video sensors into portable devices, such as camcorders, digital cameras, tablets, and smartphones. Most of these technologies now offer network connectivity and file sharing functionalities. The latter, combined with the rise and widespread use of social networks (such as Facebook, Twitter, Instagram) and video sharing platforms (such as YouTube, Vimeo, DailyMotion) resulted in an enormous increase in the number of videos captured and shared online by amateur users on a daily basis. These User-Generated Videos (UGVs) can nowadays be recorded at any time and place using smartphones, tablets, and a variety of video cameras (such as GoPro action cameras) that can be attached to sticks, body parts or even drones. The ubiquitous use of video capturing devices, supported by the convenience of the users to share videos through social networks and video sharing platforms, leads to a wealth of online available UGVs.

Over the last years, these online shared UGVs are, in many cases, the only evidence of a breaking or evolving story. The sudden and unexpected appearance of these events makes their timely coverage by news or media organization impossible. However, the existence (in most cases) of eyewitnesses capturing the story with their smartphones and instantly sharing the recorded video (even live, i.e., during its recording) via social networks, makes the UGV the only and highly valuable source of information about the breaking event. In this newly formed technological environment, that facilitates information diffusion through a variety of social media platforms, journalists and investigators alike are increasingly turning to these platforms to find media recordings of events. Newsrooms in TV stations and online news platforms make use of video to illustrate and report on news events, and since professional journalists are not always at the scene of a breaking or evolving story (as mentioned above), it is the content shared by users that can be used for reporting the story. Nevertheless, the rise of social media as a news source has also seen a rise in fake news, i.e., the spread of deliberate misinformation or disinformation on these platforms. Based on this unfortunate fact, the online shared user-generated content comes into question and people's trust in journalism is severely shaken.

One type of fakes, probably the easiest to do and thus one of the most commonly found by journalists, relies on the reuse of a video from an earlier event with the claim that it shows a contemporary event. An example of such a fake is depicted in

Fig. 3.1 Example of a fake news based on the reuse of a video from a hurricane in Uruguay (image on the left) to deliberately mislead people about the strike of hurricane Otto in Panama (image in the middle) and the strike of Hurricane Irma in the US islands (image on the right)

Fig. 3.1. In this figure, the image on the left is a screenshot of a video showing a hurricane that strikes in Dolores, Uruguay on May 29, 2016; the image on the middle is a screenshot of the same video with the claim that it shows Hurricane Otto that strikes in Bocas del Toro, Panama on November 24, 2016; and the image on the right is a screenshot of a tweet that uses the same video with the claim that it shows the activity of Hurricane Irma in the islands near the United States on September 9, 2017.

The identification and debunking of such fakes require the detection of the original video through the search for prior occurrences of this video (or parts of it) on the web. Early approaches for performing this task were based on manually taking screenshots of the video in the player and uploading these images for performing reverse image search using the corresponding functionality of popular web search engines (e.g., Google search). This process can be highly laborious and time-demanding, while its efficiency depends on a limited set of manually taken screenshots of the video. However, the in-time identification of media posted online, which (claim to) illustrate a (breaking) news event is for many journalists the foremost challenge in order to meet deadlines to publish a news story online or fill a news broadcast with content. The time needed for extensive and effective search regarding the posted video, in combination with the lack of expertise by many journalists and the time-pressure to publish the story, can seriously affect the credibility of the published news item. And the publication or republication of fake news can significantly harm the reliability of the entire news organization. An example of miss-verification of a fake video by an Italian news organization is presented in Fig. 3.2. A video from the filming of the "World War Z" movie (left part of Fig. 3.2) was used in a tweet claiming to show a Hummer attack against police in Notre-Dame, Paris, France on June 6, 2017 (middle part of Fig. 3.2) and another tweet claiming to show an attack at Gare Centrale, Brussels, Belgium two weeks later (right part of Fig. 3.2). The fake tweet about the Paris attack was used in a new item published by the aforementioned news organization, causing a strong defeat in its trustworthiness.

Several tools that enable the identification of near-duplicates of a video on the web have been developed over the last years, a fact that indicates the usefulness and applicability of this process by journalists and members of the media verification

Fig. 3.2 Example of a fake news based on the reuse of a video from the filming of the "World War Z" movie (image on the left) to deliberately mislead people about a Hummer attack in Notre-Dame, Paris (image in the middle) and at Gare Centrale in Brussels (image on the right)

community. Nevertheless, the existing solutions (presented in detail in Sect. 3.2.2) exhibit several limitations that restrict the effectiveness of the video reverse search task. In particular, some of these solutions rely on a limited set of video thumbnails provided by the video sharing platform (e.g., the YouTube DataViewer of Amnesty International[1]). Other technologies demand the extraction of video frames for performing reverse image search (e.g., the TinEye search engine[2] and the Karma Decay[3] web application). A number of tools enable this reverse search on closed collections of videos that significantly limit the boundaries of investigation (e.g., the Berify[4], the RevIMG[5], and the Videntifier[6] platforms). Last but not least, a commonality among the aforementioned technologies is that none of them supports the analysis of locally stored videos.

Aiming to offer a more effective approach for reverse video search on the web, in InVID we developed: (a) an algorithm for temporal fragmentation of (single-shot) UGVs into sub-shots (presented in Sect. 3.3.1.1), and (b) a web application that integrates this algorithm and makes possible the time-efficient and at the fragment-level reverse search for near-duplicates of a given video on the web (described in Sect. 3.3.2). The developed algorithm allows the identification of visually and temporally coherent parts of the processed video, and the extraction of a dynamic number of keyframes in a manner that secures a complete and concise representation of the defined—visually discrete—parts of the video. Moreover, the compatibility of the web application with several video sharing platforms and social networks is further extended by the ability to directly process videos that are locally stored in the user's machine. In a nutshell, our complete technology assists users to quickly discover the

---

[1] https://citizenevidence.amnestyusa.org/.

[2] https://tineye.com/.

[3] http://karmadecay.com/.

[4] https://berify.com/.

[5] http://www.revimg.com/.

[6] http://www.videntifier.com.

temporal structure of the video, extract detailed information about the video content and use this data in their reverse video search queries.

In the following, Sect. 3.2 discusses the current state of the art on methods for video sub-shot fragmentation (Sect. 3.2.1) and tools for reverse video search on the web (Sect. 3.2.2). Then Sect. 3.3 is dedicated to the presentation of two advanced approaches for video sub-shot fragmentation—the InVID method that relies on the visual resemblance of the video content (see Sect. 3.3.1.1) and another algorithm that is based on the extraction of motion information (see Sect. 3.3.1.2)—and the description of the InVID web application for reverse video search on the web (see Sect. 3.3.2). Subsequently, Sect. 3.4 reports the extracted findings regarding the performance of the aforementioned methods (see Sect. 3.4.1) and tool (see Sect. 3.4.2), while Sect. 3.5 concludes the document and presents our future plans in this research area.

3.2 Related Work

This part presents the related work, both in terms of methods for temporal fragmentation of uninterruptedly captured (i.e., single-shot) videos into sub-shots (Sect. 3.2.1) and tools for finding near-duplicates of a given video on the web (Sect. 3.2.2).

3.2.1 Video Fragmentation

A variety of methods dealing with the temporal fragmentation of single-shot videos have been proposed over the last couple of decades. Most of them are related to approaches for video summarization and keyframe selection (e.g., [1–4]), some focus on the analysis of egocentric or wearable videos (e.g., [5–7]), others aim to address the need for detecting duplicates of videos (e.g., [8]), and a number of them are related to the indexing and annotation of personal videos (e.g., [9]), while there is a group of methods that deal with the task of indexing and summarization of rushes video (e.g., [10–13]). The majority of the suggested approaches can be grouped into two main classes of methodologies.

The techniques of the first class consider a sub-shot as an uninterrupted sequence of frames within a shot that only have a small variation in visual content. Based on this assumption, they try to define sub-shots by assessing the visual similarity of consecutive or neighboring video frames. A rather straightforward approach that evaluates frames' similarity using color histograms and the x^2 test was described in [13], while a method that detects sub-shots of a video by assessing the visual dissimilarity of frames lying within a sliding temporal window using 16-bin HSV histograms (denoted as "Eurecom fragmentation") was reported in [10]. Instead of using HSV histograms, the video fragmentation and keyframe selection approach described in [14] represents the visual content of each video frame with the help of the

Discrete Cosine Transform (DCT) and assesses the visual similarity of neighboring video frames based on the cosine similarity. The generated frame-level sequence of similarity scores is then post-processed and the sequences of frames that exhibit visual and temporal coherence form the sub-shots of the video. A different approach [12] estimates the grid-level dissimilarity between pairs of frames and fragments a video by observing that the cumulative difference in the visual content of subsequent frames indicates gradual change within a sub-shot; a similar approach was presented in [11]. The method of [15] estimates the brightness, contrast, camera, and object motion of each video frame using YUV histograms and optical flow vectors, and defines sub-shot boundaries by analyzing the extracted features through a coherence discontinuity detection mechanism on groups of frames within a sliding window.

The methods of the second class fragment a video shot into sub-shots based on the rationale that each sub-shot corresponds to a different action of the camera during the video recording. Hence, these approaches aim to detect different types of camera activity over sequences of frames and define these frame sequences as the different sub-shots of the video. An early, MPEG-2 compatible, algorithm that detects basic camera operations by fitting the motion vectors of the MPEG stream into a 2D affine model was presented in [16]. Another approach that exploits the same motion vectors and estimates the camera motion via a multi-resolution scheme was proposed in [17]. More recently, the estimation of the affinity between pairs of frames for motion detection and categorization was a core idea for many other techniques. Some of them use the motion vectors of the MPEG-2 stream (e.g., [3]), while others compute the parameters of a 3×3 affine model by extracting and matching local descriptors [2] or feature points [18]. The dominant motion transformation between a pair of frames is then estimated by comparing the computed parameters against predefined models. [19] studies several approaches for optical flow field calculation, that include the matching of local descriptors (i.e., SIFT [20], SURF [21]) based on a variety of block matching algorithms, and the use of the Pyramidal Lucas Kanade (PLK) algorithm [22]. The more recently introduced algorithm of [23] performs a lightweight computation of spatiotemporal optical flow over sequences of frames and compares the frame-level motion distribution against predefined motion models. The extracted motion information is then used to detect (and categorize) a number of different video recording actions (which relate to camera movement or focal distance change) and the frame sequences that temporally correlate with each identified action are considered as the video sub-shots. Contrary to the use of experimentally defined thresholds for categorizing the detected camera motion, [24] describes a generic approach for motion-based video parsing that estimates the affine motion parameters, either based on motion vectors of the MPEG-2 stream or by applying a frame-to-frame image registration process, factorizes their values via Singular Value Decomposition (SVD) and imports them into three multi-class Support Vector Machines (SVMs) to recognize the camera motion type and direction between successive video frames. A variation of this approach [25], identifies changes in the "camera view" by estimating a simplified three-parameter global camera motion model using the Integral Template Matching algorithm [26]. Then, trained SVMs classify the camera motion of each frame, and neighboring frames with the same type of camera motion are grouped together forming a sub-shot. Another threshold-less approach [7] aims to identify specific activities in egocentric videos using hierarchical Hidden Markov Models (HMM), while the algorithm of [4] combines the concept of "camera views" and the use of HMM for performing camera motion-based fragmentation of UGVs. Finally, a study on different approaches for motion estimation was presented in [27].

Further to the aforementioned two general classes of methodologies, other approaches have been also proposed. The early approach from [28] and the more recently proposed algorithm from [1] exploit motion vector information from the compressed video stream at the macro-block level. The methods in [8, 29] extract several descriptors from the video frames (e.g., color histograms and motion features) and subdivide each shot into sub-shots by clustering its frames into an appropriately determined number of clusters with the help of the c-means and k-means clustering algorithms, respectively. A couple of techniques, presented in [30, 31], utilize data from auxiliary camera sensors (e.g., GPS, gyroscope, and accelerometers) to identify the camera motion type for every video sub-shot or a group of events in UGVs. On a slightly different context, algorithms capable to analyze egocentric or wearable videos were discussed in [5, 6]. Last but not least, the variety of introduced algorithms for video sub-shot fragmentation includes approaches based on the extraction and processing of 3D spatiotemporal slices (e.g., [32, 33]), and statistical analysis (e.g., [34–36]), while a comparative study evaluating the performance of different approaches for sub-shot fragmentation can be found in [19].

3.2.2   Reverse Video Search on the Web

Nowadays, there are a plethora of tools that support the search and retrieval of near-duplicates of an image or video on the web. The latter indicates the popularity and attractiveness of image/video-based search and highlights the usefulness of the visual content-based searching procedure for performing several media asset management tasks, including the assessment of the originality and authenticity of a given video.

One of the earliest (and most known among journalists) technologies is the YouTube DataViewer of Amnesty International[7] which enables the users to find near-duplicates of a YouTube video by performing a reverse image search using the YouTube-extracted video thumbnails. Nevertheless, this solution performs reverse video search based on a limited set of (usually) randomly selected video keyframes/thumbnails that have been associated to the video. This fact introduces the risk of excluding parts of the video that could enhance the reverse search or be of particular interest to the user, or even worse, to base the reverse search on thumbnails that are completely irrelevant to the video and have been deliberately selected for clickbait purposes. In addition, the search is supported only for videos available online, thus making impossible the reverse search of a video stored in the user's machine.

---

[7]https://citizenevidence.amnestyusa.org/.

Another (preexisting) solution that can partially support the retrieval of near-duplicates of a video is the TinEye search engine[8], which enables the online search and retrieval of a given image. The advantage of this tool is that it offers a (paid) API to anyone who wishes to perform image search requests in a more automated way instead of providing every time the URL of the image file or uploading a local copy of the file on the TinEye web application. The limitation of this technology when trying to find near-duplicates of a given video is that it requires the extraction of video frames that should be used as query images, a process which implies an overhead to the overall procedure. A variation of this platform, with significantly more restricted functionalities though, is the Karma Decay[9] web application which allows to perform reverse image search on Reddit.com. Last but not least, three recently developed platforms that assist the detection and retrieval of images and videos are the Berify, the RevIMG, and the Videntifier. Berify[10] is a paid service that, according to its developers, offers functionalities for image-driven search of online available images and videos; updates of the search results are checked and forwarded to its users on a predefined basis. RevIMG[11] is another non-free solution that offers more unique functionalities, enabling the user to specify and use a portion of an image to search. However, the reverse search is performed only within closed collections of images. Videntifier[12] is a visual search engine which can be used for the retrieval of a given image or video stream (even after being modified), but similar to RevIMG, the identification of a near-duplicate relies on the matching of the given media item against a closed reference collection of video content.

3.3   State-of-the-Art Techniques and Tools

3.3.1   Video Fragmentation

This section describes two different approaches for the fragmentation of single-shot videos into sub-shots; one that relies on the assessment of the visual resemblance between neighboring frames of the video (presented in Sect. 3.3.1.1), and another one that is based on the detection of motion which corresponds to different camera activities during the recording of the video (explained in Sect. 3.3.1.2). In terms of

---

[8]https://tineye.com/.

[9]http://karmadecay.com/.

[10]https://berify.com/.

[11]http://www.revimg.com/.

[12]http://www.videntifier.com.

the utilized strategy for defining the different segments of the video, these methods cover a major portion of the techniques reported in the literature part of the chapter (Sect. 3.2.1). Hence, the following subsections allow the reader to understand how these different approaches tackle the problem of video sub-shot fragmentation, identify the pros and cons of each approach, and get a concrete view about the efficiency of each method based on the evaluation outcomes reported in Sect. 3.4.1.

3.3.1.1 Video Sub-shot Fragmentation Based on the Visual Coherence

This algorithm (described in [14]) belongs to the first class of methods presented in Sect. 3.2.1. It decomposes a single-shot video into sub-shots based on the detection of visually and temporally coherent parts of the video, i.e., sequences of frames having only a small and contiguous variation in their visual content. This detection relies on the comparison and assessment of the visual similarity of neighboring frames of the video. For this purpose, the visual content of each video frame is represented with the help of the Discrete Cosine Transform (DCT), which is similar to the applied transformation when extracting the MPEG-7 Color Layout Descriptor [37]. More specifically, the pipeline for computing the DCT-based representation of a video frame is illustrated in Fig. 3.3 and contains the following steps:

- the video frame is initially resized to $m \times m$ dimensions for increasing the resilience of the analysis against changes in the image aspect ratio and size (step 1 in Fig. 3.3);
- the resized image is represented as a sum of cosine functions oscillating at different frequencies via a two-dimensional DCT (step 2 in Fig. 3.3), which results in an $m \times m$ matrix (for illustration purposes, $m = 8$ in Fig. 3.3) where the top left element corresponds to the DC coefficient (zero-frequency) and every other element moving from left to right and from top to bottom corresponds to an increase in the horizontal and vertical frequency by a half cycle, respectively;
- the top left $r \times r$ part ($r < m$) of the computed matrix (for illustration purposes, $r = 3$ in Fig. 3.3) is kept, thus maintaining the most of the visual information that tends to be concatenated in a few low-frequency components of DCT, while high-frequency coefficients that store information related to the visual details of the image are discarded (step 3 in Fig. 3.3);
- a matrix reshaping process is applied to piece together the rows of the extracted $r \times r$ sub-matrix to a single row vector (step 4 in Fig. 3.3);
- the first element of this vector, which corresponds to the DC coefficient, is removed (step 5 in Fig. 3.3), forming a row vector of size $r^2 - 1$ that represents the image.

Having extracted the DCT-based representation of the video frames, the visual similarity between a pair of frames is then estimated by computing the cosine similarity of their descriptor vectors. More specifically, given a pair of video frames F_i and F_j with descriptor vectors D_i and D_j, respectively, their visual resemblance $V_{i,j}$ is calculated by $V_{i,j} = \frac{D_i \cdot D_j}{\|D_i\|\|D_j\|}$, where $\cdot$ denotes the dot product of the descriptor vectors and $\|\|$ denotes their Euclidean norm. Nevertheless, a pair of subsequent video

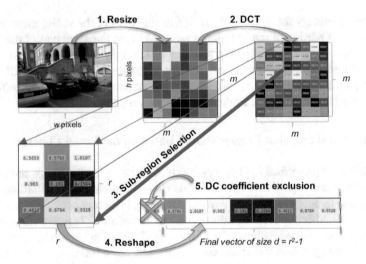

Fig. 3.3 The steps of the applied analysis for extracting the DCT-based representation of the visual content of each processed video frame

frames—even in the case of a video with the typical frame-rate of 30 fps—usually exhibits high visual similarity, and this similarity gets more and more significant for videos of higher frame-rates that users are allowed to capture with modern smartphones or other devices (such as GoPro cameras which support video recoding up to 240 fps). Driven by this observation, the algorithm does not apply the aforementioned pairwise similarity estimation on every pair of consecutive video frames, but only for neighboring frames selected via a frame-sampling strategy which keeps 3 equally distant frames per second.

The analysis of the entire set of selected video frames results in a series of similarity scores, which is then post-processed in order to identify visually coherent fragments with gradually changing visual content (that exhibit high visual resemblance), and parts of the video with more drastically altered visual content (which typically show lower visual resemblance). In particular, the computed series of similarity scores undergoes a smoothing procedure with the help of a sliding mean average window of size 3 (see the gray curve in Fig. 3.4). Through this process, the algorithm reduces the effect of sudden, short-term changes in the visual content of the video, such as the ones introduced due to camera flashlights or after a slight hand movement of the camera holder. In the following, the turning points of the smoothed series are identified by computing its second derivative (see the yellow vertical lines in Fig. 3.4). Each turning point signifies a change in the similarity tendency and therefore a sub-shot boundary—the latter implies that each video sub-shot is delimited by a pair of subsequent turning points in the smoothed series of similarity scores. Through this process, the algorithm indicates both sub-shots having none or small and slowly gradual variation in their visual content, and sub-shots with more drastically changing visual content.

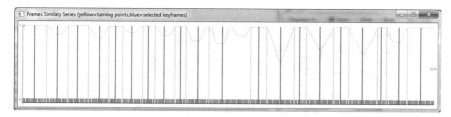

Fig. 3.4 An example of the smoothed series of similarity scores (gray curve), the identified sub-shot boundaries (yellow vertical lines), and the selected representative keyframe (blue vertical lines) for each one of them

As a final processing (keyframe extraction) step, sub-shots with low variation are represented by their middle frame and sub-shots with more drastically changing visual content are represented by the frame that corresponds to the most pronounced visual change within the sub-shot (see the blue vertical lines in Fig. 3.4). The selected keyframes can be used for supporting fragment-level reverse video search on the web, as detailed in Sect. 3.3.2.

3.3.1.2   Video Sub-shot Fragmentation Based on Motion Detection

This method (reported in [23]) belongs to the second class of techniques presented in Sect. 3.2.1. It fragments a single-shot video into sub-shots by identifying self-contained parts which exhibit visual continuity and correspond to individual elementary low-level actions that take place during the video recording. These actions include camera panning and tilting; camera movement in the 3D Euclidean space; camera zoom in/out and minor or no camera movement. The detection of sub-shot boundaries—and the identification of the performed action as an extra feature—is based on the extraction and spatiotemporal analysis of motion information.

Following the reasoning explained in Sect. 3.3.1.1 regarding the significantly high visual resemblance of successive video frames, the algorithm applies the subsequently described pairwise motion estimation on neighboring frames selected through a sampling strategy with a fixed step equal to 10% of the video frame-rate. The conducted motion between a pair of neighboring frames is estimated by computing the region-level optical flow based on the procedure depicted in Fig. 3.5, which consists of the following steps:

- each frame undergoes an image resizing process that maintains the original aspect ratio and makes the frame width equal to w, and then it is spatially fragmented into four quartiles;
- the most prominent corners in each quartile are detected based on the algorithm of [38];
- the detected corners are used for estimating the optical flow at the region-level by utilizing the Pyramidal Lucas Kanade (PLK) method;
- based on the extracted optical flow, a mean displacement vector is computed for each quartile, and the four spatially distributed vectors are treated as a region-level representation of the motion activity between the pair of frames.

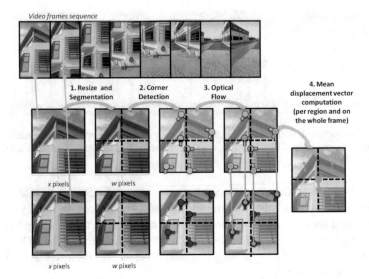

Fig. 3.5 The steps of the applied procedure for estimating the region-level optical flow between a pair of frames

To detect (and classify) any displacement of the camera in the 2D space at the frame-level, the algorithm:

- takes the computed region-level mean displacement vectors (left part of Figs. 3.6a, 3.6b, 3.6c);
- averages them producing a frame-level mean displacement vector (middle part of Fig. 3.6a, 3.6b, 3.6c);
- projects the created frame-level mean displacement vector to the horizontal and vertical axis of the Euclidean space (right part of Fig. 3.6a, 3.6b, 3.6c).

Subsequently, a single x-axis vector (Fig. 3.6a) is interpreted as a horizontal-only camera displacement to the vector's direction, a single y-axis vector (Fig. 3.6b) is recognized as a vertical-only camera displacement to the vector's direction, while a pair of x- and y-axis vectors (Fig. 3.6c) is correlated to a diagonal displacement to the frame-level mean displacement vector's direction.

For identifying camera activity at the depth level (i.e., the z-axis of the 3D space) the algorithm:

- takes the computed region-level mean displacement vectors (left part of Fig. 3.6d, 3.6e, 3.6f);
- inverts the direction of the top- and bottom-left vectors (middle part of Fig. 3.6d, 3.6e, 3.6f);
- computes the sum vector and projects it on the x-axis (right part of Fig. 3.6d, 3.6e, 3.6f).

As shown in Fig. 3.6s, the vector inversion process in the case of camera movement at the horizontal and/or vertical axes only, leads to a set of counterbalanced mean

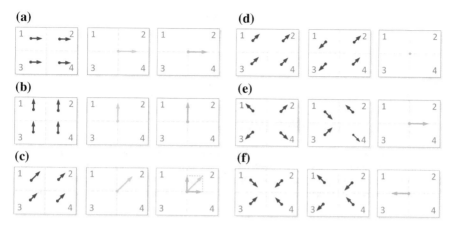

Fig. 3.6 Motion estimation process for **a** right displacement, **b** upward displacement, and **c** diagonal displacement of the camera. Focal distance change estimation process in case of **d** displacement only at horizontal and vertical axes (similar to (**c**)—thus, no change in the z-axis), **e** forward displacement or camera zoom in, and **f** backward displacement or camera zoom out

displacement vectors and thus, the magnitude of the projection is zero. However, in case of camera activity at the depth axis, the four mean displacement vectors do not maintain the same direction, but point either: to the corners of the frame (Fig. 3.6e), forming a projection vector with positive magnitude, which indicates the existence of forward camera movement or a camera zooming in; or to the center of the frame (Fig. 3.6f), forming a projection vector with negative magnitude, that denotes the occurrence of backward camera movement or a camera zooming out.

Based on the above the algorithm computes for each pair of frames three values that represent the spatial displacement in x-, y-, and z-axis. These values, denoted as V_x, V_y and V_z in the sequel, are normalized in $[-1, +1]$ where:

- V_x $(V_y) = -1$ represents left (downward) displacement of frame pixels equal to 5% of the frame width (height);
- V_x $(V_y) = +1$ signifies right (upward) displacement of frame pixels equal to 5% of the frame width (height);
- V_x $(V_y) = 0$ denotes no displacement of frame pixels;
- $V_z = -1$ $(+1)$ indicates increment (decrement) of the focal distance that causes inward (outward) spatial displacement of frame pixels equal to 5% of the frame's diagonal;
- $V_z = 0$ indicates no change of the focal distance.

The normalized spatial displacement vectors V_x, V_y, and V_z are then post-processed, as described in Algorithm 1, to detect the different sub-shots. Specifically, the values of each vector are initially subjected to low-pass filtering in the frequency domain (sample rate equals video frame-rate; cutoff frequency empirically set as 1.0Hz), which excludes sharp peaks related to wrong estimation of the PLK algorithm or quick changes in the light conditions (top row of Fig. 3.7). Each of the filtered vectors V'_x, V'_y and V'_z is then processed for finding its intersection points with the corresponding axis, and the identified intersection points are stored in vectors I_x,

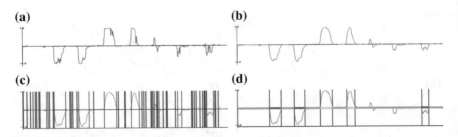

Fig. 3.7 Application of Algorithm 1 for a single normalized displacement vector: **a** initial values V_x, **b** low-pass filtered values V'_x, **c** detected candidate sub-shot boundaries in I_x, and **d** selected sub-shot boundaries in B_x; red parts denote fragments with left displacement, orange parts denote fragments with right displacement, and green parts denote fragments with no or minor movement

I_y and I_z, respectively (Fig. 3.7c). These intersection points are candidate sub-shot boundaries, since the video frames between a pair of consecutive intersection points exhibit a contiguous and single-directed camera movement, thus being a potential sub-shot according to the proposed approach.

Algorithm 1 Pseudocode of the proposed technique

Input: V_x, V_y, V_z: axes displacement vectors
Output: O': set of sub-shot boundaries
  1: **function** PROCESSVECTOR(V)
  2:    Low-pass filter V. Store in V'.
  3:    Detect intersection points in V'. Store in I.
  4:    Measure the total displacement between intersection points in I. Store in D.
  5:    Select fragments with displacement $D > t$ as sub-shots. Store in B.
  6: **end function**
  7: $B_x \leftarrow$ PROCESSVECTOR(V_x)
  8: $B_y \leftarrow$ PROCESSVECTOR(V_y)
  9: $B_z \leftarrow$ PROCESSVECTOR(V_z)
 10: Add in O the B_x and B_y fragments.
 11: Extend O by adding B_z fragments that do not coincide with B_x and B_y fragments. Mark remaining parts of the video as fragments with no or minor movement.
 12: Discard fragments less than 1 sec. Store in O'.

Driven by the observation that most (single-shot) User-Generated Videos (UGVs) are captured by amateurs without the use of any professional equipment that ensures camera's stability, the algorithm filters out fragments depicting minor motion by computing the total displacement over each fragment as the sum of the absolute values of the filtered displacement values V'_x, V'_y and V'_z of each pair of frames in the fragment. This process results in vectors D_x, D_y and D_z, which store the total displacement score of each defined fragment in the x-, y-, and z-axis, respectively. The video fragments with total displacement score less than an experimentally defined threshold $t = 12$, are discarded. The determined fragments of each axis are stored in vectors B_x, B_y and B_z (Fig. 3.7d). In the following, a simple fusion process is applied that: (i) takes the union O of B_x and B_y fragments, (ii) extends it by adding B_z fragments that do not temporally coincide (either completely or partially) with B_x and B_y fragments, and (iii) marks the remaining parts of the video as fragments with no or minor movement. The final output of the algorithm (O') is formed by discarding fragments with duration less than 1 s through a process that equally dispenses their frames in the previous and the following sub-shot. Each defined video sub-shot is finally represented by its middle frame that is selected as keyframe.

3.3.2   Reverse Video Search on the Web

The InVID project developed a web application for reverse video search on the web. This web-based tool is directly accessible at http://multimedia3.iti.gr/video_fragmentation/service/start.html, or through the "Keyframes" component of the InVID Verification Plugin.[13] Through its interactive user interface, this technology enables a user to quickly fragment a single-shot video—which is the most common case for UGVs—into visually and temporally coherent parts, using the video sub-shot fragmentation algorithm described in Sect. 3.3.1.1. The subsequent and automatic selection of a representative keyframe for each defined fragment results in a complete and concise visual summary of the video, that facilitates the time-efficient discovery of the video content and the fragment-level reverse video search on the web based on the image search functionality of popular web search engines (e.g., Google search).

Contrary to the technologies presented in Sect. 3.2.2, that rely on a preselected and limited set of video thumbnails (YouTube DataViewer), the manual extraction of video frames for performing reverse image search (TinEye, Karma Decay, Berify), or the creation of collections of (pre-analyzed) video content (RevIMG, Videntifier), this web application extracts a dynamic number of keyframes in a way which ensures that all the visually discrete parts of the video are adequately represented through the extracted set of keyframes. Furthermore, it supports the direct analysis of both online available videos from several platforms and local copies of a video from the user's machine without requiring its prior upload to any video sharing platform. In this way, it assists users to quickly discover the temporal structure of a video, to extract detailed information about the video content and to use this data in their reverse video search queries.

Through the user interface of the InVID web application for reverse video search on the web, the user is able to submit a video for (video sub-shot fragmentation) analysis, quickly get a rich and representative collection of video keyframes, and perform keyframe-based reverse video search via a "one-click" process. The submitted video can be fetched in two ways: (i) either via its URL (in case of an online available video), (ii) or by uploading a local copy of it from the user's machine (a typical environment for file browsing and selection is shown to the user through a pop-up window). The provision of the user's e-mail is optional and can be selected

---

[13] Available at: http://www.invid-project.eu/verify/.

Fig. 3.8 Provision of extracted keyframes after the completion of the analysis

in case that the user needs to be automatically notified by e-mail when the analysis
results are available.

As stated in the documentation of this tool (accessible after clicking at the "About
this tool" button), the supported online video sources include YouTube, Facebook,
Twitter, Instagram, Vimeo, DailyMotion, LiveLeak and Dropbox. However, the user
is being informed that not all videos from these platforms are accessible to the web
application, due to platform-specific or user-defined restrictions about the use of
each specific video; moreover, the provided URL should always point to a single

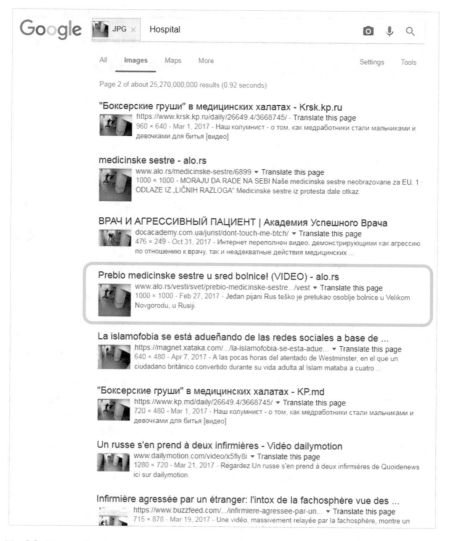

Fig. 3.9 The results after applying reverse image search on one of the extracted keyframes. Within the yellow bounding box is the result that leads to a near-duplicate of the video that corresponds to the originally published one

video, rather than a playlist of videos. Last but not least, the tool can handle videos in several video formats, including "mp4", "webm", "avi", "mov", "wmv", "ogv", "mpg", "flv", and "mkv".

After submitting a video for analysis the user is able to monitor the progress of the analysis and, after its completion, to get on the screen the collection of extracted keyframes (see Fig. 3.8). Alternatively, if the user provided an e-mail account (which is optional as described before) s/he may close the browser and be notified by e-mail

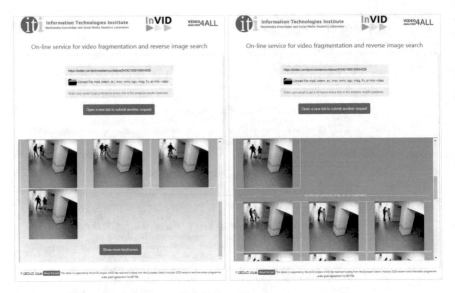

Fig. 3.10 Additional keyframes can be optionally provided to the user for more extended search

when the analysis results are ready. The provided collection of keyframes allows the user to explore the video structure (in the sub-shot-level) and perform reverse keyframe search, simply by (left) clicking on any desired keyframe. This action initiates a Google image search and the results of this search are served to the user in a new tab of his/her browser (see Fig. 3.9). In case more keyframes are needed for performing a more extended search for the video, the user can click on the "Show more keyframes" button that appears right after the initial collection of extracted keyframes (right part of Fig. 3.10); these keyframes correspond to the same video fragments with the initially provided ones, so they could contain duplicates (left part of Fig. 3.10). The generated results from the analysis (i.e., the collection of keyframes) are available only for 48 h and are automatically deleted from the server after this time period. All video rights remain with the uploader, who is assumed to have the right to submit the video to this service for analysis.

The feedback concerning the performance of this tool, received mainly from the users of the corresponding component of the InVID Verification Plugin, is very positive and encouraging. According to the analytics about the use of this web application since the public release of the plugin, more than 4, 000 users have submitted (in total) over 13, 500 requests, for analyzing more than 650 h of video content. Moreover, a group of approximately 150 "power-users"—coming mostly from news agencies, human rights organizations and media verification networks—have used the tool more than 20 times each, while the top-10 of them have used the tool more than 100 times each. The collected traffic data indicate that there is significant (and constantly raising) community of regular users that exploit the verification functionality of the tool on a frequent basis. The functionality of this component enabled the users to debunk a number of fake news that are based on the reuse of a previously pub-

Table 3.1 Indicative list of fakes debunked using the web application for video fragmentation and reverse keyframe search

Fake news	Claim	Date	Original source	Fact	Date
https://www.facebook.com/Pakkorner/videos/365709494264601/	Pakistani soldiers making a floating bridge over a river	Apr 2019	https://www.youtube.com/watch?v=mju6XUIlm6l	Troops build pontoon bridge during NATO drills in Lithuania	Jun. 2017
https://www.facebook.com/Army.Of.Pakistan/videos/417288652413285/	Firing by Pakistan's military at the border with India	Mar 2019	https://www.youtube.com/watch?v=WHIMoz2E-tw	Pakistan army random infantry fire power show	Jul. 2017
https://www.facebook.com/LogKyaKahengyy/videos/404467560327831/	Effigy of Pakistani Prime Minister Imran Khan being burnt	Feb 2019	https://www.youtube.com/watch?v=DruBl3Py3zY	Congress workers injured while burning Modi effigy in Shimla	Dec 2015
https://twitter.com/i/status/1096811492098289664	Pulwama terror attack footage	Feb 2019	https://www.youtube.com/watch?v=8l-IUqsHR9Q	Truck bomb in Iraq	Apr 2008
https://www.facebook.com/halimhusin.my/videos/2119944594692914/	China opened 880 km highway linking their country to Pakistan	Feb 2019	https://www.youtube.com/watch?v=YbzT8ycTjQc	Yaxi Highway, a 240 km-long highway in China's Sichuan province	Jan 2019
https://www.facebook.com/TimeNewsInternational/videos/2187809244837800/	Plane caught in a typhoon in China	Sep 2018	https://www.youtube.com/watch?v=AgvzhJpyn10	Video of a company specialized in digital special effects	Jun 2017
https://www.facebook.com/100009631064968/videos/730611413936554/	Muslims attack cars in Birmingham, UK	May 2018	https://www.youtube.com/watch?v=AoQTQE_YTY	Hooligans from Zurich faced off with hooligans from Basel	May 2018
https://www.youtube.com/watch?v=C4BjUoQAw5Y	Migrants attacking cars in Metz, France	May 2018			
https://twitter.com/kwilli1046/status/872106123570163712 https://www.youtube.com/watch?v=OVAxQA3gMEo	Attack in Notre-Dame, Paris	Jun. 2017	https://www.youtube.com/watch?v=W2lA9UwmHCA	World War Z making off	Sep 2012
https://twitter.com/mikethecraigy/status/877248566384873472	Attack in Brussels Central Station	Jun 2017			
https://www.youtube.com/watch?v=HD2Wj6MjY6k	Casino robbery in Manila Philippines	Jun. 2017	https://www.youtube.com/watch?v=MX3YCSpl2M	Robbery in a hotel in Suriname	Jan. 2012
https://twitter.com/tprincedelamour/status/843421609159544836	Immigrant attacks nurse in public hospital in France	Mar 2017	https://www.youtube.com/watch?v=CuyfdZKc3TQ	Drunk patient beats up doctors in Novgorod hospital in Russia	Feb 2017

(continued)

Table 3.1 (continued)

Fake news	Claim	Date	Original source	Fact	Date
https://twitter.com/FuegoNugz/status/905246797123203072	Hurricane Irma in Barbados, US	Sep. 2017	https://www.youtube.com/watch?v=0IHDVel-NPw	Hurricane Dolores in Uruguay	May 2016
https://www.youtube.com/watch?v=fmUEI0L2aIY	Hurricane Otto in Panama	Nov. 2016			
https://www.facebook.com/amisrahimrahim/videos/111375748646580/	Inside the EgyptAir airplane before the crash	May 2016	https://www.stuff.co.nz/travel/travel-troubles/79637635/severe-turbulence-injures-32-on-etihad-flight-to-indonesia	Severe turbulence injures 32 on Etihad flight to Indonesia	May 2016
https://www.youtube.com/watch?v=mZcs8-tzZ0w	Explosion in Brussels airport	Mar. 2016	https://www.youtube.com/watch?v=yhO7gZObaqY	Attack in Domodedovo airport in Russia	Jan 2011
https://www.youtube.com/watch?v=nkQ-ij3LTTM	Video showing a Hezbollah sniper	Feb. 2016	https://www.youtube.com/watch?v=Xjq5VIPdAe4	"Let's play" video from "Medal of Honor"	Aug 2012
https://www.youtube.com/watch?v=Q-yWYQLwm5M	Brave revel against tank in Syria	Jul 2015	http://www.military.com/video/operations-and-strategy/antitank-weapons/rocket-hits-syrian-tank-at-close-range/1826311054001	Rocket hits Syrian tank	Sep 2012

lished video. Indicative examples of such fakes and the corresponding original video sources that were identified with the help of the web application can be found in Table 3.1.

Last but not least, this web application has a complementary role with the near-duplicate detection utility of the InVID Verification Application, which is presented in the Chap. 4. The former allows the fragment-level reverse search of videos on the web using the extracted keyframes, while the latter enables the video-level reverse search of videos within a constantly extendible collection of selected newsworthy video material.

3.4 Performance Evaluation and Benchmarking

This part reports on the conducted experiments for evaluating the performance of the developed algorithms for video sub-shot segmentation, and for assessing the usefulness and effectiveness of the InVID web application for reverse video search on the web.

3.4.1 Video Fragmentation

Driven by the lack of publicly available datasets for evaluating the performance of video sub-shot fragmentation algorithms,[14] we built our own ground-truth dataset. This dataset is publicly available[15] and consists of:

- 15 single-shot videos of total duration 6 minutes, recorded in our facilities; these videos, denoted as "own videos" in the sequel, contain clearly defined fragments that correspond to several video recording activities.
- 5 single-shot amateur videos of total duration 17 minutes, found on YouTube; these videos are denoted as "amateur videos" in the sequel.
- 13 single-shot parts of known movies of total duration 46 minutes; these videos, denoted as "movie excerpts", represent professional video content.

Ground truth fragmentation of the employed dataset was created by human annotation of the sub-shot boundaries for each video. Adopting the most commonly used approach from the relevant literature for segmenting a single-shot video into sub-shots, each determined sub-shot boundary indicates the end of a visually and temporally contiguous activity of the video recording device and the start of the next one (e.g., the end of a left camera panning, which is followed by a camera zooming). This approach might not be strictly aligned to the fragmentation criterion of

---

[14]Some works reported in Sect. 3.2.1 use certain datasets (TRECVid 2007 rushes summarization, UT Ego, ADL and GTEA Gaze) which were designed for assessing the efficiency of methods targeting specific types of analysis, such as video rushes fragmentation [12] and the identification of everyday activities [6] and thus, ground-truth sub-shot fragmentation is not available for them.

[15]https://mklab.iti.gr/results/annotated-dataset-for-sub-shot-segmentation-evaluation.

methods relying on visual resemblance among frames, but we can claim that all sub-shots defined by the aforementioned strategy exhibit high levels of visual similarity, and thus could be identified by similarity-based fragmentation algorithms as well. Overall, our dataset contains 674 sub-shot transitions.

The performance of the algorithms presented in Sect. 3.3.1.1 (denoted as S_DCT) and Sect. 3.3.1.2 (denoted as SP_OF) was compared against other methods from the relevant literature, that include:

- A straightforward approach (denoted S_HSV in the sequel) which assesses the similarity between subsequent video frames with the help of HSV histograms and x^2 distance.
- A method (denoted B_HSV) similar to [13] that selects the first frame of the video F_a as the base frame and compares it sequentially with the following ones using HSV histograms and x^2 distance until some frame F_b is different enough, then frames between F_a and F_b form a sub-shot, and F_b is used as the next base frame in a process that is repeated until all frames of the video have been processed; a variation of this approach (denoted B_DCT) that represents the visual content of the video frames using DCT features and estimates their visual resemblance based on the cosine similarity was also implemented.
- The algorithm of [2] (denoted A_SIFT), which estimates the dominant motion between a pair of frames based on the computed parameters of a 3×3 affine model through the extraction and matching of SIFT descriptors; furthermore, variations of this approach that rely on the use of SURF (denoted A_SURF) and ORB [39] (denoted A_ORB) descriptors were also implemented for assessing the efficiency of faster alternatives to SIFT.
- An implementation of the best performing technique of [19] (denoted A_OF), which computes the optical flow using the PLK algorithm and identifies camera movement by fitting it to a 2×2 affine model containing parameters that represent the camera pan, tilt, zoom, and rotation actions.
- Variations of the local feature-based approaches documented in [19], that rely on the extraction and matching of SIFT, SURF, and ORB descriptors (denoted H_SIFT, H_SURF, and H_ORB, respectively) or the computation of the optical flow using PLK (denoted H_OF), for estimating the dominant motion based on specific parameters of the homography matrix computed by the RANSAC method [40]; an example of SURF-based homography estimation between a pair of frames is depicted in Fig. 3.11.

For each one of the tested approaches the number of correct detections (where the detected boundary can lie within a temporal window around the respective ground-truth boundary, equal to twice the video frame-rate), misdetections and false alarms were counted and the algorithms' performance was expressed in terms of precision (P), recall (R), and F-score (F), similarly to [25, 41]. Time-efficiency was evaluated by computing the ratio of processing time over the video's duration (a value below 1 indicates faster than real-time processing). All experiments were conducted on a PC with an i7-4770K CPU and 16GB of RAM.

Fig. 3.11 Local feature extraction and matching for computing the homography between a pair of frames (i.e., how the image on the left should be translated to match the one on the right), that subsequently allows motion detection and estimation. Note: Frames were extracted from the opening scene of the "Spectre" movie

Table 3.2 Evaluation results for different sub-shot fragmentation approaches (P: precision, R: recall, F: F-score)

Method	"Own videos"			"Amateur videos"			"Movie excerpts"			Overall dataset		
	P	R	F	P	R	F	P	R	F	P	R	F
S_HSV	0.31	0.28	0.30	0.23	0.09	0.13	0.28	0.44	0.34	0.28	0.36	0.32
S_DCT	0.54	0.88	0.67	0.14	**0.86**	0.25	0.25	**0.84**	0.38	0.22	**0.84**	0.36
B_HSV	0.30	0.09	0.14	**0.55**	0.09	0.16	0.43	0.12	0.18	0.44	0.11	0.18
B_DCT	0.50	0.23	0.32	0.36	0.40	0.38	0.43	0.24	0.31	0.41	0.27	0.32
A_OF	0.41	0.68	0.50	0.20	0.82	0.31	0.30	0.78	0.43	0.27	0.78	0.40
A_SIFT	0.55	0.62	0.59	0.20	0.09	0.12	0.30	0.14	0.19	0.33	0.17	0.23
A_SURF	0.54	0.64	0.58	0.29	0.30	0.29	0.36	0.25	0.30	0.36	0.29	0.33
A_ORB	0.40	0.25	0.30	0.09	0.02	0.03	0.46	0.02	0.05	0.38	0.05	0.08
H_OF	**0.98**	0.62	0.76	0.26	0.67	0.38	0.41	0.58	0.47	0.37	0.60	0.45
H_SIFT	0.90	0.74	0.82	0.27	0.78	0.39	0.35	0.63	0.45	0.34	0.66	0.45
H_SURF	0.88	0.73	0.80	0.26	0.70	0.38	0.36	0.64	0.47	0.36	0.66	0.46
H_ORB	0.85	0.67	0.75	0.18	0.76	0.30	0.30	0.73	0.43	0.28	0.72	0.40
SP_OF	0.96	**0.90**	**0.93**	0.42	0.71	**0.53**	**0.48**	0.64	**0.55**	**0.52**	0.70	**0.59**

Table 3.2 reports the evaluation results of each compared approach, both separately on each of the three parts of the dataset, as described above, and on the overall dataset. General observations regarding the different implemented methodologies are the following.

- Approaches that estimate the dominant motion based on a homography matrix seem to be more effective compared to the methods that rely on affine models or the assessment of visual similarity, with the latter ones being slightly better compared to the affine-based methods.
- Among the examined similarity-based techniques, the use of HSV histograms results in better performance in terms of precision; however, the utilization of DCT features leads to remarkably higher recall scores, and thus a better overall performance (F-score).
- Concerning the implemented affine-based techniques, the most efficient is the one that relies on the optical flow, showing the highest recall scores in all different video categories and comparable precision scores with the other related methods.
- Regarding the suitability of local descriptors for computing an affine model that helps with the identification of the performed movement, SURF are the most effective ones, SIFT perform slightly worse, and ORB exhibit the weakest performance.
- With respect to the evaluated homography-based approaches, the use of different local descriptors or optical flow resulted in similar efficiency, with ORB being the least competitive descriptor due to lower precision.
- In terms of precision, the achieved scores are rather low in general, a fact that indicates the limited robustness of all tested approaches against the challenging task of segmenting an uninterruptedly captured video in sub-shots; methods that evaluate the similarity between distant frames (B_HSV and B_DCT) achieve precision slightly over 0.4, and are being more efficient than the sequentially operating ones (S_HSV and S_DCT); motion-based methods that rely on affine transformations or homography matrices exhibit slightly worse performance, reaching a precision around 0.35; finally, the highest precision (slightly over 0.5) is scored when the video recording activities are modeled by computing and evaluating the optical flow in both the spatial and temporal dimension of the video.

Regarding the best performing approaches, the last row of Table 3.2 indicates that the most effective method is the spatiotemporal motion-based algorithm of Sect. 3.3.1.2. This algorithm achieves the highest F-score both on the overall dataset, as well as on each different part of it. On the first collection of videos, it exhibits the highest recall score, with the method of Sect. 3.3.1.1 being the second best, while its precision is slightly lower than the one achieved by the H_OF method. On "Amateur videos", the SP_OF technique is again the best performing one, while the B_HSV method and the technique of Sect. 3.3.1.1 that presented competitive precision and recall, respectively, achieved significantly lower overall performance. Similar efficiency is observed when analyzing single-shot parts of professional movies; the SP_OF approach is the best in terms of F-score and precision. The above are reflected in the last three columns of Table 3.2 which show the superiority of this algorithm over the other evaluated techniques in the overall dataset. Two indicative examples of how this algorithm fragments (a part of) two UGVs are presented in Fig. 3.12. Another finding that can be easily extracted from the results reported in Table 3.2 relates to the ability of the DCT-based algorithm of Sect. 3.3.1.1 to achieve high recall scores. This method proved to be the most effective one in terms of recall

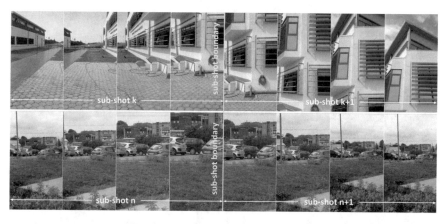

Fig. 3.12 Top row: a sequence of video frames (sampled for space and presentation efficiency) fragmented by the proposed algorithm into two sub-shots; one related to a horizontal and one related to an upward camera movement. Bottom row: a sequence of video frames (sampled for space and presentation efficiency) fragmented by the proposed algorithm into two sub-shots; one related to a camera zooming in and one related to camera zooming out

when analyzing "Amateur videos" and "Movie excerpts", while it was the second best performing approach on "Own videos" with a score slightly lower than the one achieved by the motion-based technique of Sect. 3.3.1.2. The competency of the DCT-based technique to achieve high recall scores is recorded also for the entire dataset, as shown in the penultimate column of Table 3.2.

With respect to the time-efficiency, as shown in Table 3.3, the more straightforward approaches that fragment a video based on the visual resemblance of video frames are faster than methods computing the parameters of affine models or homography matrices, as expected. Moreover, the use of DCT features, especially in the way that the method of Sect. 3.3.1.1 utilizes them, outperforms the HSV histograms, while the extraction and matching of complex local descriptors (SIFT and SURF) are more computationally expensive compared to the matching of binary descriptors (ORB) or the extraction of optical flow for computing the affine or homography matrices. The SP_OF approach of Sect. 3.3.1.2 exhibits competitive time performance, being a bit slower than the straightforward similarity-based methods and faster than almost the entire set of the evaluated affine- and homography-based techniques. Its time-efficiency permits sub-shot fragmentation to be performed nine times faster than real-time analysis, while this performance can be further improved by introducing simple parallelization in the algorithm's execution. In fact, a multi-threaded software implementation of this technique splits the group of analyzed frames into four different and non-overlapping parts which are being processed (i.e., for extracting the optical flow among each pair of frames) in parallel on the CPU. The lightweight post-processing of the computed displacement vectors for motion detection and recognition is still carried out using a single thread. Experiments on the same dataset showed a 267% speed-up compared to the single-thread version, which means that the analy-

Table 3.3 Time-efficiency of the evaluated sub-shot fragmentation approaches

Method	S_HSV	S_DCT	B_HSV	B_DCT	A_OF	A_SIFT	A_SURF	A_ORB	H_OF	H_SIFT	H_SURF	H_ORB	Proposed
Proc. time % of video length	7.1	**2.9**	3.8	6.7	7.8	127.2	56.3	12.7	14.5	132.6	70.2	16.1	11.1

sis of a single-shot video with the multi-thread implementation of the algorithm takes only 4.1% of the video's duration. This performance is comparable with the time-efficiency of the fastest approach, namely the DCT-based algorithm of Sect. 3.3.1.1, which completes the analysis in less than 3% of the video length and thus, enables video processing more than 30 times faster compared to real-time processing.

The findings concerning the detection accuracy and the time-efficiency of the comparatively evaluated approaches document that:

- the motion-based algorithm of Sect. 3.3.1.2 combines the time-efficiency of similarity-based approaches, that rely on the extraction of lightweight visual descriptors, with the detection effectiveness of more complex state-of-the-art techniques, that estimate the dominant motion with the help of affine transformations and image homography;
- the similarity-based method of Sect. 3.3.1.1 can be a reasonable choice when high recall is needed, i.e., when the over-fragmentation of the video and the creation of an over-wealthy set of representative keyframes favors the next steps of the analysis, as in the case of fragment-level reverse video search;
- there is room for further improvement (mainly in terms of Precision) of the current methods for video sub-shot fragmentation, and for this purpose, the performance of modern deep-network architectures, that capture the visual and temporal dependency among video frames (such as Recursive Neural Networks with Long Short-Term Memory (LSTM) units), could be exploited.

3.4.2 Reverse Video Search on the Web

The InVID approach for video sub-shot fragmentation and keyframe extraction (presented in Sect. 3.3.1.1) was comparatively evaluated against two alternative baseline approaches for keyframe extraction; one extracting one keyframe per second, and another one that extracts the reference frames (a.k.a. I-frames) of the mp4 video stream.[16] This benchmarking was conducted with the help of two journalists—one coming from Agence France-Presse (AFP) and one coming from Deutsche Welle (DW)—with media verification background, and its focus was bilateral. In particular, it aimed to assess:

- the efficiency of each tested approach in defining a set of keyframes that represents the visual content of the video without missing any important pieces of information, with the least amount of frames;
- the usefulness/appropriateness of each generated keyframe collection for supporting the task of finding near-duplicates of the analyzed video on the web.

Given that the evaluated InVID method is integrated into the web application for reverse video search, this testing allowed to assess how concise and complete the

---

[16]Both of these approaches were implemented using the FFmpeg framework that is available at: https://www.ffmpeg.org/.

produced collection of keyframes is, and to which extent the generated collection (and thus this web application) facilitates the quick identification of prior occurrences of a given video on the web.

According to the evaluation protocol, each tester was asked to select 10 user-generated videos; these videos could be either online available videos from the web or local videos from the testers' machines. Experimentation with non-user-generated videos (i.e., edited professional videos) was also permitted. Subsequently, each selected video should be submitted for analysis to:

- the InVID web application for reverse video search that uses the InVID approach for video fragmentation and keyframe selection;
- a variation of this tool that creates a keyframe collection by applying the first alternative and extracts one keyframe per second;
- another variation of this tool that defines a keyframe collection by applying the second alternative and extracts the reference frames (a.k.a. I-frames) of the mp4 video stream.

After analyzing each selected video with the above listed technologies, the testers had to answer the following questions:

- Q1: How many keyframes were extracted by each tested approach?
- Q2: Which collection is the most concise and complete one (i.e., represents the visual content of the video without missing any important pieces of information, with the least amount of frames)?
- Q3: If you try reverse image search: which collection helps you the most to quickly identify near-duplicates of the video on the web?
- Q4: Are the used videos publicly accessible? If so, please copy and paste the links at the end of this document.

Their feedback was provided by filling-in Tables 3.4 and 3.5, while the submitted videos by each tester are listed in Table 3.6. In the utilized ranking system for answering questions Q2 and Q3, "1" stands for the worse performance and "5" stands for the best performance.

Table 3.4 contains the evaluation results of the AFP journalist. The collected feedback showed that the InVID approach exhibits competitive performance compared to the other tested approaches. Concerning the generation of a concise and complete keyframe-based summary of the video content, the InVID algorithm was the highest voted one in seven cases, and the second best performing one in the remaining three cases. The representation efficiency of the first alternative, which extracts one keyframe per second, was positively appreciated by the AFP journalist in four cases where the algorithm was voted as the best (or among the best) performing one(s). The second alternative that selects the I-frames of the video was indicated as the least efficient one and marked as the second best in four cases only.

The good ranking of the first alternative approach reveals the AFP journalist's preference in having keyframe collections that sufficiently cover all the details of the video, even if this entails a compromise regarding the comprehensiveness of the created collection and the existence of information redundancy. As further detailed

Table 3.4 The votes of the AFP journalist regarding the tested approaches for video keyframe extraction and keyframe-based reverse video search

	Method	Q1: extracted keyframes	Q2: concise and complete					Q3: helps the most in reverse search				
			1	2	3	4	5	1	2	3	4	5
Video #1	InVID	17				X					X	
	Alt. #1	43		X						X		
	Alt. #2	12			X				X			
Video #2	InVID	6		X					X			
	Alt. #1	17				X				X		
	Alt. #2	4	X					X				
Video #3	InVID	101				X					X	
	Alt. #1	371		X					X			
	Alt. #2	127			X					X		
Video #4	InVID	4				X					X	
	Alt. #1	19					X			X		
	Alt. #2	5				X					X	
Video #5	InVID	9				X				X		
	Alt. #1	29				X				X		
	Alt. #2	46			X				X			
Video #6	InVID	10				X				X		
	Alt. #1	43			X					X		
	Alt. #2	43			X					X		
Video #7	InVID	65				X				X		
	Alt. #1	210			X					X		
	Alt. #2	92			X					X		
Video #8	InVID	13				X				X		
	Alt. #1	46			X					X		
	Alt. #2	45			X					X		
Video #9	InVID	85		X						X		
	Alt. #1	303				X					X	
	Alt. #2	72		X					X			
Video #10	InVID	31				X					X	
	Alt. #1	74			X					X		
	Alt. #2	32			X					X		

in his evaluation report, the explanation behind this choice is governed by his news verification background and relies on the fact that some video frames might contain an element that helps to confirm the location, identify a person, a scene, an event or something useful for the verification or debunking of a news video. As a consequence, the appearance of these frames in the keyframe collection, even if near-duplicates of them—that are less informative though—are already included in this collection, is positively assessed. Finally, the keyframe collections generated by the second alternative, even being comparatively sized with the ones created by the InVID algorithm (see Table 3.4), proved to be less useful than the other evaluated techniques due to more missing frames that are needed for effectively conveying the reported story in the video.

An example that illustrates the findings reported above, is depicted in Fig. 3.13 which contains the generated keyframe collections by the three evaluated algorithms for the analyzed video #4. The top left corresponds to the InVID method, the bottom left corresponds to the second alternative and the right-sided one corresponds to the first alternative. The video reports a story about the first woman in Saudi Arabia that receives her driving license, and it is recorded within an office by a (mainly) standing cameraman. The InVID-extracted keyframe collection contains three keyframes that show the provision of the license by the officer to the woman. The keyframe collection created by the second alternative conveys (visually) the same information but exhibits more redundancy, as keyframes #3 and #4 are near-duplicates of keyframes #2 and #5, respectively. Finally, the collection generated by the first alternative covers the story in much more details, but with the cost of much higher duplication of the visual information. Nevertheless, the last keyframe of this collection shows a photographer that is also in the room and takes a photo of this event. His appearance in the video does not change or affect the main subject of the video, but it can provide a hint that could help a journalist to verify or debunk this video (e.g., by observing a badge on his uniform that relates to a specific country or army). Hence, the journalist's voting (as shown in Table 3.4) rewards the existence of this keyframe in the collection, considering it as more important than the information redundancy that this collection presents.

Concluding, the keyframe selection strategy of the first alternative combined with the competitive performance of the InVID approach in most examined cases, indicates the InVID method as the most efficient one in generating keyframe-based video summaries that are well-balanced according to the determined criteria for the descriptiveness (completion) and representativeness (conciseness) of the keyframe collection.

Concerning the use of the generated keyframe collections by the three evaluated methods to facilitate the identification of near-duplicates of the processed videos on the web, the InVID method was generally determined as the most useful one. The keyframe collections extracted by this method were considered as helping the most in reverse video search in three cases, and as equally effective one with the collections produced by other approaches in five cases. The first alternative proved to be the second most appreciated method, and this finding is aligned with the journalist's interest, explained previously, to get and use any visual detail of the video that could assist its verification. Finally, the second alternative was ranked as the less efficient one since the extracted keyframe collections were denoted as less useful for video reverse search in several of the tested scenarios.

These outcomes are consistent to the findings regarding the comprehensiveness and fullness of the generated keyframe collections, and show that the InVID developed algorithm and the first alternative can (almost) equally support the users' needs when performing a fragment-level reverse search of a video on the web.

Table 3.5 includes the evaluation results of the DW journalist. The received feedback clearly indicates the InVID approach as the best performing one in producing a

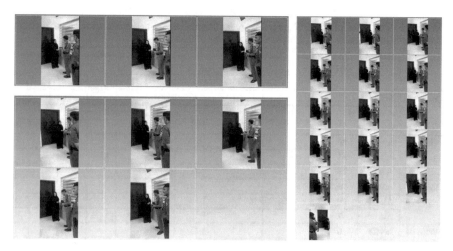

Fig. 3.13 The keyframe collections generated for an AFP-selected video by the three tested approaches. The top left corresponds to the InVID method, the bottom left corresponds to the second alternative, and the right-sided corresponds to the first alternative

concise and complete keyframe-based summary of the video. In most cases (specifically in 9 out of 10) the InVID method got the highest score compared to the other tested approaches. The keyframe collections generated by this algorithm were voted as best (four times) or well (four times) performing ones. A similar, but in some cases less efficient, performance was shown by the second alternative which extracts the I-frames of the video. This technique was evaluated as approximately equally performing one with the InVID approach in six cases, while in one case it was voted as the most effective technique. This finding is reasonable if we take under consideration that this method: (a) selects the frames of the video that are the most complete and descriptive ones in terms of visual information (in order to be used as the reference basis for the compression of the subsequent p- and b-frames of the video) and (b) usually results in a small set of keyframes that is comparable in size with the collection of keyframes extracted by the InVID method, as reported in Table 3.5 and shown in the example of Fig. 3.14 below (left column). The least competitive one was the first alternative that extracts one keyframe per second. This method results in a keyframe-based representation of the video with high amount of redundant information (due to the occurrence of near-duplicate frames) and limited usefulness when the need is to quickly discover the video content.

The above described findings are illustrated in the example Fig. 3.14 which shows the extracted keyframe collections by the three tested approaches for the submitted video #7. Once again, the top left corresponds to the InVID method, the bottom left corresponds to the second alternative and the right-sided one corresponds to the first alternative. As can be seen, the latest one offers a very detailed and complete representation of the video content; however, several keyframes exhibit high visual resemblance, thus resulting in significant information redundancy which, in case of

Table 3.5 The votes of the DW journalist regarding the tested approaches for video keyframe extraction and keyframe-based reverse video search

	Method	Q1: extracted keyframes	Q2: concise and complete					Q3: helps the most in reverse search				
			1	2	3	4	5	1	2	3	4	5
Video #1	InVID	41				X					X	
	Alt. #1	150		X					X			
	Alt. #2	31				X						X
Video #2	InVID	20				X					X	
	Alt. #1	81		X					X			
	Alt. #2	18				X					X	
Video #3	InVID	6				X					X	
	Alt. #1	20		X					X			
	Alt. #2	7				X					X	
Video #4	InVID	6			X						X	
	Alt. #1	25		X						X		
	Alt. #2	9			X						X	
Video #5	InVID	42			X						X	
	Alt. #1	153	X					X				
	Alt. #2	68		X				X				
Video #6	InVID	14			X					X		
	Alt. #1	52		X				X				
	Alt. #2	21			X					X		
Video #7	InVID	6				X					X	
	Alt. #1	26		X					X			
	Alt. #2	8			X						X	
Video #8	InVID	36				X						X
	Alt. #1	139	X						X			
	Alt. #2	53				X						X
Video #9	InVID	10		X				X				
	Alt. #1	54			X						X	
	Alt. #2	15				X					X	
Video #10	InVID	20				X		X				
	Alt. #1	64		X				X				
	Alt. #2	17				X		X				

long videos, makes the discovery of the video content a time-consuming process. On the contrary, the left-sided keyframe collections provide a concise but also complete summary of the video content, as they contain all the key parts of the presented story. The collection generated by the second alternative (at the bottom left of Fig. 3.14) includes a couple of near-duplicate frames, and thus was voted as slightly worse that then collection produced by the InVID approach.

As an overall comment, the keyframe selection strategy of the second alternative, in combination with the competitive performance that the InVID method exhibits in most cases, indicates that the developed algorithm for video sub-shot fragmenta-

Fig. 3.14 The keyframe collections generated for a DW-selected video by the three tested approaches. The top left corresponds to the InVID method, the bottom left corresponds to the second alternative, and the right-sided corresponds to the first alternative

tion and keyframe selection is highly efficient in extracting a set of keyframes that represent the visual content of the video without missing any important pieces of information, with the least amount of frames.

In terms of keyframe-based reverse search for quickly finding near-duplicates of the submitted videos on the web, the InVID approach and the second alternative were voted as equally performing ones in seven cases. Moreover, the InVID method was the best performing one in one case and the second best performing one in two cases. The second alternative was voted as the best one in two cases, while the first alternative was marked as the less efficient one in all tested cases. The later can be explained by the fact that, even providing a very fine-grained representation of the video content, this collection increases the amount of the time and effort needed to discover the keyframe collection and select the most appropriate keyframes for performing the keyframe-based reverse video search on the web.

These findings are aligned to the ones extracted regarding the conciseness and completeness of the generated keyframe collections, and indicate the InVID method and the second alternative as the best choices for performing a fragment-level reverse search of a video on the web.

Table 3.6 The submitted videos by the AFP and DW journalists for evaluating the InVID and the two alternative methods for video keyframe extraction and keyframe-based reverse video search

#	AFP journalist	DW journalist
1	https://www.youtube.com/watch?v=GhxqIITtTtU	https://www.youtube.com/watch?v=okvoLbHlaVA
2	https://www.youtube.com/watch?v=oKQiTUjHlQ4	https://www.youtube.com/watch?v=ziOvZSUwU_c
3	https://www.facebook.com/Oker.Turgut/videos/1708996762482817/	https://twitter.com/AZeckenbiss/status/1033790392037199873
4	https://twitter.com/kengarex/status/1003749477583413249	https://twitter.com/JorgeaHurtado/status/1018125444158279682
5	https://www.youtube.com/watch?v=sza-j0nubNw	https://www.facebook.com/nafisa.alharazi/videos/10156699747657790/
6	https://twitter.com/tprincedelamour/status/8434421609159544836	https://www.facebook.com/goodshitgoOdsHitthatssomegoodshitrightthere/videos/347521802658077/
7	https://www.youtube.com/watch?v=r5aBqCniQyw	https://www.youtube.com/watch?v=szKPipLRFsM
8	https://video.twimg.com/ext_tw_video/876820481919397889/pu/vid/360x640/VWTPEvrV8vVJFf4d.mp4	https://www.youtube.com/watch?v=BU9YAHigNx8
9	Local copy of the Thailand cave rescue video	https://www.youtube.com/watch?v=DeUVsmWji8g
10	https://www.youtube.com/watch?v=UTeqpMQKZaY	https://www.youtube.com/watch?v=-sWZuykJy9Q

Summing up the collected feedback regarding the competence of the developed video fragmentation approach for creating a concise and complete summary of the video content, and the appropriateness of this visual summary for supporting the task of video verification, we reach the conclusion that this technology is the best trade-off between two desirable but, to some extent, incompatible features. It results in keyframe collections that adequately maintain the visual details of the video content and can be highly valued for evidence-based video authentication or debunking through the visual inspection of such details (e.g., signs, labels, business marks, car plates, etc.), thus being aligned to the AFP journalist's focus of interest. Moreover, it secures a concise representation of the presented story that allows quick discovery of the video content and its verification through a sufficiently fine-grained, fragment-level search for finding near-duplicates of the video on the web, thus meeting the DW journalist's demand.

3.5   Conclusions and Future Work

Video content captured by amateurs and shared via social media platforms constitutes a valuable source of information, especially in the case where these amateurs
are eyewitnesses of a breaking or evolving story. Driven by this reality, journalists
and investigators alike are constantly searching these platforms to find media recordings of breaking events. Nevertheless, this rise of information diffusion via social
networks came along with a rise in fake news, i.e., the intentional misinformation
or disinformation to mislead people about a person, event or situation. Hence, the
publicly shared user-generated video comes into question and needs to be verified
before being used by a journalist for reporting the story.

One of the easiest ways to produce fake news (such fakes are known as "easy
fakes" in the media verification community) is based on the reuse of a video from
an earlier circumstance with the assertion that it presents a current event, with the
aim to deliberately misguide the viewers about the event. To detect and demystify
such a fake the investigator needs to identify the original video by looking for prior
instances of it on the web. To support the reverse video search process several tools
have been developed over the last years; however, they introduce some limitations
that relate to (a) the use of a (usually) limited group of video thumbnails provided by
the platforms that host the video, (b) the time-demanding manual extraction of video
frames for performing reverse image search, (c) the searching for near-duplicates
within closed and restricted collections of videos, and (d) the inability to handle
local copies of a video from the user's machine.

Driven by the current state of the art on tools and methods for reverse video search
on the web, in InVID we designed and developed a method that decomposes a single-
shot video (such as the majority of UGVs) into visually and temporally coherent parts
called sub-shots, and we integrated this method into a web-based interactive tool that
allows the fine-grained reverse search of a given video (either found online or locally
stored on the user's machine) on the web. This search is based on the automatic
extraction of a set of keyframes that adequately represent and summarize the video
content, and the use of these keyframes for performing a fragment-level web-based
search for near-duplicates of the video.

To give an overall view of this type of fake news and of the existing solutions for
addressing it, this chapter: discussed the main characteristics of this fake (Sect. 3.1);
provided an overview of current methods for video fragmentation and tools for reverse
video search on the web (Sect. 3.2); presented two state-of-the-art approaches for the
temporal decomposition of videos into sub-shots (the most suitable granularity when
dealing with UGVs) and a web application that facilitates the quick identification of
near-duplicates of a given video on the web (Sect. 3.3); and described the conducted
experimental evaluations concerning the performance of the aforementioned technologies (Sect. 3.4). The reported findings indicate the competitive performance of
the developed algorithms for video sub-shot fragmentation compared to other state-
of-the-art approaches, highlight the capability of the technique that relies on visual
coherence to produce a concise and complete keyframe-based summary of the video

content, and point out the competence of the InVID tool for video reverse search to facilitate the quick and effective discovery of near-duplicates of a video on the web.

Regarding the future outlook of the presented technologies, motivated by the adoption and use of the developed web application for reverse video search by hundreds of users on a daily basis (through its integration into the InVID Verification Plugin[17]), our work will focus on: (a) the user-based evaluation of the efficiency of the motion-based method of Sect. 3.3.1.2 to produce a comprehensive and thorough keyframe-based summary of the video content; (b) the possibility to combine the algorithms of Sects. 3.3.1.1 and 3.3.1.2 in order to exploit the fragmentation accuracy of the latter one and the visual discrimination efficiency of the former one (especially on the keyframe selection part of the process); (c) the exploitation of the performance of modern deep-network architectures (such as Deep Convolutional Neural Networks and Long Short-Term Memory units) for advancing the accuracy of the video fragmentation process; and (d) the further improvement of the keyframe selection process to minimize the possibility of extracting black or blurred video frames of limited usability for the user, thus aiming to an overall amelioration of the tool's effectiveness.

Acknowledgements The work reported in this chapter was supported by the EUs Horizon 2020 research and innovation program under grant agreements H2020-687786 InVID and H2020-732665 EMMA.

References

1. Kelm P, Schmiedeke S, Sikora T (2009) Feature-based video key frame extraction for low quality video sequences. In: 2009 10th workshop on image analysis for multimedia interactive services, pp 25–28 (2009). https://doi.org/10.1109/WIAMIS.2009.5031423
2. Cooray SH, Bredin H, Xu LQ, O'Connor NE (2009) An interactive and multi-level framework for summarising user generated videos. In: Proceedings of the 17th ACM international conference on multimedia, MM '09. ACM, New York, NY, USA, pp 685–688 (2009). https://doi.org/10.1145/1631272.1631388
3. Mei T, Tang LX, Tang J, Hua XS (2013) Near-lossless semantic video summarization and its applications to video analysis. ACM Trans Multimed Comput Commun Appl 9(3):16:1–16:23 (2013). https://doi.org/10.1145/2487268.2487269
4. González-Díaz I, Martínez-Cortés T, Gallardo-Antolín A, Díaz-de María F (2015) Temporal segmentation and keyframe selection methods for user-generated video search-based annotation. Expert Syst Appl 42(1):488–502. https://doi.org/10.1016/j.eswa.2014.08.001
5. Lu Z, Grauman K (2013) Story-driven summarization for egocentric video. In: Proceedings of the 2013 IEEE conference on computer vision and pattern recognition, CVPR '13. IEEE Computer Society, Washington, DC, USA, pp. 2714–2721. https://doi.org/10.1109/CVPR.2013.350
6. Xu, J., Mukherjee, L., Li, Y., Warner, J., Rehg, J.M., Singh, V.: Gaze-enabled egocentric video summarization via constrained submodular maximization. In: 2015 IEEE Conference on Computer Vision and Pattern Recognition (CVPR) [345], pp 2235–2244. http://dblp.uni-trier.de/db/conf/cvpr/cvpr2015.html#XuMLWRS15

---

[17] Available at: http://www.invid-project.eu/verify/.

7. Karaman S, Benois-Pineau J, Dovgalecs V, Mégret R, Pinquier J, André-Obrecht R, Gaëstel Y, Dartigues JF (2014) Hierarchical hidden markov model in detecting activities of daily living in wearable videos for studies of dementia. Multimed Tools Appl 69(3):743–771. https://doi.org/10.1007/s11042-012-1117-x

8. Chu WT, Chuang PC, Yu, JY (2010) Video copy detection based on bag of trajectory and two-level approximate sequence. In: Matching, Proceedings of IPPR conference on computer vision, graphics, and image processing conference (2010)

9. Luo J, Papin C, Costello K (2009) Towards extracting semantically meaningful key frames from personal video clips: From humans to computers. IEEE Transactions Circuits and Systems for Video Technology 19(2):289–301. https://doi.org/10.1109/TCSVT.2008.2009241

10. Dumont E, Merialdo B, Essid S, Bailer W et al (2008) Rushes video summarization using a collaborative approach. In: TRECVID 2008, ACM International Conference on Multimedia Information Retrieval 2008, October 27-November 01, 2008, Vancouver, BC, Canada. Vancouver, CANADA. https://doi.org/10.1145/1463563.1463579. URL http://www.eurecom.fr/publication/2576

11. Liu Y, Liu Y, Ren T, Chan K (2008) Rushes video summarization using audio-visual information and sequence alignment. In: Proceedings of the 2nd ACM TRECVid video summarization workshop, TVS '08. ACM, New York, NY, USA, pp. 114–118. https://doi.org/10.1145/1463563.1463584

12. Bai L, Hu Y, Lao S, Smeaton AF, O'Connor NE (2010) Automatic summarization of rushes video using bipartite graphs. Multimed Tools Appl 49(1):63–80. https://doi.org/10.1007/s11042-009-0398-1

13. Pan CM, Chuang YY, Hsu WH (2007) NTU TRECVID-2007 fast rushes summarization system. In: Proceedings of the international workshop on TRECVID video summarization, TVS '07. ACM, New York, NY, USA, pp 74–78. https://doi.org/10.1145/1290031.1290045

14. Teyssou D, Leung JM, Apostolidis E, Apostolidis K, Papadopoulos S, Zampoglou M, Papadopoulou O, Mezaris V (2017) The invid plug-in: web video verification on the browser. In: Proceedings of the first international workshop on multimedia verification, MuVer '17. ACM, New York, NY, USA, pp 23–30. https://doi.org/10.1145/3132384.3132387

15. Ojutkangas O, Peltola J, Järvinen S (2012) Location based abstraction of user generated mobile videos. Springer, Berlin, Heidelberg, pp 295–306. https://doi.org/10.1007/978-3-642-30419-4_25

16. Kim, J.G., Chang, H.S., Kim, J., Kim, H.M.: Efficient camera motion characterization for mpeg video indexing. In: 2000 IEEE International Conference on Multimedia and Expo. ICME2000. Proc.. Latest Advances in the Fast Changing World of Multimedia (Cat. No.00TH8532), vol. 2, pp. 1171–1174 vol.2 (2000). https://doi.org/10.1109/ICME.2000.871569

17. Durik M, Benois-Pineau J (2001) Robust motion characterisation for video indexing based on MPEG2 optical flow. In: International workshop on content-based multimedia indexing, CBMI01, pp 57–64

18. Nitta N, Babaguchi N (2013) [invited paper] content analysis for home videos. ITE Trans Media Technol Appl 1(2):91–100. https://doi.org/10.3169/mta.1.91

19. Cooray SH, O'Connor NE (2010) Identifying an efficient and robust sub-shot segmentation method for home movie summarisation. In: 2010 10th international conference on intelligent systems design and applications, pp 1287–1292. https://doi.org/10.1109/ISDA.2010.5687086

20. Lowe D.G (1999) Object recognition from local scale-invariant features. In: Proceedings of the 7th IEEE international conference on computer vision, vol 2, pp 1150–1157

21. Bay H, Ess A, Tuytelaars T, Gool LV (2008) Speeded-up robust features (SURF). Comput Vis Image Underst 110(3):346–359. https://doi.org/10.1016/j.cviu.2007.09.014

22. Bouguet JY (2001) Pyramidal implementation of the affine lucas kanade feature tracker description of the algorithm. Intel Corp 5(1–10):4

23. Apostolidis K, Apostolidis E, Mezaris V (2018) A motion-driven approach for fine-grained temporal segmentation of user-generated videos. In: Schoeffmann K, Chalidabhongse TH, Ngo CW, Aramvith S, O'Connor NE, Ho YS, Gabbouj M, Elgammal A (eds) MultiMedia modeling. Springer International Publishing, Cham, pp 29–41

24. Haller M et al (2007) A generic approach for motion-based video parsing. In: 15th European signal processing conference, pp 713–717 (2007)
25. Abdollahian G, Taskiran CM, Pizlo Z, Delp EJ (2010) Camera motion-based analysis of user generated video. IEEE Trans Multimed 12(1):28–41. https://doi.org/10.1109/TMM.2009. 2036286
26. Lan, D.J., Ma, Y.F., Zhang, H.J.: A novel motion-based representation for video mining. In: Proc. of the 2003 International Conference on Multimedia and Expo (ICME '03), vol. 3, pp. III–469–72 vol.3 (2003). https://doi.org/10.1109/ICME.2003.1221350
27. Benois-Pineau J, Lovell BC, Andrews RJ (2013) Motion estimation in colour image sequences. Springer New York, NY, pp 377–395. https://doi.org/10.1007/978-1-4419-6190-7_11
28. Koprinska I, Carrato S (1998) Video segmentation of mpeg compressed data. In: 1998 IEEE international conference on electronics, circuits and systems, vol 2. Surfing the Waves of Science and Technology (Cat No 98EX196), pp 243–246. https://doi.org/10.1109/ICECS.1998. 814872
29. Grana C, Cucchiara R (2006) Sub-shot summarization for MPEG-7 based fast browsing. In: Post-Proceedings of the second Italian research conference on digital library management systems (IRCDL 2006), Padova, 27th Jan 2006 [113], pp. 80–84
30. Wang G, Seo B, Zimmermann R (2012) Motch: an automatic motion type characterization system for sensor-rich videos. In: Proceedings of the 20th ACM international conference on multimedia, MM '12. ACM, New York, NY, USA, pp 1319–1320 (2012). https://doi.org/10. 1145/2393347.2396462
31. Cricri F, Dabov K, Curcio IDD, Mate S, Gabbouj M (2011) Multimodal event detection in user generated videos. In: 2011 IEEE international symposium on multimedia, pp 263–270 (2011). https://doi.org/10.1109/ISM.2011.49
32. Ngo CW, Pong TC, Zhang HJ (2003) Motion analysis and segmentation through spatio-temporal slices processing. IEEE Trans Image Process 12(3):341–355. https://doi.org/10.1109/ TIP.2003.809020
33. Ngo CW, Ma YF, Zhang HJ (2005) Video summarization and scene detection by graph modeling. IEEE Trans Circuits Syst Video Technol 15(2):296–305. https://doi.org/10.1109/TCSVT. 2004.841694
34. Mohanta PP, Saha SK, Chanda B (2008) Detection of representative frames of a shot using multivariate wald-wolfowitz test. In: 2008 19th international conference on pattern recognition, pp 1–4. https://doi.org/10.1109/ICPR.2008.4761403
35. Omidyeganeh M, Ghaemmaghami S, Shirmohammadi S (2011) Video keyframe analysis using a segment-based statistical metric in a visually sensitive parametric space. IEEE Trans Image Process 20(10):2730–2737. https://doi.org/10.1109/TIP.2011.2143421
36. Guo Y, Xu Q, Sun S, Luo X, Sbert M (2016) Selecting video key frames based on relative entropy and the extreme studentized deviate test. Entropy 18(3):73 (2016). http://dblp.uni-trier.de/db/journals/entropy/entropy18.html#GuoXSLS16a
37. Kasutani E, Yamada A (2001) The MPEG-7 color layout descriptor: a compact image feature description for high-speed image/video segment retrieval. In: Proceedings of 2001 international conference on image processing (Cat. No.01CH37205), vol 1, pp 674–677. https://doi.org/10. 1109/ICIP.2001.959135
38. Shi J et al (1994) Good features to track. In: Proceedigns of the IEEE conference on computer vision and pattern recognition, pp 593–600
39. Rublee E, Rabaud V, Konolige K, Bradski G (2011) ORB: an efficient alternative to SIFT or SURF. In: Proceedings of the IEEE international conference on computer vision (ICCV 2011), pp 2564–2571
40. Fischler MA, Bolles RC (1981) Random sample consensus: a paradigm for model fitting with applications to image analysis and automated cartography. ACM Commun 24(6):381–395. https://doi.org/10.1145/358669.358692
41. Apostolidis E, Mezaris V (2014) Fast shot segmentation combining global and local visual descriptors. In: Proceedings of the 2014 IEEE international conference on acoustics, speech and signal processing, pp 6583–6587 (2014)

Chapter 4
Finding Near-Duplicate Videos in Large-Scale Collections

Giorgos Kordopatis-Zilos, Symeon Papadopoulos, Ioannis Patras and Ioannis Kompatsiaris

Abstract This chapter discusses the problem of Near-Duplicate Video Retrieval (NDVR). The main objective of a typical NDVR approach is: given a query video, retrieve all near-duplicate videos in a video repository and rank them based on their similarity to the query. Several approaches have been introduced in the literature, which can be roughly classified in three categories based on the level of video matching, i.e., (i) video-level, (ii) frame-level, and (iii) filter-and-refine matching. Two methods based on video-level matching are presented in this chapter. The first is an unsupervised scheme that relies on a modified Bag-of-Words (BoW) video representation. The second is a s upervised method based on Deep Metric Learning (DML). For the development of both methods, features are extracted from the intermediate layers of Convolutional Neural Networks and leveraged as frame descriptors, since they offer a compact and informative image representation, and lead to increased system efficiency. Extensive evaluation has been conducted on publicly available benchmark datasets, and the presented methods are compared with state-of-the-art approaches, achieving the best results in all evaluation setups.

G. Kordopatis-Zilos (✉) · S. Papadopoulos · I. Kompatsiaris
Information Technologies Institute, Centre for Research and Technology Hellas,
Thessaloniki, Greece
e-mail: georgekordopatis@iti.gr

S. Papadopoulos
e-mail: papadop@iti.gr

I. Kompatsiaris
e-mail: ikom@iti.gr

G. Kordopatis-Zilos · I. Patras
School of Electronic Engineering and Computer Science, Queen Mary University,
London, UK
e-mail: i.patras@qmul.ac.uk

© Springer Nature Switzerland AG 2019
V. Mezaris et al. (eds.), *Video Verification in the Fake News Era*,
https://doi.org/10.1007/978-3-030-26752-0_4

4.1 Introduction

The problem of verifying multimedia content (images, video) that is contributed by users of social media platforms such as YouTube, Instagram, and Facebook is of increasing interest given the pervasive use of these platforms and the modern technological capabilities for real-time capturing and sharing of rich multimedia content. For instance, in the context of breaking news events, such as natural disasters or terrorist attacks multiple eyewitness reports are posted and shared through social media platforms. Yet, the reliability and veracity of such reports are often questioned due to the increasing amount of misleading or manipulated content that can quickly spread through online social networks and cause disinformation at large scale. As a result, there is a profound need for technologies that can assist the process of multimedia verification (or the inverse process of debunking fake content).

One popular verification approach adopted by journalists [1] is to try to establish the provenance of a social media post by looking for near-duplicate media items that were posted in the past. For instance, it has been found that images or videos from past events are often reposted in the context of breaking news events falsely claiming to have been captured in the new setting. For instance, the photo in the tweet in Fig. 4.1 was originally published by the Wall Street Journal on April 2011.[1] However, the same photo was shared thousands of times more than one year later during the Hurricane Sandy (October 29, 2012), supposedly depicting a dangerous storm descending in New York. To identify such cases and find the origin of an image, journalists often use online services such as Google Images[2] and TinEye.[3] Yet, there is currently no available service or tool to support reverse video search. The research field focusing on this problem is Near-Duplicate Video Retrieval (NDVR).

Due to the exponential growth of social media applications and video sharing websites, NDVR is increasingly important, yet it poses a highly challenging task. At the moment, YouTube reports almost two billion users and more than one billion hours of video viewed per day.[4] Due to the uncontrolled nature of publishing in video platforms, a very common phenomenon is the publication of multiple videos that are either near or partial duplicates of an original video. To this end, our goal is to build an NDVR approach that is able to efficiently and effectively retrieve all such videos in order to support the multimedia verification process.

Being a relatively new research topic, there is a variety of definitions and interpretations of NDVR among the multimedia research community. The definitions vary with respect to the level of resemblance that determines whether a pair of videos are considered related. These range from a very narrow scope, where only the almost identical videos are considered positive pairs [2], to very broad where videos from the same event [3] or with the same semantic content [4] are considered as related. The

---

[1]https://blogs.wsj.com/metropolis/2011/04/28/weather-journal-clouds-gathered-but-no-tornado-damage/ (accessed on March 2019).

[2]https://images.google.com/ (accessed on March 2019).

[3]https://www.tineye.com/ (accessed on March 2019).

[4]https://www.youtube.com/yt/about/press/ (accessed on March 2019).

Fig. 4.1 Tweet example of reposted image claiming to be breaking news

definition that is closer to the needs of multimedia verification is the one provided in [2]. Based on this, Near-Duplicate videos (NDVs) are considered those that originate from the same source, but can be different in terms of photometric variations (color, light changes), editing operations (caption, logo insertion), encoding parameters (file format), different lengths, or camera settings (camera viewpoint). A number of such NDV examples are presented in Fig. 4.2.

Considerable effort has been invested from the research community to the NDVR problem. Yet, many of the proposed methods are computationally intensive and thus not easy to apply in a setting where many videos need to be verified in very short time. Another limitation is the lack of flexibility, in a sense that near-duplicate search is often too strict (returns only almost exact copies of the input videos) and in some cases it is not catered for the specific requirements of the problem (e.g., when a user needs support for partial near-duplicate search or for frame-to-video search). Another issue of many state-of-the-art methods is that they adopt a dataset-specific approach: the same dataset is used for both development and evaluation. This leads to specialized solutions that typically exhibit poor performance when used on different video collections.

As a result, the challenge in building an effective NDVR solution is to offer flexibility with respect to the definition of near-duplicate videos and additionally support different requirements of relevance for the verification setting, namely partial-duplicate search), very high precision and recall scores, and at the same time the

Fig. 4.2 Examples of queries and near-duplicate videos from the CC_WEB_VIDEO dataset

possibility for scalable indexing of massive collections of multimedia and achieving low response times.

Motivated by the excellent performance of deep learning in a wide variety of multimedia problems, we have developed two NDVR approaches that incorporate deep learning and can be used in different application scenarios. For both schemes, we use features from intermediate convolutional layers [5, 6] of pretrained Convolutional Neural Networks (CNNs) based on the Maximum Activations of Convolutions (MAC). The first approach is unsupervised and is a variation of the traditional Bag-of-Words (BoW) scheme. It uses two feature aggregation techniques and an inverted video-feature structure for fast retrieval. This method does not need annotated data, and as a result, it can be applied on any video corpus. However, due to several limitations of this approach (i.e., volatile performance), we also built a second supervised solution leveraging Deep Metric Learning (DML). We set up a DML framework based on a triplet-wise scheme to learn a compact and efficient embedding function. A significant benefit of the learning scheme is that it gives the opportunity to be trained in various scenarios; thus, it provides us with the required flexibility with respect to the NDV definition. Both approaches outperform several state-of-the-art methods on the widely used CC_WEB_VIDEO dataset, and the recently published FIVR-200K dataset.

The remainder of the chapter is organized as follows. In Sect. 4.2, we review the related literature in the field of NDVR by providing an outline of the major trends in the field. In Sect. 4.3, we present the two aforementioned NDVR approaches that have been developed within the InVID project [7, 8]. In Sect. 4.4, we report on the results of a comprehensive experimental study, including a comparison with five state-of-the-art methods. In Sect. 4.5, we summarize the findings of our work and offer an outlook into future work in the area.

4.2   Literature Review

In this section, we review several representative works in the literature. NDVR is a challenging problem and has attracted increasing research interest during the last two decades. For a comprehensive overview of the NDVR literature, the reader is referred to Liu et al. [9]. The definition of the NDVR problem is discussed and compared to those of similar research problems (Sect. 4.2.1). Additionally, a variety of approaches are presented and classified based on the type of similarity computed between videos (Sect. 4.2.2). Finally, several publicly available benchmark datasets used to evaluate such approaches are described (Sect. 4.2.3).

4.2.1   Definition and Related Research Problems

There is a variety of definitions and interpretations among the multimedia research community regarding the concept of NDVs, as pointed in [10]. The representative and predominant definitions are those proposed in Wu et al. [2], Shen et al. [11] and Basharat et al. [4]. These vary with respect to the level of resemblance that determines whether a pair of videos are considered to be near-duplicates.

Wu et al. [2] adopted the most narrow scope among the definitions: *NDVs were considered only those that are identical or approximately identical videos, i.e., close to being exact duplicates of each other, but different in terms of file format, encoding parameters, minor photometric variations, editing operations, length, and other modifications.* By contrast, the definition in Shen et al. [11] extended this to videos with *the same semantic content but different in various aspects introduced during capturing time, including photometric or geometric settings.* Another definition was suggested by Basharat et al. [4], which *considered NDVs as videos originating from the same scene.* The same semantic concept can occur under different illumination, appearance, scene settings, camera motion, etc.

Cherubini et al. [12] conducted a large-scale online survey to formulate the definition of NDVs based on the human perception. The results revealed that the technical definitions with respect to manipulations of visual content in Wu et al. [2] and Shen et al. [11] agree to the human perception. However, videos differing with respect to overlaid or added visual content were not perceived as near-duplicates. It is evidenced that users perceive as near-duplicate those videos that are both visually similar and semantically very close [12].

Additionally, NDVR is closely related with other research fields, such as Video Copy Detection (VCD) [13] and Event Video Retrieval (EVR) [3]. The definition of video copies in VCD is very close to the one of NDVR, yet it is slightly narrower. Videos derived from the same source video and differing only with respect to photometric or geometric transformations are considered as copies based on Law-To et al. [13]. Also, the objective of a VCD approach is to identify the copied videos and detect the particular video segments that have been copied. The EVR problem was formulated by Revaud et al. [3]. The objective of EVR is the retrieval of videos that capture the same event. The definition of same-event videos is very broad, including videos that have either spatial or temporal relationship.

4.2.2 NDVR Approaches

The NDVR approaches can be classified based on the level of matching performed to determine near-duplicity into video-level (Sect. 4.2.2.1), frame-level (Sect. 4.2.2.2), and filter-and-refine matching (Sect. 4.2.2.3)

4.2.2.1 Video-Level Matching

Video-level approaches have been developed to deal with web-scale retrieval. In such approaches, videos are usually represented with a global signature such as an aggregated feature vector [2, 14, 18–20] or a hash code [15–17, 21, 22]. The video matching is based on the similarity computation between the video representations. Table 4.1 displays the performance of five video-level approaches on CC_WEB_VIDEO.

A common process to generate a video representation is by the combination of visual features extracted from the video frames into a single feature vector. Wu et al. [2] introduced a simple approach for the video signature generation. They

Table 4.1 Video representation and mean Average Precision (mAP) on CC_WEB_VIDEO dataset of five video-level matching methods. GV stands for global vectors and HC for hash codes

Research	Video rep.	mAP
Wu et al. [2]	GV	0.892
Shang et al. [14]	GV	0.953
Song et al. [15]	HC	0.958
Hao et al. [16]	HC	0.971
Jing et al. [17]	HC	0.972

extracted HSV features from the video keyframes and averaged them to create a single vector. The distance between two video signatures was computed based on their Euclidean distance. Huang et al. [19] proposed a video representation model called Bounded Coordinate System (BCS), which extended Principal Component Analysis (PCA) over the color histograms of the video frames. To compute the similarity between two BCS signatures, scaling and rotation were both considered for matching videos. To improve retrieval efficiency, a two-dimensional transformation method was introduced based on the bidirectional axes in BCS. Liu et al. [18] proposed a method where each video was compared with a set of seed vectors, derived from a number of reference videos. The percentage of video frames that were close to the corresponding reference video was calculated based on the Euclidean distance of their color histograms and used to determine the video similarity. Shang et al. [14] introduced compact spatiotemporal features based on Local Binary Patterns (LBP) [23], called STF-LBP, to represent videos and constructed a modified inverted file index. These spatiotemporal features were extracted based on a feature selection and w-shingling scheme. They adopted Jaccard similarity to rank videos. Cai et al. [20] presented a large-scale BoW approach by applying a scalable K-means clustering technique on the color correlograms [24] of a sample of frames and using inverted file indexing [25] for the fast retrieval of candidate videos. They used cosine similarity to measure similarity between two candidate videos.

Hashing schemes have been extensively used for NDVR. Song et al. [21] presented an approach for Multiple Feature Hashing (MFH) based on a supervised method that employed multiple frame features (i.e., LBP and HSV features) and learned a group of hash functions that map the video keyframe descriptors into the Hamming space. The video signatures were generated by averaging the keyframe hash codes. The Hamming distance was employed to calculate video distances. They extended their approach in [15] by including information of the keyframe groups into the objective function, so as to introduce temporal information in the learning process of the hash functions, which led to a marginal performance increase. Hao et al. [16] combined multiple keyframe features to learn a group of mapping functions that projected the video keyframes into the Hamming space. The combination of the keyframe hash codes generated a video signature that constituted the video representation in the dataset. The Kullback–Leibler (KL) divergence measure was used to approximate the retrieval scores. They extended their work in [22] by employing t-distribution to estimate the similarity between the relaxed hash codes and introduced a deep hashing architecture based on a 3-layer CNN. Jing et al. [17] proposed a supervised hashing method called Global-View Hashing (GVH), which utilized relations among multiple features of video keyframes. They projected all features into a common space and learned multi-bit hash codes for each video using only one hash function. The Hamming distance of the learned hash codes was used to rank the retrieved videos with respect to an input query.

4.2.2.2 Frame-Level Matching

In the case of frame-level matching approaches, the near-duplicate videos are determined by the comparison between individual video frames or sequences. Typical frame-level approaches [9, 26–29] calculate the frame-by-frame similarity and then employ sequence alignment algorithms to compute similarity at the video-level. Moreover, a lot of research effort has been invested in methods that exploit spatiotemporal features to represent video segments in order to facilitate video-level similarity computation [3, 30–33]. Table 4.2 displays the performance of four approaches on the VCDB dataset.

Frame-level methods usually extract local information of video frames and generate a global frame representation for similarity calculation and video matching. Tan et al. [26] introduced an approach based on Temporal Networks (TN). They embedded temporal constraints into a network structure and formulated the partial video alignment problem into a network flow problem. The near-duplicate video segments were determined based on the longest network's paths. Also, to precisely decide the boundaries of the overlapping segments, pairwise constraints generated from keypoint matching were applied. Douze et al. [27] detected points of interest using the Hessian-affine region detector [35], and extracted SIFT [36] and CS-LBP [37] descriptors, in order to create a BoW codebook [25] for Hamming Embedding with weak geometric consistency [38]. Using post-filtering, they verified retrieved matches with spatiotemporal constraints and devised the so-called temporal Hough Voting (HV). Jiang et al. [28] employed a pretrained CNN to extract global features for the video frames and they also trained another CNN with pairs of image patches that captures the local information of frames. They experimented with TN and HV in order to detect the copied video segments. Wang et al. [29] proposed a compact video representation by combining features extracted from pretrained CNN architectures with sparse coding to encode them into a fixed-length vector. To determine the copied video segments, they constructed TNs based on the distance between the extracted features.

Some works utilized spatiotemporal features to accelerate the matching process and improve the performance by considering not only the spatial information of frames but also the temporal relations among frames. Huang et al. [30] proposed a one-dimensional Video Distance Trajectory (VDT) based on the continuous changes

Table 4.2 Employed features and F1 score (%) on VCDB of four frame-level matching methods. HC stands for handcrafted, DL for deep learning, and ST for spatiotemporal features

Research	Features	F1 score (%)
Jiang et al. [34]	HC	60.0
Jiang et al. [28]	DL	65.0
Wang et al. [29]	DL	70.4
Baraldi et al. [33]	DL+ST	68.7

of consecutive frames with respect to a reference point. VDT was further segmented and represented by a sequence of compact signatures called Linear Smoothing Functions (LSFs), which utilized the compound probability to combine three independent video factors and compute sequence similarity. Wu and Aizawa [31] proposed a self-similarity-based feature representation called Self-Similarity Belt (SSBelt), which derived from the Self-Similarity Matrix (SSM). The interest corners were detected and described by a BoW representation. Revaud et al. [3] proposed the Circulant Temporal Encoding (CTE) that encodes frame features in a spatiotemporal representation with Fourier transform. The videos are compared in the frequency domain based on the properties of circulant matrices. Poullot et al. [32] introduced the Temporal Matching Kernel (TMK) that encodes sequences of frames with periodic kernels that take into account the frame descriptor and timestamp. A score function was introduced for video matching that maximizes both the similarity score and the relative time offset by considering all possible relative timestamps. Baraldi et al. [33] built a deep learning layer component based on TMK and set up a training process to learn the feature transform coefficients in the Fourier domain. A triplet loss that takes into account both the video similarity score and the temporal alignment was used in order to train the proposed network.

4.2.2.3   Filter-and-Refine Matching

To overcome the bottleneck of video-level approaches and to achieve efficient NDVR implementations, researchers developed hybrid approaches by combining the advantages of frame-level and video-level methods. Table 4.3 displays the performance of four filter-and-refine approaches on TRECVID 2011. Wu et al. [2] generated video signatures by averaging the HSV histograms of keyframes. Then, they applied a hierarchical filter-and-refine scheme to cluster and filter out near-duplicate videos. When a video could not be clearly classified as NDV, they calculated video similarity based on an expensive local feature-based scheme. Tian et al. [43] extracted audiovisual features. They applied a BoW scheme on the local visual features (SIFT [36], SURF [44]) and a locality sensitive hashing (LSH) scheme on global visual features (DCT) and audio features (WASF [45]). A sequential pyramid matching

Table 4.3 Multimodal approach and F1 score on TRECVID 2011 of four filter-and-refine matching methods. If the approach is not multimodal, then the F1 score is calculated based on the video transformations only

Research	Multimodal	F1 score
Tian et al. [39]	✓	0.950
Jiang et al. [40]	✓	0.962
Tian et al. [41]	✓	0.952
Chou et al. [42]	✗	0.938

(SPM) algorithm was devised to localize the similar video sequences. In contrast, Jiang et al. [40] presented a soft cascade framework utilizing multiple hashed features to filter out non-NDVs. They modified the SPM to introduce temporal information in a temporal pyramid matching (TPM). To further improve performance, they proposed in [39] a multi-scale sequence matching method by LSH using WASF, DCT, and the dense color version SIFT (DC-SIFT), combined with TPM to match near-duplicate segments. Including the concept of transformation-awareness, copy units, and soft decision boundary, Tian et al. [41] extended the multimodal detector cascading framework [39, 40] to a more general approach. Chou et al. [42] proposed a spatiotemporal indexing structure utilizing index patterns, termed Pattern-based Index Tree (PI-tree), to early filter non-near-duplicate videos. In the refine stage, an m-Pattern-based Dynamic Programming scheme was devised to localize near-duplicate segments and to re-rank results of the filter stage. Yang et al. [46] proposed a multi-scale video sequence matching method, which gradually detected and located similar segments between videos from coarse to fine scales. Given a query, they used a maximum weight matching algorithm to rapidly select candidate videos in the coarser scale, then extracted the similar segments in the middle scale to find the NDVs. In the fine scale, they used bidirectional scanning to check the matching similarity of video parts to localize near-duplicate segments.

4.2.3 Benchmark Datasets

Although the problem of NDVR has been investigated for at least two decades, few benchmark datasets have been published. Table 4.4 presents an overview of several publicly available datasets developed for related retrieval tasks. Many researchers constructed their own datasets and did not release them. For instance, Shen et al. [11] collected and manually annotated more than 11,000 TV commercials with an average length of about 60 s.

The most popular and publicly available dataset related to the NDVR problem is CC_WEB_VIDEO [2]. It was published by the research groups of City University

Table 4.4 Publicly available video datasets developed for retrieval tasks related to NDVR

Dataset	Queries	Videos	User-gen.	Retrieval task
CC_WEB_VIDEO [2]	24	12,790	✓	Near-duplicate video retrieval
UQ_VIDEO [21]	24	169,952	✓	Near-duplicate video retrieval
MUSCLE-VCD [13]	18	101	✗	Video copy detection
TRECVID 2011 [47]	11,256	11,503	✗	Video copy detection
VCDB [48]	528	100,528	✓	Partial video copy detection
EVVE [3]	620	102,375	✓	Event video retrieval
FIVR-200K [49]	100	225,960	✓	Fine-grained incident video retrieval

of Hong Kong and Carnegie Mellon University and consists of 13,129 generated videos collected from the Internet. For the dataset collection, 24 popular text queries were submitted to popular video platforms, such as YouTube, Google Video, and Yahoo! Video. A set of videos were collected for each query and the video with the most views was selected as the query video. Then, videos in the collected sets were manually annotated based on their relation to the query video. It is noteworthy that video sets contain high amounts of near-duplicates. On average, there are 27% videos per query that are considered near-duplicates to the most popular version of a video in the search results. However, for certain queries, the redundancy of non-near-duplicates can be as high as 94%.

Several variations of the CC_WEB_VIDEO dataset were developed [14, 20, 21, 42]. In order to make the NDVR problem more challenging and benchmark the scalability of their approaches, researchers usually extend the core CC_WEB_VIDEO dataset with many thousands of distractor videos. The most well-known public dataset that was created through this process is UQ_VIDEO [21]. For the dataset collection, they chose the 400 most popular queries based on Google Zeitgeist Archives from years 2004 to 2009. Each query was fed to YouTube search and they limited the returned videos to one thousand. After filtering out videos with size greater than 10 MB, the combined dataset contains 169,952 videos (including those of the CC_WEB_VIDEO) in total with 3,305,525 keyframes and the same 24 query videos contained in CC_WEB_VIDEO. Unfortunately, only the HSV and LBP histograms of the video keyframes are provided by the authors.

Another popular public benchmark is the Muscle-VCD, created by Law-To et al. [13]. This dataset was designed for the problem of VCD. It consists of 100 h of videos that include Web video clips, TV archives, and movies with different bitrates, resolutions, and video format. A set of original videos and their corresponding transformed videos are given for the evaluation of copy detection algorithms. Two kinds of transformation were applied on the queries: (a) entire video copy with a single transformation, where the videos may be slightly recoded and/or noised; (b) partial video copy with a mixture of transformations, where two videos only share one or more short segments. Both transformations were simulated by using video-editing software to apply the transformations. The transformed videos or segments were used as queries to search their original versions in the dataset.

The annual TRECVID [50] evaluation included a task on copy detection in years 2008 to 2011. Each year a benchmark dataset was generated and released only to the registered participants of the task. The TRECVID datasets were constructed in a very similar way to the Muscle-VCD dataset. The latest edition of the dataset [47] contained 11,503 reference videos of over 420 h. Query videos were categorized into three types: (i) a reference video only, (ii) a reference video embedded into a non-reference video, and (iii) a non-reference video only. Only the first two types of query videos were near-duplicates to videos in the dataset. Each query was generated using a software to randomly extract a segment from a dataset video and impose a few predefined transformations. The contestants were asked to find the original videos and detect the copied segment.

A more recent dataset that is relevant to our problem is the VCDB [48]. This dataset is composed of videos derived from popular video platforms (i.e., YouTube and Metacafe) and has been compiled and annotated as a benchmark for the partial copy detection problem, which is highly related to the NDVR problem. VCDB contains two subsets, the core and the distractor subset. The core subset contains 28 discrete sets of videos composed of 528 query videos and over 9,000 pairs of partial copies. Each video set was manually annotated by seven annotators and the video chunks of the video copies were extracted. The distractor subset is a corpus of approximately 100,000 distractor videos that is used to make the video copy detection problem more challenging.

Moreover, the EVVE (EVent VidEo) [3] dataset was developed for the problem of event video retrieval. The main objective of the systems evaluated on this dataset is the retrieval of all videos that capture a particular event given a query video. The dataset contains 13 major events that were provided as queries to YouTube. A total number of 2,375 videos were collected and 620 of them were selected as video queries. Each event was annotated by one annotator, who first produced a precise definition of the event. In addition to the videos collected for specific events, the authors also retrieved a set of 100,000 distractor videos by querying YouTube with unrelated terms. These videos were collected before a certain date to ensure that the distractor set did not contain any of the relevant events of EVVE, since all events were temporally localized after that date.

Finally, the FIVR-200K [49] dataset was developed to simulate the problem of Fine-grained Incident Video Retrieval (FIVR). For the dataset collection, the major events occurring in the time span from January 2013 to December 2017 were collected by crawling Wikipedia. The event headlines were then used to query YouTube. In total, 225,960 videos were collected from 4,687 events, and 100 query videos were selected using a systematic process. Then the videos in the dataset were manually annotated based on their relation to the queries. FIVR-200K includes three different tasks: (a) the Duplicate Scene Video Retrieval (DSVR) task which is highly related to the NDVR problem and it only accepts as positive matches videos that contain at least one identical scene, (b) the Complementary Scene Video Retrieval (CSVR) task which is a broader variant of the NDVR problem where videos that contain scenes captured at the same time but from different camera viewpoints are considered related, and (c) the Incident Scene Video Retrieval (ISVR) task where all videos with scenes displaying the same incident are considered positive matches.

4.3 NDVR Approaches in InVID

In InVID, two video-level solutions have been developed, since video-level NDVR appeared to offer the best trade-off between computational cost and retrieval effectiveness. Additionally, most video-level methods can be adapted to a corresponding frame-level approach in a straightforward manner if even higher retrieval accuracy is needed. Of the two developed video-level approaches, one is unsupervised

(Sect. 4.3.1) and the other supervised (Sect. 4.3.2). The former is a modified BoW scheme based on the extracted CNN features. The latter is based on Deep Metric Learning (DML), which learns an embedding function that maps the CNN descriptors into a feature space where the NDVs are closer than the other videos.

4.3.1 Bag-of-Words Approach

The proposed unsupervised NDVR approach relies on a Bag-of-Words (BoW) scheme [7]. In particular, two aggregation variations are proposed: a vector aggregation where a single codebook of visual words is used, and a layer aggregation where multiple codebooks of visual words are used. The video representations are organized in an inverted file structure for fast indexing and retrieval. Video similarity is computed based on the cosine similarity of the *tf-idf* weighted vectors of the extracted BoW representations.

4.3.1.1 CNN-Based Feature Extraction

In recent research [6, 51], pretrained CNN models are used to extract visual features from intermediate convolutional layers. These features are computed through the forward propagation of an image over the CNN network and the use of an aggregation function (e.g., VLAD encoding [52], max/average pooling) on the convolutional layer.

We adopt a compact representation for frame descriptors that is derived from activations of all intermediate convolutional layers of a pretrained CNN by applying the function called Maximum Activation of Convolutions (MAC) [5, 6]. A pretrained CNN network $\mathscr{C}$ is considered, with a total number of L convolutional layers, denoted as $\mathscr{L}^1, \mathscr{L}^2, ..., \mathscr{L}^L$. Forward propagating a frame through network $\mathscr{C}$ generates a total of L feature maps, denoted as $\mathscr{M}^l \in \mathbb{R}^{n_d^l \times n_d^l \times c^l}$ ($l = 1, ..., L$), where $n_d^l \times n_d^l$ is the dimension of every channel for convolutional layer $\mathscr{L}^l$ (which depends on the size of the input frame) and c^l is the total number of channels. To extract a single descriptor vector from every layer, an aggregation function is applied on the above feature maps. In particular, we apply max pooling on every channel of feature map $\mathscr{M}^l$ to extract a single value. The extraction process is formulated in:

$$v^l(i) = \max \mathscr{M}^l(\cdot, \cdot, i), \quad i = \{1, 2, ..., c^l\} \tag{4.1}$$

where layer vector v^l is a c^l-dimensional vector that is derived from max pooling on every channel of feature map $\mathscr{M}^l$. The layer vectors are then ℓ_2-normalized.

We extract and concatenate frame descriptors only from activations in intermediate layers, since we aim to construct a visual representation that preserves local structure at different scales. Activations from fully connected layers are not used, since they are considered to offer a global representation of the input. A positive side effect of this decision is that the resulting descriptor is compact, reducing the total processing time and storage requirements. For the VGGNet and GoogLeNet architectures, we do not use the initial layer activations as features, since those layers are expected to capture very primitive frame features (e.g., edges, corners, etc.) that could lead to false matches.

Uniform sampling is applied to select one frame per second for every video and extract the respective features for each of them. Hence, given an arbitrary video with N frames $\{F_1, F_2, ..., F_N\}$, the video representation is a set that contains all feature vectors of the video frames $v = \{v_{F_1}, v_{F_2}, ..., v_{F_N}\}$, where v_{F_i} contains all layer vectors of frame F_i. Although v_{F_i} stands for a set of vectors, we opted to use this notation for convenience.

4.3.1.2 Feature Aggregation

We follow two alternative feature aggregation schemes (i.e., ways of aggregating features from layers into a single descriptor for the whole frame): (a) *vector aggregation* and (b) *layer aggregation*. The outcome of both schemes is a frame-level histogram H_F that is considered as the representation of a frame. Next, a video-level histogram H_V is derived from the frame representations by aggregating frame-level histograms to a single video representation. Figure 4.3 illustrates the two schemes.

Vector aggregation: A bag-of-words scheme is applied on the vector v^c resulting from the concatenation of individual layer features to generate a single codebook of K visual words, denoted as $C_K = \{t_1, t_2, ..., t_K\}$. The selection of K, a system parameter, has critical impact on the performance of the approach. Having generated the visual codebook, every video frame is assigned to the nearest visual word. Accordingly, every frame F_i with feature descriptor $v^c_{F_i}$ is aggregated to the nearest visual word $t_{F_i} = NN(v^c_{F_i})$, hence its H_{F_i} contains only a single visual word.

Layer aggregation: To preserve the structural information captured by intermediate layers $\mathscr{L}$ of the CNN network $\mathscr{C}$, we generate L layer-specific codebooks of K words (denoted as $C_K^l = \{t_1^l, t_2^l, ..., t_K^l\}, l = 1, ..., L$), which we then use to extract separate bag-of-words representations (one per layer). The layer vectors $v_{F_i}^l$ of frame F_i are mapped to the nearest layer words $t_{F_i}^l = NN(v_{F_i}^l), (l = 1, 2, ..., L)$. In contrast to the previous scheme, every frame F_i is represented by a frame-level histogram H_{F_i} that results from the concatenation of the individual layer-specific histograms, thus comprising L words instead of a single one.

The final video representation is generated based on the BoW representations of its frames. In particular, given an arbitrary video with N frames $\{F_1, F_2, ..., F_N\}$, its video-level histogram H_V is derived by summing the histogram vectors corresponding to its frames, i.e., $H_V = \sum_{i \in [1,N]} H_{F_i}$. Note that for the two aggregation schemes, histograms of different sizes are generated. In the first case, the total number of visual words equals K, whereas in the second case, it equals to $K \cdot L$.

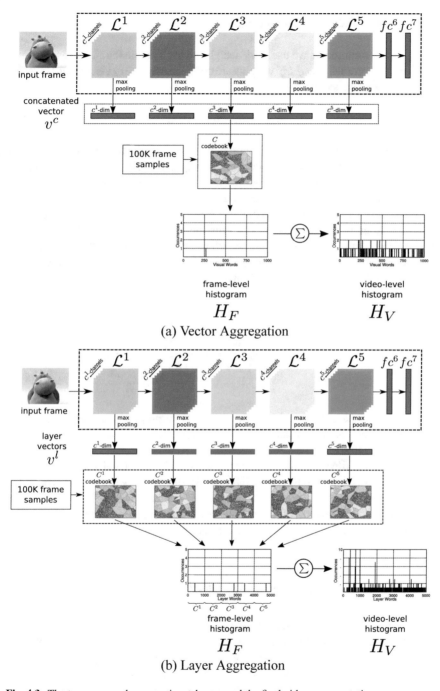

(a) Vector Aggregation

(b) Layer Aggregation

Fig. 4.3 The two proposed aggregation schemes and the final video representation

4.3.1.3   Video Indexing and Querying

In the proposed approach, we use *tf-idf* weighting to calculate the similarity between
two video histograms. The *tf-idf* weights are computed for every visual word in every
video in a video collection C_b:

$$w_{td} = n_{td} \cdot \log |C_b|/n_t \qquad (4.2)$$

where w_{td} is the weight of word t in video d, n_{td} and n_t are the number of occurrences
of word t in video d and the entire collection, respectively, while $|C_b|$ is the number
of videos in the collection. The former factor of the equation is called *term frequency*
(tf) and the latter is called *inverted document frequency* (idf).

   Video querying is the online part of the approach. Let q denote a query video. Once
the final histogram H_v^q is extracted from the query video, an inverted file indexing
scheme [25] is employed for fast and efficient retrieval of videos that have at least
a common visual word with the query video. For all these videos (i.e., videos with
non-zero similarity), the cosine similarity between the respective *tf-idf* representations is computed:

$$sim(q, p) = \frac{\mathbf{w}_q \cdot \mathbf{w}_p}{\|\mathbf{w}_q\| \|\mathbf{w}_p\|} = \frac{\sum_{i=0}^{K} w_{iq} w_{ip}}{\sqrt{\sum_{i=0}^{K} w_{iq}^2} \sqrt{\sum_{i=0}^{K} w_{ip}^2}} \qquad (4.3)$$

where $\mathbf{w}_q$ and $\mathbf{w}_p$ are the weight vectors of videos q and p, respectively, and $\|\mathbf{w}\|$ is
the norm of vector $\mathbf{w}$. The collection videos are ranked in descending order based on
their similarity to the query.

   In the inverted file structure, each entry corresponds to a visual word and contains
its ID, the *idf* value and all the video IDs in which the visual word occurs. The video
IDs map to a video in the collection C_b where the occurrences (*tf*) of the visual words
are stored. With this inverted file structure, all the needed values for the calculation
of the similarity between a query and a dataset video can be retrieved.

4.3.2 Deep Metric Learning Approach

The unsupervised approach has several limitations. The most important is that it
offers a dataset-specific solution, i.e., the extracted knowledge is not transferable, and
rebuilding the model is computationally expensive. To observe no performance loss,
a sufficiently large and diverse dataset to create vocabularies is required, which needs
significant effort to be collected or sometimes is not even possible. Hence, we also
developed a Deep Metric Learning (DML) approach to overcome this limitation [8].
This involves training a Deep Neural Network (DNN) to approximate an embedding

function for the accurate computation of similarity between two candidate videos. For training, we devised a novel triplet generation process.

For feature extraction, we build upon the same process as the one presented in Sect. 4.3.1.2. Hence, given an arbitrary video with N frames $\{F_1, F_2, ..., F_N\}$, we extract one feature descriptor for each video frame by concatenating the layer vector to a single vector. Global video representations v are then derived by averaging and normalizing (zero-mean and ℓ_2-normalization) these frame descriptors. Keep in mind that feature extraction is not part of the training (deep metric learning) process, i.e., the training of the network is not end-to-end, and as a result, the weights of the pretrained network used for feature extraction are not updated.

4.3.2.1   Problem Formulation

We address the problem of learning a pairwise similarity function for NDVR from the relative information of pairwise/triplet-wise video relations. For a given query video and a set of candidate videos, the goal is to quantify the similarity between the query and every candidate video and use it for the ranking of the entire set of candidates with the goal of retrieving the NDVs at the top ranks. We first define the similarity between two arbitrary videos q and p as the squared Euclidean distance in the video embedding space:

$$D(f_\theta(q), f_\theta(p)) = \|f_\theta(q) - f_\theta(p)\|_2^2 \tag{4.4}$$

where $f_\theta(\cdot)$ is the embedding function that maps a video to a point in the Euclidean space, θ are the system parameters, and $D(\cdot, \cdot)$ is the squared Euclidean distance in this space. Additionally, we define a pairwise indicator function $I(\cdot, \cdot)$ that specifies whether a pair of videos are near-duplicate.

$$I(q, p) = \begin{cases} 1 & \text{if } q, p \text{ are NDVs} \\ 0 & \text{otherwise} \end{cases} \tag{4.5}$$

Our objective is to learn an embedding function $f_\theta(\cdot)$ that assigns smaller distances to NDV pairs than others. Given a video with feature vector v, an NDV with v^+ and a dissimilar video with v^-, the embedding function $f_\theta(\cdot)$ should map video vectors to a common space $\mathbb{R}^d$, where d is the dimension of the feature embedding, in which the distance between query and positive videos is always smaller than the distance between query and negative. This is formulated as

$$\begin{aligned} D(f_\theta(v), f_\theta(v^+)) &< D(f_\theta(v), f_\theta(v^-)), \\ \forall v, v^+, v^- \text{ such that } I(v, v^+) &= 1, I(v, v^-) = 0 \end{aligned} \tag{4.6}$$

4.3.2.2   Triplet Loss

To implement the learning process, we create a collection of N training instances organized in the form of triplets $\mathscr{T} = \{(v_i, v_i^+, v_i^-), i = 1, ..., N\}$, where v_i, v_i^+, v_i^- are the feature vectors of the query, positive (NDV), and negative (dissimilar) videos respectively. A triplet expresses a relative similarity order among three videos, i.e., v_i is more similar to v_i^+ in contrast to v_i^-. We define the following hinge loss function for a given triplet called "triplet loss":

$$L_\theta(v_i, v_i^+, v_i^-) = \max\{0, \mathrm{D}(f_\theta(v_i), f_\theta(v_i^+)) - \mathrm{D}(f_\theta(v_i), f_\theta(v_i^-)) + \gamma\} \qquad (4.7)$$

where γ is a margin parameter to ensure a sufficiently large difference between the positive-query distance and negative-query distance. If the video distances are calculated correctly within margin γ, then this triplet will not be penalized. Otherwise, the loss is a convex approximation of the loss that measures the degree of violation of the desired distance between the video pairs specified by the triplet. To this end, we use batch gradient descent to optimize the objective function:

$$\min_\theta \sum_{i=1}^{m} L_\theta(v_i, v_i^+, v_i^-) + \lambda \|\theta\|_2^2 \qquad (4.8)$$

where λ is a regularization parameter to prevent overfitting, and m is the total size of a triplet mini-batch. Minimizing this loss will narrow the query-positive distance while widening the query-negative distance, and thus lead to a representation satisfying the desirable ranking order. With an appropriate triplet generation strategy in place, the model will eventually learn a video representation that improves the effectiveness of the NDVR solution.

4.3.2.3   DML Network Architecture

For training the DML model, a triplet-based network architecture is proposed (Fig. 4.4) that optimizes the triplet loss function in Eq. 4.7. The network is provided with a set of triplets $\mathscr{T}$ created by the triplet generation process of Sect. 4.3.2.5. Each triplet contains a query, a positive, and a negative video with v_i, v_i^+ and v_i^- feature vectors, respectively, which are fed independently into three siamese DNNs with identical architecture and parameters. The DNNs compute the embeddings of $v : f_\theta(v) \in \mathbb{R}^d$. The architecture of the deployed DNNs is based on three dense *fully connected layers* and a *normalization layer* at the end leading to vectors that lie on a d-dimensional unit length hypersphere, i.e., $\|f_\theta(v)\|_2 = 1$. The size of each hidden layer (number of neurons) and the d-dimension of the output vector $f_\theta(v)$ depends on the dimensionality of input vectors, which is in turn dictated by the employed CNN architecture. The video embeddings computed from a batch of triplets are then given to a triplet loss layer to calculate the accumulated cost based on Eq. 4.7.

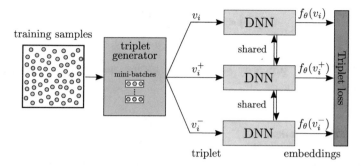

Fig. 4.4 Illustration of DML network architecture

4.3.2.4 Video-Level Similarity Computation

The learned embedding function $f_\theta(\cdot)$ is used for computing similarities between videos in a target video corpus. Given an arbitrary video with $v = \{v_{F_1}, v_{F_2}, ..., v_{F_N}\}$, two variants are proposed for fusing similarity computation across video frames: early and late fusion.

Early fusion: Frame descriptors are averaged and normalized into a global video descriptor before they are forward propagated to the network. The global video signature is the output of the embedding function $f_\theta(\cdot)$:

$$f_\theta(v) = f_\theta\left(\frac{1}{N}\sum_{i=1}^{N} v_{F_i}\right) \tag{4.9}$$

Late fusion: Each extracted frame descriptor of the input video is fed forward to the network, and the set of their embedding transformations is averaged and normalized:

$$f_\theta(v) = \frac{1}{N}\sum_{i=1}^{N} f_\theta(v_{F_i}) \tag{4.10}$$

There are several pros and cons for each scheme. The former is computationally lighter and more intuitive; however, it is slightly less effective. Late fusion leads to better performance and is amenable to possible extensions of the base approach (i.e., frame-level approaches). Nonetheless, it is slower since the features extracted from all selected video frames are fed to the DNN.

Finally, the similarity between two videos derives from the distance of their representations. For a given query q and a set of M candidate videos $\{p_i\}_{i=1}^{M} \in P$, the similarity within each candidate pair is determined by normalizing the distance with respect to the maximum value and then subtracting the result from the unit to map the similarity scores to the range $[0, 1]$. This process is formulated in:

$$S(q, p) = 1 - \frac{D(f_\theta(q), f_\theta(p))}{\max_{p_i \in P}(D(f_\theta(q), f_\theta(p_i)))} \tag{4.11}$$

where $S(\cdot, \cdot)$ is the similarity between two videos, and $\max(\cdot)$ is the maximum function.

4.3.2.5 Triplet Generation

A crucial part of the proposed approach is the generation of the video triplets. It is important to provide a considerable amount of videos for constructing a representative triplet training set. However, the total number of triplets that can be generated equals the total number of 3-combinations over the size N of the video corpus, i.e.,

$$\binom{N}{3} = \frac{N \cdot (N - 1) \cdot (N - 2)}{6} \tag{4.12}$$

We have empirically determined that only a tiny portion of videos in a corpus could be considered as near-duplicates for a given video query. Thus, it would be inefficient to randomly select video triplets from this vast set (for instance, for $N = 1,000$, the total number of triplets would exceed 160M). Instead, a sampling strategy is employed as a key element of the triplet generation process, which is focused on selecting hard candidates to create triplets.

The proposed sampling strategy is applied on a development dataset. Such a dataset needs to contain two sets of videos: $\mathcal{P}$, a set of near-duplicate video pairs that are used as query-positive pairs, and $\mathcal{N}$, a set of dissimilar videos that are used as negatives. We aim at generating *hard triplets*, i.e., negative videos (*hard negatives*) with distance to the query that is smaller than the distance between the query and positive videos (*hard positives*). The aforementioned condition is expressed in:

$$\mathcal{T} = \{(q, p, n) | (q, p) \in \mathcal{P}, n \in \mathcal{N}, D(q, p) > D(q, n)\} \tag{4.13}$$

where $\mathcal{T}$ is the resulting set of triplets. The global video features are first extracted following the process in Sect. 4.3.1.1. Then, the distance between every query in $\mathcal{P}$ and every dissimilar video in $\mathcal{N}$ is calculated. If the query-positive distance is greater than a query-negative distance, then a hard triplet is formed composed of the three videos. The distance is calculated based on the Euclidean distance of the initial global video descriptors.

4.4 Evaluation

In this section, the two developed approaches are evaluated. The experimental setup is described in Sect. 4.4.1, where we present the datasets used, the evaluation metrics, several implementation details, and a number of competing approaches from the state of the art. Extensive experimental evaluation is conducted and reported under various evaluation settings in Sect. 4.4.2.

4.4.1 Experimental Setup

4.4.1.1 Evaluation Datasets

Experiments were performed on the CC_WEB_VIDEO dataset [2], which is available by the research groups of City University of Hong Kong and Carnegie Mellon University. The collection consists of a sample of videos retrieved by submitting 24 popular text queries to popular video sharing websites (i.e., YouTube, Google Video, and Yahoo! Video). For every query, a set of video clips were collected and the most popular video was considered to be the query video. Subsequently, all videos in the collected set were manually annotated based on their near-duplicate relation to the query video. Table 4.5 depicts the types of near-duplicate types and their annotation. In the present work, all videos annotated with any symbol but X are considered near-duplicates. The dataset contains a total of 13,129 videos consisting of 397,965 keyframes.

In addition, we use the FIVR-200K [49] dataset for validating the results on a second independent dataset. It consists of 225,960 videos collected based on the 4,687 events and contains 100 video queries. Table 4.5 depicts the annotation labels used in the dataset and their definitions. FIVR-200K includes three different tasks: (a) the Duplicate Scene Video Retrieval (DSVR) task where only videos annotated with ND and DS are considered relevant, (b) the Complementary Scene Video Retrieval (CSVR) task which accepts only the videos annotated with ND, DS or CS as relevant, and (c) Incident Scene Video Retrieval (ISVR) task where all labels (with the exception of DI) are considered relevant.

4.4.1.2 Development Dataset

For generating triplets to train the supervised DML approach, we leverage the VCDB dataset [34]. This dataset is composed of videos from popular video platforms (YouTube and Metacafe) and has been compiled and annotated as a benchmark for the partial copy detection task, which is highly related to the NDVR problem setting. VCDB contains two subsets, the core $\mathcal{C}_c$ and the distractor subset $\mathcal{C}_d$. Subset $\mathcal{C}_c$ contains discrete sets of videos composed of 528 query videos and over 9,000

Table 4.5 Annotation labels of CC_WEB_VIDEO and FIVR-200K datasets

(a) CC_WEB_VIDEO

Label	Transformation
E	Exactly duplicate
S	Similar video
V	Different version
M	Major change
L	Long version
X	Dissimilar video

(b) FIVR-200K

Label	Definition
ND	Near-duplicate
DS	Duplicate scene
CS	Complementary scene
IS	Incident scene
DI	Distractor

pairs of partial copies. Each video set has been annotated and the chunks of the video copies extracted. Subset $\mathscr{C}_d$ is a corpus of approximately 100,000 distractor videos that is used to make the video copy detection problem more challenging.

For the triplet generation, we retrieve all video pairs annotated as partial copies. We define an overlap criterion to decide whether to use a pair for the triplet generation: if the duration of the overlapping content is greater than a certain threshold t compared to the total duration of each video, then the pair is retained, otherwise discarded. Each video of a given pair can be used once as query and once as positive video. Therefore, the set of query-positive pairs $\mathscr{P}$ is generated based on

$$\mathscr{P} = \{(q, p) \cup (p, q) | q, p \in \mathscr{C}_c, o(q, p) > t\} \tag{4.14}$$

where $o(\cdot, \cdot)$ determines the video overlap. We found empirically that the selection of the threshold t has considerable impact on the quality of the resulting DML model. Subset $\mathscr{C}_d$ is used as the set $\mathscr{N}$ of negatives. To generate hard triplets, the negative videos are selected based on Eq. 4.13.

4.4.1.3 Evaluation Metrics

To evaluate retrieval performance, we build upon the evaluation scheme described in [2]. We first employ the interpolated *Precision–Recall* (PR) curve. *Precision* is determined as the fraction of retrieved videos that are relevant to the query, and *Recall* as the fraction of the total relevant videos that are retrieved:

$$Precision = \frac{TP}{TP + FP}, \quad Recall = \frac{TP}{TP + FN} \tag{4.15}$$

where *TP*, *FP*, and *FN* are the true positives (correctly retrieved), false positives (incorrectly retrieved), and false negatives (missed matches), respectively. The interpolated PR-curve derives from the averaging of the Precision scores over all queries for given Recall ranges. The maximum Precision score is selected as the representative value for each Recall range. We further use *mean Average Precision* (mAP) as defined in [2] to evaluate the quality of video ranking. For each query, the *Average Precision* (AP) is calculated based on

$$AP = \frac{1}{n} \sum_{i=0}^{n} \frac{i}{r_i} \tag{4.16}$$

where n is the number of relevant videos to the query video, and r_i is the rank of the i-th retrieved relevant video. The mAP is computed from the averaging of the AP across all queries.

4.4.1.4 Implementation Details

We experiment with three deep network architectures: AlexNet [53], VGGNet [54] and GoogLeNet [55]. The AlexNet is an eight-layer network that consists of five convolutional/pooling layers, two fully connected layers, and one softmax layer. VGGNet has the same number of fully connected layers, although the number of convolutional layers may vary. In this paper, the version with 16-layers is employed as it gives similar performance to the 19-layer version. Finally, GoogLeNet is composed of 22 layers in total. In this architecture, multiple convolutions are combined in an intersection module called "inception". There are nine inception modules in total that are sequentially connected, followed by an average pooling and a softmax layer at the end. All three architectures receive as input images of size 224×224. For all the experiments, the input frames are resized to fit these dimensions, even though this step is not mandatory. Table 4.6 depicts the employed CNN architectures and the number of channels in the respective convolutional layers.

For feature extraction, we use the Caffe framework [48], which provides pretrained models on ImageNet for both employed CNN networks.[5] Regarding the unsupervised approach, the visual codebooks are generated based on scalable K-Means++ [56]—the Apache Spark[6] implementation of the algorithm is used for efficiency and scalability—in both aggregation schemes, and a sample of 100K randomly selected video frames is used for training. The implementation of the supervised deep model is built on Theano [57]. We use [800, 400, 250], [2000, 1000, 500] and [2500, 1000, 500] neurons for the three hidden layers for AlexNet, VGGNet, and GoogLeNet, respectively. Adam optimization [58] is employed with learning rate $l = 10^{-5}$. For the triplet generation, we set $t = 0.8$ which generates approximately 2K pairs in $\mathcal{P}$ and 7M, 4M and 5M triplets in $\mathcal{T}$, for AlexNet, VGGNet, and GoogLeNet, respectively. Other parameters are set to $\gamma = 1$ and $\lambda = 10^{-5}$.

---

[5]https://github.com/BVLC/caffe/wiki/Model-Zoo (accessed on March 2019).
[6]http://spark.apache.org (accessed on March 2019).

Table 4.6 Deep CNN architectures and total number of channels per layer used in the proposed approach

(a) AlexNet		(b) VGGNet		(c) GoogleNet	
Layer $\mathscr{L}^l$	c^l-dim	Layer $\mathscr{L}^l$	c^l-dim	Layer $\mathscr{L}^l$	c^l-dim
conv1	96	conv2_1	128	inception_3a	256
conv2	256	conv2_2	128	inception_3b	480
conv3	384	conv3_1	256	inception_4a	512
conv4	384	conv3_2	256	inception_4b	512
conv5	256	conv3_3	256	inception_4c	512
total	1376	conv4_1	512	inception_4d	528
		conv4_2	512	inception_4e	832
		conv4_3	512	inception_5a	832
		conv5_1	512	inception_5b	1024
		conv5_2	512	total	5488
		conv5_3	512		
		total	4096		

4.4.1.5   State-of-the-Art Approaches

We compare the proposed approach with five widely used content-based NDVR approaches. Three of those were developed based on frames of videos sampled from the evaluation set. These are the following.

Auto-Color Correlograms (ACC)—Cai et al. [20] use uniform sampling to extract one frame per second for the input video. The auto-color correlograms [24] of each frame are computed and aggregated based on a visual codebook generated from a training set of video frames. The retrieval of near-duplicate videos is performed using tf-idf weighted cosine similarity over the visual word histograms of a query and a dataset video.

Pattern-based approach (PPT)—Chou et al. [42] build a pattern-based indexing tree (PI-tree) based on a sequence of symbols encoded from keyframes, which facilitates the efficient retrieval of candidate videos. They use m-pattern-based dynamic programming (mPDP) and time-shift m-pattern similarity (TPS) to determine video similarity.

Stochastic Multi-view Hashing (SMVH)—Hao et al. [16] combine multiple keyframe features to learn a group of mapping functions that project video keyframes into the Hamming space. The combination of keyframe hash codes generates a video signature that constitutes the final video representation. A composite Kullback–Leibler (KL) divergence measure is used to compute similarity scores.

The remaining two, which are based on the work of Wu et al. [2], are not built based on any development dataset:

Color Histograms (CH)—This is a global video representation based on the color histograms of keyframes. The color histogram is a concatenation of 18 bins for Hue, 3 bins for Saturation, and 3 bins for Value, resulting in a 24-dimensional vector representation for every keyframe. The global video signature is the normalized color histogram over all keyframes in the video.

Local Structure (LS)—Global signatures and local features are combined using a hierarchical approach. Color signatures are employed to detect near-duplicate videos with high confidence and to filter out very dissimilar videos. For the reduced set of candidate videos, a local feature-based method was developed, which compares the keyframes in a sliding window using their local features (PCA-SIFT [59]).

4.4.2 Experimental Results

4.4.2.1 Comparison of Global Feature Descriptors

In this section, we benchmark the proposed intermediate CNN features with a number of global frame descriptors used in NDVR literature. The compared descriptors are divided into two groups: handcrafted and learned features.[7] The handcrafted features include RGB histograms, HSV histograms, Local Binary Patterns (LBP), Auto Color Correlograms (ACC) and Histogram of Oriented Gradients (HOG). For the learned features, we extract the intermediate CNN features, as described in Sect. 4.3.1.1, and concatenate the layer vectors to generate a single descriptor. Additionally, we experiment with the global features derived from the activations of the first fully connected layer after the convolutional layers, for each architecture. To compare the NDVR performance, a standard bag-of-words scheme with vector aggregation (Sect. 4.3.1.2) is built based on each global feature descriptor.

Table 4.7 presents the mAP of each model built on a different global descriptor for two different values of K. The intermediate features of GoogLeNet and VGGNet achieved the best results with 0.958 and 0.886 for $K = 1,000$ and $K = 10,000$, respectively. In general, learned features lead to considerably better performance than handcrafted ones in both setups. Furthermore, intermediate CNN features outperformed the ones derived from the fully connected layers in almost all cases. One may notice that there is a correlation between the dimensions of the descriptors and the performance of the model. Hence, due to the considerable performance difference, we focused our research on the exploration of the potential of intermediate CNN features.

---

[7]The features have been learned on the ImageNet dataset, since pretrained networks are utilized. However, ImageNet is a comprehensive dataset, so the learned features can be used in other computer vision tasks (i.e., NDVR) without the need of retraining.

Table 4.7 mAP and dimensionality of 11 global frame descriptors

Descriptor/network	Layers	Dimensions	K	
			1,000	10,000
RGB	–	64	0.857	0.813
HSV	–	162	0.902	0.792
LBP	–	256	0.803	0.683
ACC	–	256	0.936	0.826
HOG	–	1764	**0.940**	**0.831**
AlexNet	conv	1376	0.951	0.879
	fc	4096	0.953	0.875
VGGNet	conv	4096	0.937	**0.886**
	fc	4096	0.936	0.854
GoogLeNet	inc	5488	**0.958**	0.857
	fc	1000	0.941	0.849

4.4.2.2 Evaluation of BoW Approach

In this section, we study the impact of the feature aggregation scheme, the underlying CNN architecture and the size of the visual vocabulary on the BoW approach. Regarding the first aspect, we benchmark the three CNN architectures with both aggregation schemes using $K = 1,000$ words.

Figure 4.5 depicts the PR curves of the different CNN architectures with the two aggregation schemes. For every CNN architecture, layer-based aggregation schemes outperform vector-based ones. GoogLeNet achieves the best vector-based results with a precision close to 100% up to a 70% recall. In terms of recall, all three architectures have similar results in the value range 80–100%. All three benchmarked

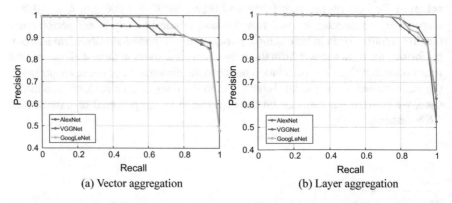

(a) Vector aggregation   (b) Layer aggregation

Fig. 4.5 Precision–recall curve of the proposed approach based on three CNN architectures and for the two aggregation schemes

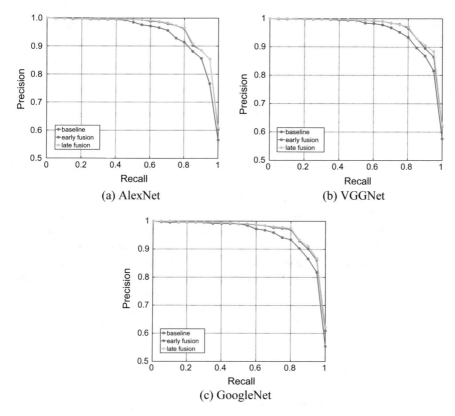

Fig. 4.6 Precision–recall curve of the baseline and two DML fusion schemes for the three benchmarked CNN architectures

Table 4.8 mAP per CNN architecture and aggregation scheme

Method	K	AlexNet	VGGNet	GoogLeNet
Vector aggr.	1000	0.951	0.937	**0.958**
	10,000	0.879	0.886	0.857
Layer aggr.	1000	0.969	**0.976**	0.974
	10,000	0.948	0.959	0.958

architectures have almost perfect performance up to 75% recall when the layer-based aggregation scheme is employed.

As presented in Table 4.8, similar results are obtained in terms of mAP for the CNN architectures and the aggregation schemes. In the case of vector-based aggregation, the results are the same as in Table 4.7, hence GoogLeNet outperforms the other two architectures with a mAP of 0.958, and VGGNet reports the worst performance with 0.937 mAP. However, when the layer-based aggregation is employed, VGGNet achieves the best results with a mAP score of 0.976. The lowest, yet competitive

Table 4.9 mAP of the baseline and two DML fusion schemes for the three benchmarked CNN architectures

Architecture	Baseline	Early fusion	Late fusion
AlexNet	0.948	0.964	0.964
VGGNet	0.956	0.970	**0.971**
GoogLeNet	0.952	0.968	0.969

results in the case of layer-based aggregation, are obtained for AlexNet with 0.969 mAP.

The two schemes are compared with $K = 1,000$ and $K = 10,000$ (Table 4.8) in order to test the impact of vocabulary size. Results reveal that the performance of vector-based aggregation for $K = 10,000$ is lower compared to the case when $K = 1,000$ words are used. It appears that the vector-based aggregation suffers considerably more from the increase of K compared to the layer-based aggregation, which appears to be less sensitive to this parameter. Due to this fact, we did not consider to use the same amount of visual words for the vector-based and the layer-based aggregation, since the performance gap between the two types of aggregation with the same number of visual words would be much more pronounced.

4.4.2.3 Evaluation of DML Approach

In this section, we study the performance of the supervised DML approach in the evaluation dataset in relation to the underlying CNN architecture and the different fusion schemes. The three CNN architectures are benchmarked. For each of them, three configurations are tested: (i) *baseline*: all frame descriptors are averaged to a single vector which is used for retrieval without any transformation, (ii) *early fusion*: all frame descriptors are averaged to a single vector which is then transformed by applying the learned embedding function to generate the video descriptor, (iii) *late fusion*: all frame descriptors are transformed by applying the learned embedding function and the generated embeddings are then averaged.

Figure 4.6 and Table 4.9 present the PR curves and the mAP, respectively, of the three CNN architectures with the three fusion setups. Late fusion schemes consistently outperform the other two fusion schemes for all CNN architectures. VGGNet achieves the best results for all three settings with a small margin compared to the GoogLeNet, with precision more than 97% up to 80% recall and mAP scores of 0.970 and 0.971 for early and late fusion, respectively. Performance clearly increases in both trained fusion schemes compared to the baseline for all three architectures. The early and late fusion schemes achieve almost identical results, which is an indication that the choice of the fusion scheme is not critical.

4.4.2.4   Comparison Against State-of-the-Art NDVR Approaches

For comparing the performance of the two approaches with the five NDVR approaches from the literature, we select the setup using VGGNet features with layer aggregation for the BoW approach, denoted as LBoW, and the setup using VGGNet features with late fusion for the DML approach, denoted as DML_{vcdb}, since they achieved the best results in each case. We separate the compared approaches in two groups based on the developed dataset, i.e., whether the evaluation dataset is used for development or not. For the sake of comparison and completeness, the results of the DML method trained on a triplet set derived from both VCDB (similar to DML_{vcdb}) and also videos sampled from CC_WEB_VIDEO are denoted as DML_{cc}. This simulates the situation where the DML-based approach has access to a portion of the evaluation corpus, similar to the setting used by the competing approaches.

In Table 4.10, the mAP scores of the competing methods are reported. The DML approach outperforms all methods in each group with a clear margin. A similar conclusion is reached by comparing the PR curves illustrated in Fig. 4.7, with the light blue line (DML approach) lying upon all others up to 90% recall in both cases. The DML approach trained on VCDB dataset outperforms four out of five state-of-the-art methods. It achieves similar results to the SMVH, even though the latter has been developed with access to the evaluation dataset during training. The LBoW approach

Table 4.10 mAP comparison between the two developed approaches against five state-of-the-art methods. The approaches are divided based on the dataset used for development

| Method | Same dataset | | | | | No/different dataset | | |
	ACC	PPT	SMVH	LBoW	DML_{cc}	CH	LS	DML_{vcdb}
mAP	0.944	0.958	0.971	0.976	**0.982**	0.892	0.954	**0.971**

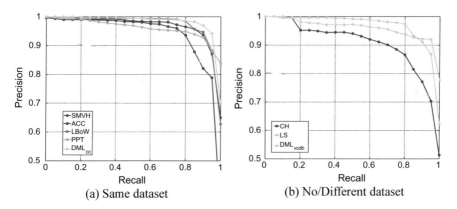

(a) Same dataset   (b) No/Different dataset

Fig. 4.7 Precision–recall curve comparison between the two developed approaches against five state-of-the-art methods. The approaches are divided based on the dataset used for development

is in the second place consistently outperforming all five competing approaches by a considerable margin.

4.4.2.5   In-Depth Comparison of the Two Approaches

In this section, we compare the two implemented NDVR approaches in two evaluation settings. To this end, in addition to the existing experiments, we implement the BoW approach with VGGNet features and layer aggregation based on information derived from the VCDB dataset, i.e., we build the layer codebooks from a set of video frames sampled from the aforementioned dataset. We then test two variations, the $LBoW_{cc}$ that was developed on the CC_WEB_VIDEO dataset (same as Sect. 4.4.2.2) and the $LBoW_{vcdb}$ developed on the VCDB dataset. For each of the 24 queries of CC_WEB_VIDEO, only the videos contained in its subset (the dataset is organized in 24 subsets, one per query) are considered as candidate and used for the calculation of retrieval performance. To emulate a more challenging setting, we created CC_WEB_VIDEO* in the following way: for every query in CC_WEB_VIDEO, the set of candidate videos is the entire dataset instead of only the query subset.

Figure 4.8 depicts the PR curves of the four runs and the two setups. There is a clear difference between the performance of the two variants of the LBoW approach, for both dataset setups. The DML approach outperforms the LBoW approach for all runs and setups at any recall point by a large margin. Similar conclusions can be drawn from the mAP scores of Table 4.11. The performance of LBoW drops by more than 0.02 and 0.062 when the codebook is learned on VCDB, for each setup, respectively. Again, there is a considerable drop in performance in CC_WEB_VIDEO* setup for both approaches, with the DML being more resilient to the setup change. As a result, it has been demonstrated to be highly competitive and possible to transfer to different datasets with relatively lower performance loss.

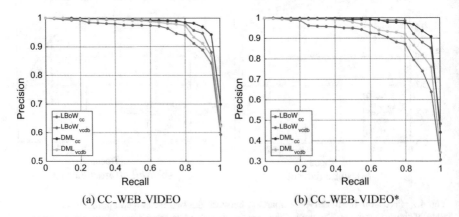

(a) CC_WEB_VIDEO   (b) CC_WEB_VIDEO*

Fig. 4.8 Precision–recall curve comparison of the two developed approaches on two dataset setups

Table 4.11 mAP comparison of the two developed approaches on two different dataset setups

	CC_WEB_VIDEO	CC_WEB_VIDEO*
$LBoW_{vcdb}$	0.957	0.906
DML_{vcdb}	**0.971**	**0.936**
$LBoW_{cc}$	0.976	0.960
DML_{cc}	**0.982**	**0.969**

Table 4.12 mAP of the two developed approaches on the FIVR-200K dataset

Task	DSVR	CSVR	ISVR
LBoW	0.378	0.361	0.297
DML	0.398	0.378	0.309

In addition, the developed approaches are also benchmarked on the FIVR-200K [49] dataset. As described in Sect. 4.2.3 it includes three tasks that accept different type of video results as relevant. To compare the two methods, we implemented them with frame features derived from the VGGNet and built them with videos from the VCDB dataset. Table 4.12 presents the mAP of the two developed approaches on the FIVR-200K dataset. It is evident that the DML approach achieves noticeably better performance in comparison to the LBoW, when they are both developed on a different dataset other than the evaluation. For the DSVR task, the two methods achieve 0.398 and 0.378 mAP for DML and LBoW, respectively. The performance of both approaches marginally drops for the CSVR task in comparison to DSVR with a reduction of about 0.02 in terms of mAP. On the ISVR task, both runs have a considerable drop in their performance, with 0.309 and 0.297 mAP for DML and LBoW, respectively. Hence, the performance of both methods is significantly reduced in comparison to CC_WEB_VIDEO dataset, revealing that the FIVR-200K dataset is much more challenging. The main reason is that the vast majority of positive video pairs are partially related, i.e., the videos are not related in their entirety but in particular segments. The competing approaches from the NDVR literature lead to even lower performance, since they are based on video-level schemes that employ handcrafted frame descriptors with limited representation capability.

Both presented approaches are limited in similar ways which lead to similar errors in the retrieval process. The major issue of both approaches is that they do not function effectively when the near-duplicate segment between two videos is small relative to their total size. As revealed from the evaluation in the FIVR-200K dataset, video-level solutions suffer in such setups. Even the LBoW approach where the video-level representation contains frame-level information fails to retrieve relevant videos, especially when it has been built on different datasets than the evaluation. Another category of videos that the proposed schemes fail is when heavy transformations have been applied on the source video. Typically, the extracted frame descriptors are not close enough, so as such videos to be retrieved and ranked with high similarity score.

Even the DML scheme that should learn to handle such case fails to recognize this kind of duplicate pairs, especially when heavy edits or overlays have been applied. A solution to this issue is the use of frame descriptors that better capture local information within frames. This can be achieved with end-to-end training of the CNN models and/or use of another aggregation function (other than MAC) that better preserves local information.

Finally, we compare the two approaches in terms of processing time on the large-scale FIVR-200K dataset. The results have been measured using the open-source library Scikit-learn [60] in Python, on a Linux PC with a 4-core i7-4770K and 32GB of RAM. The DML approach is significantly faster than the LBoW approach. It needs 333 ms to perform retrieval for one query on the FIVR-200K dataset, compared to 1,155 ms needed for the LBoW approach. However, both methods are significantly faster than common frame-level approaches, which usually need several minutes to process all videos in the dataset.

4.5   Conclusions and Future Work

In this chapter, we focused on the problem of Near-Duplicate Video Retrieval (NDVR). First, we presented a review of NDVR definitions, approaches, and datasets existing in the literature. The state-of-the-art methods were grouped into three major categories based on the level of video matching they perform: video-level, frame-level, and filter-and-refine matching. Moreover, we proposed two different video-level approaches (an unsupervised and a supervised) based on deep neural networks. For both methods, we used CNN features extracted from the intermediate convolutional layers by applying Maximum Activations of Convolutions (MAC). We found that this setup led to the best results among many other features, both handcrafted and learned.

The first approach is an unsupervised scheme that relies on a Bag-of-Words (BoW) video representation. A layer-based aggregation scheme was introduced in order to generate the global video representation, and then store it in an inverted file index for fast indexing and retrieval. To quantify video similarity, we calculated the cosine similarity on *tf-idf* weighted versions of the extracted vectors and ranked the results in descending order. However, we found that there are several limitations regarding the BoW approach, i.e., it is a dataset-specific solution and is hard to be re-trained on new data. To address these issues, we developed a second supervised approach based on DML. This method approximates an embedding function that transforms input frame descriptors and leads to more accurate computation of the distance between two candidate videos. For each video in the dataset, we sampled one frame per second and extracted its CNN features to generate a global video vector. The global video vectors are then transformed based on the embedding function to the learned feature space. The video retrieval is performed based on the Euclidean distance of the video embeddings.

We conducted extensive evaluations with different experimental setups, testing the performance of the developed approaches under various settings. Through the evaluation process, it was evident that the developed approaches exceed the performance of five established state-of-the-art NDVR approaches. Finally, we empirically determined that the DML approach overcomes the limitations imposed by the BoW approach, i.e., it achieves better performance even without access to the evaluation dataset (even though further improvements are possible if such access is possible).

In the future, we will focus on the improvement of the retrieval performance of the developed system. Initially, we are going to put effort on the design of sophisticated similarity calculation functions that take into account the spatial structure of video frames and, at the same time, the temporal relations within frame sequences, in order to precisely compute the similarity between two compared videos. To achieve these goals, we will modify the developed DML approach to perform frame-level matching, e.g., by considering more effective fusion schemes (compared to early and late fusion), so as to capture the temporal relations between videos. To capture the spatial structure of video frames during the similarity calculation process, we are going to devise a solution that computes similarity at region level. Moreover, we plan to exploit the spatiotemporal information contained in consecutive video frames by employing 3D and/or two-steam CNN network architectures to extract video features. These networks are able to encode the depicted actions in videos to compact feature representations. We anticipate that such features will have considerable impact on the performance of the systems, especially in more general retrieval tasks such as ISVR. Finally, we will assess the performance of the developed approach on the problem of Partial Duplicate Video Retrieval (PDVR).

References

1. Silverman C et al (2014) Verification handbook. European Journalism Center, EJC
2. Wu X, Hauptmann AG, Ngo CW (2007) Practical elimination of near-duplicates from web video search. In: Proceedings of the 15th ACM international conference on multimedia. ACM, pp 218–227
3. Revaud J, Douze M, Schmid C, Jégou H (2013) Event retrieval in large video collections with circulant temporal encoding. In: 2013 IEEE conference on computer vision and pattern recognition (CVPR). IEEE, pp 2459–2466
4. Basharat A, Zhai Y, Shah M (2008) Content based video matching using spatiotemporal volumes. Computer Vision and Image Understanding 110(3):360–377
5. Sharif Razavian A, Azizpour H, Sullivan J, Carlsson S (2014) CNN Features off-the-shelf: an astounding baseline for recognition. In: Proceedings of the IEEE conference on computer vision and pattern recognition workshops, pp 806–813
6. Zheng L, Zhao Y, Wang S, Wang J, Tian Q (2016) Good practice in CNN feature transfer. arXiv preprint arXiv:1604.00133
7. Kordopatis-Zilos G, Papadopoulos S, Patras I, Kompatsiaris Y (2017) Near-duplicate video retrieval by aggregating intermediate CNN layers. In: International conference on multimedia modeling. Springer, Berlin, pp 251–263

8. Kordopatis-Zilos G, Papadopoulos S, Patras I, Kompatsiaris Y (2017) Near-duplicate video retrieval with deep metric learning. In: 2017 IEEE international conference on computer vision workshop (ICCVW). IEEE, pp 347–356

9. Liu H, Lu H, Xue X (2013) A segmentation and graph-based video sequence matching method for video copy detection. IEEE Trans Knowl Data Eng 25(8):1706–1718

10. Liu J, Huang Z, Cai H, Shen HT, Ngo CW, Wang W (2013) Near-duplicate video retrieval: Current research and future trends. ACM Comput Surv (CSUR) 45(4):44

11. Shen HT, Zhou X, Huang Z, Shao J, Zhou X (2007) UQLIPS: a real-time near-duplicate video clip detection system. In: Proceedings of the 33rd international conference on very large data bases. VLDB Endowment, pp 1374–1377

12. Cherubini M, De Oliveira R, Oliver N (2009) Understanding near-duplicate videos: a user-centric approach. In: Proceedings of the 17th ACM international conference on multimedia. ACM, pp 35–44

13. Law-To J, Joly A, Boujemaa N (2007) Muscle-VCD-2007: a live benchmark for video copy detection

14. Shang L, Yang L, Wang F, Chan KP, Hua XS (2010) Real-time large scale near-duplicate web video retrieval. In: Proceedings of the 18th ACM international conference on multimedia. ACM, pp 531–540

15. Song J, Yang Y, Huang Z, Shen HT, Luo J (2013) Effective multiple feature hashing for large-scale near-duplicate video retrieval. IEEE Trans Multimedia 15(8):1997–2008

16. Hao Y, Mu T, Hong R, Wang M, An N, Goulermas JY (2017) Stochastic multiview hashing for large-scale near-duplicate video retrieval. IEEE Trans Multimedia 19(1):1–14

17. Jing W, Nie X, Cui C, Xi X, Yang G, Yin Y (2018) Global-view hashing: harnessing global relations in near-duplicate video retrieval. World wide web, pp 1–19

18. Liu, L., Lai, W., Hua, X.S., Yang, S.Q.: Video histogram: a novel video signature for efficient web video duplicate detection. In: International conference on multimedia modeling. Springer, pp 94–103

19. Huang Z, Shen HT, Shao J, Zhou X, Cui B (2009) Bounded coordinate system indexing for real-time video clip search. ACM Trans Inf Syst (TOIS) 27(3):17

20. Cai Y, Yang L, Ping W, Wang F, Mei T, Hua XS, Li S (2011) Million-scale near-duplicate video retrieval system. In: Proceedings of the 19th ACM international conference on multimedia. ACM, pp 837–838

21. Song J, Yang Y, Huang Z, Shen HT, Hong R (2011) Multiple feature hashing for real-time large scale near-duplicate video retrieval. In: Proceedings of the 19th ACM international conference on multimedia. ACM, pp 423–432

22. Hao Y, Mu T, Goulermas JY, Jiang J, Hong R, Wang M (2017) Unsupervised t-distributed video hashing and its deep hashing extension. IEEE Trans Image Process 26(11):5531–5544

23. Zhao G, Pietikainen M (2007) Dynamic texture recognition using local binary patterns with an application to facial expressions. IEEE Trans Pattern Anal Mach Intell 29(6):915–928

24. Huang J, Kumar SR, Mitra M, Zhu WJ, Zabih R (1997) Image indexing using color correlograms. In: 1997 IEEE computer society conference on computer vision and pattern recognition, 1997. Proceedings. IEEE, pp 762–768

25. Sivic J, Zisserman A (2003) Video Google: a text retrieval approach to object matching in videos. In: Ninth IEEE international conference on computer vision, 2003. Proceedings. IEEE, pp 1470–1477

26. Tan HK, Ngo CW, Hong R, Chua TS (2009) Scalable detection of partial near-duplicate videos by visual-temporal consistency. In: Proceedings of the 17th ACM international conference on multimedia. ACM, pp 145–154

27. Douze M, Jégou H, Schmid C (2010) An image-based approach to video copy detection with spatio-temporal post-filtering. IEEE Trans Multimedia 12(4):257–266

28. Jiang YG, Wang J (2016) Partial copy detection in videos: A benchmark and an evaluation of popular methods. IEEE Trans Big Data 2(1):32–42

29. Wang L, Bao Y, Li H, Fan X, Luo Z (2017) Compact CNN based video representation for efficient video copy detection. In: International conference on multimedia modeling. Springer, pp 576–587

30. Huang Z, Shen HT, Shao J, Cui B, Zhou X (2010) Practical online near-duplicate subsequence detection for continuous video streams. IEEE Trans Multimedia 12(5):386–398
31. Wu Z, Aizawa K (2014) Self-similarity-based partial near-duplicate video retrieval and alignment. Int J Multimed Inf Retr 3(1):1–14
32. Poullot S, Tsukatani S, Phuong Nguyen A, Jégou H, Satoh S (2015) Temporal matching kernel with explicit feature maps. In: Proceedings of the 23rd ACM international conference on multimedia. ACM, pp 381–390
33. Baraldi L, Douze M, Cucchiara R, Jégou H (2018) LAMV: learning to align and match videos with kernelized temporal layers. In: Proceedings of the IEEE conference on computer vision and pattern recognition, pp 7804–7813
34. Jiang YG, Jiang Y, Wang J (2014) VCDB: a large-scale database for partial copy detection in videos. In: European conference on computer vision. Springer, pp 357–371
35. Mikolajczyk K, Schmid C (2004) Scale and affine invariant interest point detectors. Int J Comput Vis 60(1):63–86
36. Lowe DG (2004) Distinctive image features from scale-invariant keypoints. Int J Comput Vis 60(2):91–110
37. Heikkilä M, Pietikäinen M, Schmid C (2009) Description of interest regions with local binary patterns. Pattern Recognit 42(3):425–436
38. Jegou H, Douze M, Schmid C (2008) Hamming embedding and weak geometric consistency for large scale image search. In: European conference on computer vision (ECCV 2008). Springer, pp 304–317
39. Tian Y, Huang T, Jiang M, Gao W (2013) Video copy-detection and localization with a scalable cascading framework. IEEE MultiMedia 20(3):72–86
40. Jiang M, Tian Y, Huang T (2012) Video copy detection using a soft cascade of multimodal features. In: Proceedings of the 2012 IEEE international conference on multimedia and expo. IEEE, pp 374–379
41. Tian Y, Qian M, Huang T (2015) Tasc: a transformation-aware soft cascading approach for multimodal video copy detection. ACM Trans Inf Syst (TOIS) 33(2):7
42. Chou CL, Chen HT, Lee SY (2015) Pattern-based near-duplicate video retrieval and localization on web-scale videos. IEEE Trans Multimedia 17(3):382–395
43. Tian Y, Jiang M, Mou L, Rang X, Huang T (2011) A multimodal video copy detection approach with sequential pyramid matching. In: 2011 18th IEEE international conference on image processing. IEEE, pp 3629–3632
44. Bay H, Ess A, Tuytelaars T, Gool LV (2008) Speeded-up robust features (SURF). Comput Vis Image Underst 110(3):346–359. http://dx.doi.org/10.1016/j.cviu.2007.09.014
45. Chen J, Huang T (2008) A robust feature extraction algorithm for audio fingerprinting. In: Pacific-rim conference on multimedia. Springer, pp 887–890
46. Yang Y, Tian Y, Huang T (2018) Multiscale video sequence matching for near-duplicate detection and retrieval. Multimed Tools Appl, 1–26
47. Kraaij W, Awad G (2011) TRECVID 2011 content-based copy detection: task overview. Online Proceedigs of TRECVid 2010
48. Jia Y, Shelhamer E, Donahue J, Karayev S, Long J, Girshick R, Guadarrama S, Darrell T (2014) Caffe: convolutional architecture for fast feature embedding. In: Proceedings of the 22nd ACM international conference on multimedia. ACM, pp 675–678
49. Kordopatis-Zilos G, Papadopoulos S, Patras I, Kompatsiaris I (2019) FIVR: fine-grained incident video retrieval. IEEE Trans Multimedia
50. TREC Video Retrieval Evaluation: TRECVID (2018) https://trecvid.nist.gov/
51. Yue-Hei Ng J, Yang F, Davis LS (2015) Exploiting local features from deep networks for image retrieval. In: Proceedings of the IEEE conference on computer vision and pattern recognition workshops, pp 53–61
52. Jégou H, Douze M, Schmid C, Pérez P (2010) Aggregating local descriptors into a compact image representation. In: 2010 IEEE conference on computer vision and pattern recognition (CVPR). IEEE, pp 3304–3311

53. Krizhevsky A, Sutskever I, Hinton GE (2012) Imagenet classification with deep convolutional neural networks. In: Advances in neural information processing systems (2012), pp 1097–1105
54. Simonyan K, Zisserman A (2014) Very deep convolutional networks for large-scale image recognition. CoRR arXiv:abs/1409.1556
55. Szegedy C, Liu W, Jia Y, Sermanet P, Reed S, Anguelov D, Erhan D, Vanhoucke V, Rabinovich A (2015) Going deeper with convolutions. In: Proceedings of the IEEE conference on computer vision and pattern recognition (CVPR 2015), pp 1–9
56. Bahmani B, Moseley B, Vattani A, Kumar R, Vassilvitskii S (2012) Scalable k-means++. Proc VLDB Endowment 5(7):622–633
57. Theano Development Team (2016) Theano: A Python framework for fast computation of mathematical expressions. arXiv e-prints arXiv:abs/1605.02688
58. Kingma D, Ba J (2014) Adam: a method for stochastic optimization. arXiv preprint arXiv:1412.6980
59. Ke Y, Sukthankar R (2004) PCA-SIFT: a more distinctive representation for local image descriptors. In: Proceedings of the 2004 IEEE computer society conference on computer vision and pattern recognition, 2004. CVPR 2004, vol 2. IEEE, pp II–II
60. Van der Walt S, Schönberger JL, Nunez-Iglesias J, Boulogne F, Warner JD, Yager N, Gouillart E, Yu T (2014) scikit-image: image processing in python. PeerJ 2:e453

Chapter 5
Finding Semantically Related Videos in Closed Collections

Foteini Markatopoulou, Markos Zampoglou, Evlampios Apostolidis, Symeon Papadopoulos, Vasileios Mezaris, Ioannis Patras and Ioannis Kompatsiaris

Abstract Modern newsroom tools offer advanced functionality for automatic and semi-automatic content collection from the web and social media sources to accompany news stories. However, the content collected in this way often tends to be unstructured and may include irrelevant items. An important step in the verification process is to organize this content, both with respect to what it shows, and with respect to its origin. This chapter presents our efforts in this direction, which resulted in two components. One aims to detect semantic concepts in video shots, to help annotation and organization of content collections. We implement a system based on deep learning, featuring a number of advances and adaptations of existing algorithms to increase performance for the task. The other component aims to detect logos in videos in order to identify their provenance. We present our progress from a keypoint-based detection system to a system based on deep learning.

F. Markatopoulou · M. Zampoglou (✉) · E. Apostolidis · S. Papadopoulos · V. Mezaris
I. Kompatsiaris
Information Technologies Institute, Centre for Research and Technology Hellas,
Thessaloniki, Greece
e-mail: markzampoglou@iti.gr

F. Markatopoulou
e-mail: markatopoulou@iti.gr

E. Apostolidis
e-mail: apostolid@iti.gr

S. Papadopoulos
e-mail: papadop@iti.gr

V. Mezaris
e-mail: bmezaris@iti.gr

I. Kompatsiaris
e-mail: ikom@iti.gr

E. Apostolidis · I. Patras
School of Electronic Engineering and Computer Science, Queen Mary University,
London, UK
e-mail: i.patras@qmul.ac.uk

© Springer Nature Switzerland AG 2019
V. Mezaris et al. (eds.), *Video Verification in the Fake News Era*,
https://doi.org/10.1007/978-3-030-26752-0_5

5.1   Problem Definition and Challenge

News events typically give rise to the creation and circulation of User-Generated Content (UGC). This media content, typically in the form of images or videos, spreads in social media and attracts the attention of news professionals and investigators. Such events generate multiple different media items, often published on different platforms, and at different times following the breaking of the event.

In many cases, news organizations use automatic or semi-automatic tools to collect such content. These tools crawl the web and various media-sharing platforms and collect potentially related content based on search queries. This leads to the formation of unstructured media collections, which may contain both relevant and irrelevant content. It may include content from different aspects of event, possibly taken at different times and displaying different scenes. It may also include content from different sources, each of which may focus on a different aspect or exhibit different forms of bias.

As a way of assisting the verification process, it is very helpful to organize the collected videos according to what they depict, or based on who published them. This organization step is assumed to take place after the near-duplicate retrieval step (see Chap. 4), which can identify near-duplicates and remove or aggregate them. Consecutively, the semantic-level analysis described in this chapter can allow grouping, comparison, and contrasting, as well as cross-referencing to spot videos that may be altered, misleading, or irrelevant. To this end, we developed two components within InVID that semantically analyse content, the first performing Semantic Video Annotation and the second Logo Detection. The former analyses videos or video segments, and annotates them with detected concept labels, such as 'car', 'dancing' or 'beach'. The second looks for logos in the video, which can reveal the group, agency or institution sharing (or re-sharing) it, and this, in turn, can reveal possible biases or intentions behind the posting of the item, as well as allow the investigator to link it to past content published by the same party. In this sense, these two components of InVID cover similar needs from different aspects, offering ways to automatically annotate videos or video segments with semantic tags on their content and origin, allowing more nuanced search within closed collections.

With respect to semantic annotation, video content can be annotated with simple concept labels that may refer to objects (e.g. 'car' and 'chair'), activities (e.g. 'running' and 'dancing'), scenes (e.g. 'hills' and 'beach'), etc. Annotating videos with concepts is a very important task that facilitates many applications such as finding semantically related videos in video collections, semantics-based video segmentation and retrieval, video event detection, video hyperlinking and concept-based video search [1–9]. Concept-based video search refers to the retrieval of video fragments (e.g. keyframes) that present specific simple concept labels from large-scale video collections. Thus, within InVID, the task entails creating a module that will be able to reliably annotate videos by taking their keyframes and detecting any known concepts found within them.

With respect to logo detection, the ability to annotate videos with respect to their provenance can be an important part of verification. Knowing who first produced the video or is responsible for its dissemination can help determine potential bias in the content or form an initial impression about its trustworthiness. Furthermore, identifying the source of the video can help establish contact, in order to ask permissions or verify the authenticity of content. Even when no direct contact with the content creator or owner is possible, determining the content's origin can provide important context for the verification process. Since many times content tends to be reproduced not by sharing but by re-uploading, it is commonly hard to find the original source. However, in this process of tracing the video, logos can play an important role, provided they can be identified.

While many logos—and especially, the ones belonging to the most popular news channels—are well known, especially among news professionals, there exist many organizations which are not so easy to identify, whether less well-known channels, or unofficial groups such as paramilitary organizations or independent journalist groups. There exist more than 27,000 TV broadcast stations in the world according to the CIA World Factbook,[1] and a very large—and hard to estimate—number of paramilitary groups. Those cases are aggravated by the large numbers of such logos that a professional might have to memorize, and a certain degree of instability which leads to groups merging or splitting (this is the case with militant groups in the Syrian Civil War, for example). As a result, identifying one logo among the multitude of possible candidates is very challenging for human investigators (Fig. 5.1). In those cases, automatically identifying the logo and providing information about its owner can significantly speed up the analysis and verification process.

It is important to note that, in cases where we have to deal with videos consisting of multiple shots, each shot should be treated independently, since it may contain different logos and entirely different semantic concepts. Thus, both components are aimed to operate at the shot level, after the videos have been analysed by the video shot fragmentation component of the InVID platform.

5.2 Semantic Video Annotation

5.2.1 Related Work

To deal with concept-based video search, concept-based video annotation methods have been developed that automatically annotate video fragments, e.g. keyframes extracted from video shots, with semantic labels (concepts), chosen from a pre-defined concept list [1]. A typical concept-based video annotation system mainly follows the process presented in Fig. 5.2. A video is initially segmented into meaningful fragments, called shots; each shot is represented by one or more characteristic

---

[1] https://www.nationsencyclopedia.com/WorldStats/CIA-Television-broadcast-stations.html, accessed 08 April 2019.

Fig. 5.1 Top: Two video frames with easily identifiable news channel sources; Bottom: Two video frames where the logos cannot be easily identified

keyframes. Then, several hand-crafted or DCNN-based (Deep Convolutional Neural Network) features are extracted from the generated representation of each shot; e.g. visual features from the extracted keyframes, and audio and textual features from the audio representation of the shot. Given a ground truth annotated video training set, supervised machine learning algorithms are then used to train concept classifiers independently for each concept, using the extracted features and ground truth annotations. The trained classifiers can subsequently be applied to an unlabelled video shot, following feature extraction, and return a set of confidence scores for the appearance of the different concepts in the shot. A recent trend in video annotation is to learn features directly from the raw keyframe pixels using DCNNs. DCNNs consist of many layers of feature extractors, and are thus able to model more complex structures in comparison to handcrafted representations. DCNN layers can learn different types of features without requiring feature engineering, in contrast to the hand-crafted features that are designed by humans to capture specific properties of video frames, e.g. edges and corners. DCNNs can be used both as standalone classifiers (Fig. 5.2, bottom), i.e. unlabelled keyframes are passed through a pre-trained DCNN that performs the final class label prediction directly, using typically a softmax or a hinge loss layer [10, 11], and also as extractors for video keyframe features (Fig. 5.2, top), i.e. the output of a hidden layer of the pre-trained DCNN is used as a global keyframe representation [10]. This latter type of features is referred to as DCNN-based, and in that case, DCNN features are used to train binary classifiers (e.g. SVMs) separately for each concept.

While significant progress has been made during the last years in the task of video annotation and retrieval, it continues to be a difficult and challenging task. This is due

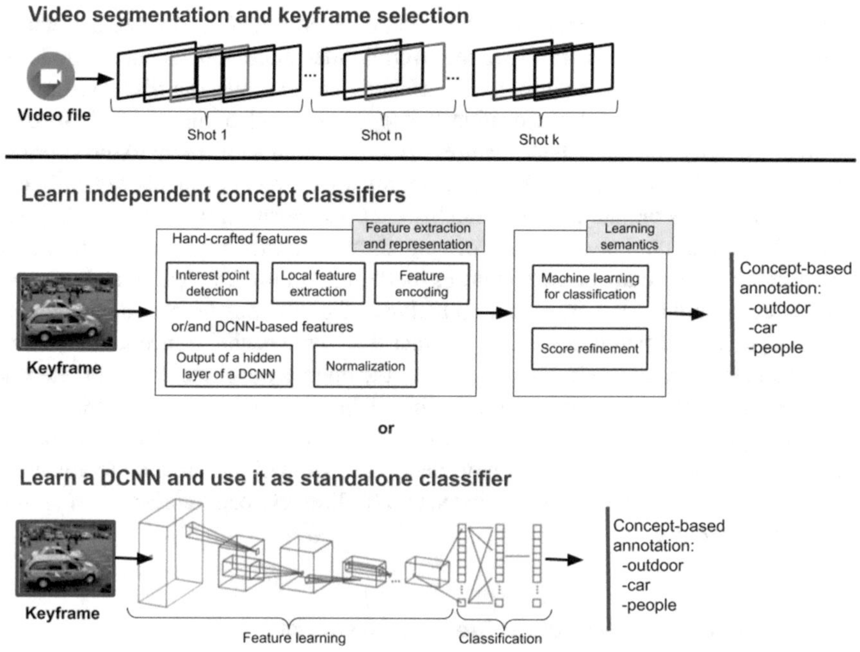

Video segmentation and keyframe selection

Learn independent concept classifiers

or

Learn a DCNN and use it as standalone classifier

Fig. 5.2 Video concept annotation pipelines: After temporal video segmentation, e.g. using automatic video shot detection and extracting one representative keyframe per shot, the upper part shows a typical concept-based video annotation pipeline that is based on hand-crafted or DCNN-based features and supervised classifiers trained separately for each concept. The lower part is based on features that can be learned directly from the raw keyframe pixels using an DCNN, and subsequently using the DCNN as standalone classifier to perform the final class label prediction

to the diversity in form and appearance exhibited by the majority of semantic concepts and the difficulty to express them using a finite number of representations. The system needs to learn a practically limitless number of different patterns that characterize the different concepts (e.g. landscapes, faces, actions). As a result, generality is an important property that a concept-based video annotation system should present in order to generalize its performance across many different heterogeneous concepts. Finally, computational requirements are another major challenge. The large number of concepts that a video annotation system should learn is computationally expensive requiring lightweight and fast methods. Finally, there are by far more labelled datasets available that contain still images than datasets extracted from video keyframes. Typically classifiers are trained on the former still image datasets and applied on video datasets, which is a suboptimal practice.

It has been shown that combining many different features for the same concept, instead of using a single feature, improves the concept annotation accuracy. However, which subsets of features to use for the needs of a specific task, and which classification scheme to follow, is a challenging problem that will affect the accuracy and computational complexity of the complete concept-based video annotation system. Other methods also improve the overall video annotation accuracy by looking for existing semantic relations, e.g. concept correlations. As discussed above the dominant approach for performing concept-based video annotation is to train DCNNs whereby concepts share features within the architectures up to the very last layer, and then branch off to T different classification branches (using typically one layer), where T is the number of concepts [12]. However, in this way, the implicit feature-level relations between concepts, e.g. the way in which concepts such as a *car* and *motorcycle* share lower level features modelling things like their wheels, are not directly considered. Also, in such architectures, the relations or inter-dependencies of concepts at a semantic level, i.e. the fact that two specific concepts may often appear together or, inversely, the presence of the one may exclude the other, are also not directly taken into consideration. In this chapter, we will refer to methods that have been proposed for exploiting in a more elaborate way one of these two different types of concept relations. Then, in Sect. 5.2.2 we will present a more advanced method that jointly exploits visual- and semantic-level concept relations in a unified DCNN architecture.

5.2.1.1 Supervised Learning Using Deep Networks

Concept-based video annotation is a multi-label classification (MLC) problem (one keyframe may be annotated with more than one semantic concepts). One way to solve this problem is to treat it as multiple independent binary classification problems where for each concept a model can be learned to distinguish keyframes where the concept appears from those where the concept does not appear. Given feature-based keyframe representations that have been extracted from different keyframes and also the ground truth annotations for each keyframe (i.e. the concepts presented) any supervised machine learning algorithm that solves classification problems can be used in order to learn the relations between the low-level image representations and the high-level semantic concepts.

We can distinguish two main categories of visual features: hand-crafted features and features based on Deep Convolutional Networks (DCNN-based). With respect to hand-crafted features, binary (ORB [13]) and non-binary (SIFT [14], SURF [15]) local descriptors, as well as colour extensions of them [16] have been examined for concept-based video annotation. Local descriptors are aggregated into global image representations by employing feature encoding techniques such as Fisher Vector (FV) [17] and VLAD [18]. With respect to DCNN-based features, one or more hidden layers of a pre-trained DCNN are typically used as a global keyframe representation [10]. Several DCNN software libraries are available in the literature, e.g. Caffe [19], MatConvNet, TensorFlow [20] and different DCNN architectures have been proposed, e.g. AlexNet [11], VGGNet [10], GoogLeNet [21], ResNeXt [22], ResNet [23]. DCNN-based descriptors present high discriminative power and generally outperform local descriptors [24, 25].

The most commonly used machine learning algorithms are Support Vector Machines (SVM), Logistic Regression (LR) and Random Forests (RF). A recent trend in video annotation is to learn features directly from the raw keyframe pixels using DCNNs. DCNNs were derived from simple neural networks so here we will briefly explain how neural networks and subsequently deep networks work. Neural networks consist of artificial neurons that have learnable weights and biases. Neurons are connected to each other, each neuron receives some inputs from other neurons, and outputs a new signal, i.e. a value, that can be used to activate or deactivate other neurons connected to its output. Pairs of neurons are assigned with weights that represent their connection relation. In order to calculate the output value of a neuron, i.e. its activation, we calculate the weighted sum of the activations of all neurons that are fed into it. This sum is subsequently given as input to an activation function that outputs the final neuron's activation value. In an DCNN, neurons are arranged in layers with each neuron in a single layer being connected to all or a subset of neurons in the previous layer. The connections go only from lower to top layers and this is why DCNNs are also referred as feedforward networks. In a concept-based video annotation task, an DCNN consists of an input layer, a number of intermediate layers, a.k.a. hidden layers, and the output layer. The input layer takes a keyframe, it forward propagates it to the hidden layers and based on the neurons that are activated, the keyframe's class labels are finally triggered in the output layer that consists of as many neurons as the number of concepts that the network aims to learn. A deep network has millions of parameters and for this reason a large set of inputs is needed to train the network without overfitting on the data. In addition, during training, a loss function is used (e.g. hinge loss, softmax) in order to measure how well the network's output fits the real ground truth values. Then, randomly selected keyframes are provided to it and the network's weights are adjusted based on the output that is returned in order to reduce the value of the loss function. To update the weights the popular technique of backpropagation is used. A few years before, training networks with many hidden layers was computationally infeasible. However, the great success on the development of powerful GPUs was a driver for the evolution of this field and now it is common to train networks with many hidden layers in hours or days.

The small number of labelled training examples is a common problem in video datasets, making it difficult to train a deep network from scratch without over-fitting its parameters on the training set [26]. For this reason, it is common to use transfer learning that uses the knowledge captured in a source domain in order to learn a target domain without caring about the improvement in the source domain. When a small-sized dataset is available for training an DCNN, a transfer learning technique is followed, where a conventional DCNN, e.g. [23], is first trained on a large-scale dataset and then the classification layer is removed, the DCNN is extended by one or more fully connected layers that are shared across all of the tasks, and a new classification layer is placed on top of the last extension layer (having size equal to the number of concepts that will be learned in the target domain). Then, the extended network is fine-tuned in the target domain [12]. Experiments presented in [12] show that extending by one or more fully connected layers works better than simply re-learning some of the pre-trained fully connected layers.

5.2.1.2   Multi-task Learning and Structured Outputs

As described in Sect. 5.2.1.1, video concept annotation is a challenging multi-label classification problem that in recent years is typically addressed using DCNN models that choose a specific DCNN architecture [10, 23] and put a multi-label cost function on top of it [27–29]. As is the case in other multi-label problems, there exist relations between different concepts, and several methods attempt to model and leverage these relations so as to improve the performance or reduce the complexity of classification models that treat each concept independently. These methods can be roughly divided into two main categories. In the first category, methods that fall under the framework of Multi-task Learning (MTL), attempt to learn representations or classification models that, at some level, are shared between the different concepts (tasks) [30–42]. In the second category, methods that fall under the framework of structured output prediction attempt to learn models that make multidimensional predictions that respect the structure of the output space using either label constraints or post-processing techniques [41, 43–48, 48–62]. Label constraints refer to regularizations that are imposed on the learning system in order to exploit label relations (e.g. correlations) [41, 48, 49, 60–63]. Post-processing techniques refer to re-calculating the concept prediction results using either meta-learning classifiers or other re-weighting schemes [43–47].

5.2.2   Methodology

As discussed in Sect. 5.2.1.1, the dominant approach for performing concept-based video annotation is training DCNN architectures where the concepts share features up to the very last layer, and then branch off to T different classification branches (using typically one layer), where T is the number of concepts [12]. However, in this way, the implicit feature-level relations between concepts, e.g. the way in which concepts such as a *car* and *motorcycle* share lower level features modelling things like their wheels, are not directly considered. Also, in such architectures, the relations or inter-dependencies of the concepts at a semantic level, i.e. the fact that two specific concepts may often appear together or, inversely, the presence of the one may exclude the other, are also not directly taken into consideration.

In this section, we present an DCNN architecture that addresses the problem of video/image concept annotation by exploiting concept relations at two different levels. More specifically, it captures both implicit and explicit concept relations, i.e. both visual-level and semantic-level concept relations, as follows. First, implicit concept relations are modelled in an DCNN architecture that learns T concept-specific feature vectors that are themselves linear combinations of $k < T$ latent concept feature vectors. In this way, in the shared representations (i.e. the latent concepts feature vectors), higher level concepts may share visual features—for example, concepts such as *car*, *motorcycle*, and *airplane* may share features encoding the *wheels* in their depiction [64]. This bears similarities to multi-task learning (MTL) schemes, like GO-MTL [39] and the two-sided network proposed in [41] that factorize the 2D weight matrix to encode concept-specific features. However, in contrast to GO-MTL [39], in our case the factorization is achieved in two standard convolutional network layers, and in contrast to [41], our network does not only verify whether a certain concept that is given as input to the one side of the network is present in the video/image that is given as input to the other side. Instead, it provides scores for all concepts in the output, similar to classical multi-label DCNNs. Second, explicit concept relations are introduced by a new cost term, implemented using a set of standard CNN layers that penalize differences between the matrix encoding the correlations among the ground truth labels of the concepts, and the correlations between the concept label predictions of our network. In this way, we introduce constraints on the structure of the output space by utilizing the label correlation matrix—this explicitly captures, for example, the fact that *daytime* and *nighttime* are negatively correlated concepts. Both of the above types of relations are implemented using standard convolutional layers and are incorporated in a single DCNN architecture that can then be trained end to end with standard backpropagation. This method was originally presented in [65] and the source code is available on GitHub.[2]

5.2.2.1 Problem Formulation and Method Overview

We consider a set of concepts $C = \{c_1, c_2, \ldots, c_T\}$ and a multi-label training set $\mathscr{P} = \{(x_i, y_i) : x_i \in \mathscr{X}, y_i \in \{0, 1\}^{T \times 1}, i = 1 \ldots N\}$, where x_i is a 3-channel keyframe/image, y_i is its ground truth annotation (i.e. contains the T labels of the ith keyframe/image), and N is the number of training examples. A video/image concept annotation system learns T supervised learning tasks, one for each target concept c_j, i.e. it learns a real-valued function $f : \mathscr{X} \to \mathscr{Y}$, where $\mathscr{Y} = [0, 1]^{T \times N}$. The main symbols used in this paper are presented in Table 5.1.

Figure 5.3 presents an DCNN architecture that exploits both implicit visual-level and explicit semantic-level concept relations for video/image concept annotation by building on ideas from MTL and structured output prediction, respectively. Specifically, Fig. 5.3 (i) shows a typical $(\Pi + 1)$-layer DCNN architecture, e.g. ResNet, that shares all the layers but the last one [10, 23]; Fig. 5.3 (ii) shows how the typical DCNN architecture of Fig. 5.3 (i) can be extended by one FC extension layer, to improve the results in transfer learning problems [12]; and finally, Fig. 5.3 (iii) shows the adopted DCNN architecture. In the next subsections, we briefly introduce the parts of this architecture. For more details, the interested reader can refer to our original paper [65]. Specifically, we first introduce the FV-MTL approach for learning implicit visual-level concept relations; this is done using the multi-task learning subnetwork shown in Figs. 5.3 and 5.5. Second, we introduce the CCE-LC cost function that learns explicit semantic-level concept relations. CCE-LC predicts structured outputs by exploiting concept correlations that we can acquire from the ground truth annotations of a training dataset.

---

[2]https://github.com/markatopoulou/fvmtl-ccelc.

Table 5.1 Definition of main symbols

Symbol	Definition
x	A keyframe/image
y	A vector containing the ground truth concept annotations for a keyframe/image
N	The number of training keyframes/images
c	A concept
T	The number of concepts, i.e. number of tasks
$\hat{y}$	A vector containing the concept prediction scores for a keyframe/image
L_x	Latent concept feature vectors of a keyframe/image
S	Concept-specific weight matrix, each column corresponds to a task containing the coefficients of the linear combination with L_x
$L_x S$	Concept-specific feature vectors incorporating information from k latent concept representations
U	Concept-specific parameter matrix for the final classification
k	The number of latent tasks
d_1	The size of the output of the previous network layer
Φ	The concept correlation matrix calculated from the ground truth annotated training set
m	A cost vector utilized for data balancing

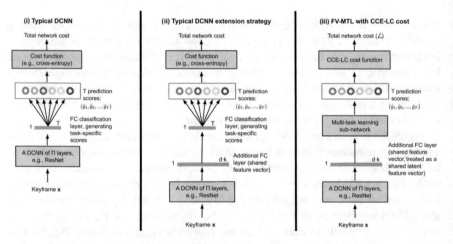

Fig. 5.3 (i) The typical DCNN architecture (e.g. ResNet [23]). (ii) The typical DCNN extension strategy proposed in [12]. (iii) The FV-MTL with CCE-LC cost function approach of [65].

5.2.2.2   Shared Latent Feature Vectors Using Multi-task Learning (FV-MTL)

In the FV-MTL approach, similarly to GO-MTL [39], we assume that the parameter vectors of the tasks that present visual-level concept relations lie in a low-dimensional subspace, thus sharing information; and, at the same time, dissimilar tasks may also partially overlap by having one or more bases in common. To allow this sharing of information, we learn T concept-specific feature vectors that are linear combinations of a small number of latent concept feature vectors that are themselves learned as well (Fig. 5.4). Specifically, we use a shared latent feature vector $\boldsymbol{L_x} \in \mathbb{R}^{d \times k}$ for all task models, where the columns of $\boldsymbol{L_x}$ correspond to d-dimensional feature representations of k latent tasks; and we produce T different concept-specific feature vectors $\boldsymbol{L_x}s_j$, for $j = 1 \ldots T$, where each of them incorporates information from relevant latent tasks, with $s_j \in \mathbb{R}^{k \times 1}$ being a task-specific weight vector that contains the coefficients of the linear combination. Each linear combination is assumed to be sparse, i.e. s_j's are sparse vectors; in this way, we assume that there exist a small number of latent basis tasks, and each concept-specific feature vector is a linear combination of them. The overlap between the weight vectors s_j and $s_{j'}$ controls the amount of information-sharing between the corresponding tasks.

The above are implemented in an DCNN architecture by using the network layers depicted in Figs. 5.3 and 5.5. Specifically, an input training set keyframe is processed by any chosen DCNN architecture (e.g. ResNet) and a fully connected layer, to produce a shared representation of the keyframe across all of the tasks. Subsequently, the output of the fully connected layer is reshaped to the matrix $\boldsymbol{L_x}$ (Fig. 5.5: step (a)); thus, the reshaped layer outputs k feature vectors that correspond to k latent concepts. Those representations are shared between the T concepts. The subsequent layer calculates T concept-specific feature vectors, where T is the number of the concepts we want to detect. Each of those feature vectors is a combination of k latent concept feature vectors, with coefficients that are specific to the concept in question. This is implemented as a 1D convolutional layer on the k feature masks (Fig. 5.5: step (b)). Once T feature vectors are extracted, then an additional layer (Fig. 5.5: step

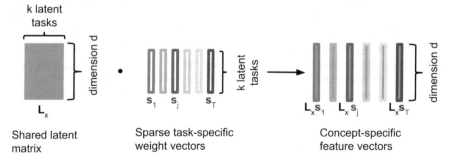

Fig. 5.4   Shared latent feature vectors using multi-task learning (FV-MTL)

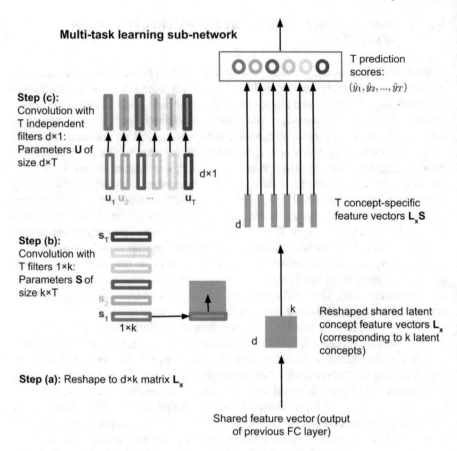

Fig. 5.5 MTL part of the proposed FV-MTL with CCE-LC cost function

(c)) transforms each of the T feature vectors into T concept annotation scores, one for each of the concepts that we want to detect. This process leads to a *soft* feature sharing, because the latent concept feature vectors adjust how much information and across which tasks are shared. By contrast, both the typical DCNN and the DCNN extension architecture of [12] (Fig. 5.3 (i) and (ii)) output a single feature vector that is shared across all of the target concepts and it is subsequently *hard* translated into concept annotation scores independently for each concept. Finally, a sigmoid cross-entropy cost term is used at the top of the network in order to optimize the sigmoid cross-entropy between the predictions and the ground truth labels; we refer to this classification cost term as λ_1.

5.2.2.3 Label Constraints for Structured Output Prediction

The cross-entropy cost is not adequate for capturing semantic concept relations. For this reason in [65], we proposed an additional cost term that constitutes an effective way to integrate structural information. By structural information, we refer to the inherently available concept correlations in a given ground truth annotated collection of training videos/images. It should be noted that information from other external sources, such as WordNet [66] or other ontologies, could also be used but we have not tried it in our experiments. In order to consider this information, we first calculate the correlation matrix $\boldsymbol{\Phi} \in [-1, 1]^{T \times T}$ from the ground truth annotated data of the training set. Each position of this matrix corresponds to the ϕ-correlation coefficient between two concepts $c_j, c_{j'}$ calculated as discussed in [65]. The auxiliary concept correlation cost term uses the above correlation matrix $\boldsymbol{\Phi}$, however, the way that this term is formed is omitted here because this is out of the scope of this book chapter. It should only be noted that this term works as a label-based constraint and its role is to add a penalty to concepts that are positively correlated but were assigned with different concept annotation scores. Similarly, it adds a penalty to concepts that are negative-correlated but were not assigned with opposite annotation scores. Contrarily, it does not add a penalty to non-correlated concepts.

We implement the auxiliary concept correlation cost term, noted as λ_2, using a set of standard CNN layers, as presented in Fig. 5.6. One matrix layer encodes the correlations between the ground truth labels of the concepts (denoted as $\boldsymbol{\Phi}$), and the other matrix layer contains the correlations between the concept label predictions of our network in the form of squared differences (denoted as $\boldsymbol{Q} \in \mathbb{R}^{T \times T}$, i.e. the matrix $\boldsymbol{Q}$ contains the differences of activations from the previous layer). Matrix $\boldsymbol{Q}$ gets multiplied, by element-wise multiplication, with the correlation matrix $\boldsymbol{\Phi}$, i.e. $\boldsymbol{Q} \circ \boldsymbol{\Phi}$, and all the rows in the resulting $T \times T$ matrix is added, leading to a single row vector.

5.2.2.4 FV-MTL with Cost Sigmoid Cross-Entropy with Label Constraint (FV-MTL with CCE-LC)

The two cost terms discussed in Sects. 5.2.2.2 and 5.2.2.3, and also denoted in Fig. 5.6 as λ_1 and λ_2 respectively, can be added in a single cost function that forms our total FV-MTL with CCE-LC network's cost. In our overall network architecture, an additional layer is used to implement the complete FV-MTL with CCE-LC cost function. In this way, the complete DCNN architecture learns by considering both the actual ground truth annotations and also the concept correlations that can be inferred from it. In contrast, a typical DCNN architecture simply incorporates knowledge learned from each individual ground truth annotated sample. For more details on this cost function, the interested reader can refer to our original paper [65].

CCE-LC cost function (structured output prediction)

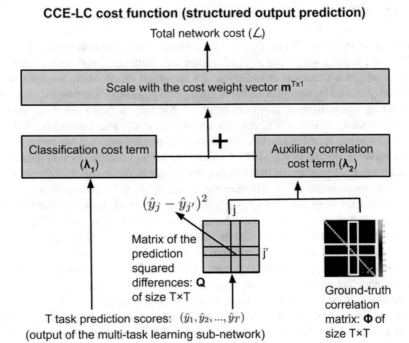

Total network cost ($\mathcal{L}$)

Scale with the cost weight vector $\mathbf{m}^{T\times1}$

Classification cost term (λ_1)

$+$

Auxiliary correlation cost term (λ_2)

$(\hat{y}_j - \hat{y}_{j'})^2$

Matrix of the prediction squared differences: $\mathbf{Q}$ of size T×T

Ground-truth correlation matrix: $\mathbf{\Phi}$ of size T×T

T task prediction scores: $(\hat{y}_1, \hat{y}_2, ..., \hat{y}_T)$
(output of the multi-task learning sub-network)

Fig. 5.6 Structured output prediction part of the proposed FV-MTL with CCE-LC cost function

5.2.3 *Results*

5.2.3.1 Datasets and Experimental Setup

Our experiments were performed on the TRECVID SIN 2013 dataset [67]. For assessing concept annotation performance, the indexing problem as defined in [67] was evaluated, i.e. given a concept, the goal was to retrieve the 2000 video shots that are mostly related to it. The TRECVID SIN 2013 [67] dataset consists of approximately 600 and 200 h of Internet archive videos for training and testing, respectively. The training set is partially annotated with 346 semantic concepts. The test set is evaluated on 38 concepts for which ground truth annotations exist, i.e. a subset of the 346 concepts.

Since the available ground truth annotations for this dataset are not adequate in number in order to train a deep network from scratch without overfitting its parameters, similarly to other studies [12], we used transfer learning, i.e. we used as a starting point the ResNet-50 network [23], which was originally trained on 1000 ImageNet categories [68], and fine-tuned its parameters towards our dataset. In order to evaluate the methods' performance, we used the mean extended inferred average precision

(MXinfAP) [69], which is an approximation of MAP. MXinfAP is suitable for the
partial ground truth that accompanies this dataset.

5.2.3.2 Visual-Level and Semantic-Level Concept Relations of the Presented DCNN Architecture

According to our preliminary experimental results presented in our journal paper [65],
FV-MTL with CCE-LC for k equal to 32 and d equal to 64 was the pair that reached
the best overall MXinfAP. In this subsection, we will try to visualize what this model
has learned with respect to visual-level and semantic-level concept relations. As
explained in Sect. 5.2.2.2, the overlap in the sparsity patterns of any two tasks, (i.e.
the overlap between task-specific weight vectors s_j and $s_{j'}$) controls the amount of
sharing between them. Based on this in Fig. 5.7, we recovered sparsity patterns (the
matrix S) using FV-MTL with CCE-LC for 15 selected concepts of the TRECVID
SIN dataset (darker colour indicates higher absolute value of the coefficient). The
horizontal axis depicts the 15 observed concepts and the vertical axis the latent tasks
($k = 32$) in this case. It is difficult to recover the grouping and overlap structure for

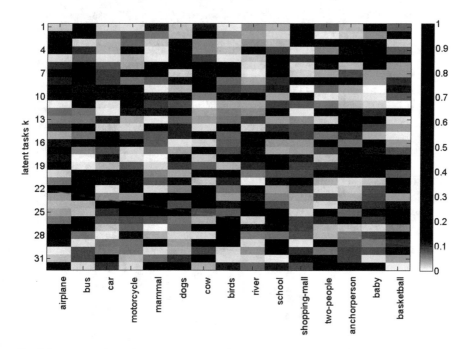

Fig. 5.7 Recovered sparsity patterns (the matrix S) with FV-MTL with CCE-LC, for k equal to
32 and d equal to 64, for 15 selected concepts of the TRECVID SIN 2013 dataset. Darker colour
indicates higher absolute value of the coefficient. The horizontal axis depicts the 15 observed
concepts and the vertical axis the 32 latent tasks

the observed concepts based on this figure, but some interesting observations can be made. For example, concepts with the same sparsity pattern can be considered as belonging to the same group, while concepts with orthogonal sparsity patterns can be considered as belonging to different groups. The 9th and 10th latent tasks are always active for the transport-related concepts (e.g. airplane, car, bus, motorcycle) but they are inactive, at least one of the two, for any of the other concepts. Transport-related concepts can be considered as belonging to the same group. In addition, those latent tasks that are active for the concept 'river' are always inactive for the concept 'shopping-mall' (except for the 11th latent task), which indicates that these are two disjoint groups.

Regarding the semantic-level concept relations, Fig. 5.8 presents the colour map of the phi-correlation coefficients, when calculated on the final prediction scores of the model when applied on the TRECVID SIN 2013 test dataset for 20 selected concepts. We can see that the model has captured many pairs of positively correlated concepts

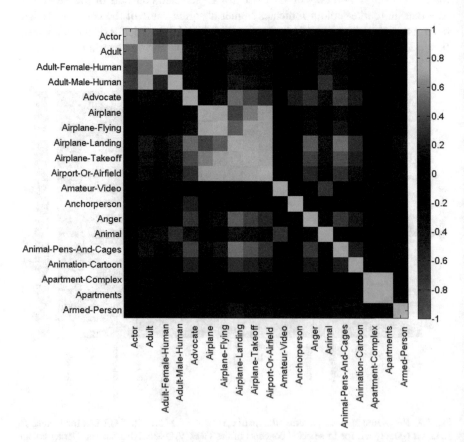

Fig. 5.8 Colour map of the phi-correlation coefficient calculated on the final prediction scores of the proposed FV-MTL with CCE-LC, for k equal to 32 and d equal to 64, when applied on the TRECVID-SIN 2013 test dataset for 20 selected concepts

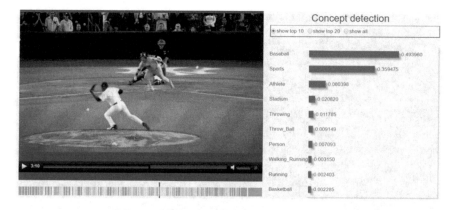

Fig. 5.9 Visual inspection of the results of our DCNN trained model, when applied on a specific video (downloaded from YouTube); here we are considering the concept-based keyframe annotation problem, i.e. whether we can annotate a given keyframe with the most relevant concepts

such as 'adult'-'actor', 'adult'-'female human person' (green areas of the figure), pairs of negatively correlated concepts such as 'animal'-'airplane landing' (red areas of the figure), and non-correlated concepts such as 'animal'-'actor', 'anger'-'actor' (black areas of the figure). According to the observations recovered from Figs. 5.7 and 5.8, we can see that our proposed method is able to capture both visual-level and semantic-level concept relations.

Finally, Figs. 5.9 and 5.10 present examples of concept-based keyframe annotation and retrieval results of our method, respectively. We can see that our method works very well for both problems retrieving correct results on top positions.

5.2.3.3   Main Findings—Comparisons with Related Methods

Figure 5.11 presents some of our main findings. The interested reader can refer to our original paper [65], where an extensive experimental evaluation has been performed. It should be noted that in [65] the FV-MTL with CCE-LC method, presented in this chapter, has been extensively evaluated and compared with many other concept-based video annotation methods. The compared methods have been categorized into three groups (i) those that do not consider neither MTL nor SO, (ii) those that either consider MTL or SO and (iii) those that consider both MTL and SO.

The FV-MTL with CCE-LC cost method presented in this chapter jointly exploits implicit visual-level and explicit semantic-level concept relations. This integrated DCNN architecture that emerges from combining these approaches was shown to improve concept annotation accuracy and outperformed the related state-of-the-art methods. Specifically, according to the left diagram of Fig. 5.11, it outperforms methods that do not impose any concept relations from 1.5 to 5%, methods that solely

Fig. 5.10 Visual inspection of the results of our DCNN trained model, when applied on a specific video (downloaded from YouTube); here we are considering the concept-based keyframe retrieval problem, i.e. whether we can retrieve all the relevant keyframes of a video, for a given concept

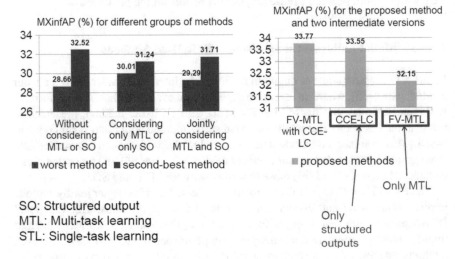

Fig. 5.11 Main findings on the TRECVID-SIN 2013 dataset. Evaluation in terms of MXinfAP

introduce either MTL or structured outputs by ∼2%, and finally methods that jointly consider MTL and structured outputs by ∼4%, in the TRECVID SIN dataset.

In addition, we evaluate the two intermediate versions of the integrated DCNN architecture (right part of Fig. 5.11): (a) Extension strategy [12] for DCNNs with the proposed CCE-LC cost, i.e. the typical complete DCNN architecture illustrated in Fig. 5.3 (ii), but replacing the sigmoid cross-entropy cost with the proposed CCE-LC cost, and (b) a subset of the FV-MTL with CCE-LC method, in which only the MTL part is used (i.e. without considering concept correlations). We observe that the two intermediate versions of our proposed method perform quite well; however, jointly considering both of them into a single architecture further improves the concept-based video retrieval accuracy.

To sum up, FV-MTL with CCE-LC always presents the best accuracy in terms of MXinfAP, which is equal to 33.77% (as presented on the right part of Fig. 5.11. All the other methods perform worse. Due to lack of space, we did not present all these comparisons, so on the left part of Fig. 5.11 we show the performance of the second best method and also the performance of the worst method from each of the different groups evaluated in our original paper [65].

Finally, it should be noted that a thorough analysis of the execution times of the proposed method appears in our original paper [65] that shows that our method is not considerably more computationally expensive than DCNN methods that use single-task learning cost functions. In terms of scalability, if we provide more concepts, then the network could model more and stronger task and label relations. So, we expect that the proposed method could work very well for larger number of concepts. In addition, in our preliminary experiments presented in the original paper of the method we have shown that parameters k and d are not sensitive to the number of concepts so the complexity of this part would not significantly increase when more concepts are to be learned. However, more experimentation towards this direction is needed.

5.3 Logo Detection

5.3.1 Related Work

The problem of detecting overlaid logos in videos is essentially a sub-problem of object detection in images. However, the problem definition of our particular case has a number of inherent constraints, which simplify the task, making it relatively easier than general object detection. By definition, object detection [70, 71] describes the task of identifying broad object categories (e.g. 'helicopter', 'human', 'airplane') in images. These object categories have extremely high within-class variation in comparison to detecting overlaid video/image logos, which are expected to be near-identical in every instance they appear. In this sense, the problem is more relevant to the task of logo detection [72, 73], which, despite the common name, has certain differences from the InVID use case. In the task commonly referred to as *logo*

Fig. 5.12 Top: An example of a generic logo detection task; Bottom: An example of the much more specific TV logo detection task

detection, the aim is to detect trademark logos on depicted objects, e.g. the brand of a shoe or a poster on a building. This includes perspective distortions and variants of the same logo, which again make the task broader than what we have to tackle within InVID. Our problem concerns logos that typically appear on the screen at the same angle, usually at approximately the same size, and often at the same position (Fig. 5.12). We will use the term *TV logo detection*, as it is established in literature, although it is clear that in our case we are often not dealing with actual TV channels and, in fact, the most important part of the task is identifying the logos of unofficial video sources, such as paramilitary groups. The case of TV logo detection is a much more narrow field than logo detection, and the respective methods exploit the constraints of the task to increase detection accuracy and speed.

The most common assumption of such methods is that the logo remains static throughout a video shot, while the rest of the frame contents change through time. Thus, approaches such as frame accumulation and thresholding [74] and brightness variance thresholding [75, 76] have been proposed to take advantage of these characteristics of the specific task. While seemingly a reasonable approach, a major issue with such approaches is that this assumption does not hold consistently, especially when dealing with arbitrary logos. It is not uncommon, for example, in the case of middle eastern paramilitary or clandestine political organizations to use animated logos (Fig. 5.13). In that case, any method based on the static logo assumption would fail entirely.

Fig. 5.13 Three frames from a Free Syrian Army clip displaying a rotating and changing logo

We thus decided to explore more powerful and robust algorithms for the problem. The options we considered were drawn from current literature, namely keypoint-based methods, sliding windows, region proposal methods, and object detection Convolutional Neural Networks (CNNs).

Keypoint-based approaches have been quite popular in the past, and generally provided relatively robust solutions to the task [77–80]. To learn a candidate logo, the algorithm extracts keypoints from a logo template, and retains their relative coordinates and local descriptors. For detection in an unknown image, keypoints are similarly extracted from the candidate image, and then their descriptors are matched against those of the candidate logos. Generally, these methods combine the matching of keypoints with some geometrical analysis of the feature location to ensure a match between the query and the candidates, and take into account possible geometrical transformations (in the case of logos positioned on objects, which may be distorted due to perspective.

Another option is a sliding window approach [81, 82], where a global descriptor is extracted from each logo. Then candidate overlapping windows are extracted from the image, at multiple scales, and the corresponding descriptor is extracted from each window. Consecutively, the descriptor is compared to the descriptors of all candidate logos. The comparison step is much faster than in keypoint-based methods, and can achieve much higher accuracy. However, due to the need of extracting descriptors from multiple overlapping windows, such approaches are prohibitively slow for real-time operational settings.

A much faster variant to sliding windows is region proposal. In that case, we can use a region proposal algorithm to extract a small number of candidate regions from the image, which are more likely to contain objects of interest (i.e. logos). We then only evaluate these regions [83, 84] as candidate windows. While faster than sliding window methods, these approaches often still require several seconds to propose the candidate windows for a single image. Furthermore, the success of the algorithm depends strongly on how strictly at least one of the proposed regions corresponds to the logo in the image. However, preliminary experiments showed that in many cases none of the proposed regions contained the logo, and thus the algorithms would simply not work in these cases.

Currently, the best performance in object detection is achieved using Deep Neural Networks, and specifically Region proposal Convolutional Neural Networks (R-CNN) [85, 86]. These methods train a region proposal network together with a classification network, and are very fast in terms of detection time since they only

require a single forward pass to return both classification and localization information. While Faster-RCNN remains a dominant architecture for object detection, other
variants such as YOLO attempt to further reduce complexity [87], while recently a
novel loss function was proposed to allow simpler and faster networks to reach the
accuracy of R-CNN and its variants. However, a common issue with deep learning
architectures is that they typically require a lot of annotated training data which are
not easily available.

5.3.2 Methodology

In the first steps of the project, the possibility of using Deep Learning to solve the
problem was not considered viable, since the large amount of annotated data that
would be required by the system was unavailable. Thus, based on speed considerations, the first approach we opted to use was a point matching method that compared
an image or video keyframe under investigation with a collection of stored logo
templates. An implementation of a keypoint-based algorithm was developed and
deployed for quantitative evaluations and as a first version of the service.

However, as the project progressed, it became apparent that the main limitation
of the keypoint-based method was scalability. Each new template that would be
added to the database would need to be compared to the image, which would lead
to the computational cost rising linearly with the number of known logos. Thus,
during the second year of InVID we decided to move to a Deep Learning solution
which, due to the parallelized, single-pass nature of the model, would retain its time
complexity constant, independent of the number of known logos. This was combined
with an innovative solution that generated ample artificial training examples using
data augmentation, to address the need of the network for large numbers of annotated
examples.

Both implementations are image-based. They were designed to deal with both
single images and video frames. For videos, the approach relies on integration with
the Video Fragmentation component of InVID, and operates at the shot level by
processing keyframes of each shot and producing a separate set of estimates per
shot. The approach allows for multiple logos to be present in the same image or shot.
The main reason for this is that, as videos are shared or re-transmitted, organizations
may add their own logos alongside the original ones, and the identities of all agencies
involved may be important information for an investigator. In the case of videos, since
each shot may contain different logos, the detection was done on a per-shot basis. In
that case, the detection process can take place on one or more individual keyframes
per shot.

5.3.2.1 Keypoint-Based Method

In our keypoint-based implementation, detection is performed against a list of logo templates. Each potentially detectable logo is linked with one template image and a corresponding database entry. Each entry contains the name of the organization the logo belongs to, the name of the corresponding template image file, the link to the Wikipedia article corresponding to the organization/group, and the dimensions of the frame size from which the logo template was extracted. While following an inherently multi-scale representation, the advantage of dealing with TV logos is that, in the vast majority of cases, they tend to appear at roughly the same dimensions in the frame. In our preliminary investigations, we found that resizing all candidate images to roughly the same dimensions as the image from which the template was extracted can provide a performance boost without increasing the computational complexity, while the fact that we use a scale-invariant representation means that we can still deal with certain scale variations.

For each logo in our list, we applied a preprocessing step where we extracted SURF [15] features from the corresponding template image. The features and the corresponding logo information were then stored to be used for detection. At detection time, when presented with a new candidate image, the image is rescaled to the appropriate dimensions, and SURF features are also extracted from it. Feature matching is then performed between the logo template and the candidate image using a k-nearest neighbours approach. The process is repeated for all logos in the list, and only logos returning a number of matches $\geqslant M$ are retained, where M is an experimentally determined threshold.

For all logos where a sufficient number of matching points are found, a second-level processing step takes place, where the geometrical consistency of the matches is evaluated. A RANSAC approach is then used to find the optimal perspective projection modelling the point correspondences, and to keep only the subset of matched points that conformed to the model. If the number of points surpasses a second threshold N (in our current implementation, $M = N$), the logo is considered to exist in the image.

For the keypoint-based implementation, it was found to be beneficial for accuracy to get more than one keyframe per shot and consecutively average them, to get a more salient version of the logo. Given a static logo, we can assume that in the averaged image the logo will remain intact while the rest of the image will appear blurred out. As a result, this will produce fewer salient keypoints in the overall image. Having fewer candidate SURF points in the image means much smaller chance of false matches. However, this option can only work for static logos. Thus while this approach was used in the method's offline evaluations, it had to be abandoned during integration with InVID, and instead, the middle keyframe of each shot was used for detection.

5.3.2.2   Deep Learning Method

As network architecture, we chose the Faster Region proposal Convolutional Neural Network (Faster-RCNN) [86]. This architecture simultaneously outputs a large number of region proposals and classification estimates for each region in a single pass, making it extremely fast during detection. Furthermore, the region proposal and the classification parts are trained simultaneously, making its training faster than its counterparts. Its performance is among the best in the state-of-the-art, and open-source implementations exist for the Caffe[3] and Tensorflow[4] frameworks. Thus, it was straightforward to experiment and adapt to the project's needs.

The main challenge with Deep Neural Networks is training. They tend to require large amounts of annotated data and generally require a lot of time to train. However, the task at hand is significantly simpler than most detection tasks, since in our case the candidate object (i.e. a logo) has very little variability between instances. This characteristic allowed us to use an innovative training technique that removes the need for manually annotated data.

Normally for an object detection task, we would require a large number of annotated images (hundreds or thousands) containing each object, and each image would have to be annotated with the class and the localization coordinates of the object. Creating such a training dataset for logos would be impossible within the scope of InVID, and impractical when extending the dataset with new logos. However, since in our case all appearances of a logo would be expected to be very similar, we were able to devise a way to automatically generate training images on the fly using a single logo example. A training image can be generated by taking a random base image from any realistic image dataset (such as MIRFlickr[5]), and a logo from our collection, and placing the logo at a random position on the image. To account for variations of the logo, a set of data augmentation techniques are applied, such as scaling (sometimes non-proportional), blurring by a random-sized kernel, brightness and colour modification. In this way, we can generate a practically infinite number of training images. To further speed up the training process, we place a number of logos in each training image, in a non-overlapping manner, ranging from 1 to 3 (Fig. 5.14). This process allows us to train a classifier without going through the process of collecting and manually annotating a dataset. It also allows for extensibility, since adding a new entry in the list of known logos does not require additional examples, but only the new logo template. It also solves the problem of a channel using many variants of its logo, since the addition of more examples adds little complexity to the task. Similarly, in the case of animated logos such as those depicted in Fig. 5.13, it is easy to add multiple frames from the animation into the known logo dataset, which means that we will be able to match the logo in a random keyframe from the video, whatever part of the animation it may contain. It should be noted that, roughly at the

---

[3]https://github.com/rbgirshick/py-faster-rcnn/.

[4]https://github.com/tensorflow/models/tree/master/research/object_detection/.

[5]http://press.liacs.nl/mirflickr/.

Fig. 5.14 Three artificially generated training samples with logos, some of which are semi-transparent

same time that we were implementing this approach, a publication presented a very similar data generation method for logo detection [88].

Following training, the detection process is simple: an image is passed through the trained model, and the model outputs a list of region estimates, plus the estimate of the logo class that was detected within them.

A further advantage of the CNN-based approach is that it is much more robust with respect to the logo background and potential transparency. When the keypoint-based approach detected points along the logo borders (generally a common case), the corresponding local descriptors were also affected by the colour of the background. In some cases, it was necessary to extend the template collection with instances of the same logo over different backgrounds, to cover all such eventualities. Furthermore, in the keypoint-based algorithm both the keypoint detection and the description steps were strongly affected by semi-transparent logos, which returned different results depending on the background they appeared on. In contrast, the CNN-based approach can easily learn to recognize such logos, provided it can be trained with enough artificially generated examples containing the logo overlaid on different backgrounds.

5.3.3 Results

Both approaches were implemented in Python. The SURF-based keypoint-based approach was implemented using methods from the OpenCV[6] library, and fast feature matching was done with the KDTree algorithm using OpenCV's FLANN-based[7] implementation. Faster-RCNN was implemented using existing frameworks, namely the Caffe-based `py-faster-rcnn`[8] implementation during the second year of the project, and the TensorFlow object detection framework[9] during the third year.

---

[6]http://opencv.org/.

[7]http://www.cs.ubc.ca/research/flann/.

[8]https://github.com/rbgirshick/py-faster-rcnn.

[9]See footnote 4.

Table 5.2 Logo detection evaluation results

	Videos			Shots		
	Keypoints	Fr-RCNN 1	Fr-RCNN 2	Keypoints	Fr-RCNN 1	Fr-RCNN 2
True detections	0.83	0.80	0.85	0.63	0.64	0.72
False detections	0.06	0.06	0.13	0.004	0.01	0.01

TensorFlow has comparably fewer library dependencies, its Python integration is simpler, and the object detection framework is part of the official release, unlike `py-faster-rcnn` which is a custom adaptation. Thus, as InVID approached its final release stage, TensorFlow was a more reliable choice for future maintenance.

The template list developed for the keypoint-based approach contained 503 logo templates from 169 channels and news sources. The number of logo templates was generally higher than for the deep learning approach, since in the keypoint-based approach we need to include many more variants of the templates (e.g. with different backgrounds). For the Faster-RCNN method, all the logos associated with a particular channel were grouped together, thus the network had 169 classes for our evaluation experiments. The training of the Faster-RCNN was done with roughly 200,000 automatically generated examples.

The evaluation dataset we used consisted of 2,752 videos originating from various YouTube channels, containing videos that featured at least one of the known logos in at least one shot. The videos were then separated in 54,986 shots using the InVID Video Fragmentation and Annotation service.

Table 5.2 shows the comparison between the performance of the keypoint-based approach and two CNN models. As shown in Table 5.2, the Faster-RCNN version of the algorithm is currently comparable to the keypoint-based approach. We tested two RCNN models, one trained with early stopping (Fr-RCNN 1) and one trained for longer period of time (Fr-RCNN 2). Fr-RCNN 1 shows slightly lower True Detection (TD) rates than keypoint-based methods, and comparable False Detections (FD). On the other hand, Fr-RCNN 2 has better TD rates, but significantly higher FD rates. One explanation is that the logo template collection contains several images of relatively low quality that are blurred. For the keypoint-based method these were necessary, in order to be able to detect logos in low-quality images. However, in Faster-RCNN training, especially after the potential additional blurring of the augmentation step, the network might be trained on extremely blurred templates, which could lead to finding false matches on arbitrary regions. Another observation is that the false positives appear disproportionately higher per video than per shot. This means that the relatively few false positives in the shots (0.01) are very scattered across the shots, with few (usually one at most) in each video. Thus in practice, these spurious matches are not distracting for professionals, since they can be easily discarded by visual inspection.

Overall, we consider the Faster-RCNN approach to be a superior choice, for two reasons: (1) the results for Faster-RCNN have significant potential for improve-

Table 5.3 Logo detection time requirements (in seconds)

	Image	Shot	Video
Keypoint-based	8.47	6.56	383.50
Faster-RCNN	4.17	1.18	69.00
Speedup (%)	203	556	556

ment by improving the template dataset—with the help of the user partners—and by tweaking the training parameters and (2) the Faster-RCNN approach is significantly faster, and its detection speed is much less dependent on the number of logos that are possible to detect. To confirm this hypothesis, we ran a series of evaluations with respect to detection speed. For fairness, we had to account for certain additional computational costs that the Faster-RCNN algorithm requires. Specifically, as the neural network runs on a PC equipped with a GPU, it had to be placed on a separate server, and it is possible that the communication between the logo detection server and the neural network server may incur additional delays. This means that the reported times include the service communication delays, which reflects the actual user experience. Table 5.3 gives the current differences in speed between the two services, per single image, per video shot, and per video. The reasons that the performance per shot is improved more than the performance per image, is that (a) the keypoint-based method was run on both the middle image and the mean image of the shot in order to reach its optimal performance, while the Faster-RCNN algorithm only runs on the middle image of each shot and (b) the impact of the communication overhead is much smaller, since the major load is accessing the image/video, which only happens once per video. In fact, the speed of the new service is so superior that it outweighs even the added time requirements of fragmenting the video (which we do not have in images), leading to the much higher per-shot improvement compared to the per-image one.

While it is conceivable that adding many new logos may increase training time, we consider that any potential increase will be manageable. Furthermore, it is possible that the overall training time can be reduced by tweaking the training hyperparameters and improving the data augmentation procedure.

5.4 Conclusions and Future Work

In this chapter, we explored two tasks to assist investigators in identifying and organizing semantically related items in unstructured collections gathered from the web in order to assist verification. One component was a concept-based annotation system, while the other was a logo detection system. Following an analysis of the state of the art, a choice of the most relevant approaches, and significant improvements, refinements and innovations beyond state-of-the-art methods, both systems were implemented and integrated into the final InVID platform.

Specifically, with respect to concept detection, we presented a machine learning architecture that is based on deep learning, referring to it as FV-MTL with CCE-LC. Overall, the lesson we learned is that a good video annotation and retrieval architecture can be developed by carefully taking into account many different directions such as feature extraction, classifier combination, feature-level and semantic-level concept relations. Deep learning architectures are the best way of jointly considering all these, with the presented FV-MTL with CCE-LC deep architecture consistently outperforming other related state-of-the-art approaches.

With respect to logo detection, we designed an innovative way to generate enough training data in order to fine-tune the existing object detection systems to the task of logo detection, even in the absence of a large annotated training set. Given than the InVID logo detection component will have to be kept up to date by adding new logos submitted by users, such an approach is the only way to be able to extend the classifier in the future. Since research into data augmentation is still ongoing, and recent methods based on Generative Adversarial Networks have yielded very promising results [89, 90], it might be a promising future path with respect to improving the classification accuracy of the system.

For our next step, we will continue to advance both components, to improve their efficiency and accuracy. With respect to semantic video annotation, we will continue to experiment with deep learning architectures, to exploit concept relations and yield better accuracy, and we will also reconsider whether the TRECVID semantic concepts are the most appropriate for the task or another set of concepts (given a correspondingly annotated dataset for training) would be more appropriate for the needs of newsworthy video annotation and retrieval. With respect to logo detection, we will keep experimenting with the automatic training data generation process in order to improve the performance of the algorithm. We will also continue expanding the known logo dataset with user-submitted logos. Finally, we will attempt to expand the synthetic training data creation process by introducing perspective-like transforms into the logos. This will allow us to move from detecting overlaid logos to detecting logos within the scene, e.g. on clothing or walls. Such an extension of the component capabilities would empower journalists to have a more complete understanding of the provenance and history of the video, and even allow them to verify aspects of the depicted content and the associated claims.

References

1. Snoek CGM, Worring M (2009) Concept-based video retrieval. Found Trends Inf Retr 2(4):215–322
2. Markatopoulou F, Moumtzidou A, Tzelepis C, Avgerinakis K, Gkalelis N, Vrochidis S, Mezaris V, Kompatsiaris I (2013) ITI-CERTH participation to TRECVID 2013. In: TRECVID 2013 workshop, Gaithersburg, MD, USA, vol 1, p 43

3. Gkalelis N, Mezaris V, Kompatsiaris I (2010) A joint content-event model for event-centric multimedia indexing. In: IEEE international conference on semantic computing (ICSC), pp 79–84

4. Sidiropoulos P, Mezaris V, Kompatsiaris I, Meinedo H, Bugalho M, Trancoso I (2011) Temporal video segmentation to scenes using high-level audiovisual features. IEEE Trans Circuits Syst Video Technol 21(8):1163–1177. https://doi.org/10.1109/TCSVT.2011.2138830

5. Tzelepis C, Galanopoulos D, Mezaris V, Patras I (2016) Learning to detect video events from zero or very few video examples. Image Vision Comput 53(C):35–44. https://doi.org/10.1016/j.imavis.2015.09.005

6. Tzelepis C, Ma Z, Mezaris V, Ionescu B, Kompatsiaris I, Boato G, Sebe N, Yan S (2016) Event-based media processing and analysis. Image Vision Comput 53(C), 3–19. https://doi.org/10.1016/j.imavis.2016.05.005

7. Markatopoulou F, Galanopoulos D, Mezaris V, Patras I (2017) Query and keyframe representations for ad-hoc video search. In: Proceedings of the 2017 ACM on international conference on multimedia retrieval, ICMR '17, pp 407–411. ACM, NY, USA. https://doi.org/10.1145/3078971.3079041, http://doi.acm.org/10.1145/3078971.3079041

8. Galanopoulos D, Markatopoulou F, Mezaris V, Patras I (2017) Concept language models and event-based concept number selection for zero-example event detection. In: Proceedings of the 2017 ACM on international conference on multimedia retrieval, ICMR '17, pp 397–401. ACM, New York, NY, USA. https://doi.org/10.1145/3078971.3079043, http://doi.acm.org/10.1145/3078971.3079043

9. Gkalelis N, Mezaris V (2017) Incremental accelerated kernel discriminant analysis. In: Proceedings of the 25th ACM international conference on multimedia, MM '17, pp 1575–1583. ACM, New York, USA. https://doi.org/10.1145/3123266.3123401, http://doi.acm.org/10.1145/3123266.3123401

10. Simonyan K, Zisserman A (2014) Very deep convolutional networks for large-scale image recognition. arXiv:abs/1409.1556

11. Krizhevsky A, Sutskever I, Hinton GE (2012) Imagenet classification with deep convolutional neural networks. In: Advances in neural information processing systems, pp 1097–1105

12. Pittaras N, Markatopoulou F, Mezaris V, Patras I (2017) Comparison of fine-tuning and extension strategies for deep convolutional neural networks. In: Proceedings of the 23rd international conference on MultiMedia modeling (MMM 2017), pp 102–114. Springer, Reykjavik, Iceland

13. Rublee E, Rabaud V, Konolige K, Bradski G (2011) ORB: an efficient alternative to SIFT or SURF. In: Proceedings of the IEEE International Conference on Computer Vision (ICCV 2011), pp 2564–2571

14. Lowe DG (2004) Distinctive image features from scale-invariant keypoints. Int J Comput Vis 60(2):91–110

15. Bay H, Ess A, Tuytelaars T, Gool LV (2008) Speeded-up robust features (SURF). Comput Vis Image Underst 110(3):346–359. https://doi.org/10.1016/j.cviu.2007.09.014

16. Van de Sande KEA, Gevers T, Snoek CGM (2010) Evaluating color descriptors for object and scene recognition. IEEE Trans Pattern Anal Mach Intell 32(9):1582–1596

17. Csurka G, Perronnin F (2011) Fisher vectors: beyond bag-of-visual-words image representations. In: Richard P, Braz J (eds) Computer vision, imaging and computer graphics theory and applications, vol 229. Communications in computer and information science. Springer, Berlin, pp 28–42

18. Jégou H, Douze M, Schmid C, Pérez P (2010) Aggregating local descriptors into a compact image representation. In: 2010 IEEE Conference on Computer Vision and Pattern Recognition (CVPR), pp 3304–3311. IEEE

19. Jia Y, Shelhamer E, Donahue J, Karayev S, Long J, Girshick R, Guadarrama S, Darrell T (2014) Caffe: convolutional architecture for fast feature embedding. In: Proceedings of the 22nd ACM international conference on multimedia, pp 675–678. ACM

20. Abadi M, Agarwal A, Barham P et al (2015) TensorFlow: large-scale machine learning on heterogeneous systems. Software available from https://www.tensorflow.org/

21. Szegedy C, Liu W, Jia Y, Sermanet P, Reed S, Anguelov D, Erhan D, Vanhoucke V, Rabinovich A (2015) Going deeper with convolutions. In: Proceedings of the IEEE conference on computer vision and pattern recognition (CVPR 2015), pp 1–9
22. Xie S, Girshick R, Dollár P, Tu Z, He K (2016) Aggregated residual transformations for deep neural networks. arXiv:1611.05431
23. He K, Zhang X, Ren S, Sun J (2016) Deep residual learning for image recognition. In: Proceedings of the IEEE conference on computer vision and pattern recognition (CVPR 2016), pp 770–778. https://doi.org/10.1109/CVPR.2016.90
24. Safadi B, Derbas N, Hamadi A, Budnik M, Mulhem P, Qu G (2014) LIG at TRECVid 2014 : semantic indexing tion of the semantic indexing. In: TRECVID 2014 workshop, Gaithersburg, MD, USA
25. Snoek C, Sande K, Fontijne D, Cappallo S, Gemert J, Habibian A, Mensink T, Mettes P, Tao R, Koelma D et al (2014) Mediamill at trecvid 2014: searching concepts, objects, instances and events in video
26. Snoek CGM, Cappallo S, Fontijne D, Julian D, Koelma DC, Mettes P, van de Sande KEA, Sarah A, Stokman H, Towal RB (2015) Qualcomm research and university of Amsterdam at TRECVID 2015: recognizing concepts, objects, and events in video. In: Proceedings of TRECVID 2015. NIST, USA (2015)
27. Wei Y, Xia W, Lin M, Huang J, Ni B, Dong J, Zhao Y, Yan S (2016) Hcp: a flexible cnn framework for multi-label image classification. IEEE Trans Pattern Anal Mach Intell 38(9):1901–1907. https://doi.org/10.1109/TPAMI.2015.2491929
28. Wang X, Zheng WS, Li X, Zhang J (2016) Cross-scenario transfer person reidentification. IEEE Trans Circuits Syst Video Technol 26(8):1447–1460
29. Bishay M, Patras I (2017) Fusing multilabel deep networks for facial action unit detection. In: Proceedings of the 12th IEEE international conference on automatic face and gesture recognition (FG)
30. Argyriou A, Evgeniou T, Pontil M (2007) Multi-task feature learning. Advances in neural information processing systems (NIPS 2007)
31. Obozinski G, Taskar B (2006) Multi-task feature selection. In: the 23rd international conference on machine learning (ICML 2006). Workshop of structural knowledge transfer for machine learning. Pittsburgh, Pennsylvania
32. Mousavi H, Srinivas U, Monga V, Suo Y, Dao M, Tran T (2014) Multi-task image classification via collaborative, hierarchical spike-and-slab priors. In: the IEEE international conference on image processing (ICIP 2014), pp 4236–4240. Paris, France
33. Evgeniou T, Pontil M (2004) Regularized multi–task learning. In: the 10th ACM SIGKDD international conference on knowledge discovery and data mining (KDD 2004), pp 109–117. Seattle, WA
34. Daumé III H (2009) Bayesian multitask learning with latent hierarchies. In: Proceedings of the 25th conference on uncertainty in artificial intelligence (UAI 2009), pp 135–142. AUAI Press, Quebec, Canada
35. Argyriou A, Evgeniou T, Pontil M (2008) Convex multi-task feature learning. Mach Learn 73(3):243–272
36. Zhou J, Chen J, Ye J (2011) Clustered multi-task learning via alternating structure optimization. Advances in neural information processing systems (NIPS 2011)
37. Sun G, Chen Y, Liu X, Wu E (2015) Adaptive multi-task learning for fine-grained categorization. In: Proceedings of the IEEE international conference on image processing (ICIP 2015), pp 996–1000
38. Markatopoulou F, Mezaris V, Patras I (2016) Online multi-task learning for semantic concept detection in video. In: Proceedings of the IEEE international conference on image processing (ICIP 2016), pp 186–190
39. Kumar A, Daume H (2012) Learning task grouping and overlap in multi-task learning. In: the 29th ACM international conference on machine learning (ICML 2012), pp 1383–1390. Edinburgh, Scotland

40. Zhang Z, Luo P, Loy CC, Tang X (2014) Facial landmark detection by deep multi-task learning. In: The 13th European conference on computer vision (ECCV 2014). Springer, Zurich, Switzerland, pp 94–108
41. Markatopoulou F, Mezaris V, Patras I (2016) Deep multi-task learning with label correlation constraint for video concept detection. In: Proceedings of the international conference ACM multimedia (ACMMM 2016), pp 501–505. ACM, Amsterdam, The Netherlands
42. Yang Y, Hospedales TM (2015) A unified perspective on multi-domain and multi-task learning. In: The international conference on learning representations (ICLR 2015), San Diego, California
43. Smith J, Naphade M, Natsev A (2003) Multimedia semantic indexing using model vectors. In: Proceedings of the international conference on multimedia and expo (ICME 2003), pp 445–448. IEEE, New York. https://doi.org/10.1109/ICME.2003.1221649
44. Weng MF, Chuang YY (2012) Cross-domain multicue fusion for concept-based video indexing. IEEE Trans Pattern Anal Mach Intell 34(10):1927–1941
45. Deng J, Ding N, Jia Y, Frome A, Murphy K, Bengio S, Li Y, Neven H, Adam H (2014) Large-scale object classification using label relation graphs, pp 48–64. Springer, Zrich, Switzerland
46. Ding N, Deng J, Murphy KP, Neven H (2015) Probabilistic label relation graphs with ising models. In: Proceedings of the 2015 IEEE international conference on computer vision (ICCV 2015), pp 1161–1169. IEEE, Washington, DC, USA
47. Markatopoulou F, Mezaris V, Pittaras N, Patras I (2015) Local features and a two-layer stacking architecture for semantic concept detection in video. IEEE Trans Emerg Top Comput 3:193–204
48. Qi GJ et al (2007) Correlative multi-label video annotation. In: Proceedings of the 15th international conference on multimedia, pp 17–26. ACM, New York
49. Yang Y, Wu F, Nie F, Shen HT, Zhuang Y, Hauptmann AG (2012) Web and personal image annotation by mining label correlation with relaxed visual graph embedding. IEEE Trans Image Process 21(3):1339–1351
50. Wang H, Huang H, Ding C (2011) Image annotation using bi-relational graph of images and semantic labels. In: Proceedings of the IEEE conference on computer vision and pattern recognition (CVPR 2011), pp 793–800
51. Wang H, Huang H, Ding C (2009) Image annotation using multi-label correlated green's function. In: Proceedings of the IEEE conference on computer vision and pattern recognition (CVPR 2009), pp 2029–2034
52. Zhang ML, Zhang K (2010) Multi-label learning by exploiting label dependency. In: Proceedings of the 16th ACM SIGKDD international conference on knowledge discovery and data mining (KDD 2010), pp 999–1008. ACM, New York, USA
53. Lu Y, Zhang W, Zhang K, Xue X (2012) Semantic context learning with large-scale weakly-labeled image set. In: Proceedings of the 21st ACM international conference on information and knowledge management, pp 1859–1863. ACM, New York, USA
54. Baumgartner M (2009) Uncovering deterministic causal structures: a boolean approach. Synthese 170(1):71–96
55. Luo Q, Zhang S, Huang T, Gao W, Tian Q (2014) Superimage: packing semantic-relevant images for indexing and retrieval. In: Proceedings of the international conference on multimedia retrieval (ICMR 2014), pp 41–48. ACM, New York, USA
56. Cai X, Nie F, Cai W, Huang H (2013) New graph structured sparsity model for multi-label image annotations. In: Proceedings of the IEEE international conference on computer vision (ICCV 2013), pp 801–808
57. Taskar B, Guestrin C, Koller D (2003) Max-margin markov networks. In: Proceedings of the 16th international conference on neural information processing systems (NIPS 2003). MIT Press
58. Deng J, Satheesh S, Berg AC, Li F (2011) Fast and balanced: efficient label tree learning for large scale object recognition. In: Advances in neural information processing systems, pp 567–575. Curran Associates, Inc

59. Sucar LE, Bielza C, Morales EF, Hernandez-Leal P, Zaragoza JH, Larra P (2014) Multi-label classification with bayesiannetwork-based chain classifiers. Pattern Recognit Lett 41:14–22
60. Schwing AG, Urtasun R (2015) Fully connected deep structured networks. arXiv:abs/1503.02351
61. Deng Z, Vahdat A, Hu H, Mori G (2015) Structure inference machines: recurrent neural networks for analyzing relations in group activity recognition. arXiv:abs/1511.04196
62. Zheng S, Jayasumana S et al (2015) Conditional random fields as recurrent neural networks. In: Proceedings of the international conference on computer vision (ICCV 2015)
63. Zhao X, Li X, Zhang Z (2015) Joint structural learning to rank with deep linear feature learning. IEEE Trans Knowl Data Eng 27(10):2756–2769
64. Jalali A, Sanghavi S, Ruan C, Ravikumar PK (2010) A dirty model for multi-task learning. In: Advances in neural information processing systems, pp 964–972. Curran Associates
65. Markatopoulou F, Mezaris V, Patras I (2019) Implicit and explicit concept relations in deep neural networks for multi-label video/image annotation. IEEE Trans Circuits Syst Video Technol 29(6):1631–1644. https://doi.org/10.1109/TCSVT.2018.2848458
66. Fellbaum C (1998) WordNet: an electronic lexical database. Bradford Books
67. Over P et al (2013) TRECVID 2013 – An overview of the goals, tasks, data, evaluation mechanisms and metrics. In: TRECVID 2013. NIST, USA
68. Russakovsky O, Deng J, Su H et al (2015) ImageNet large scale visual recognition challenge. Int J Comput Vis (IJCV 2015) 115(3):211–252. https://doi.org/10.1007/s11263-015-0816-y
69. Yilmaz E, Kanoulas E, Aslam JA (2008) A simple and efficient sampling method for estimating ap and ndcg. In: the 31st ACM international conference on research and development in information retrieval (SIGIR 2008), pp 603–610, Singapore
70. Erhan D, Szegedy C, Toshev A, Anguelov D (2014) Scalable object detection using deep neural networks. In: Proceedings of the IEEE conference on computer vision and pattern recognition (CVPR 2014), pp 2155–2162. IEEE Computer Society
71. Dollár P, Appel R, Belongie SJ, Perona P (2014) Fast feature pyramids for object detection. IEEE Trans Pattern Anal Mach Intell 36(8):1532–1545
72. Hoi SCH, Wu X, Liu H, Wu Y, Wang H, Xue H, Wu Q (2015) LOGO-net: large-scale deep logo detection and brand recognition with deep region-based convolutional networks. arXiv:abs/1511.02462
73. Oliveira G, Frazão X, Pimentel A, Ribeiro B (2016) Automatic graphic logo detection via fast region-based convolutional networks. arXiv:abs/1604.06083
74. Ku D, Cheng J, Gao G (2013) Translucent-static TV logo recognition by SUSAN corner extracting and matching. In: 2013 Third international conference on innovative computing technology (INTECH), pp 44–48. IEEE
75. Zhang X, Zhang D, Liu F, Zhang Y, Liu Y, Li J (2013) Spatial HOG based TV logo detection. In: Lu K, Mei T, Wu X (eds) International conference on internet multimedia computing and service, ICIMCS '13, Huangshan, China - 17–19 August 2013, pp 76–81. ACM
76. Shen L, Wu W, Zheng S (2012) TV logo recognition based on luminance variance. In: IET international conference on information science and control engineering 2012 (ICISCE 2012), pp 1–4. IET
77. Romberg S, Lienhart R (2013) Bundle min-hashing for logo recognition. In: Proceedings of the 3rd ACM international conference on multimedia retrieval, pp 113–120. ACM
78. Revaud J, Douze M, Schmid C (2012) Correlation-based burstiness for logo retrieval. In: Proceedings of the 20th ACM international conference on Multimedia, pp 965–968. ACM
79. Rusinol M, Llados J (2009) Logo spotting by a bag-of-words approach for document categorization. In: 2009 10th international conference on document analysis and recognition, pp 111–115. IEEE
80. Le VP, Nayef N, Visani M, Ogier JM, De Tran C (2014) Document retrieval based on logo spotting using key-point matching. In: 2014 22nd international conference on pattern recognition, pp 3056–3061. IEEE
81. Chum O, Zisserman A (2007) An exemplar model for learning object classes. In: Proceedings of the IEEE conference on computer vision and pattern recognition (CVPR 2007), pp 1–8. IEEE

82. Ferrari V, Fevrier L, Jurie F, Schmid C (2008) Groups of adjacent contour segments for object detection. IEEE Trans Pattern Anal Mach Intell 30(1):36–51
83. Gu C, Lim JJ, Arbeláez P, Malik J (2009) Recognition using regions. In: IEEE conference on computer vision and pattern recognition (CVPR 2009), pp 1030–1037. IEEE
84. Bianco S, Buzzelli M, Mazzini D, Schettini R (2015) Logo recognition using CNN features. In: Proceedings of 2015 international conference on image analysis and processing, pp 438–448. Springer
85. Girshick R (2015) Fast R-CNN. In: Proceedings of the IEEE international conference on computer vision (ICCV 2015), pp 1440–1448
86. Ren S, He K, Girshick RB, Sun J (2015) Faster R-CNN: Towards real-time object detection with region proposal networks. In: Cortes C, Lawrence ND, Lee DD, Sugiyama M, Garnett R (eds) Advances in neural information processing systems 28: annual conference on neural information processing systems 2015, 7–12 December 2015, Montreal, Quebec, Canada, pp 91–99. http://papers.nips.cc/book/advances-in-neural-information-processing-systems-28-2015
87. Redmon J, Divvala S, Girshick R, Farhadi A (2016) You only look once: unified, real-time object detection. In: Proceedings of the IEEE conference on computer vision and pattern recognition (CVPR 2016), pp 779–788
88. Su H, Zhu X, Gong S (2017) Deep learning logo detection with data expansion by synthesising context. In: 2017 IEEE winter conference on applications of computer vision (WACV), pp 530–539. IEEE
89. Ratner AJ, Ehrenberg H, Hussain Z, Dunnmon J, Ré C (2017) Learning to compose domain-specific transformations for data augmentation. In: Advances in neural information processing systems, pp 3236–3246
90. Mariani G, Scheidegger F, Istrate R, Bekas C, Malossi C (2018) Bagan: Data augmentation with balancing GAN. arXiv:1803.09655

Chapter 6
Detecting Manipulations in Video

Grégoire Mercier, Foteini Markatopoulou, Roger Cozien,
Markos Zampoglou, Evlampios Apostolidis, Alexandros I. Metsai,
Symeon Papadopoulos, Vasileios Mezaris, Ioannis Patras
and Ioannis Kompatsiaris

Abstract This chapter presents the techniques researched and developed within
InVID for the forensic analysis of videos, and the detection and localization of
forgeries within User-Generated Videos (UGVs). Following an overview of state-of-
the-art video tampering detection techniques, we observed that the bulk of current
research is mainly dedicated to frame-based tampering analysis or encoding-based
inconsistency characterization. We built upon this existing research, by designing
forensics filters aimed to highlight any traces left behind by video tampering, with

G. Mercier · R. Cozien
eXo maKina, Paris, France
e-mail: gregoire.mercier@exomakina.fr

R. Cozien
e-mail: roger.cozien@exomakina.fr

F. Markatopoulou · M. Zampoglou (✉) · E. Apostolidis · A. I. Metsai
S. Papadopoulos · V. Mezaris · I. Kompatsiaris
Information Technologies Institute, Centre for Research and Technology Hellas,
Thessaloniki, Greece
e-mail: markzampoglou@iti.gr

F. Markatopoulou
e-mail: markatopoulou@iti.gr

E. Apostolidis
e-mail: apostolid@iti.gr

A. I. Metsai
e-mail: alexmetsai@iti.gr

S. Papadopoulos
e-mail: papadop@iti.gr

V. Mezaris
e-mail: bmezaris@iti.gr

I. Kompatsiaris
e-mail: ikom@iti.gr

E. Apostolidis · I. Patras
School of Electronic Engineering and Computer Science, Queen Mary University,
London, UK
e-mail: i.patras@qmul.ac.uk

© Springer Nature Switzerland AG 2019
V. Mezaris et al. (eds.), *Video Verification in the Fake News Era*,
https://doi.org/10.1007/978-3-030-26752-0_6

161

a focus on identifying disruptions in the temporal aspects of a video. As for many other data analysis domains, deep neural networks show very promising results in tampering detection as well. Thus, following the development of a number of analysis filters aimed to help human users in highlighting inconsistencies in video content, we proceeded to develop a deep learning approach aimed to analyze the outputs of these forensics filters and automatically detect tampered videos. In this chapter, we present our survey of the state of the art with respect to its relevance to the goals of InVID, the forensics filters we developed and their potential role in localizing video forgeries, as well as our deep learning approach for automatic tampering detection. We present experimental results on benchmark and real-world data, and analyze the results. We observe that the proposed method yields promising results compared to the state of the art, especially with respect to the algorithm's ability to generalize to unknown data taken from the real world. We conclude with the research directions that our work in InVID has opened for the future.

6.1 Introduction

Among the InVID requirements, a prominent one has been to provide state-of-the-art technologies to support video forensic analysis, and in particular, manipulation, detection, and localization. Video manipulation detection refers to the task of using video analysis algorithms to detect whether a video has been tampered with video processing software, and if yes, to provide further information on the tampering process (e.g., where in the video the tampering is located and what sort of tampering took place).

InVID deals with online content, primarily User-Generated Content (UGC). The typical case concerns videos captured with hand-held devices (e.g., smartphones) by amateurs, although it is not uncommon to include semiprofessional or professional content. These videos are presented as real content captured on the scene of a newsworthy event, and usually do not contain any shot transitions but instead consist of a single shot. This is an important aspect of the problem, as a video that contains multiple shots has by definition already been edited, which may lessen its value as original eyewitness material. The videos are typically uploaded on social media-sharing platforms (e.g., Facebook, YouTube), which means that they are typically in H.264 format, and often suffer from low resolution, and relatively strong quantization.

When considering the task, we should keep in mind that image modifications are not always malicious. Of course, such cases are possible, such as the insertion or removal of key people or objects, which may alter the meaning of a video, and these are the cases that InVID video forensics was mostly aimed at. However, there are many more types of tampering that can take place in a video, which can be considered innocuous. These may include, for example, whole-video operations such as sharpening or color adjustments for esthetic reasons, or the addition of logos and watermarks on the videos. Of course, contextually such post-processing steps do partly diminish the originality and usefulness of a video, but in the case that such videos are the only available evidence on a breaking event, they become important for news organizations.

The detection of manipulations in video is a challenging task. The underlying rationale is that a tampering operation leaves a trace on the video—usually invisible to the eye and pertaining to some property of the underlying noise or compression patterns of the video—and that trace may be detectable with an appropriate algorithm. However, there are multiple complications in this approach. Overall, there are many different types of manipulation that can take place (object removal, object copy–paste from the same scene or from another video, insertion of synthetic content, frame insertion or removal, frame filtering or global color/illumination changes, etc.), each potentially leaving different sorts of traces on the video. Furthermore, we are dealing with the fact that video compression consists of a number of different processes, all of which may disrupt the tampering traces. Finally, especially in the case of online UGVs, these are typically published on social networks, which means that they have been repeatedly re-encoded and are often of low quality, either due to the resulting resolution or due to multiple compression steps. So, in order to succeed, detection strategies may often need to be able to detect very weak and fragmented traces of manipulation. Finally, an issue that further complicates the task is non-malicious editing. As mentioned above, occasionally videos are published with additional logos or watermarks. While these do not constitute manipulation or tampering, they are the result of an editing process identical to that of tampering and thus may trigger a detection algorithm, or cover up the traces of other, malicious modifications.

With these challenges in mind, we set out to implement the InVID video forensics component, aiming to contribute a system that could assist professionals in identifying tampered videos, or to advance the state of the art toward this direction. We began by exploring the state of the art in image forensics, based on the previous expertise of some of InVID partners (CERTH-ITI, eXo maKina) in this area. We then extended our research into video forensics, and finally proceeded to develop the InVID video forensics component. This consists of a number of algorithms, also referred to as *Filters*, aimed to process the video and help human users localize suspect inconsistencies. These filters are integrated in the InVID Verification Application and their outputs made visible to the users, to help them visually verify the videos. Finally, we tried to automate the detection process by training a deep neural network architecture to spot these inconsistencies and classify videos as authentic or tampered.

This chapter focuses on video tampering detection and does not deal with other forms of verification, e.g., semantically analyzing the video content, or considering metadata or contextual information. It is dedicated to the means that are adopted to track weak traces (or *signatures*) left by the tampering process in the encoded video content. It accounts for encoding integrity, space, time, color and quantization coherence. Two complementary approaches are presented, one dealing with tampering localization, i.e., using filters to produce output maps aimed to highlight where the image may have been tampered, and designed to be interpreted by a human user, and one dealing with tampering detection, aiming to produce a single-value output per video indicating the probability that the video is tampered.

The rest of the chapter is organized as follows. Section 6.2 briefly presents the necessary background, Sect. 6.3 presents an overview of the most relevant approaches that can be found in the literature. Section 6.4 details the methodologies developed in InVID for detecting tampering in videos. Specifically, subsection 6.4.1 presents the filters developed for video tampering localization, while Sect. 6.4.2 presents our approach for automatic video tampering detection. Section 6.5 then presents and analyses the evaluation results from the automatic approach over a number of experimental datasets. Finally, Sect. 6.6 presents our conclusions from our work in video forensics during the InVID project.

6.2   Background

Image and Video forensics are essentially subfields of image and video processing, and thus certain concepts from these fields are particularly important to the tasks at hand. In this section, we will briefly go over the most relevant of these concepts, as necessary background for the rest of the chapter.

While an image (or video frame) can in our case be treated as a 2D array of (R, G, B) values, the actual color content of the image is often irrelevant for forensics. Instead, we are often interested in other less prominent features, such as the noise, luminance-normalized color, or acuity of the image.

The term **image noise** refers to the random variation of brightness or color information, and is generally a combination of the physical characteristics of the capturing device (e.g., lens imperfections) and the image compression (in the case of lossy compression which is the norm). One way to isolate the image noise is to subtract a low-pass filtered version of the image from itself. The residue of this operation tends to be dominated by image noise. In cases where we deal with the luminance rather than the color information of the image, we call the output **luminance noise**. Another high-frequency aspect of the image is the **acuity** or **sharpness**, which is is a combination of focus, visibility, and image quality, and can be isolated using high-pass filtering.

With respect to video, certain aspects of MPEG compression are important for forensics and will be presented in short here. MPEG compression in its variants (MPEG-1, MPEG-2, MPEG-4 Part 2, and MPEG-4 part 10, also known as AVC or H.264) is essentially based on the difference between frames that are encoded using only information contained within them, also known as intra-frame compression, and frames that are encoded using information from other frames in the video, known as inter-frame compression. Intra-frame compression is essentially image compression, and in most cases is based on algorithms that resemble JPEG encoding. The concept of inter-frame encoding is more complicated. Given other frames in the sequence, the compression algorithm performs block-matching between these frames and the frame to be encoded. The vectors linking these blocks are known as **motion vectors** and, besides providing a way to reconstruct a frame using similar parts from other frames, can also provide a rough estimate of the motion patterns in the video, by

Fig. 6.1 Two example GOPs with I, P, and B frames. The GOP size, in this case, is 6 for both GOPs

studying the displacements of objects through time. The reconstruction of a frame is done by combining the motion-compensated blocks from the reference frames, with a residue image which is added to it to create the final frame.

Frames in MPEG-encoded videos are labeled **I**, **P**, or **B frames**, depending on their encoding. I signifies intra-frame encoding, P signifies inter-frame encoding using only data from previous frames, while B signifies bidirectional inter-frame encoding using data from both previous and future frames. Within a video, these are organized in **Groups of Pictures (GOPs)**, starting with an I-frame and containing P- and B-frames (Fig. 6.1). The distance between two I-frames is the GOP length, which is fixed in earlier encodings but can vary in the modern formats. Similarly, modern formats allow much more flexibility in other aspects of the encoding, such as the block size and shape, which means that algorithms with strict assumptions on the workings of the algorithm (e.g., expecting a fixed GOP size) will not work on modern formats.

6.3   Related Work

6.3.1   Image Forensics

Multimedia forensics is a field with a long research history, and much progress has been achieved in the past decades. However, most of this progress concerned the analysis of images rather than videos. Image forensics methods are typically organized in one of the two categories: *active forensics*, where a watermark or similar (normally invisible) piece of information is embedded in the image at the time of capture, of which the integrity ensures that the image has not been modified since capture [1–3], and *passive forensics*, where no such prior information exists, and the analysis of whether an image has been tampered depends entirely on the image content itself. While the latter is a much tougher task, it is also the most relevant in the majority of use cases, where we typically have no access to any information about the image capturing process.

One important distinction in image forensics algorithms is between tampering *detection* and tampering *localization*. In the former case, the algorithm only reports knowledge on whether the image has been tampered or not, and typically returns a scalar likelihood estimate. In the latter case, the algorithm attempts to inform the user *where* the tampering has taken place, and returns a map corresponding to the shape of the image and highlighting the regions of the image that are likely to have been tampered—ideally, a per-block or per-pixel probability estimate.

Passive image forensics approaches can be categorized with respect to the type of modification they intend to detect and/or localize. Three main groups of modifications are copy–moving, splicing or in-painting, and whole-image operations. In the first case, a part of the image is replicated and placed elsewhere in it—for example, the background is copied to remove an object or person, or a crowd is duplicated to appear larger. Copy–move detection algorithms attempt to capture the forgery by looking for self-similarities within the image [4, 5]. In the case of splicing, a part of one image is placed within another. Splicing detection and localization algorithms are based on the premise that, on some possibly invisible level, the spliced area will differ from the rest of the image due to their different capturing and compression histories. The case with in-painting, i.e., when part of the image is erased and then automatically filled using an in-painting algorithm is in principle similar, since the computer-generated part will carry a different profile than the rest of the image. Algorithms designed to detect such forgeries may exploit inconsistencies in the local JPEG compression history [6, 7], in local noise patterns [8, 9], or in the traces left by the capturing devices' Color Filter Array (CFA) [10, 11]. It is interesting to note that, in many cases, such algorithms are also able to detect copy–move forgeries, as they also often cause detectable local disruptions. For cases where localization is not necessary, tampering detection algorithms combining filtering and machine learning have been proposed in the past, reaching very high accuracy within some datasets [12, 13]. Finally, whole-image operations such as rescaling, recompression, or filtering cannot be localized and thus are generally tackled with tampering detection algorithms [14–16].

Recently, with the advent of deep learning, new approaches began to appear, attempting to leverage the power of convolutional neural networks for tampering localization and detection. One approach is to apply a filtering step on the image, and then use a Convolutional Neural Network to analyze the filter output [17]. Other methods have attempted to incorporate the filtering step into the network, through the introduction of a Constrained Convolutional Layer, of which the parameters are normalized at each iteration of the training process. This ensures that the first layer always operates as a high-pass filter, but is still trained alongside the rest of the network. Networks having this layer as their first convolutional layer were proposed for tampering detection [18] and resampling detection [19] with promising results, while a multi-scale approach was proposed in [20]. Recently, an integrated model was proposed, re-implementing an approach similar to [21], but exclusively using deep learning architectures [22].

A major consideration with image forensics, and especially in the use cases tackled through InVID, where we deal with online content from web and social media sources, is the degradation of the tampering traces as the content circulates from platform to platform. The traces that most algorithms look for are particularly fragile, and are easily erased through resampling or recompression. Since most online platforms perform such operations on all images uploaded to them, this is a very important consideration for news-related multimedia forensics, and a recent study attempted to evaluate the performance of splicing localization algorithms in such environments [23].

6.3.2 Video Forensics

With respect to video-related disinformation, the types of tampering that we may encounter are, to an extent, similar to the ones encountered in images. Thus, we may encounter copy–moving, splicing, in-painting, or whole-video operations such as filtering or illumination changes. An important difference is that such operations may have a temporal aspect, e.g., splicing is typically the insertion of a second video consisting of multiple green-screen frames depicting the new object in motion. Similarly, a copy–move may be temporally displaced, i.e., an object of a video from some frames reappearing in other frames, or spatially displaced, i.e., an object from a frame reappearing elsewhere on the same frame. Furthermore, there exists a type of forgery that is only possible in videos, namely inter-frame forgery, which essentially consists of frame insertion or deletion.

Inter-frame forgery is a special type of video tampering, because it is visually identifiable in most cases as an abrupt cut or shot change in the video. There exist two types of videos where such a forgery may actually succeed to deceive viewers: One is the case of a video that already contains cuts, i.e., edited footage. There, a shot could be erased or added among the existing shots, if the audio track can be correspondingly edited. The other is the case of CCTV video or other video footage taken from a static camera. There, frames could be inserted, deleted, or replaced without being visually noticeable. However, the majority of InVID use cases concern UGV, which is usually taken by hand-held capturing devices and consists of unedited single shots. In those cases, inter-frame forgeries cannot be applied without being immediately noticeable. Thus, inter-frame forgery detection was not a high priority for InVID.

When first approaching video forensics, one could conceptualize the challenge as an extension of image forensics, which could be tackled with similar solutions. For example, video splicing could be detected based on the assumption that the inserted part carries a different capturing and compression history than the video receiving it. However, our preliminary experimentation showed that the algorithms designed for images do not work on videos, and this even applies to the most generic noise-based algorithms. It goes without saying that algorithms based specifically on the JPEG image format are even more inadequate to detect or localize video forgeries. The main reason for this is that a video is much more than a sequence of images. MPEG compression—which is the dominant video format today—encodes information by exploiting temporal interrelations between frames, essentially reconstructing most frames by combining blocks from other frames with a residual image. This process essentially destroys the traces that image-based algorithms aim to detect. Furthermore, the re-quantization and recompression performed by online platforms such as

YouTube, Facebook, and Twitter are much more disruptive for the fragile traces of tampering than the corresponding recompression algorithms for images. Thus, video tampering detection requires the development of targeted, video-based algorithms. Even more so, algorithms designed for MPEG-2 will often fail when encountered with MPEG-4/H.264 videos [24], which are the dominant format for online videos nowadays. Thus, when reviewing the state of the art, we should always evaluate the potential robustness of the algorithm with respect to online videos.

When surveying the state of the art, a similar taxonomy that we used for image forensics can be used for videos-based algorithms. Thus, we can find a large number of active forensics approaches [25–29], which however are not applicable in most InVID use cases, where we have no control of the video capturing process. As mentioned above, passive video forensics can be organized in a similar structure as passive image forensics, with respect to the type of forgery they aim to detect: splicing/object insertion, copy–moving/cloning, whole-video operations, and inter-frame insertion/deletion. The following subsections present an overview of these areas, while two comprehensive surveys can be found in [24, 30].

6.3.2.1 Video Splicing and In-Painting

Video splicing refers to the insertion of a part of an image or video in some frames of a recipient video. Video in-painting refers to the replacement of a part of the video frames with automatically generated content, presumably to erase the objects depicted in those parts of the frame. In principle, video splicing detection algorithms operate similarly to image splicing detection algorithms, i.e., by trying to identify local inconsistencies in some aspect of the image, such as the noise patterns or compression coefficients.

Other strategies focus on temporal noise [31] or correlation behavior [32]. It is not clear if those methods could process video encoded in a constant bit rate strategy, since imposing a constant bit rate compression induces a variable quantization level over time, depending on the video content. Nevertheless, the noise estimation induces a predictable feature shape or background, which imposes an implicit hypothesis such as a limited global motion (the fact is that those methods work better with still background). The Motion-Compensated Edge Artifact is an interesting alternative to deal with temporal behavior of residuals between I, P, and B frames without requiring strong hypotheses on the motion or background contents. Those periodic artifacts in the DCT coefficients may be extracted through a thresholding technique [33] or spectral analysis [34].

6.3.3 Detection of Double/Multiple Quantization

When we detect that a video has been re-quantized more than once, it does not mean that the video was tampered between the two compressions. In fact, it may well be possible that the video was simply rescaled, or changed format, or was simply uploaded on a social media platform which re-encoded the video. Thus, detection of double/multiple quantization does not give tampering information as such, but gives a good indication that the video has been reprocessed and may have been edited. Of course, as InVID primarily deals with social media content, all analyzed videos will have been quantized twice. Thus, from our perspective, it is more important to know if the video has been quantized more than two times, and if yes, to know the exact number of quantizations it has undergone.

Video multiple quantization detection is often based on the quantization analysis of I-frames. This is similar to techniques used for recompression analysis of JPEG images, although, as explained above, it should be kept in mind that an I-frame cannot always be treated as a JPEG image, as its compression is often much more complex, and a JPEG-based algorithm may be inadequate to address the problem.

In JPEG compression, the distribution of DCT coefficients before quantization follows the Generalized Gaussian distribution, thus its quantized representation is given by Benford's law and its generalized version [35]. The degree to which the DCT coefficient distribution conforms with Benford's law may be used as an indication of whether the image has been re-quantized or not. In a more video-specific approach, the temporal behavior of the parameters extracted from Benford's law may also be exploited to detect multi-compression of the video [36, 37].

Other approaches propose to detect multiple quantization of a video stream by considering the link between the quantization level and the motion estimation error, especially on the first P frame following a (re-quantized) I-frame [38, 39]. However, such approaches are designed to work with fixed-size GOPs, which is more relevant for MPEG-2 or the simpler Part 2 of MPEG-4, rather than the more complex modern formats such as H.264/AVC/MPEG-4 Part 10.

6.3.4 Inter-frame Forgery Detection

This kind of tampering is characterized by the insertion (or removal) of entire frames in the video stream. Such cases arise for instance in video surveillance systems where, due to the static background, frames can be inserted, deleted, or replaced without being detectable, with malicious intent. Many approaches are based on the detection of inconsistencies in the motion prediction error along frames, the mean displacement over time, the evolution of the percentage of intra-coded macro blocks, or the evolution of temporal correlation of spatial features such as Local Binary Patterns (LBP) or velocity fields [40–43].

However, inter-frame forgery is generally not very common in UGVs, as we have found through the InVID use cases. The Fake Video Corpus [44], a dataset of fake and real UGC videos collected during InVID shows that, on the one hand, most UGV content presented as original is typically unedited and single shot, which means that it is hard to insert frames without them being visually detectable. On the other hand, multi-shot video by nature includes frame insertions and extractions, without this constituting some form of forgery. Thus, for InVID, such methods are not particularly relevant.

6.3.5 Video Deep Fakes and Their Detection

Recently, the introduction of deep learning approaches has disrupted many fields including image and video classification and synthesis. Of particular relevance has been the application of such approaches for the automatic synthesis of highly realistic videos with impressive results. Among them, a popular task with direct implications on the aims of InVID is face swapping, where networks are trained to replace human faces in videos with increasingly more convincing results [45, 46]. Other tasks include image-to-image translation [47, 48], where the model learns to convert images from one domain to another (e.g., take daytime images and convert them to look as if they were captured at night), and image in-painting [49, 50], where a region of the image is filled by automatically generated content, presumably with erasing objects and replacing them with background.

Those approaches are bringing new challenges in the field of video forensics, since in most of these cases the tampered frames are synthesized from scratch by the network. As a consequence, in these cases, it is most likely that content inconsistencies are no longer relevant with respect to tampering detection. Thus, all strategies based on the statistical analysis of video parameters (such as quantization parameters, motion vectors, heteroscedasticity, etc.) may have been rendered obsolete. Instead, new tampering detection strategies need to account for scene, color and shape consistencies, or to look for possible artifacts induced by forgery methods. Indeed, detecting deep fakes may be a problem more closely linked to the detection of computer-generated images (a variant of which is the detection of computer graphics and 3D rendered scenes) [51–53] than to tampering detection. Face swaps are an exception to this, as in most cases the face is inserted in an existing video frame, thus the established video splicing scenario still holds. Recently, a study on face swap detection was published, testing a number of detection approaches against face swaps produced by three different algorithms, including one based on deep learning [54]. This work, which is an extension of a previous work on face swap detection [55], shows that in many cases image splicing localization algorithms such as XceptionNet [56] and MesoNet [57] can work, at least for the raw images and videos having undergone one compression step. During the course of the InVID project, the discourse on the potential of deep fakes to disrupt the news cycle and add to the amount of online disinformation has risen from practically nonexistent in 2016 to central in 2018. The timing and scope of the project did not allow to devote resources to tackling the challenge. Instead, the InVID forensics component was dedicated to analyzing forgeries committed using more traditional means. However, as the technological capabilities of generative networks increase, and their outputs become increasingly more convincing, it is clear that any future ventures into video forensics would have to take this task very seriously as well.

6.4   Methodology

6.4.1   Video Tampering Localization

The first set of video forensics technologies developed within InVID concerned a number of forensics filters aimed to be interpreted by trained human investigators in order to spot inconsistencies and artifacts, which may highlight the presence of tampering. In this work, we followed the practice of a number of image tampering localization approaches [8, 58] that do not return a binary map or a bounding box giving a specific answer to the question, but rather a map of values that need to be visualized and interpreted by the user in order to decide if there is tampering, and where.

With this in mind, eXo maKina developed a set of novel filters aimed at generating such output maps by exploiting the parameters of the MPEG-4 compression, as well as the optical and mathematical properties of the video pixel values. The outputs of these filters are essentially videos themselves, with the same duration as the input videos, allowing temporal and spatial localization of any highlighted inconsistencies in the video content. In line with their image forensics counterparts, these filters do not include direct decision-making on whether the video is tampered or not, but instead highlight various aspects of the video stream that an investigator can visually analyze for inconsistencies. However, since these features can be used by analysts to visually reach a conclusion, we deduce that it is possible for a system to be trained to automatically process these traces and come to a similar conclusion without human help. This reduces the need for training investigators to analyze videos. Therefore, in parallel to developing filters for human inspection, we also investigated machine learning processes that may contribute to decision-making based on the outputs of those filters. Section 6.4.1 presents these filters and the type of tampering artifacts they aim to detect, while Sect. 6.4.2 presents our efforts to develop an automatic system that can interpret the filter outputs in order to assist investigators.

The filters developed by eXo maKina for the video forensics component of InVID are organized into three broad groups: Algebraic, optical, and temporal filters.

1. Algebraic filters: The term *algebraic filters* refers to any algebraic approaches that allow projecting information into a sparse feature space that makes forensic interpretation easier.

   - The **Q4** filter is used to analyze the decomposition of the image through the Discrete Cosine Transform. The 2D DCT converts an $N \times N$ block of an image into a new $N \times N$ block in which the coefficients are calculated based on their frequency. Specifically within each block, the first coefficient situated at position $(0, 0)$ represents the lowest frequency information and its value is therefore related to the average value of the entire block, the coefficient $(0, 1)$ next to it characterizes a slow evolution from dark to light in the horizontal direction, etc.

If we transform all $N \times N$ blocks of an image with the DCT, we can build for example a single-channel image of the coefficients $(0, 0)$ of each block. This image will then be N times smaller per dimension. More generally, one can build an image using the coefficients corresponding to position (i, j) of each block for any chosen pair of i and j. Additionally, one may create false color images by selecting three block positions and using the three resulting arrays as the red, green, and blue channel of the resulting image, as shown in the following equation:

$$\begin{pmatrix} \text{red} \\ \text{green} \\ \text{blue} \end{pmatrix} = \begin{pmatrix} \text{coefficients} \#1 \\ \text{coefficients} \#2 \\ \text{coefficients} \#3 \end{pmatrix}. \tag{6.1}$$

For the implementation of the Q4 filter used in InVID, we chose to use blocks of size 2×2. Since the coefficient corresponding to block position $(0, 0)$ is not relevant for verification and only returns a low-frequency version of the image, we have the remaining three coefficients with which we can create a false color image. Thus, in this case, the red channel corresponds to horizontal frequencies $(0, 1)$, the green channel corresponds to vertical frequencies $(1, 0)$, and the blue corresponds to frequencies along the diagonal direction $(1, 1)$ (Fig. 6.2).

- The **Chrome** filter (Fig. 6.3) is dedicated to analyzing the luminance noise of the image. It highlights noise homogeneity, which is expected in a normal and naturally illuminated observation system. It is mainly based on a nonlinear filter in order to capture impulsive noise. Hence, the Chrome filter is mainly based on the following operation applied on each frame of the video:

$$I_{\text{Chrome}}(x) = |I(x) - \text{median}(W(I(x)))|, \tag{6.2}$$

(a)   **(b)**

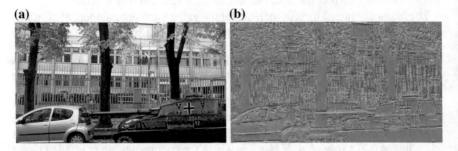

Fig. 6.2 Output of the **Q4** filter on the edited tank video. **a** Edited frame, **b** filter output. According to Eq. (6.1), the image in (**b**) shows in red the strength of vertical transition (corresponding to transitions along the lines), in green the horizontal transitions and in blue the diagonal transitions (which can be mainly seen in the leaves of the trees)

(a)   **(b)**

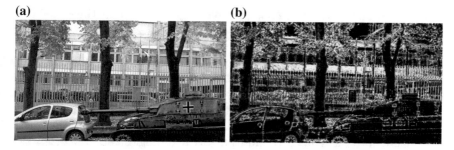

Fig. 6.3 Output of the **Chrome** filter on the edited tank video. **a** Edited frame, **b** filter output. The image in (**b**) appears to be black and white but remains with color information. As it comes from Eq. (6.2), it shows that the noise is of the same level independent of the input color bands

where $I(x)$ signifies an image pixel, and $W(I(x))$ stands for a 3×3 window around that pixel.

This filter resembles the Median Noise algorithm for image forensics, implemented in the Image Forensics Toolbox,[1] where the median filter residue image is used to spot inconsistencies in the image. Essentially, as it isolates high-frequency noise, this approach gives an overview of the entire frame where items with different noise traces can be spotted and identified as standing out from the rest of the frame.

2. Optical filters: Videos are acquired from an optical system coupled with a sensor system. The latter has the sole purpose of transforming light and optical information into digital data in the form of a video stream. A lot of information directly related to the light and optical information initially captured by the device is hidden in the structure of the video file. The purpose of **optical** filters is to extract this information and to allow the investigator to look for anomalies in the optical information patterns. It must be kept in mind that these anomalies are directly related to optical physics. Some knowledge of these phenomena is therefore required for an accurate interpretation of the results.

- The **Fluor** filter is used to study the colors of an image regardless of its luminance level. The filter produces a *normalized* image where the colors of the initial image have been restored independently of the associated luminance. The underlying transformation is the following:

$$\begin{pmatrix} \text{red} \\ \text{green} \\ \text{blue} \end{pmatrix} = \begin{pmatrix} \frac{\text{red}}{\text{red+green+blue}} \\ \frac{\text{green}}{\text{red+green+blue}} \\ \frac{\text{blue}}{\text{red+green+blue}} \end{pmatrix} \tag{6.3}$$

---

[1] https://github.com/MKLab-ITI/image-forensics.

As shown in Fig. 6.4, in 2D or 3D, colored pixels with Red, Green, and Blue components are projected on the sphere centered on the black color so that the norm of the new vector (red, green, and blue) is always equal to 1.

We see on the 2D image that the points in black represent different colors but their projections on the arc of a circle are located in the same region which induces the same hue of the image **Fluor**. On the other hand, dark pixels, drawn as points in gray in the image, may appear similar to the eye, but may actually have a different hue and their projection on the arc enhances these differences and may allow the user to distinguish between them. This normalization performed by the Fluor filter makes it possible to break the similarity of colors as it is perceived by the human visual system and to highlight colors with more pronounced differences based on their actual hue (Fig. 6.5).

- The **Focus** filter is used to identify and visualize the sharp areas in an image or areas of stronger *acuity*. When an image is sharp, it has the characteristic

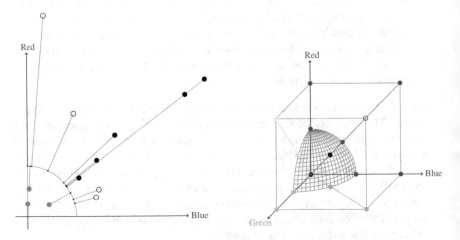

Fig. 6.4 Projection principle performed by the **Fluor** filter

Fig. 6.5 Output of the **Fluor** filter on the edited tank video. **a** Edited frame, **b** filter output. Image on (**b**) shows the colors of the original according to Eq. (6.3)

(a)   (b)

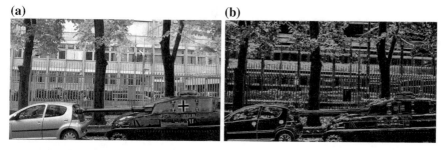

Fig. 6.6 Output of the **Focus** filter on the edited tank video. **a** Edited frame, **b** filter output. In the (**b**) image, vertical sharpness is shown in red and horizontal sharpness in green

(a)   (b)

Fig. 6.7 Output of the **Acutance** filter on the edited tank video. **a** Edited frame, **b** filter output. The image (**b**) stresses that the tank appears much more sharp than the rest of the image

of containing *abrupt* transitions as opposed to a *smooth* level evolution of color at the boundaries of an object. An image with high acuity contains a higher amount of high frequencies, while in contrast, the high frequencies are insignificant when the object is blurred or out of focus. This sharpness estimation for the Focus filter is performed through the wavelet transform [59]. The **Focus** filter considers the wavelet coefficients only through a nonlinear filtering based on the processing of the three RGB planes of each frame. It yields a false color composition where blurred low-frequency areas remain in gray and the sharp contours appear in color (Fig. 6.6).

• The **Acutance** filter (Fig. 6.7) refers to the physical term for the sharpness in photography. Normally, it is a simple measure of the slope of a local gradient but, here, it is normalized with the local value of the gray levels, which distinguishes it from the **Focus** filter. The Acutance filter is computed as the ratio between the outputs of a high-pass filter and a low-pass filter. In practice, we use two Gaussian filters with different sizes. Hence, the following equation characterizes the **Acutance** filtering process:

$$\text{frame}_{\text{Acutance}} = \frac{\text{frame}_{\text{HighPass}}}{\text{frame}_{\text{LowPass}}}. \tag{6.4}$$

(a)   **(b)**

Fig. 6.8 Output of the **Cobalt** filter on the edited tank video. **a** Edited frame, **b** filter output

3. Temporal filters: These filters aim at highlighting the behavior of the video stream over time. MPEG-4 video compression exploits temporal redundancy to reduce the compressed video size. This is the reason a compressed video is much more complex than a sequence of compressed images. Moreover, in many frames, MPEG-4 mixes up the intra/inter predictions in one direction or in a forward/backward strategy, so that the frame representation is highly dependent on the frame contents and the degree of quantization. Thus, the analysis of the temporal behavior of the quantization parameters may help us detect inconsistencies in the frame representation.

- The **Cobalt** filter compares the original video with a modified version of the original video re-quantized by MPEG-4 with a different quality level (and a correspondingly different bit rate). The principle of the Cobalt filter is simple. One observes the video of errors[2] between the initial video and the video re-quantized by MPEG-4 with a variable quality level or a variable bit rate level. If the quantization level coincides with the quality level actually used on the small modified area, there will be no error right there (Fig. 6.8). This practice is quite similar to the JPEG Ghosts algorithm [6] where a JPEG image is recompressed and the new image is subtracted from the original, to locally highlight inconsistencies ("ghosts") that correspond to added objects from images of different qualities. The ELA algorithm[3] follows a similar approach.
- The **Motion Vectors** filter yields a color-based representation of block motions as encoded into the video stream (Fig. 6.9). Usually, this kind of representation uses arrows to show block displacements. It is worth noting that the encoding system does not recognize "objects" but handles blocks only (namely macro blocks). The motion vectors are encoded in the video stream to reconstruct all frames which are not keyframes (i.e., not intra-coded frames but inter-coded frames that are essentially encoded by using information from other frames). Then, an object of the scene has a set of motion vectors associated to each macro block inside it. These motions as represented by the Motion

---

[2] Video of errors: a video constructed by per-pixel differences of frames between the two videos.
[3] https://fotoforensics.com/tutorial-ela.php.

(a)   (b)

Fig. 6.9 Output of the **Motion Vectors** filter on the edited tank video. **a** Edited frame, **b** filter output. Instead of a usual arrow-based representation of the motion vectors, image (**b**) shows macro blocks displacements according to a vector orientation definition that uses the Hue angular definition of the HLS color representation. This representation allows better visualization for human investigators, and potential processing by automatic systems

(a)   (b)

Fig. 6.10 Output of the **Temporal Filter** on the edited tank video. **a** Edited frame, **b** filter output. The frame-to-frame difference shown in image (**b**) highlights the tank displacement as well as the light shift of the camera

Vectors filter have to be homogeneous and coherent, otherwise there is a high likelihood that some suspicious operation has taken place.

- The **Temporal Filter** is used to apply temporal transformation on the video, such as smoothing or temporal regulation (Fig. 6.10). It should also be used to make a frame-to-frame comparison to focus on the evolution of the luminance in time only. The Temporal Filter is computed as the frame-to-frame difference over time as stated by the following equation:

$$\text{frame}_{\text{Temporal Filter}}(t) = \text{frame}(t) - \text{frame}(t-1)$$

which is applied on each color channel of the frames so that the output of the filter is also a color image.

6.4.2 Tampering Detection

Besides the development of video-specific forensics filters, we also dedicated effort toward developing an automatic detection system, which would be able to assist investigators in their work. Similar to other tampering detection approaches, our methodology is to train a machine learning system using a set of input features to distinguish between tampered and non-tampered items. The approach presented in [60] is based on image classification. Since the filters produce colorized sequences of outputs in the form of digital videos, we decided to use image classification networks in order to model the way a human investigator would look for inconsistencies in the filter outputs.

Deep networks generally require very large training sets. This is the reason the authors of [55] resorted to (semi-)automatically generated face swap videos for training and evaluation. However, for the general case of video tampering, such videos do not exist. On the other hand, in contrast to other methods which are based on filter outputs that are not readable by humans, the outputs produced by our filters are designed to be visually interpreted by users. This means that we can treat the task as a generic image classification task, and refine networks that have been pretrained on general image datasets.

Even in this case, there is need for a large number of items, which was not available. Similar to [54], we decided to deal with the problem at the frame level. Thus, each frame was treated as a separate item, and accordingly, the system was trained to distinguish between tampered and untampered frames. There are admittedly strong correlations between consecutive video frames, which reduces the variability in the training set, but operating at the frame level remains the only viable strategy given the limited available data. Of course, during training and evaluation, caution needs to be applied so as to ensure that all the frames from the same video remain exclusively either in the training or test set, and that no information leak takes place.

For classification, we chose Convolutional Neural Networks (CNNs) which are currently the dominant approach for this type of task. Specifically, we chose GoogLeNet [61] and ResNet [62], which are two very successful models for image classification. In order to apply them to tampering detection, we initialize the models with pretrained weights from the ImageNet dataset, and fine-tune them using annotated filter outputs from our datasets.

To produce the outputs, we chose the Q4 and Cobalt filters for classification, which represent two complementary aspects of digital videos: Q4 provides us with frequency analysis through the DCT transform, and Cobalt visualizes the re-quantization residue. The CNNs are designed to accept inputs in a fixed resolution of 224×224 pixels. We thus rescaled all filter outputs to match these dimensions. Generally, in multimedia forensics, rescaling is a very disruptive operation that tends to erase the—usually very sensitive—traces of tampering. However, in our case, the forensics filters we are using are designed to be visually inspected by humans and, as a result, exhibit no such sensitivities. Thus, we can safely adjust their dimensions to the CNNs.

One final note on the CNNs is that, instead of using their standard architecture, we extend them using the proposed approach of [63]. The work of [63] shows that, if we extend the CNN with an additional Fully Connected (FC) layer before the final FC layer, the network classification performance is improved significantly. We chose to add a 128-unit FC layer to both networks, and we also replaced the final 1000-unit layer, aimed at the 1000-class ImageNet task, with a 2-unit layer appropriate for the binary (tampered/untampered) task.

6.5 Results

6.5.1 Datasets and Experimental Setup

This section is dedicated to the quantitative evaluation of the proposed tampering detection approach. We drew videos from two different sources to create our training and evaluation datasets. One source was the NIST 2018 Media Forensics Challenge[4] and specifically, the annotated development datasets provided for the *Video Manipulation Detection* task. The development videos provided by NIST were split into two separate datasets, named Dev1 and Dev2. Out of those datasets, we kept all tampered videos, plus their untampered sources, but did not take into account the various distractor videos included in the sets, which would lead to significant class imbalances, and also because we decided to train the model using corresponding pairs of tampered videos and their sources, which are visually similar to a large extent. The aim was to allow the network to ignore the effects of the visual content—since it would not allow it to discriminate between the two—and focus on the impact of the tampering.

In our experiments, Dev1 consists of 30 tampered videos and their 30 untampered sources, while Dev2 contains 86 tampered videos, and their 86 untampered sources. The two datasets contain approximately 44,000 and 134,000 frames respectively, which are generally evenly shared between tampered and untampered videos. It should be kept in mind that the two datasets originate from the same source (NIST), and thus, while during our experiments we treat them as different sets, it is very likely that they exhibit similar feature distributions.

The other source was the InVID Fake Video Corpus [64], a collection of real and fake videos developed in the course of the InVID project. The version of the FVC used in these experiments consists of 110 "real" and 117 "fake" news-related, user-generated videos from various social media sources. These are videos that convey factual or counterfactual information, but the distinction between tampered and untampered is not clear, since many "real" videos contain watermarks or logos, which means they should be detected as tampered, and in contrast many "fake" videos are untampered user-captured videos that were circulated out of context. Out of that

---

[4]https://www.nist.gov/itl/iad/mig/media-forensics-challenge-2018.

Fig. 6.11 Indicative videos from the FVC dataset. Top (tampered videos): "Bear attacks cyclist", "Lava selfie", "Bear attacks snowboarder", "Eagle drops snake". Bottom (untampered videos): "Stockholm attack", "Hudson landing", "Istanbul attack", and "Giant aligator in golf field"

collection, we selected 35 "real", unedited videos, and 33 "fake" videos that were tampered with the aim of deceiving viewers, but with no obvious edits such as logos, watermarks, or cuts/transitions. In total, the subset of the FVC dataset we created contains 163,000 frames, which are approximately evenly shared between tampered and untampered videos (Fig. 6.11).

One major problem with the dataset is that we do not have accurate temporal annotations for most videos. That is, in many cases where only part of the video contains tampered areas, and the rest is essentially identical to the untampered version, we do not have specific temporal or per-frame annotations. As an approximation in our experiments, we labeled all the frames that we drew from tampered videos as tampered, and all the frames we drew from untampered videos as untampered. This is a weak assumption, and we can be certain that a percentage of our annotations will be wrong. However, based on manual inspection, we concluded that it is indeed true for the majority of videos—meaning, in most cases, the tampering appears on the frame from the beginning to the end of the video—and thus we consider the quality of annotations adequate for the task.

6.5.2 Experiments and Results

For our evaluation experiments, we first applied the two chosen filters, namely Q4 and Cobalt, on all videos, and extracted all frames of the resulting output sequences to use as training and test items. Then, each of the two chosen networks—GoogLeNet and ResNet—was trained on the task using these outputs. For comparison, we also implemented three more features from related approaches, to be used for classification in a similar manner. These features are:

- *rawKeyframes* [55]. The video is decoded into its frames and the raw keyframes (without any filtering process) are given as input to the deep network.
- *high-pass frames* [21]. The video is decoded into its frames, each frame is filtered by a high-pass filter and the filtered frame is given as input to the deep network.

- *frameDifference* [65]. The video is decoded into its frames, the frame difference between two neighboring frames is calculated, the new filtered frame is also processed by a high-pass filter and the final filtered frame is given as input to the deep network.

As explained, during training each frame is treated as an individual image. However, in order to test the classifier, we require a per-video result. To achieve this, we extract the classification scores for all frames, and calculate the average score separately for each class (tampered, untampered). If the average score for the "tampered" class is higher than the average score for the "untampered" class, then the video is classified as tampered.

We ran two types of experiments. In one case, we trained and evaluated the algorithm on the same dataset, using fivefold cross-validation, and ensuring that all frames from a video are placed either in the training or in the evaluation set to avoid information leak. In the other case, we used one of the datasets for training, and the other two for testing. These cross-dataset evaluations are important in order to evaluate an algorithm's ability to generalize, and to assess whether any encouraging results we observe during within-dataset evaluations are actually the result of overfitting on the particular dataset's characteristics, rather than a true solution to the task. In all cases, we used three performance measures: Accuracy, Mean Average Precision (MAP), and Mean Precision for the top-20 retrieved items (MP@20). A preliminary version of these results has also been presented in [60].

6.5.2.1   Within-Dataset Experiments

For the within-dataset evaluations, we used the two NIST datasets (Dev1, Dev2) and their union. This resulted in three separate runs, the results of which are presented in Table 6.1.

As shown on the Table 6.1, Dev1 consistently leads to poorer performance in all cases, for all filters and both models. The reason we did not apply the MP@20 measure on Dev1 is that the dataset is so small that the test set in all cases contains less than 20 items, and thus is inappropriate for the specific measure. Accuracy is between 0.58 and 0.68 in all cases in Dev1, while it is significantly higher in Dev2, ranging from 0.79 to 0.88. MAP is similarly significantly higher in Dev2. This can be explained by the fact that Dev2 contains many videos that are taken from the same locations, so we can deduce that a degree of leakage occurs between training and test data, which leads to seemingly more successful detections.

We also built an additional dataset by merging Dev1 and Dev2. The increased size of the Dev1 + Dev2 dataset suggests that cross-validation results will be more reliable than for the individual sets. As shown in Table 6.1, Mean Average Precision for Dev1 + Dev2 falls between that for Dev1 and Dev2, but is much closer to Dev2. On the other hand, MP@20 is higher than for Dev2, although that could possibly be the result of Dev2 being relatively small. The cross-validation Mean Average Precision for Dev1 + Dev2 reaches 0.937, which is a very high value and can be

Table 6.1 Within-dataset evaluations

Dataset	Filter-DCNN	Accuracy	MAP	MP@20
Dev1	cobalt-gnet	**0.6833**	0.7614	–
	cobalt-resnet	0.5833	0.6073	–
	q4-gnet	0.6500	**0.7856**	–
	q4-resnet	0.6333	0.7335	–
Dev2	cobalt-gnet	0.8791	**0.9568**	**0.82**
	cobalt-resnet	0.7972	0.8633	0.76
	q4-gnet	**0.8843**	0.9472	0.79
	q4-resnet	0.8382	0.9433	0.76
Dev1 + Dev2	cobalt-gnet	**0.8509**	0.9257	0.91
	cobalt-resnet	0.8217	0.9069	0.87
	q4-gnet	0.8408	**0.9369**	**0.92**
	q4-resnet	0.8021	0.9155	0.87

considered promising with respect to the task. It is important to note that, for this set of evaluations, the two filters yielded comparable results, with Q4 being superior in some cases and Cobalt in others. Simultaneously, with respect to the two CNN models there seems to be a significant difference between GoogLeNet and ResNet, with the former yielding much better results.

6.5.2.2 Cross-Dataset Experiments

Within-dataset evaluations using cross-validation is the typical way to evaluate automatic tampering detection algorithms. However, as we are dealing with machine learning, it does not account for the possibility of the algorithm actually learning specific features of a particular dataset, and thus remaining useless for general application. The most important set of algorithm evaluations for InVID automatic tampering detection concerned cross-dataset evaluation, with the models being trained on one dataset and tested on another.

The training-test sets were based on the three datasets we described above, namely Dev1, Dev2, and FVC. Similar to Sect. 6.5.2.1, we also combined Dev1 and Dev2 to create an additional dataset, named Dev1 + Dev2. Given that Dev1 and Dev2 are both taken from the NIST challenge, although different, we would expect that they would exhibit similar properties and thus should give relatively better results than when testing on FVC. In contrast, evaluations on the FVC correspond to the most realistic and challenging scenario, that is training on benchmark, lab-generated content, and testing on real-world content encountered on social media. Given the small size and the extremely varied content of the FVC, we opted not to use it for training, but only as a challenging test set.

Table 6.2 Cross-dataset evaluations (training set: Dev1)

Training	Testing	Filter-DCNN	Accuracy	MAP	MP@20
Dev1	Dev2	cobalt-gnet	0.5818	0.7793	0.82
		cobalt-resnet	0.6512	0.8380	0.90
		q4-gnet	0.5232	0.8282	0.90
		q4-resnet	0.5240	0.8266	**0.93**
		rawKeyframes-gnet [55]	0.5868	0.8450	0.85
		rawKeyframes-resnet [55]	0.4512	0.7864	0.75
		highPass-gnet [21]	0.5636	0.8103	0.88
		highPass-resnet [21]	0.5901	0.8026	0.84
		frameDifference-gnet [65]	**0.7074**	**0.8585**	0.87
		frameDifference-resnet [65]	0.6777	0.8240	0.81
	FVC	cobalt-gnet	0.5147	0.5143	0.48
		cobalt-resnet	0.4824	0.5220	0.50
		q4-gnet	0.5824	0.6650	0.64
		q4-resnet	**0.6441**	**0.6790**	**0.69**
		rawKeyframes-gnet [55]	0.5265	0.5261	0.49
		rawKeyframes-resnet [55]	0.4882	0.4873	0.44
		highPass-gnet [21]	0.5441	0.5359	0.51
		highPass-resnet [21]	0.4882	0.5092	0.49
		frameDifference-gnet [65]	0.5559	0.5276	0.46
		frameDifference-resnet [65]	0.5382	0.4949	0.51

The results are shown in Tables 6.2, 6.3 and 6.4. Using Dev1 to train and Dev2 to test, and vice versa, yields comparable results to the within-dataset evaluations for the same dataset, confirming our expectation that, due to the common source of the two datasets, cross-dataset evaluation for these datasets would not be particularly challenging. Compared to other approaches, it seems that our proposed approaches do not yield superior results in those cases. Actually, the *frameDifference* feature seems to outperform the others in those cases.

The situation changes in the realistic case where we are evaluating on the Fake Video Corpus. In that case, the performance drops significantly. In fact, most algorithms drop to an Accuracy of almost 0.5. One major exception, and the most notable finding in our investigation, is the performance of the Q4 filter. In this case, the performance is significantly higher than in any other case, and remains promising with respect to the potential of real-world application. Being able to generalize into new data with unknown feature distributions is the most important feature in this respect, since it is very unlikely at this stage that we will be able to create a large-scale training dataset to model any real-world case.

Trained on Dev1 + Dev2, the Q4 filter combined with GoogLeNet yields a MAP of 0.711. This is a promising result and significantly higher than all competing alternatives. However, it is not sufficient for direct real-world application, and further refinement would be required to improve this.

Table 6.3 Cross-dataset evaluations (training set: Dev2)

Training	Testing	Filter-DCNN	Accuracy	MAP	MP@20
Dev2	Dev1	cobalt-gnet	0.5433	0.5504	0.55
		cobalt-resnet	0.5633	0.6563	0.63
		q4-gnet	0.6267	0.6972	**0.71**
		q4-resnet	0.5933	0.6383	0.63
		rawKeyframes-gnet	**0.6467**	0.6853	0.65
		rawKeyframes-resnet	0.6200	0.6870	0.62
		highPass-gnet [21]	0.5633	0.6479	0.66
		highPass-resnet [21]	0.6433	0.6665	0.65
		frameDifference-gnet [65]	0.6133	**0.7346**	0.70
		frameDifference-resnet [65]	0.6133	0.7115	0.67
	FVC	cobalt-gnet	0.5676	0.5351	0.58
		cobalt-resnet	0.5059	0.4880	0.49
		q4-gnet	**0.6118**	**0.6645**	**0.70**
		q4-resnet	0.5000	0.4405	0.39
		rawKeyframes-gnet [55]	0.5206	0.6170	0.66
		rawKeyframes-resnet [55]	0.5971	0.6559	0.69
		highPass-gnet [21]	0.4794	0.5223	0.47
		highPass-resnet [21]	0.5235	0.5541	0.58
		frameDifference-gnet [65]	0.4882	0.5830	0.64
		frameDifference-resnet [65]	0.5029	0.5653	0.59

Table 6.4 Cross-dataset evaluations (training set: Dev1 + Dev2)

Training	Testing	Filter-DCNN	Accuracy	MAP	MP@20
Dev1 + Dev2	FVC	cobalt-gnet	0.5235	0.5178	0.54
		cobalt-resnet	0.5029	0.4807	0.47
		q4-gnet	**0.6294**	**0.7017**	**0.72**
		q4-resnet	0.6000	0.6129	0.64
		rawKeyframes-gnet	0.6029	0.5694	0.53
		rawKeyframes-resnet	0.5441	0.5115	0.52
		highPass-gnet	0.5147	0.5194	0.53
		highPass-resnet	0.5294	0.6064	0.70
		frameDifference-gnet	0.5176	0.5330	0.55
		frameDifference-resnet	0.4824	0.5558	0.54

6.6   Conclusions and Future Work

We presented our efforts toward video forensics, and the development of the tampering detection and localization components of InVID. We explored the state of the art in video forensics, identified the current prospects and limitations of the field, and then proceeded to advance the technology and develop novel approaches.

We first developed a series of video forensics filters aimed to analyze videos from various perspectives, and highlight potential inconsistencies in different spectrums that may correspond to traces of tampering. These filters are aimed to be interpreted by human investigators and are based on three different types of analysis, namely algebraic processing of the video input, optical features, and temporal video patterns.

With respect to automatic video tampering detection, we developed an approach based on combining the video forensics filters with deep learning models designed for visual classification. The aim was to evaluate the extent to which we could automate the process of analyzing the filter outputs using deep learning algorithms. We evaluated two of the filters developed in InVID, combined with two different deep learning architectures. The conclusion was that, while alternative features performed better in within-dataset evaluations, the InVID filters were more successful in realistic cross-dataset evaluations, which are the most relevant in assessing the potential for real-world application.

Still, more effort is required to reach the desired accuracy. One major issue is the lack of accurate temporal annotations for the datasets. By assigning the "tampered" label on all frames of tampered videos, we are ignoring the fact that tampered videos may also contain frames without tampering, and as a result, the labeling is inaccurate. This may be resulting in noisy training, which may be a cause of reduced performance. Furthermore, given the per-frame classification outputs, currently we calculate the per-video score by comparing the average "tampered" score with the average "untampered" score. This approach may not be optimal, and different ways of aggregating per-frame to per-video scores need to be investigated.

Currently, given the evaluation results, we cannot claim that we are ready for real-world application, nor that we have exhaustively evaluated the proposed automatic detection algorithm. In order to improve the performance of the algorithm and run more extensive evaluations, we intend to improve the temporal annotations of the provided datasets and continue collecting real-world cases to create a larger scale evaluation benchmark. Finally, given that the current aggregation scheme may not be optimal, we will explore more alternatives in the hope of improving the algorithm performance and should extend our investigations into more filters and CNN models, including the possibility of using feature fusion by combining the outputs of multiple filters in order to assess each video.

References

1. Qi X, Xin X (2015) A singular-value-based semi-fragile watermarking scheme for image content authentication with tamper localization. J Vis Commun Image Represent 30:312–327
2. Qin C, Ji P, Zhang X, Dong J, Wang J (2017) Fragile image watermarking with pixel-wise recovery based on overlapping embedding strategy. Signal Process 138:280–293
3. Shehab A, Elhoseny M, Muhammad K, Sangaiah AK, Yang P, Huang H, Hou G (2018) Secure and robust fragile watermarking scheme for medical images. IEEE Access 6:10269–10278
4. Warif NBA, Wahab AWA, Idris MYI, Ramli R, Salleh R, Shamshirband S, Choo KKR (2016) Copy-move forgery detection: survey, challenges and future directions. J Netw Comput Appl 100(75):259–278
5. Soni B, Das PK, Thounaojam DM (2017) CMFD: a detailed review of block based and key feature based techniques in image copy-move forgery detection. IET Image Process 12(2):167–178
6. Farid H (2009) Exposing digital forgeries from JPEG ghosts. IEEE Trans Inf Forens Secur 4(1):154–160
7. Iakovidou C, Zampoglou M, Papadopoulos S, Kompatsiaris Y (2018) Content-aware detection of JPEG grid inconsistencies for intuitive image forensics. J Vis Commun Image Represent 54:155–170
8. Mahdian B, Saic S (2009) Using noise inconsistencies for blind image forensics. Image Vis Comput 27(10):1497–1503
9. Cozzolino D, Poggi G, Verdoliva L (2015) Splicebuster: a new blind image splicing detector. In: 2015 IEEE international workshop on information forensics and security (WIFS). IEEE, pp 1–6
10. Dirik AE, Memon N (2009) Image tamper detection based on demosaicing artifacts. In: Proceedings of the 2009 IEEE international conference on image processing (ICIP 2009). IEEE, pp 1497–1500
11. Ferrara P, Bianchi T, De Rosa A, Piva A (2012) Image forgery localization via fine-grained analysis of CFA artifacts. IEEE Trans Inf Forens Secur 7(5):1566–1577
12. Cozzolino D, Gragnaniello D, Verdoliva L (2014) Image forgery detection through residual-based local descriptors and block-matching. In: 2014 IEEE international conference on image processing (ICIP). IEEE, pp 5297–5301
13. Muhammad G, Al-Hammadi MH, Hussain M, Bebis G (2014) Image forgery detection using steerable pyramid transform and local binary pattern. Mach Vis Appl 25(4):985–995
14. Zhang Y, Li S, Wang S, Shi YQ (2014) Revealing the traces of median filtering using high-order local ternary patterns. IEEE Signal Process Lett 3(21):275–279
15. Birajdar GK, Mankar VH (2014) Blind method for rescaling detection and rescale factor estimation in digital images using periodic properties of interpolation. AEU-Int J Electron Commun 68(7):644–652
16. Vázquez-Padín D, Comesana P, Pérez-González F (2015) An SVD approach to forensic image resampling detection. In: 2015 23rd European signal processing conference (EUSIPCO). IEEE, pp 2067–2071
17. Chen J, Kang X, Liu Y, Wang ZJ (2015) Median filtering forensics based on convolutional neural networks. IEEE Signal Process Lett 22(11):1849–1853
18. Bayar B, Stamm MC (2016) A deep learning approach to universal image manipulation detection using a new convolutional layer. In: Proceedings of the 4th ACM workshop on information hiding and multimedia security. ACM, pp 5–10
19. Bayar B, Stamm MC (2017) On the robustness of constrained convolutional neural networks to JPEG post-compression for image resampling detection. In: 2017 IEEE international conference on acoustics, speech and signal processing (ICASSP). IEEE, pp 2152–2156
20. Liu Y, Guan Q, Zhao X, Cao Y (2018) Image forgery localization based on multi-scale convolutional neural networks. In: Proceedings of the 6th ACM workshop on information hiding and multimedia security. ACM, pp 85–90

21. Fridrich J, Kodovsky J (2012) Rich models for steganalysis of digital images. IEEE Trans Inf Forens Secur 7(3):868–882
22. Cozzolino D, Poggi G, Verdoliva L (2017) Recasting residual-based local descriptors as convolutional neural networks: an application to image forgery detection. In: Proceedings of the 5th ACM workshop on information hiding and multimedia security. ACM, pp 159–164
23. Zampoglou M, Papadopoulos S, Kompatsiaris Y (2017) Large-scale evaluation of splicing localization algorithms for web images. Multim Tools Appl 76(4):4801–4834
24. Sitara K, Mehtre BM (2016) Digital video tampering detection: an overview of passive techniques. Digit Investig 18:8–22
25. Singh R, Vatsa M, Singh SK, Upadhyay S (2009) Integrating SVM classification with svd watermarking for intelligent video authentication. Telecommun Syst 40(1–2):5–15
26. Zhi-yu H, Xiang-hong T (2011) Integrity authentication scheme of color video based on the fragile watermarking. In: 2011 international conference on electronics, communications and control (ICECC). IEEE, pp 4354–4358
27. Fallahpour M, Shirmohammadi S, Semsarzadeh M, Zhao J (2014) Tampering detection in compressed digital video using watermarking. IEEE Trans Instrum Meas 63(5):1057–1072
28. Tong M, Guo J, Tao S, Wu Y (2016) Independent detection and self-recovery video authentication mechanism using extended NMF with different sparseness constraints. Multim Tools Appl 75(13):8045–8069
29. Sowmya K, Chennamma H, Rangarajan L (2018) Video authentication using spatio temporal relationship for tampering detection. J Inf Secur Appl 41:159–169
30. Piva A (2013) An overview on image forensics. ISRN Signal Process:1–22
31. Pandey R, Singh S, Shukla K (2014) Passive copy-move forgery detection in videos. In: IEEE international conference on computer and communication technology (ICCCT), pp 301–306
32. Lin CS, Tsay JJ (2014) A passive approach for effective detection and localization of region-level video forgery with spatio-temporal coherence analysis. Digit Investig 11(2):120–140
33. Su L, Huang T, Yang J (2015) A video forgery detection algorthm based on compressive sensing. Multim Tools Appl 74:6641–6656
34. Dong Q, Yang G, Zhu N (2012) A MCEA based passive forensics scheme for detecting frame based video tampering. Digit Investig:151–159
35. Fu D, Shi Y, Su W (2009) A generalized Benford's law for JPEG coefficients and its applications in image forensics. In: Proceedings of SPIE, security, steganography and watermarking of multimedia contents IX, vol 6505, pp 39–48
36. Milani S, Bestagini P, Tagliasacchi M, Tubaro S (2012) Multiple compression detection for video sequences. In: MMSP. IEEE, pp 112–117. http://ieeexplore.ieee.org/xpl/mostRecentIssue.jsp?punumber=6331800
37. Xu J, Su Y, liu Q (2013) Detection of double MPEG-2 compression based on distribution of DCT coefficients. Int J Pattern Recognit Artif Intell 27(1)
38. Wang W, Farid H (2006) Exposing digital forgery in video by detecting double MPEG compression. In: Proceedings of the 8th workshop on multimedia and security. ACM, pp 37–47
39. Su Y, Xu J (2010) Detection of double compression in MPEG-2 videos. In: IEEE 2nd international workshop on intelligent systems and application (ISA)
40. Shanableh T (2013) Detection of frame deletion for digital video forensics. Digit Investig 10(4):350–360. https://doi.org/10.1016/j.diin.2013.10.004
41. Zhang Z, Hou J, Ma Q, Li Z (2015) Efficient video frame insertion and deletion detection based on inconsistency of correlations between local binary pattern coded frames. Secur Commun Netw 8(2)
42. Gironi A, Fontani M, Bianchi T, Piva A, Barni M (2014) A video forensic technique for detecting frame deletion and insertion. In: ICASSP
43. Wu Y, Jiang X, Sun T, Wang W (2014) Exposing video inter-frame forgery based on velocity field consistency. In: 2014 IEEE international conference on acoustics, speech and signal processing (ICASSP)
44. Papadopoulou O, Zampoglou M, Papadopoulos S, Kompatsiaris I (2018) A corpus of debunked and verified user-generated videos. Online Inf Rev

45. Choi Y, Choi M, Kim M, Ha JW, Kim S, Choo J (2018) StarGAN: unified generative adversarial networks for multi-domain image-to-image translation. In: IEEE conference on computer vision and pattern recognition (CVPR)
46. Baek K, Bang D, Shim H (2018) Editable generative adversarial networks: generating and editing faces simultaneously. CoRR. arXiv:1807.07700
47. Bansal A, Ma S, Ramanan D, Sheikh Y (2018) Recycle-GAN: unsupervised video retargeting. In: Ferrari V, Hebert M, Sminchisescu C, Weiss Y (eds) Computer vision—ECCV 2018—15th European conference, Munich, Germany, September 8–14, 2018, Proceedings, Part V. Lecture notes in computer science, vol 11209. Springer, pp 122–138
48. Lee HY, Tseng HY, Huang JB, Singh M, Yang MH (2018) Diverse image-to-image translation via disentangled representations. In: Proceedings of the European conference on computer vision (ECCV), pp 35–51
49. Wang Y, Tao X, Qi X, Shen X, Jia J (2018) Image inpainting via generative multi-column convolutional neural networks. In: Advances in neural information processing systems, pp 331–340
50. Yu J, Lin Z, Yang J, Shen X, Lu X, Huang TS (2018) Generative image inpainting with contextual attention. In: Proceedings of the IEEE conference on computer vision and pattern recognition, pp 5505–5514
51. Dehnie S, Sencar HT, Memon ND (2006) Digital image forensics for identifying computer generated and digital camera images. In: Proceedings of the 2006 IEEE international conference on image processing (ICIP 2006). IEEE, pp 2313–2316. http://ieeexplore.ieee.org/xpl/mostRecentIssue.jsp?punumber=4106439
52. Dirik AE, Bayram S, Sencar HT, Memon ND (2007) New features to identify computer generated images. In: Proceedings of the 2007 IEEE international conference on image processing (ICIP 2007). IEEE, pp 433–436. http://ieeexplore.ieee.org/xpl/mostRecentIssue.jsp?punumber=4378863
53. Wang J, Li T, Shi YQ, Lian S, Ye J (2017) Forensics feature analysis in quaternion wavelet domain for distinguishing photographic images and computer graphics. Multim Tools Appl 76(22):23721–23737
54. Rössler A, Cozzolino D, Verdoliva L, Riess C, Thies J, Nießner M (2019) Faceforensics++: learning to detect manipulated facial images. arXiv:1901.08971
55. Rössler A, Cozzolino D, Verdoliva L, Riess C, Thies J, Nießner M (2018) Faceforensics: a large-scale video dataset for forgery detection in human faces. CoRR. arXiv:1803.09179v1
56. Chollet F (2017) Xception: deep learning with depthwise separable convolutions. In: Proceedings of the IEEE conference on computer vision and pattern recognition, pp 1251–1258
57. Afchar D, Nozick V, Yamagishi J, Echizen I (2018) MesoNet: a compact facial video forgery detection network. CoRR. arXiv:1809.00888
58. Ye S, Sun Q, Chang EC (2007) Detecting digital image forgeries by measuring inconsistencies of blocking artifact. In: 2007 IEEE international conference on multimedia and expo. IEEE, pp 12–15
59. Mallat S (2009) A wavelet tour of signal processing, 3rd edn. Academic Press
60. Zampoglou M, Markatopoulou F, Mercier G, Touska D, Apostolidis E, Papadopoulos S, Cozien R, Patras I, Mezaris V, Kompatsiaris I (2019) Detecting tampered videos with multimedia forensics and deep learning. In: International conference on multimedia modeling. Springer, pp 374–386
61. Szegedy C, Liu W, Jia Y, Sermanet P, Reed S, Anguelov D, Erhan D, Vanhoucke V, Rabinovich A (2015) Going deeper with convolutions. In: Proceedings of the IEEE conference on computer vision and pattern recognition (CVPR 2015), pp 1–9
62. He K, Zhang X, Ren S, Sun J (2016) Deep residual learning for image recognition. In: Proceedings of the IEEE conference on computer vision and pattern recognition (CVPR 2016), pp 770–778. https://doi.org/10.1109/CVPR.2016.90
63. Pittaras N, Markatopoulou F, Mezaris V, Patras I (2017) Comparison of fine-tuning and extension strategies for deep convolutional neural networks. In: Proceedings of the 23rd international conference on multimedia modeling (MMM 2017). Springer, Reykjavik, Iceland, pp 102–114

64. Papadopoulou O, Zampoglou M, Papadopoulos S, Kompatsiaris Y, Teyssou D (2018) Invid fake video corpus v2.0 (version 2.0). Dataset on Zenodo
65. Yao Y, Shi Y, Weng S, Guan B (2017) Deep learning for detection of object-based forgery in advanced video. Symmetry 10(1):3

Chapter 7
Verification of Web Videos Through Analysis of Their Online Context

**Olga Papadopoulou, Markos Zampoglou, Symeon Papadopoulos
and Ioannis Kompatsiaris**

Abstract This chapter discusses the problem of analysing the online 'context' of User-Generated Videos (UGVs) with the goal of extracting clues that help analysts with the video verification process. As video context, we refer to information surrounding the video, i.e. information about the video itself, user comments below the video, information about the video publisher and any dissemination of the video through other video platforms or social media. As a starting point, we present the Fake Video Corpus, a dataset of debunked and verified UGVs that aims at serving as reference for qualitative and quantitative analysis and evaluation. Next, we present a web-based service, called Context Aggregation and Analysis, which supports the collection, filtering and mining of contextual pieces of information that can serve as verification signals. This service aims to assist Internet users in their video verification efforts.

7.1 Introduction

User-Generated Content (UGC) currently plays a major role in news reporting since publishing information and media content on the web has become very accessible to Internet users. Recent surveys[1] showed that smartphone users worldwide reached

---

[1] From the Pew Research Center (http://www.journalism.org/2018/09/10/news-use-across-social-media-platforms-2018/—accessed on April 2019).

O. Papadopoulou · M. Zampoglou (✉) · S. Papadopoulos · I. Kompatsiaris
Information Technologies Institute, Centre for Research and Technology Hellas,
Thessaloniki, Greece
e-mail: markzampoglou@iti.gr

O. Papadopoulou
e-mail: olgapapa@iti.gr

S. Papadopoulos
e-mail: papadop@iti.gr

I. Kompatsiaris
e-mail: ikom@iti.gr

V. Mezaris et al. (eds.), *Video Verification in the Fake News Era*,
https://doi.org/10.1007/978-3-030-26752-0_7

2.5 billion in 2018. Bystanders who happen to witness newsworthy events often act as journalists and share content about the event in their personal social media profiles (e.g. Facebook, Twitter) and to well-known video platforms (e.g. YouTube, Vimeo). This uncontrolled spread of information has exacerbated the challenge of disinformation, also known as 'fake news', but has also created a source of important information for news stories, including images and videos, that would otherwise be inaccessible to news organizations. While the term 'fake' (typically in association with news) is very popular, it may be misleading in light of the complexity of the problem of online disinformation. In this chapter, we will use the term to refer to inaccurate, decontextualized, misleading or fabricated videos, due to its simplicity and recognition, but the reader should be aware of the nuances of the problem [1].

A top-level categorization of 'fake' videos includes (a) tampered videos, which have undergone digital processing, typically with malicious purpose and (b) out-of-context videos, which are genuine but disseminated with false contextual information. The first step towards understanding the challenge of video verification begins by investigating and analysing existing cases of fake videos from the past. To this end, we collected and annotated the first, to our knowledge, dataset of debunked and verified UGVs, called Fake Video Corpus (FVC). The first version of this dataset consisted of 104 videos, of which 55 were fake and 49 real. In Sect. 7.3.1, a description of the first release of the FVC [2] is provided together with the methodology that was subsequently followed to extend the dataset to a much larger number of cases and to extend its coverage to multiple platforms. The scale of the latest release of the FVC, called FVC-2018 [3], is large enough ($\sim5K$) to make it suitable for both qualitative and quantitative evaluations.

Most research on video verification focuses on the development of *video forensics* algorithms [4], which aim to find traces of forgery inside the multimedia content of videos. In addition, there are methods that assess video credibility by analysing the information surrounding the video, e.g. video metadata, the user who posted the video. Following the latter direction, we aim to deal with video verification of UGVs and specifically with the problem of discerning whether a suspect video conveys factual information or tries to spread disinformation—in other words, for the sake of brevity, if the video is 'real' or 'fake'. As a first attempt to assist news professionals with the verification of UGC, we developed the *Context Aggregation and Analysis* (CAA) service, which facilitates the verification of user-generated video content posted on social media platforms by collecting and analysing the online context around a video post. Specifically, the information collected directly from the corresponding video platform API is aggregated along with information that is extracted or computed by the module to form a first-level verification report. The goal of this tool is to present all the information about the video on one page in order to ease inspection and analysis of the available data by the investigator who is the one in charge of making the final decision regarding the video veracity.

CAA is a tool that aids with the investigation of both tampered and out of context videos. For instance, a tampered fake video was posted on YouTube claiming to show a tornado hitting Cape Town, South Africa. The video circulated on the web but was

Fig. 7.1 Left: the original footage of a tornado hitting Texas. Right: the doctored video of a tornado hitting Cape Town

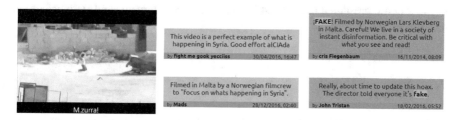

Fig. 7.2 Video depicting a Syrian boy running through gunfire and trying to rescue a girl. Blue: video comments posted below the video. Green: comments labelled as verification-related

finally debunked.[2] In Fig. 7.1, the original footage of a tornado in Texas (left) was used to digitally create the video of a tornado in Cape Town (right). CAA aggregates information about the video and provides indicators that can help investigators decide about the video veracity. One of those indicators derives from reverse image search, which may retrieve the original tornado footage and can provide evidence that there are two videos from different events merged in a single video. Videos associated with misleading contextual information could either be genuine videos from old events that are reposted as breaking news and/or staged videos that are created with the intention to mislead, or could be associated with other more nuanced cases of disinformation. For instance, a well-known fake video of a Syrian boy running through gunfire and trying to rescue a girl can be debunked with the assistance of the CAA service by leveraging the service facilities for video comment aggregation and filtering (Fig. 7.2). A case of reposting an old video claiming to capture the Brussels airport explosion in 2016, which was actually a video from the Domodedovo airport explosion in 2011, can be debunked with the help of the CAA tool by obtaining pointers to the original footage of Domodedovo (Fig. 7.3).

These are all cases where the CAA tool can assist investigators. Detailed description of the CAA functionalities and usage is provided in Sect. 7.4. While it is not easy

---

[2]https://www.snopes.com/fact-check/tornadoes-in-cape-town/—accessed on April 2019.

Fig. 7.3 A footage of the Domodedovo airport explosion in 2011 shared as footage of the explosion in Brussels airport in 2016. Reverse image search retrieves references to the original video

to devise a way to quantify the usefulness of such a tool, some qualitative evaluations of the tool are presented in Sect. 7.4.2, based on user comments and statistics of the tool usage.

7.2 Related Work

The area of multimedia verification consists of various fields of study depending on the type of disinformation under study. A large body of research concerns the detection of traces of forgery and tampering in multimedia items (InVID work in this area is further presented in Chap. 6 of the book). A family of algorithms, known as 'active forensics' attempt to deal with image modifications by embedding watermarks in multimedia content and monitoring their integrity [5, 6]. Another strand of work focuses on searching for telltale self-repetitions [7, 8] or inconsistencies in the image, without making any further assumptions. With respect to image forensics, a recent survey and evaluation of algorithms dealing with these challenges was presented by Zampoglou et al. [4]. The survey explains how these algorithms fail due to limited robustness with respect to image transformation, recompression and rescaling, as it is often the case with social media uploads, where tampering traces quickly disappear as a result of such underlying transformations.

However, there are cases where a multimedia item is used to convey false information not by altering its content, but by presenting it out of its context. In order to confirm or debunk any newsworthy item (text, photo, video), reporters will typically resort to practices such as tracking down the original author that posted the item and ideally contacting them, or looking for inconsistencies between contextual characteristics of the posted item (date, location) and external knowledge about the event. Given the complexity of the problem at hand, there are several multimedia verification fields of study, tackling various aspects of the problem from different viewpoints.

In the rest of the section, we summarize the strategies, tools and algorithms, which are introduced for dealing with the different types of disinformation. First, an analysis from a journalistic point of view is conducted, concluding that journalists are often cautious of automatic algorithms for content verification. However, they follow guides and tutorials for consulting online tools and decide about an online content veracity (see detailed description in the *Journalistic practices* subsection). Then, a description of semi-automatic and automatic content verification techniques based on *machine learning approaches* is provided. The analysis refers to the extraction of feature/characteristics of the item that is questioned and machine (often deep) learning methods for building verification-oriented classification models. We split this analysis in three categories based on the online item that is questioned; (a) rumour analysis, where machine learning practices on hand-crafted features, propagation-based approaches and neural network techniques are examined to detect rumours, (b) tweet verification, where features are extracted from the tweet text and the Twitter account that posted it and (c) clickbait content, where similarly characteristics of the post are extracted and machine learning algorithms are used for deciding whether the post is clickbait or not. Finally, the *Verification support* subsection lists fact-checking services and verification tools that exist online and can help with the verification of online content.

7.2.1 Journalistic Practices

Automatic verification methods have shown great potential in automatically distinguishing between credible news and disinformation. While journalists generally tend to distrust black box and fully automatic methods [9, 10], preferring to retain a degree of control over the verification process, such tools can provide valuable assistance to them when deciding on the veracity of online content. Journalists are often turning to social networks to extract information and for that reason, they need to use verification strategies to verify suspicious social media content and sources [11]. The first attempts to replace ad hoc initiatives with a structured framework consisted of guides and tutorials on what pieces of information are integral for verification, and how to exploit various existing online tools such as Google search,[3] reverse image search,[4] or Street View,[5] for the purposes of verification. One of these reference guides, which is still highly relevant today, is The Verification Handbook by the European Journalism Centre, edited by Craig Silverman.[6] Google News Lab provides its own set of tutorials on how to use Google tools for verification[7] and has also announced its Fact Check feature [12]. The online investigative organization Bellingcat also provides its own guides, including one specific for UGVs.[8]

Previous works in the literature try to analyse the behaviour of journalists and the practices that they use to collect and verify UGC from social platforms. For

---

[3] https://www.google.com/.

[4] Google: https://www.google.com/imghp?hl=EN, Yandex: https://yandex.com/images/.

[5] https://www.google.com/streetview/.

[6] https://firstdraftnews.com/curriculum_resource/the-verification-handbook/.

[7] https://newslab.withgoogle.com/course/verification—accessed on April 2019.

[8] https://www.bellingcat.com/resources/how-tos/2017/06/30/advanced-guide-verifying-video-content/—accessed on April 2019.

example, Rauchfleisch et al. [13] describe how journalists verify UGC during terrorist incidents, by focusing on the Brussels attacks in March 2016 and the dissemination of UGC through Twitter. With respect to Twitter as a social network for serving and disseminating news content, Heravi et al. [14] analyse the attitudes of journalists in Ireland in order to come up with a set of patterns and practices to serve as global journalistic standards. On the other hand, it is interesting how journalists and social media users approach the various technologies that have been developed for verifying social news content. Looking at the outcomes of a recent work by Brandtzaeg et al. [15], we can see that both professional journalists and citizens are at odds: while some underline the usefulness of the available tools and services for verification, others express significant levels of distrust towards them.

7.2.2 Machine Learning Approaches

Rumours are pieces of information with truthfulness that is ambiguous or never confirmed. The task of *rumour detection* concerns the accumulation and analysis of a collection of items posted around a claim. According to Zubiaga et al. [16], rumours circulating on social media can be separated into two types: (a) long-standing rumours that circulate for long periods of time and (b) newly emerging rumours such as breaking news. Automatic rumour detection methods are categorized by Cao et al. [17] into: (a) classification approaches using hand-crafted features, (b) propagation-based approaches and (c) approaches based on neural networks. Several studies have been carried out that analyse user behaviour, text features and external sources to assess the credibility of a set of tweets comprising a rumour [18–21]. Moreover, there are approaches that move beyond the extraction of features and focus on modelling the propagation of an event in social networks [22, 23]. In [22], Wu et al. present a novel approach for inferring social media user embeddings from social network structures and utilize an approach based on Long Short-Term Memory and Recurrent Neural Networks (LSTM-RNN) for classifying the propagation of news items. With regards to neural networks, RNNs are used by Ma et al. [24] to learn hidden representations of posts, without the need of extracting hand-crafted features. The task of early detection of social media rumours is investigated by Song et al. [25] proposing a model called Credible Early Detection. In contrast to existing methods, which typically need all reposts of a rumour for making the prediction, this work aims to make credible predictions soon after the initial suspicious post.

Similarly, previous works on *content verification* rely on extracting characteristics of the text surrounding the multimedia item. In Fig. 7.4, a number of such typical text-based features are presented and categorized in five main groups. A typical case is the work of Boididou et al. [26] where text-based features are used to classify a tweet as 'fake' or 'real', and show promising results by experimenting with supervised and semi-supervised learning approaches. The approach of Gupta et al. [27] deals with 14 news events from 2011 that propagated through Twitter, and extracts 'content-based' (e.g. number of unique characters, pronouns) and "source-based"

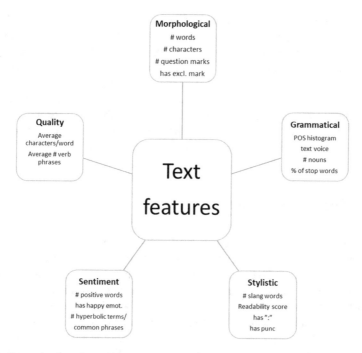

Morphological
words
characters
question marks
has excl. mark

Quality
Average
characters/word
Average # verb
phrases

Grammatical
POS histogram
text voice
nouns
% of stop words

Text features

Sentiment
positive words
has happy emot.
hyperbolic terms/
common phrases

Stylistic
slang words
Readability score
has ":"
has punc

Fig. 7.4 Categorization of text features for characterizing a news item

(e.g. number of followers, length of username) features. The approach is evaluated using RankSVM and a relevance feedback approach, showcasing that both groups of features are important for assessing tweet credibility. A comparison of the top-performing approaches of the 'Verifying Multimedia Use' benchmark task, which took place in MediaEval 2015 [28] and 2016 [29], is presented by Boididou et al. [26] showing promising results in the challenge of automatic classification of multimedia Twitter posts into credible or misleading. The work of Wang et. al [30] presents a large-scale dataset of manually annotated statements from PolitiFact where a hybrid Convolutional Neural Network (CNN) is proposed to integrate metadata with text, showing promising results on the problem of fake news detection. The International Workshop on Semantic Evaluation (SemEval) has introduced tasks dealing with disinformation such as the SemEval-2017 Task 8 'RumourEval: Determining the rumour veracity and support for rumours' [31] and the SemEval-2019 Task 4 'Hyperpartisan News Detection' [32]. Both tasks have attracted interest and participation and several machine and deep learning approaches were introduced for dealing with the challenges.

In parallel, there exist a number of techniques designed for detecting *clickbait* content. One such approach is presented by Potthast et al. [33], where 215 features were extracted and evaluated using three classifiers; Logistic Regression, Naive Bayes and Random Forests. Moreover, the authors presented the first clickbait dataset of tweets.

SVMs and Naive Bayes are employed by Chen et al. [34] to tackle clickbait detection using a variety of linguistic features. In [35], Chakraborty et al. present an extensive analysis of linguistic features such as sentence structure, hyperbolic and common phrases, determiners, part of speech tags. The features are evaluated in combination with three different classifiers (SVM, Decision Trees, Random Forests), leading to a 93% accuracy in detecting clickbait. Anand et al. [36] used word embeddings and character level word embeddings as features and an RNN-based scheme as a classifier. RNN and CNNs based on linguistic and network features were used by Volkova et al. [37] to detect satire, hoaxes, clickbait and propaganda.

7.2.3 Verification Support

Several means of verification support have been introduced in the recent years to assist journalists and other news professionals to decide on the veracity of news-related UGC. These can be broadly grouped in two types: (a) fact-checking services and (b) verification tools. With the spread of unverified information, fact-checking services have gained popularity [38] and based on a Duke Reporters Lab server in 2017 [39], the number of active fact-checking teams was 114. In *automated fact checking* [40], statements are isolated and their veracity is evaluated using reliable databases providing structured knowledge such as FreeBase and DBpedia. Such approaches are generally useful for assessing claims pertaining to historical truths rather than unfolding events. For breaking news, credible fact-checking websites such as FactCheck.org,[9] Snopes,[10] and StopFake[11] can contribute to the verification. A survey of automatic fact-checking approaches is presented in [41]. Thorne et al. try to unify the definitions presented in related works, which use inconsistent terminology, and identify common concepts by discussing fact-checking in the context of journalism. Then, related works on automated fact-checking approaches are collected and organized considering the input, output, and the evidence used in the fact-checking process. Social media platforms such as Facebook and Twitter have acknowledged their potential role as means of spreading disinformation, and as a result, anti-rumour mechanisms are being designed. Facebook intended to ask users to indicate possible rumours, which would then be sent by the platform to fact-checking organizations such as the AP, FactCheck.org and Snopes.com for verification [42]. Recently, Facebook approached Bloomsbury AI, a London-based startup, with the intention to collaborate and deal together against fake news.[12]

With regard to *verification tools*, the image verification tool of Elkasrawi et al. [43] has been proposed to assess the credibility of online news stories by applying a

[9]https://www.factcheck.org.
[10]http://snopes.com.
[11]http://stopfake.org.
[12]https://thenextweb.com/artificial-intelligence/2018/07/02/facebook-just-bought-an-ai-startup-to-help-it-fight-fake-news/—accessed on April 2019.

semi-automatic approach using image and text clustering techniques for analysing the image authenticity and consequently the online news story authenticity. The work of Pasquini et al. [44], leveraging the images attached to a news article, tries to identify the visual and semantic similarity between images that appear in articles of the same topic. Fakebox[13] is another tool for verifying news articles by providing information about the title, the content and the domain of the article. The more information is provided, the more accurate the assessment of the article will be. Similarly to Google reverse image search, TinEye[14] supports searches for similar images on the Web, which may be useful for journalists when conducting provenance analysis of online video and images.

For *video verification*, Amnesty International's 'YouTube Data Viewer'[15] returns the video upload time/date, plus a number of thumbnails (extracted from YouTube) with links to Google reverse image search. Enrique Piracés's Video Vault[16] allows archiving online videos to save them from being taken down, and provides information in four parts: thumbnails, the metadata of the video as it appeared online, the video footage and audio. It also provides a meeting room where multiple users can share these components and discuss about them in real time. It also allows links for reverse image search on the thumbnails, and a toolbar to slow down playback, speed it up, zoom in on particular areas, rotate the video and take a snapshot of particular moments.

In a relevant problem, TruthNest[17] and the Tweet Verification Assistant[18] provide solutions for *Tweet verification* using contextual information. In [45], the Twitter-Trails web-based tool is introduced in order to help users study the propagation of rumours on Twitter by collecting relevant tweets and important information such as the originator, burst characteristics, propagators and main actors with regard to the rumour. Two more tools have been proposed to help with rumour analysis: Hoaxy [46], which studies the social dynamics of online news sharing, and RumourFlow [47], which integrates visualizations and modelling tools in order to expose rumour content and the activity of the rumour participants.

7.3 Fake Video Corpus

7.3.1 Dataset Collection and Overview

The first, to the best of our knowledge, annotated dataset of debunked and verified user-generated videos (UGVs), was created in the context of the InVID project over[19]

---

[13]https://machinebox.io/docs/fakebox#uses-for-fakebox.

[14]http://tineye.com.

[15]https://citizenevidence.org/2014/07/01/youtube-dataviewer/—accessed on April 2019.

[16]https://www.bravenewtech.org/.

[17]http://www.truthnest.com/.

[18]http://reveal-mklab.iti.gr/reveal/fake/.

[19]https://www.invid-project.eu/.

Fig. 7.5 Examples of mis-/dis-information through video. Top: (i) The Pope slaps Donald Trump's hand away (Satire/Parody), (ii) Guy Verhofstadt is calling for more migration to Europe (Manipulated content), (iii) A real dragon found on a beach (False connection). Bottom: (iv) Explosion moment in Brussels airport in 2016 (False Context), (v) Syrian boy rescuing a girl amid gunfire (Fabricated content), (vi) Walmart Throws Away Good Food (Misleading content), (vii) Boko Haram leader Abubakar Shekau surrendering on camera (Imposter content)

an extended period of time (2016–2018) in cooperation with media experts from the InVID project, and the use of the Context Aggregation and Analysis (CAA) service.[20] The latter is a tool for video verification developed within the InVID project and presented in detail in Sect. 7.4. The service has drawn attention from the news verification community and has been receiving a large number of video submissions for analysis, which enables the anonymous logging and analysis of videos that were of interest to the verification community.

The first release of the dataset, called Fake Video Corpus (FVC) and introduced by Papadopoulou et al. [2], consisted of 104 videos posted on YouTube, of which 55 were annotated as fake and 49 as real. As the number of cases in this dataset was rather small, the next step was to try and expand the dataset with more fake and real cases. While attempting to expand the dataset, we had to better understand the different types of disinformation. After careful investigation of the literature, we decided to follow the categorization introduced by Wardle et al. [1]. Below, we provide some examples of videos of the FVC[21] assigned to one of the seven types of mis- and disinformation (Fig. 7.5):

(i) **Satire or Parody**: A piece of content obviously intended to amuse viewers that can be misinterpreted as fact, without the intention to cause harm. Example: A video claiming that Pope Francis slapped Donald Trump's hand away, a day

---

[20]http://caa.iti.gr.

[21]https://mklab.iti.gr/results/fake-video-corpus/.

after Melania Trump had also slapped his hand away. The latter event was real and was captured in a widely disseminated video. The video with the Pope, on the other hand, does not show a real interaction between Donald Trump and Pope Francis but was created by the late-night television show 'Jimmy Kimmel Live'.

(ii) **Manipulated content**: Content that presents real information but is manipulated in some way to tell a different story. For example, a video with dramatic music and a voice-over decrying migration in Europe, with a shot of the Member of European Parliament Guy Verhofstadt saying 'we need migration' in order to frame him as 'out of touch' and 'dangerous'. However, the phrase is cut from an interview with Verhofstadt and taken out of context, removing the nuance of the original statement.

(iii) **False connection**: Content that connects two unrelated things, where the video, the caption, or the headline promoting a story does not actually match up with the content. For example, a video claiming that a real dragon was found on a beach. It was watched more than 1.5 million times within three days of its initial posting, and many viewers speculated that the depicted creature was indeed real. The video actually shows a dragon sculpture created for Cuarto Milenio, a Spanish television show.

(iv) **False Context**: Genuine content disseminated with false contextual information (taken out of context). For example, a video claiming to depict the moment of an explosion during the attack in Brussels airport in 2016. In truth, it was an older video, shot in 2011 at Domodedovo Airport (Moscow, Russia), and misleadingly shared as footage from the 2016 attack in Brussels.

(v) **Fabricated content**: Everything in this type of story is fake and designed with the intention to spread disinformation. It could be either Computer-Generated Imagery (CGI) or staged videos, where actors perform scripted actions under direction, published as UGC. For example, a video supposedly showing a young Syrian boy rescuing a girl amid gunfire. The video was staged, and was in truth filmed by Norwegian Lars Klevberg in Malta.

(vi) **Misleading content**: Misleading use of information. For example, a video that purports to show wasted food at a store in Celina, Ohio, in fact, shows the aftermath of a devastating tornado and the ensuing loss of power. According to the company, due to a tornado, the food being disposed of was unsafe to eat after the store lost power for 14 h.

(vii) **Imposter content**: Fake content that purports to come from a real news site or recognized person. For example, a video showing Boko Haram's leader Abubakar Shekau telling his followers to end their violent tactics and to embrace peace. The video turns out to have been fabricated with propagandistic intent.

By analysing the categories listed above and the videos that fall into each one, we can get a glimpse of the breadth and complexity of the problem. On the other hand, there are also real UGVs—that is, videos that convey actual news-related facts with an appropriate context. Collecting such videos from past events is also important in

Fig. 7.6 Examples of real videos. Left: a video of a pod of Dolphins washed ashore and subsequently saved by people; Middle: live footage of a volcano eruption; Right: a bear and a man sitting next to each other

order to have a better perspective of how real and false information gets disseminated and what patterns may distinguish one from the other. Furthermore, since the dataset may also serve as a benchmark for automatic video verification, the inclusion of real (verified) videos is meant to allow evaluations against potential false detections by automatic algorithms (i.e. measure how many real videos will be erroneously classified as fake). From the perspective of creating a representative dataset, this means that the videos need to have been verified first. Videos of which the veracity could not be confirmed with confidence were not included in the dataset. Figure 7.6 presents indicative examples of newsworthy, real videos. The first video shows an extremely rare event of a pod of around 30 Dolphins that were washed ashore and stranded on the beach and then saved by local people at Arraial do Cabo (Brazil). The second video shows a volcano island on the north coast of Papua New Guinea erupting and captured on camera by tourists. The third video, the veracity of which was strongly questioned at the time of its posting, shows a man sitting in his camping chair when a big brown bear walks right up to him and calmly takes a seat.

The need for a dataset more suitable for quantitative evaluation of automatic approaches and the idea to create a large-scale index of fake and real UGVs triggered the extension of the dataset besides more fake and real cases to also more video sources. Between April and July 2017, a second version of the FVC was released, containing 117 fake videos and 110 real videos. Initially, snopes.com and other debunking sites were consulted in order to collect more debunked fake videos. However, due to the limitations of manually gathering news-related UGVs, a semi-automatic procedure was then followed in order to achieve a larger scale. Between November 2017 and January 2018, all videos submitted to the InVID Context Aggregation and Analysis service were collected, forming a pool of approximately 1600 videos. This set was filtered to remove non-UGC and other irrelevant content, and consecutively, every video within it was annotated as real or fake. In order to annotate the dataset, we used debunking sites to label fake videos, while for real videos, we relied on the general consensus from respectable news sources. The resulting FVC-2018, presented in [3], consists of 380 videos (200 'fake', 180 'real'), which were used as a basis for retrieving near-duplicate instances of them on three video platforms (i.e. YouTube, Facebook and Twitter). The following steps were executed, resulting into 5,575 near-duplicates of the initial 380 videos:

- For each of the 380 videos, the video title is reformulated in a more general form (called the 'event title'). For example, a video with title 'CCTV: Manila casino attackers last moments as he enters casino, sets it on fire' was assigned the event title 'Manila casino attack'.
- The event title is then translated using Google Translate from English into four languages (Russian, Arabic, French and German). The languages were selected after preliminary tests showed that these were the most frequently appearing in the near-duplicate videos.
- The video title, event title and the four translations are submitted as search queries to the three target platforms (YouTube, Facebook, Twitter) and all results are aggregated in a common pool.
- Using the near-duplicate retrieval algorithm of Kordopatis-Zilos et al. [48], we filter the pool of videos in order to discard unrelated ones.
- Finally a manual confirmation step is used to remove erroneous results of the automatic method and only retain actual near-duplicates.

The first posted video and all its near-duplicates (temporally ordered by publication time) constitute a *video cascade*. Examples of a real (top) and a fake (bottom) video cascade are presented in Fig. 7.7. During the manual confirmation step, an additional labelling of the near-duplicates of the 200 *fake* videos was applied into the following categories:

- **Fake/Fake**: near-duplicate videos that reproduce the same false claims
- **Fake/Uncertain**: near-duplicate videos that express doubts on the reliability of the fake claim; e.g. the title or the description of the video state that it is fake
- **Fake/Debunk**: near-duplicate videos that attempt to debunk the original claim
- **Fake/Parody**: near-duplicate videos that use the content for fun/entertainment; e.g. by adding funny music effects or slow motion
- **Fake/Real**: near-duplicate videos that contain the earlier, original source from which the fake was inspired.

Fig. 7.7 Examples of video cascade. Top: a real video of a truck driving into the crowd at a major pedestrian street in central Stockholm, Sweden, on 7 April 2017; Bottom: a fake video of a lion supposedly chasing a trophy hunter to take revenge

Table 7.1 Categories of real and fake near-duplicate videos collected from YouTube (YT), Facebook (FB) and Twitter (TW). TW shares refer to tweets that share the target YouTube or Facebook videos as a link

Fake videos	YT	FB	TW	Total	TW shares
Initial	189	11	0	200	-
Fake	1,675	928	113	2,716	44,898
Private	-	467	-	467	-
Uncertain	207	122	10	339	3,897
Debunk	66	19	0	87	170
Parody	43	2	1	46	0
Real	22	51	1	74	0
Total	**2,204**	**1,133**	**125**	**3,462**	**48,965**

Real videos	YT	FB	TW	Total	TW shares
Initial	158	22	0	180	-
Real	993	901	16	1,910	28,263
Private	-	350	-	350	-
Uncertain	0	1	0	1	30
Debunk	2	0	0	2	0
Parody	14	6	0	20	0
Total	**1,167**	**930**	**16**	**2,113**	**28,293**

For the 180 initial *real* videos of the FVC-2018, their near-duplicates were manually assigned to one of the corresponding categories:

- **Real/Real**: near-duplicate videos that reproduce the same factual claims
- **Real/Uncertain**: near-duplicate videos that express doubts on the reliability of the claim
- **Real/Debunk**: near-duplicate videos that attempt to debunk their claims as false
- **Real/Parody**: near-duplicate videos that use the content for fun/entertainment.

In Table 7.1, the number of videos per category is summarized. The category 'Private' is a special category assigned only to Facebook videos in cases where the video is posted by a Facebook User or Group, and its context cannot be extracted due to Facebook API limitations. These videos are not further considered in our analysis.

Another step followed to expand the dataset was to submit the URL of the videos of each cascade to Twitter search, and collect all tweets sharing the video as a link. It is a common case, especially for YouTube videos, to be posted on Twitter either as a link or as a link accompanied with text. This step was applied only to the earliest video of each cascade due to the large number of collected tweets (see Table 7.1). The type of Twitter traffic that a video attracts can be a useful indicator of its credibility, but it is a link pointing to a video in the cascade and not another instance of the video. While all types of videos were retained in the FVC-2018 dataset for potential future analysis, the ones considered relevant to the analysis are those which retain the same claims as the initial post, i.e. Fake/Fake and Real/Real. For the rest of this work, all observations and analysis concern exclusively these types of video.

Overall, the scale of the FVC-2018 dataset is comparable to existing datasets for rumour verification. In comparison, the dataset of Gupta et al. [49] contains 16,117 tweets with fake and real images, while the MediaEval 2016 verification corpus contains 15,629 tweets of fake and real images and videos. The data set of Vosoughi et al. [50] contains 209 rumours with—on average—more than 3,000 tweets each, the collection of which was carried out automatically in order to reach this scale. One important distinction between FVC-2018 and rumour verification datasets is that the FVC-2018 cascades were assembled from disassociated videos using visual similarity, and not from a network of replies or retweets. This is important, since in platforms such as YouTube, such relations between items are not available, making their collection rather challenging.

7.3.2 Dataset Analysis

7.3.2.1 Video and Description Characteristics

We first analysed the characteristics of the fake and real videos in terms of the videos themselves, their accompanying text and the account that posted them. We compare feature distributions among fake and real videos and present the mean, when normal distribution is followed, or median, otherwise. To further evaluate the statistical significance of the differences between fake and real videos, we compare the mean values using Welch's t-test or the Mann Whitney Wilcoxon test and report the associated p-values. Regarding video information, a feature of interest is the video *duration*. The analysis is conducted separately on the first video of each cascade and the overall set of videos in a cascade. We find that, for real videos, the average duration concerning only the first video is 149 s and including the near-duplicates the average duration decreases to 124 s. On the other hand, for the initial fake videos, the average duration is 92 s ($p < 10^{-3}$) and for the cascades 77 s ($p < 10^{-3}$). Fake videos tend to be remarkably shorter than real ones.

Concerning the *video poster*, the analysis is conducted on the YouTube channel and the Twitter Users (both native Twitter videos and tweets sharing a video link). Facebook pages are excluded since there is no available information due to Facebook API limitations. First, we examined the age of the channel/account posting the video per video platform, including the near-duplicates. For YouTube real videos, the channel median age is 811 days prior to the day that the video was published, while the corresponding value for fake videos is 425 ($p < 10^{-3}$). The values for Twitter videos are 2,325 and 473 days ($p = 10^{-3}$) respectively. For Twitter shares (tweets containing the link to the initial videos), the difference is minor (1,297 days for real and 1,127 days for fake links) but given the size of the sample it is still statistically significant ($p < 10^{-3}$). Overall, newly created YouTube channels and Twitter users are more likely to post fake videos compared to older accounts. We also find that the YouTube channel subscriber count is 349 users for real videos and 92 ($p < 10^{-3}$) for fake ones. The corresponding value for Twitter accounts is the median follower count of 163,325 users. This particularly high value is due to the fact that only 16 well-established Twitter accounts with many followers were found to have re-uploaded the content as a native Twitter video. In contrast, the median number of followers of the Twitter accounts that shared the video as a link is just 333. For fake videos, the median follower count is 2,855 ($p < 10^{-3}$) for Twitter videos and 297 ($p < 10^{-3}$) for Twitter shares.

Table 7.2 FVC-2018 statistics. The upper table contains the video duration calculated over the first video of the cascades and over all videos of the cascades. The lower table contains statistics per video platform. Dash indicates that there was not enough data for calculating the feature for that video platform (YT: YouTube, FB: Facebook, TW: Twitter)

	All video platforms (YT, FB, TW)	
	Fake	Real
First video duration (seconds)	92	149
All videos duration (seconds)	77	124

	YT		FB		TW		Tw shares	
	Fake	Real	Fake	Real	Fake	Real	Fake	Real
Channel/user age (days)	425	811	-	-	2.325	473	1.127	1.297
Subscribers/Followers (#)	92	349	-	-	2.855	163.325	297	333
Video title and description in English (percentage)	38	63	28	41	43	75	52	62
Videos with not enough text (percentage)	28	13	51	48	0	0	4	5
Polarity (float within the range [-1.0, 1.0])	0.091	0.036	0.022	0.056	0.059	0.009	0.078	0.058
Subjectivity (float within the range [0.0, 1.0])	0.390	0.376	0.333	0.307	0.347	0.379	0.452	0.391
Flesh reading ease (float within the range [0, 100])	44.13	37.72	69.27	65.70	35.19	40.89	49.03	48.14
ColemanLiau index (grade level)	15.12	15.01	8.940	11.32	21.64	18.84	17.85	18.22
Time difference (days) between initial video and near-duplicates	62	1	148	3	0	1	27	6
Comments that appear in the first video (percentage)	81	69	22	9	-	-	-	-

Besides user features, linguistic analysis was carried out on the *text* that accompanies the video. Initially the text, specifically the video description for YouTube and Facebook videos and the post text for Twitter, was processed for language detection.[22] For both real and fake videos, the most frequent language is English. However, for fake videos, the percentages are lower (see Table 7.2), namely 38% for fake YT videos and 63% for real ones. A high number of posts/descriptions, generally smaller for real videos than fake ones, did not contain enough text for language detection, that is 28% for fake YT videos and 13% for real ones. Other extracted languages which appear at a minor frequency of less than 6% are Russian, Spanish, Arabic, German, Catalan, Japanese and Portuguese, with the exception of Russian fake Twitter videos which are strikingly high (28%).

---

[22]The Python langdetect (https://pypi.org/project/langdetect/) library is used.

Building on previous related studies, we studied the following textual features: (a) Polarity, (b) Subjectivity,[23] (c) Flesh reading ease [51] and (d) ColemanLiau index [52].[24] Despite the expectation that fake posts should have distinctive linguistic qualities, e.g. stronger sentiment and poorer language [18], no noticeable differences were found between fake and real videos in our dataset (cf. Table 7.2).

Furthermore, we studied the *temporal distribution* of video cascades. A timeline was created in Fig. 7.8 to show how the near-duplicates of real and fake videos are distributed. Each line corresponds to a video cascade (i.e. the original video and its near-duplicates), while the horizontal axis is the log-scale time between the posting of the initial video and its near-duplicates. Each dot in Fig. 7.8 represents a near-duplicate posted at that time. For clarity, videos are sorted from top to bottom from the most disseminated (more near-duplicate instances) to the least. The time range of near-duplicate spread ranges from a couple of minutes after the initial video was posted up to 10 years; the most important part is that of the difference between fake and real near-duplicates distributions. There are relatively few near-duplicates of real videos posted on YouTube after 10 days from the original post, in contrast to fake videos where near-duplicates are posted at a much higher rate for a much longer interval. This observation also holds for Twitter shares. By calculating the median time difference between the initial video and its near-duplicate, we also confirm this difference. Specifically, for YouTube, the median temporal distance is one day for real and 62 $(p < 10^{-3})$ for fake videos, while the values for Facebook videos are 3 and 148 $(p < 10^{-3})$. Regarding Twitter videos, although the values are comparable, one and zero days for real and fake videos respectively, the difference is still significant $(p = 3 \times 10^{-2})$. Finally, for tweets sharing the initial video link, the median distance is 6 and 27 days for real and fake videos, respectively $(p < 10^{-3})$.

A valuable source of information surrounding the videos is the *comments* (or replies in the case of Twitter) that users post below the video. Several comments, such as the verification-related comments described in Sect. 7.4, may provide clues that support or refute the video content or claim. Additionally, past work by Papadopoulou et al. [3] offered evidence in favour of the potential of user comments for improving automatic video verification. Overall, 598,016 comments were found on the entire dataset for fake videos, from which 491,639 came from YouTube, 105,816 from Facebook and 561 from Twitter videos. Regarding the real videos, the comments are 433,139 on YouTube videos, 86,326 on Facebook and 215 on Twitter, adding up to a total number of 519,680 comments. Figure 7.9 presents the cumulative average number of comments overtime per video for the three video platforms. One may make the following observations: (a) a major percentage of comments, especially for YouTube videos, appears in the first video of the cascade with 81% for fake videos against 69% for real, and 22% against 9% for Facebook, respectively; (b) the comparison between the number of comments of fake and real videos reveals that

---

[23]The TextBlob Python library (http://textblob.readthedocs.io/en/dev/) was used to calculate Polarity and Subjectivity scores.

[24]The textstat Python library (https://pypi.org/project/textstat/) was used to calculate the Flesh reading ease and ColemanLiau index.

Real videos with Twitter shares

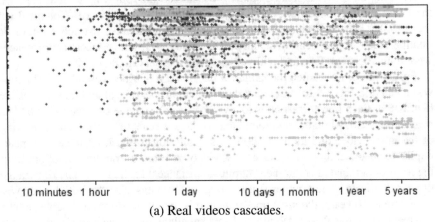

10 minutes 1 hour   1 day   10 days 1 month   1 year   5 years

(a) Real videos cascades.

Fake videos with Twitter shares

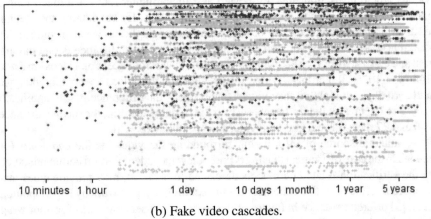

10 minutes 1 hour   1 day   10 days 1 month   1 year   5 years

(b) Fake video cascades.

Fig. 7.8 Temporal distribution of video cascades. The near-duplicates are from YouTube (red), Facebook (blue), Twitter (green) and Twitter shares (light blue)

the former prevail; (c) there is a steep increase in the number of YouTube comments in real videos for a certain period of time (between 12 h and 10 days after the video is posted), which consecutively tapers off; (d) fake videos maintain a steadier rate of accumulation, which, especially after one year from the posting, ends up relatively steeper than for real videos.

The results of the above statistical analysis are summarized in Table 7.2.

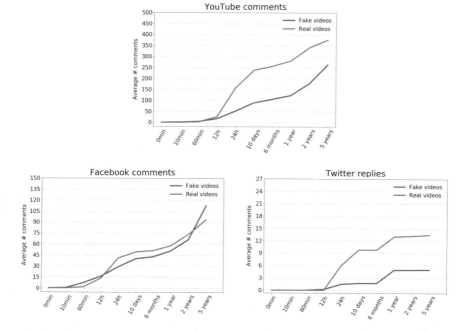

Fig. 7.9 Cumulative average number of comments/replies over time per video for YouTube, Facebook and Twitter

7.4 Context Aggregation and Analysis

7.4.1 Tool Description

The Context Aggregation and Analysis (CAA) tool gathers, filters and summarizes several credibility cues to help investigators verify videos shared in online platforms.

In early 2016, the first version of the CAA service was released as part of the InVID project, only supporting the analysis of YouTube videos. The need to extend the tool to more video platforms became apparent following a recent survey from the Pew Research Center,[25] which showed that 68% of Americans report that they get at least some of their news on social media, while a majority (57%) say that these news are expected to be largely inaccurate. Given the survey results, YouTube covers a large proportion of the population being informed about news from social networks (23%), but Facebook by far leads with 43%. Twitter follows the other two with 12% and other social media sources, including Instagram, Snapchat, LinkedIn, Reddit, WhatsApp and Tumblr, follow with lower percentages. These observations led us to

---

[25]http://www.journalism.org/2018/09/10/news-use-across-social-media-platforms-2018/—accessed on April 2019.

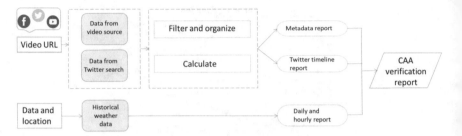

Fig. 7.10 Structure of contextual cues that make up the first-level verification report

extend the tool to support Facebook and Twitter videos. In that way, the tool will be useful for the majority of Internet users.

The starting point for using the CAA tool is a URL of a YouTube, Facebook or Twitter video.[26] Then, the tool generates a verification report following the structure of Fig. 7.10. To enrich the verification report, the date and location where the event supposedly happened could be provided as input and the historical weather data of that time and place are included in the report. Overall, the information that the service collects for a submitted video includes:

- Data from source: Information about the video and the channel/user posting the video derived directly from the corresponding video source API.
- Data from Twitter search: Tweets sharing the target video.
- Weather information at the time and place where the event supposedly took place.

The above are provided as input to the different analysis processes of the tool where they are analysed to extract three reports (metadata, Twitter timeline, daily and hourly weather) that together make up the overall CAA verification report.

At first, an extensive analysis was carried out over the metadata derived by the APIs of the three video platforms. The amount of data that each video source provides is large and raised the need to carefully filter the information. We concluded to a small, but helpful for verification, list of indicators per video source that are organized into three categories: (a) indicators that refer to the video itself (e.g. video title, description); (b) indicators providing information about the channel/user that posted the video (e.g. channel description, created time); and (c) video comments, where all comments (replies for Twitter videos) posted below the video are aggregated along with the users who posted them and the dates when they were posted. With respect to Facebook, the Graph API is the primary way to get data in and out of Facebook's social graph. There are essentially three types of accounts that may post a video: (a) 'Facebook User', representing a person on Facebook, (b) 'Facebook Page', corresponding to a community, organization, business or other non-person entity and (c) 'Facebook Group', representing a page where multiple users may post. Facebook User and Group are restricted types and no information can be retrieved

---

[26]The service supports both Native Twitter videos and tweets with embedded YouTube videos.

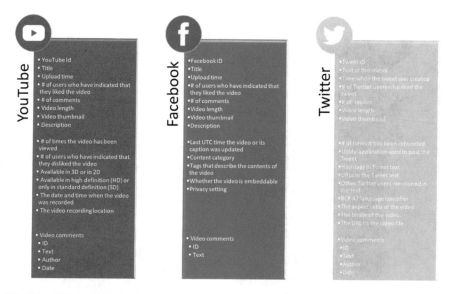

Fig. 7.11 Video verification indicators derived directly by each video platform API. Video indicators refer to information about the video itself

for videos posted by these types; some pieces of information are provided by the API only for the case of videos posted by Facebook Pages.

The next step was to map the information across the platforms and create a common reference for all videos. A considerable number of fields could be mapped across all three platforms (e.g. video title and upload time), but there are several indicators that appear in just one or two of them. For example, the 'number of times the video has been viewed' is a field provided by the YouTube API, but no such field appears in the Facebook API response; for Twitter, this was mapped to the field 'number of times this tweet has been retweeted'. For clarity, we created separate metadata reports for videos posted on different video platforms. The video indicators per platform are presented in Fig. 7.11, where on the top are the fields that are common to all video platforms and below are the platform-specific ones. Similarly, Fig. 7.12 illustrates the channel and user indicators for YouTube and Twitter, respectively.

Part of the report includes a set of credibility indicators that are calculated using the aforementioned metadata fields as presented next.

Verification comments: Users tend to comment on posted videos to express excitement or disappointment about the video content, to share their opinion or a personal experience in relation to what the video shows, and sometimes to doubt or support the veracity of the video. A list of predefined verification-related keywords[27] is used to filter the comments that may contain useful information for deciding upon video veracity. For example, the fake video entitled 'SYRIAN HERO BOY rescue girl

---

[27]The following list is currently used: 'fake', 'false', 'lie', 'lying', 'liar', 'misleading', 'propaganda', 'wrong', 'incorrect', 'confirm', 'where', 'location'.

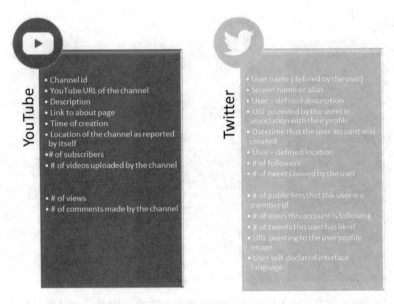

Fig. 7.12 Channel/User verification indicators derived directly by each video platform API. Channel/User indicators refer to the information about the channel (for YouTube) or user (for Twitter) that posted the video. Due to Facebook API limitations, no information about the page posting the video is available

Fig. 7.13 The fake video of a golden eagle that snatches a kid in a park in Montreal is disseminated in multiple languages. Actual video titles in English, Spanish and Russian are listed at the right

in shootout', which claims that a young Syrian boy is rescuing a girl amid gunfire, has a comment which contains the keyword 'fake' and therefore is labelled as a verification-related comment: *'FAKE! Filmed by Norwegian Lars Klevberg in Malta. Careful! We live in a society of instant disinformation. Be critical with what you see and read!'*. The comment explains that the video is staged and shot by a professional film-maker. The verification-related list was initially created in English but fake content is disseminated in multiple languages. Figure 7.13 illustrates the fake video of a golden eagle that snatches a kid in a park in Montreal. This video went viral and was spread around the Web through multiple video platforms and social media, but also in different languages. To address such cases, we translated the verification-related keywords in six languages (German, Greek, Arabic, French, Spanish and Farsi).

Number of Verification comments: The number of verification comments is an important indicator. The higher the number of verification comments, the more likely the video is unreliable or at least worth further investigation.

Locations mentioned: The location where the captured event took place can often provide helpful clues to investigators. Posting a video and claiming that it was captured at a location other than the actual one is a common case of disinformation. In CAA, location extraction from the text metadata of the video is based on Recognyze [53]. Recognyze identifies location-related named entities by searching and aligning them with established knowledge bases such as GeoNames and DBpedia, and refines the results by exploiting structure and context to solve abbreviations and ambiguities, achieving state-of-the-art performance.

Average number of videos per month uploaded by the channel: The number of videos per month is a feature of the YouTube channel. The frequency of activity of the channel for real videos is considerably larger than that of fake ones, with the average number of videos per month being 0.018 for fakes and 0.0019 for reals (based on the 380 initial videos of the FVC). Recently created channels posting sensational videos create doubts about the authenticity and reliability of the video. A viral video of a girl being chased by a bear while snowboarding was posted 5 days after the channel was created. The video gained millions of views before it was debunked.[28] The average number of videos per month uploaded by the channel is calculated by dividing the total number of videos posted by the channel to the number of months that this channel is alive.

Reverse Google/Yandex image search: CAA automatically creates a list of links to easily query Google and Yandex image search engines with the video thumbnails. Apart from the thumbnails that are documented and returned by the YouTube API, there are four additional thumbnails which are automatically constructed by YouTube under the default URL.[29] For YouTube and Twitter, the number of thumbnails is fixed, while for Facebook it varies. In cases where the video under consideration is a repost of a previously published video but someone is claiming that it was captured during an unfolding event, reverse image search makes it possible to retrieve the original video and debunk the reposted. Moreover, articles or other videos debunking the video may appear in the results, which could also offer valuable clues.

Twitter search URL: This is a query submitted to Twitter search in order to retrieve tweets that contain a link to the submitted YouTube or Facebook video.

An additional aggregation step is triggered for each submitted video to collect the ids of the tweets containing a link to that video and use them to generate a Twitter timeline report (an example of which is shown in Fig. 7.14). The tweet IDs can be useful indicators using existing online tools for tweet verification, such as the Tweet Verification Assistant [26]. The Tweet Verification Assistant provides a User Interface[30] that takes a single tweet as input and returns an estimate of the

---

[28]https://www.snopes.com/fact-check/snowboarder-girl-chased-by-bear/—accessed on April 2019.

[29]https://img.youtube.com/vi/youtube_video_id/number.jpg.

[30]http://reveal-mklab.iti.gr/reveal/fake/.

Fig. 7.14 Visualization of Twitter timeline report for a YouTube video. A tweet containing the link of the YouTube video was posted couple of minutes after its upload (vertical red line). Three more tweets were posted in the next few days

probability that the information contained within the tweet and any associated media (images, videos) is real. It is based exclusively on stylistic features, such as language and punctuation, as well as the profile of the user posting the tweet, and it returns a single value indicating the overall credibility estimate for the tweet as well as the contribution of each individual feature. For Facebook videos, we have experimentally observed that it is in general not such a common case to share them through tweets. Nonetheless, the module searches for tweets sharing the Facebook video and, if they exist, it creates a Twitter timeline report similar to the one created for YouTube videos. With respect to Twitter videos, the retweets of the submitted tweet are similarly used.

Finally, a feature that is calculated only for Twitter videos is included in the verification report. This is a verification label (fake/real), as provided by the Tweet Verification Assistant API.

Another part of the CAA verification report is dedicated to the weather data for a given location and time. We selected the Dark Sky service[31] among the few free online services to obtain weather data. To this end, the CAA module requires as input the time (in the form of a Unix timestamp) and location where the video was supposedly captured. As Dark Sky requires the location in latitude/longitude format, the CAA service converts the location name to lat/lon using the Google Maps service[32] and then submits it to Dark Sky. With respect to the time field, if the exact time (date and time of the day) is given, an hourly report is created for the specific time. Otherwise,

---

[31] https://darksky.net/.

[32] https://developers.google.com/maps/documentation/geolocation/intro—accessed on April 2019.

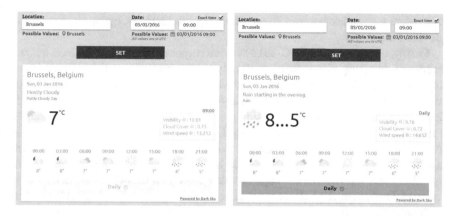

Fig. 7.15 Visual example of the hourly (right) and daily (left) weather report for a certain location. The daytime is split into groups of three hours and the temperature along with an icon indicating the weather condition at that group are presented

if only the date is given, the report refers to the whole day. The Dark Sky service provides various properties but only those relevant to verification are selected by the CAA module.

Figure 7.15 illustrates the daily (left) and hourly (right) weather reports. In both cases, the following features are extracted: (a) a short summary of the weather condition, (b) the average visibility in km, capped at 10 miles, (c) a machine-readable text summary of this data point, suitable for selecting an icon for display. If defined, this property will have one of the values 'clear-day', 'clear-night', 'rain', 'snow', 'sleet', 'wind', 'fog', 'cloudy', 'partly-cloudy-day', or 'partly-cloudy-night', (d) the percentage of sky occluded by clouds, between 0 and 1 (inclusive), (e) the wind speed in km per hour and also converted to Beaufort,[33] which is a more easy-to-understand measurement, and (f) the type of precipitation occurring at the given time. If defined, this property will have one of the values 'rain', 'snow' or 'sleet' (which refers to each of freezing rain, ice pellets, and wintery mix). The different features of these reports refer to the temperature, which for the daily report is a range from maximum to minimum temperature of the whole day, while in the hourly report the exact temperature per hour is provided grouped in 3-hour intervals.

Taking into account media experts' and other users' feedback, we extracted two new features. Although the verification comments have proven very useful for the verification process, there are cases where the predefined verification-related keywords are not suitable. Thus, in addition to the predefined keywords and the subset of comments which is automatically extracted by these words, we provide the user with the ability to create a new subset of comments filtered by keywords of their own choice. The user may provide as many keywords as he/she considers to be useful

---

[33]https://en.wikipedia.org/wiki/Beaufort_scale.

and define a complex boolean query using logical AND/OR operators among the provided keywords.

Finally, considering the FVC-2018 as a rich corpus of fake and real videos, a novel feature of detecting videos that has already been used for (mis-) disinformation is exposed as part of the service. In short, the FVC-2018 dataset includes several cases of debunked videos along with their near-duplicates, accompanied with comments about the false claim, a label indicating the type of the manipulation and optionally a link to an article or a video debunking it. The near-duplicate algorithm of [48] is used to search within the pool of already debunked videos of the FVC-2018. If there is a match, then CAA checks whether the video is unique or has near-duplicates. In the latter case, the URL of the earliest video among all near-duplicate instances is returned. Otherwise, the URL of the matched video is provided. Additionally, as part of the FVC-2018, the accompanying information (i.e. the type of manipulation and the explanation of the false claim) is also included in the report. Some special cases are handled by the CAA service in the following way:

(i) The matched video is earlier but has been removed from the video source and is currently not available online. In this case, the report contains the video metadata, specifically the date that it was published and the publisher (channel in the case of YouTube, page in the case of Facebook and user in the case of Twitter video). Moreover, URLs of other near-duplicate instances are provided, if they exist.

(ii) The matched video is later than the submitted one. There are cases where more near-duplicates of an event exist but are not part of the FVC-2018 due to the semi-automatic method used to gather the videos. In this particular case, the submitted video is either a near-duplicate which retains the same claim as the matched one or it might be the original video which was later reused to mislead.

The idea of this feature is to protect users from falling again for the same fake videos that were already debunked by reputable sources.

To sum up, the CAA tool does not provide a final decision and does not label the video as fake or real. It creates a verification report that the user should take into account, evaluate its different pieces of information and make the final decision.

7.4.2 Evaluation

The Context Aggregation and Analysis service was evaluated as: (a) standalone tool, (b) part of the InVID Verification Plugin (see Chap. 9) and (c) part of the InVID Verification Application (see Chap. 11). In InVID, applications and components are tested and evaluated in various editorial cases and trials. For CAA, tests and evaluations focused on UGVs emerging on YouTube, Facebook and Twitter. Nine Test Cycles were organized and conducted during the InVID project and the CAA service participated in most of them either as a standalone tool or as part of the aforementioned applications. The team of testers consisted of both people with journalistic background and IT specialists for testing the technical interfaces.

In addition to fixing bugs and applying technical refinements, a lot of important feedback was provided by the end users. Some of the most important recommendations include the following:

- The extension to video sources other than YouTube (which was initially the only supported platform) was a strong suggestion. At the second release of the module, we covered the most popular and used video platforms in addition to YouTube—Facebook and Twitter.
- Several variations of the input video URLs were noticed. To recognize all the different variations, a preprossessing step was implemented that takes the video URL and extracts the video platform and video id.
- In terms of error handling, the updated version provides more details when an error occurs or when a video cannot be processed.
- The possibility of reprocessing an already submitted video was added. Since new information might become available regarding an online video at any moment (e.g. new comments, likes, etc.), the ability to reprocess the video at any time and collect the new information is essential.
- Performing reverse image search of the video thumbnails was initially supported only using Google image search. After user feedback and investigation of available image search engines, we also included support for Yandex.
- Initially, just the comment/reply text was collected and presented to the user. However, the author of the comment/reply and the date that it was published was proposed as an important clue. This information is available for YouTube and Twitter videos, while the Facebook API does not provide such information.
- With respect to verification comments, requests for additional keywords and multilanguage support were taken into account and the verification-related list was extended both in terms of number of keywords and supported languages. Moreover, an additional feature was implemented where the user can define his/her own keywords to perform a comment search.

We use GoAccess[34] and GWSocket[35] for logging and browsing the service statistics. The requests come from direct calls to the CAA API, a UI of CAA developed for demonstration purposes and the InVID tools that use the CAA API (InVID Verification Plugin and InVID Verification Application). Over a period of 15 months, the service was used by more than 12,000 unique users, from all over the world (United States, France, India, Saudi Arabia and other countries), to assess the veracity of more than 17,000 unique videos.

---

[34]https://goaccess.io/.
[35]http://gwsocket.io/.

7.5 Conclusions and Future Work

This chapter presented an analysis of the challenge of verifying online videos, and ways to tackle it using contextual online information. Our starting point was the creation of a large-scale dataset of user-generated videos (200 fake and 180 real videos), along with numerous near-duplicate versions of them that were collected using a semi-automatic process. The value of the dataset to the problem at hand is twofold: (a) it provides a realistic and representative sample of past cases of disinformation based on video content; (b) it supports the development of semi-automatic and automatic tools that solve parts of the problem.

Next, we presented the Context Aggregation and Analysis tool, which has been developed within InVID. This collects and analyses the information around an input video and creates a verification report, which aims to assist investigators in their verification efforts. We experimented towards developing a video verification system that could provide the investigator with a direct estimate of whether the video is likely real or fake. Due to the challenge of the problem, we do not have yet an automatic process implemented within the CAA service. The tool is currently applicable to three popular video sharing platforms, YouTube, Facebook and Twitter. However, there are several platforms (e.g. Instagram, WhatsApp), which are currently widely used or are emerging as sources of eyewitness media. These are not possible to analyse using the CAA service due to limitations or lack of their APIs.

One pertinent issue that we faced during the development of the tool was the challenge of setting up appropriate data collection mechanisms. More often than not, platform APIs did not offer access to information that would be valuable for the task of verification. In addition, during the operation of InVID, Facebook considerably restricted access to their Graph API, as a response to the Cambridge Analytica incident.[36] This considerably reduced the amount of helpful clues that the CAA could collect about the source pages of Facebook videos. Overall, this was another strong case of the well-known Walled Garden issue.[37] The fact that popular Internet platforms such as YouTube and Facebook are in the position to control who has programmatic access to data that is otherwise publicly available makes it very challenging to build automated solutions and tools that could help mitigate the problem of disinformation.

Finally, it is worth noting that the problem of disinformation on the Web is much more nuanced compared to a simplistic 'fake'-'real' dichotomy. In fact, as became clear by the examples presented in this chapter, several kinds of video-based disinformation abound on the Internet, each with its own particularities.

The presented CAA tool combines existing metadata fields derived directly from the source video platforms along with several calculated indicators, and it aims to generate verification reports, which can be helpful when dealing with most types

---

[36]https://en.wikipedia.org/wiki/Facebook-Cambridge_Analytica_data_scandal—accessed on April 2019.

[37] A Walled Garden is a closed ecosystem, in which all the operations are controlled by the ecosystem operator.

of disinformation. The tool has been tested by many hundreds of actual end users and its increased use indicates that it is of value to the community of journalists and citizens with interest in verifying multimedia content on the Web. Yet, more research is required along the lines of (a) extending the verification report with new indicators and features and (b) making the tool output more easy to digest and interpret by non-trained users.

References

1. Wardle C, Derakhshan H (2017) Information disorder: toward an interdisciplinary framework for research and policymaking. Council of Europe report, DGI 9
2. Papadopoulou O, Zampoglou M, Papadopoulos S, Kompatsiaris Y (2017) Web video verification using contextual cues. In: Proceedings of the 2nd international workshop on multimedia forensics and security. ACM, pp 6–10
3. Papadopoulou O, Zampoglou M, Papadopoulos S, Kompatsiaris I (2018) A corpus of debunked and verified user-generated videos. Online information review
4. Zampoglou M, Papadopoulos S, Kompatsiaris Y (2017) Large-scale evaluation of splicing localization algorithms for web images. Multimed Tools Appl 76(4):4801–4834
5. Dadkhah S, Manaf AA, Hori Y, Hassanien AE, Sadeghi S (2014) An effective SVD-based image tampering detection and self-recovery using active watermarking. Signal Process Image Commun 29(10):1197–1210
6. Botta M, Cavagnino D, Pomponiu V (2015) Fragile watermarking using Karhunen-Loève transform: the KLT-F approach. Soft Comput 19(7):1905–1919
7. Zandi M, Mahmoudi-Aznaveh A, Talebpour A (2016) Iterative copy-move forgery detection based on a new interest point detector. IEEE Trans Inf Forensics Secur 11(11):2499–2512
8. Ferreira A, Felipussi SC, Alfaro C, Fonseca P, Vargas-Munoz JE, dos Santos JA, Rocha A (2016) Behavior knowledge space-based fusion for copy-move forgery detection. IEEE Trans Image Process 25(10):4729–4742
9. Teyssou D, Leung JM, Apostolidis E, Apostolidis K, Papadopoulos S, Zampoglou M, Papadopoulou O, Mezaris V (2017) The InVID plug-in: web video verification on the browser. In: Proceedings of the first international workshop on multimedia verification, MuVer'17. ACM, New York, pp 23–30. https://doi.org/10.1145/3132384.3132387
10. Zampoglou M, Papadopoulos S, Kompatsiaris Y, Bouwmeester R, Spangenberg J (2016) Web and social media image forensics for news professionals. In: Tenth international AAAI conference on web and social media
11. Brandtzaeg PB, Lüders M, Spangenberg J, Rath-Wiggins L, Følstad A (2016) Emerging journalistic verification practices concerning social media. Journal Pract 10(3):323–342
12. Kosslyn J, Yu C (2017) Fact check now available in google search and news around the world
13. Rauchfleisch A, Artho X, Metag J, Post S, Schäfer MS (2017) How journalists verify user-generated content during terrorist crises. Analyzing Twitter communication during the Brussels attacks. Soc Media Soc 3(3):2056305117717888
14. Heravi BR, Harrower N (2016) Twitter journalism in Ireland: sourcing and trust in the age of social media. Inf Commun Soc 19(9):1194–1213
15. Brandtzaeg PB, Følstad A, Chaparro Domínguez MÁ (2018) How journalists and social media users perceive online fact-checking and verification services. Journal Pract 12(9):1109–1129
16. Zubiaga A, Aker A, Bontcheva K, Liakata M, Procter R (2018) Detection and resolution of rumours in social media: a survey. ACM Comput Surv (CSUR) 51(2):32
17. Cao J, Guo J, Li X, Jin Z, Guo H, Li J (2018) Automatic rumor detection on microblogs: a survey. arXiv:1807.03505

18. Castillo C, Mendoza M, Poblete B (2011) Information credibility on Twitter. In: Proceedings of the 20th international conference on World Wide Web. ACM, pp 675–684
19. Qazvinian V, Rosengren E, Radev D, Mei Q (2011) Rumor has it: identifying misinformation in microblogs. In: Proceedings of the conference on empirical methods in natural language processing, EMNLP'11. Association for Computational Linguistics, Stroudsburg, PA, USA, pp 1589–1599
20. Zollo F, Novak PK, Del Vicario M, Bessi A, Mozetič I, Scala A, Caldarelli G, Quattrociocchi W (2015) Emotional dynamics in the age of misinformation. PLoS ONE 10(9):e0138740
21. Wu K, Yang S, Zhu KQ (2015) False rumors detection on Sina Weibo by propagation structures. In: 2015 IEEE 31st international conference on data engineering (ICDE). IEEE, pp 651–662
22. Wu L, Liu H (2018) Tracing fake-news footprints: characterizing social media messages by how they propagate. In: Proceedings of the eleventh ACM international conference on web search and data mining. ACM, pp 637–645
23. Kwon S, Cha M, Jung K, Chen W, Wang Y (2013) Aspects of rumor spreading on a microblog network. In: International conference on social informatics. Springer, Berlin, pp 299–308
24. Ma J, Gao W, Mitra P, Kwon S, Jansen BJ, Wong KF, Cha M (2016) Detecting rumors from microblogs with recurrent neural networks. In: IJCAI, pp 3818–3824
25. Song C, Tu C, Yang C, Liu Z, Sun M (2018) CED: credible early detection of social media rumors. arXiv:1811.04175
26. Boididou C, Papadopoulos S, Zampoglou M, Apostolidis L, Papadopoulou O, Kompatsiaris Y (2018) Detection and visualization of misleading content on Twitter. Int J Multimed Inf Retr 7(1):71–86
27. Gupta A, Kumaraguru P (2012) Credibility ranking of tweets during high impact events. In: Proceedings of the 1st workshop on privacy and security in online social media. ACM, p 2
28. Boididou C, Andreadou K, Papadopoulos S, Dang-Nguyen DT, Boato G, Riegler M, Kompatsiaris Y et al (2015) Verifying multimedia use at MediaEval 2015. In: MediaEval
29. Boididou C, Papadopoulos S, Dang-Nguyen DT, Boato G, Riegler M, Middleton SE, Petlund A, Kompatsiaris Y (2016) Verifying multimedia use at MediaEval 2016. In: Working notes proceedings of the MediaEval 2016 workshop, Hilversum, The Netherlands, 20–21 October 2016, vol 1739. http://CEUR-WS.org
30. Wang WY (2017) Liar, liar pants on fire: a new benchmark dataset for fake news detection
31. Derczynski L, Bontcheva K, Liakata M, Procter R, Hoi GWS, Zubiaga A (2017) SemEval-2017 task 8: RumourEval: determining rumour veracity and support for rumours. arXiv:1704.05972
32. Kiesel J, Mestre M, Shukla R, Vincent E, Adineh P, Corney D, Stein B, Potthast M (2019) SemEval-2019 task 4: hyperpartisan news detection. In: Proceedings of the 13th international workshop on semantic evaluation (SemEval 2019). Association for Computational Linguistics
33. Potthast M, Köpsel S, Stein B, Hagen M (2016) Clickbait detection. In: European conference on information retrieval. Springer, Berlin, pp 810–817
34. Chen Y, Conroy NJ, Rubin VL (2015) Misleading online content: recognizing clickbait as false news. In: Proceedings of the 2015 ACM on workshop on multimodal deception detection. ACM, pp 15–19
35. Chakraborty A, Paranjape B, Kakarla S, Ganguly N (2016) Stop clickbait: detecting and preventing clickbaits in online news media. In: Proceedings of the 2016 IEEE/ACM international conference on advances in social networks analysis and mining. IEEE Press, pp 9–16
36. Anand A, Chakraborty T, Park N (2017) We used neural networks to detect clickbaits: you won't believe what happened next! In: European conference on information retrieval. Springer, Berlin, pp 541–547
37. Volkova S, Shaffer K, Jang JY, Hodas N (2017) Separating facts from fiction: linguistic models to classify suspicious and trusted news posts on Twitter. In: Proceedings of the 55th annual meeting of the association for computational linguistics (Volume 2: Short Papers), vol 2, pp 647–653

38. Graves L, Nyhan B, Reifler J (2016) Understanding innovations in journalistic practice: a field experiment examining motivations for fact-checking. J Commun 66(1):102–138
39. Stencel M (2017) International fact checking gains ground, Duke census finds. Duke Reporters' Lab, Duke University, Durham, NC, 28 Feb 2017
40. Hassan N, Adair B, Hamilton JT, Li C, Tremayne M, Yang J, Yu C (2015) The quest to automate fact-checking. World
41. Thorne J, Vlachos A (2018) Automated fact checking: task formulations, methods and future directions. arXiv:1806.07687
42. Jamieson A, Solon O (2016) Facebook to begin flagging fake news in response to mounting criticism. The Guardian
43. Elkasrawi S, Dengel A, Abdelsamad A, Bukhari SS (2016) What you see is what you get? Automatic image verification for online news content. In: 2016 12th IAPR workshop on document analysis systems (DAS). IEEE, pp 114–119
44. Pasquini C, Brunetta C, Vinci AF, Conotter V, Boato G (2015) Towards the verification of image integrity in online news. In: Proceedings of the 2015 IEEE international conference on multimedia & expo workshops (ICMEW). IEEE, pp 1–6
45. Finn S, Metaxas PT, Mustafaraj E (2014) Investigating rumor propagation with TwitterTrails. arXiv:1411.3550
46. Shao C, Ciampaglia GL, Flammini A, Menczer F (2016) Hoaxy: a platform for tracking online misinformation. In: Proceedings of the 25th international conference companion on World Wide Web. International World Wide Web Conferences Steering Committee, pp 745–750
47. Dang A, Moh'd A, Milios E, Minghim R (2016) What is in a rumour: combined visual analysis of rumour flow and user activity. In: Proceedings of the 33rd computer graphics international. ACM, pp 17–20
48. Kordopatis-Zilos G, Papadopoulos S, Patras I, Kompatsiaris Y (2017) Near-duplicate video retrieval with deep metric learning. In: 2017 IEEE international conference on computer vision workshop (ICCVW). IEEE, pp 347–356
49. Gupta A, Lamba H, Kumaraguru P, Joshi A (2013) Faking sandy: characterizing and identifying fake images on Twitter during hurricane sandy. In: Proceedings of the 22nd international conference on World Wide Web. ACM, pp 729–736
50. Vosoughi S, Mohsenvand M, Roy D (2017) Rumor gauge: predicting the veracity of rumors on Twitter. ACM Trans Knowl Discov Data (TKDD) 11(4):50
51. Kincaid JP, Fishburne RP Jr, Rogers RL, Chissom BS (1975) Derivation of new readability formulas (automated readability index, fog count and flesch reading ease formula) for navy enlisted personnel
52. Coleman M, Liau TL (1975) A computer readability formula designed for machine scoring. J Appl Psychol 60(2):283
53. Weichselbraun A, Kuntschik P, Braşoveanu AM (2018) Mining and leveraging background knowledge for improving named entity linking. In: Proceedings of the 8th international conference on web intelligence, mining and semantics, WIMS'18. ACM, New York, pp 27:1–27:11. https://doi.org/10.1145/3227609.3227670

Chapter 8
Copyright Management of User-Generated Video for Journalistic Reuse

Roberto García, Maria Teixidor, Paloma de Barrón, Denis Teyssou, Rosa Gil, Albert Berga and Gerard Rovira

Abstract To review the copyright scope of the reuse for journalistic purposes of User-Generated Videos, usually found in social media, the starting point is the analysis of current practices in the news industry. Based on this analysis, we provide a set of recommendations for social media reuse under copyright law and social networks' terms of use. Moreover, we describe how these recommendations have been used to guide the development of the InVID Rights Management module, focusing on EU copyright law given the context of the project and the involved partners.

R. García (✉) · R. Gil
Computer Science and Engineering Department, Universitat de Lleida,
Lleida, Spain
e-mail: rgarcia@diei.udl.cat

R. Gil
e-mail: rgil@diei.udl.cat

M. Teixidor · A. Berga · G. Rovira
Universitat de Lleida, Lleida, Spain
e-mail: maria.teixidor@udl.cat

A. Berga
e-mail: albert.berga@udl.cat

G. Rovira
e-mail: gerard.rovira@udl.cat

P. de Barrón
Private Law Department, Universitat de Lleida, Lleida, Spain
e-mail: pbarron@dpriv.udl.cat

D. Teyssou
Agence France-Presse, Paris, France
e-mail: denis.teyssou@afp.com

© Springer Nature Switzerland AG 2019
V. Mezaris et al. (eds.), *Video Verification in the Fake News Era*,
https://doi.org/10.1007/978-3-030-26752-0_8

8.1 Introduction

Whilst technology is moving fast and creating new possibilities every single day, the law is far from following quickly and addressing these high-speed changes. Never in human history has law been so far from the reality it tries to regulate [1]. This is especially true when referring to copyright legislation.

Copyright has its origins in printed copies of texts, where printers found the first protection of their business through the grant of an exclusive license to print (the 'right to copy'): it was back in the eighteenth century when the legislators granted them a time-limited privilege to print. A new industry boomed allowing new actors to benefit from the generated revenues. Not only the printer who had made an investment obtained a return through the monopoly it had been granted but also authors began to have a reward for their creative effort.

Copyright evolved, following industrial developments and inventions, covering more objects (graphic prints, films, performances, etc.) and more beneficiaries (photographers, directors, musicians, etc.). Laws developed nationally, following two main systems: the Anglo-Saxon model and the Continental approach. In the first model, works are conceived as the authors' creations from which they benefit economically. In the Continental model, in addition to economic exploitation rights, moral rights are vested in the authors. These rights cannot be waived, are perpetual and legally protected.

Copyright always refers to material objects: the idea of the author is not conceivable or understood (and therefore not protected) unless it is materialised in a physical object (a writ, a painting, a picture, a film, etc.) and exploitation is not possible unless limited copies or representations of such first fixations of the work is made (a book, a poster, a music record, a film registration, etc.). But the current and ongoing technological revolution, which began at the end of the twentieth century has brought mainly two dramatic changes to this copyright system: first, the unlimited possibility for any person (not only industries) to access and make identical copies of any existing work protected under copyright at any time; second, the dilution of territorial borders. Both changes undermine current copyright legislation grounds. National legislation cannot afford a global market and traditional copyright categories, such as rights definitions or copyright exceptions, do no longer fit in the ongoing revolution.

While legislators seek to build an adapted legislative corpus to deal with this new reality (because it is still agreed that copyright is the main incentive to encourage creation, reward creators and industries that allow their works to reach the public and allow humanity to boom and progress), many technological companies like Google or Twitter have started building their own private regulations mainly in the form of Terms and Conditions that apply to the services they provide to the Information Society we are in. Therefore, and in general terms, the first assumption to make before we start any legal analysis is to recognise that we have a totally non-adapted legal framework that is being permanently questioned and that is under an ongoing discussion and revision.

In this legal context, we focus our analysis on the news industry use of copyrighted content contributed by users of social networks like YouTube, Twitter and Facebook. This kind of content contributed by users, usually not professional creators, is called User-Generated Content (UGC). In the case of multimedia content, User-Generated Video (UGV).

Nowadays, more and more news media are feeding their channels with eyewitness UGV that are uploaded to social networks. Since news media do not always directly know the owners, creators and/or uploaders of these contents, they need to find ways to ensure two very important things: first, verification of contents; second, clearance of rights so that exploitation of UGV is made without legal risks. Clearance of rights needs to be made mainly in the context of breaking news needs. Therefore, this should be done in the shortest time frame possible, since events are or need to be reported as they happen. Therefore, the objective is to study if there is a legal coverage that allows an EU-wide platform to provide (1) legal treatment of UGV for verification purposes and (2) legal use of UGV.

The rest of this chapter is organised as follows. This section continues with an overview of the applicable law from the point of view of the reuse of digital social media content from social networks, focusing on copyright law. Though a general overview is provided, the focus is placed on regulations at the European level because it is from where InVID platform services will be mainly offered. Then, an overview of current practices regarding the reuse of User-Generated Video by the news industry is provided. To better define the scope under consideration, a survey about current practices in the news industry when reusing social media has been conducted. The survey, as well as desk research and internal discussions among consortium participants, has helped prioritise the social networks to target and the kind of copyright agreements required to clear the most common kinds of content and reuses. Based on the main sources of UGV identified, YouTube, Twitter and Facebook, their terms of services have been also analysed. To conclude this chapter, a set of closing remarks and guidelines for the future development of InVID regarding rights management are presented.

8.1.1 Copyright

There is not an EU-wide copyright law that ensures a unique and common treatment of copyright in the whole EU territory. Instead, the EU has as many copyright Copyright legislations as Member States. Territoriality, as a basic principle of copyright protection, entails that copyright and related rights to copyright are conferred by national laws and enforced within the limit of each state. The object, definition and scope of copyright vary in each jurisdiction.

The need to establish a European internal market, as well as systems that ensure that competition is not distorted within it, has brought the European legislator to enact several directives on copyright EU Directives on Copyright. These directives set harmonised standards that reduce national discrepancies in specific aspects focused by each directive, but they need to be transposed into national legislation in order to be applied. This means that each state introduces the directive adapting it to its internal legislation but with some freedom to phrase it and to adopt standards in different degrees. One result is that differences between jurisdictions do exist and do not guarantee a common treatment of copyright issues within the EU.[1]

However, all European countries have signed all relevant World Intellectual Property Organization World Intellectual Property Organization (WIPO) Treaties.[2] Consequently, international standards and definitions have been introduced in their jurisdictions, which allows a common understanding of basic copyright concepts. According to this, some important concepts to understand copyright in the context of InVID are presented in the following subsections.

---

[1]The main European Union Directives include:

- Directive on the harmonisation of certain aspects of copyright and related rights in the information society ('InfoSoc Directive'), 22 May 2001. Available at http://ec.europa.eu/internal_market/copyright/copyright-infso/index_en.htm.
- Directive on the enforcement of intellectual property rights ('IPRED'), 29 April 2004. Available from http://ec.europa.eu/growth/industry/intellectual-property/enforcement/index_en.htm.
- Directive on the legal protection of databases ('Database Directive'), 11 March 1996. Available from http://ec.europa.eu/internal_market/copyright/prot-databases/index_en.htm.
- Directive on the term of protection of copyright and certain related rights amending the previous 2006 Directive ('Term Directive'), 27 September 2011. Available from: http://ec.europa.eu/internal_market/copyright/term-protection/index_en.htm.
- Directive on certain permitted uses of orphan works ('Orphan Works Directive'), 25 October 2012. Available from http://ec.europa.eu/internal_market/copyright/orphan_works/index_en.htm.

[2]Including the following:

- The Berne Convention for the Protection of Literary and Artistic Works (1886).
- The Rome Convention for the Protection of Performers, Producers of Phonograms and Broadcasting Organisations (1961).
- The Copyright Treaty, Geneva (1996), which was signed directly by the EU.

8.1.1.1 Subject Matter of Copyright

Copyright extends to both Subject Matter of Copyright:

- Works[3] understood as the product of human creativity embodied in a material form (that is, expressed); it includes cinematographic works to which works expressed by a process analogous to cinematography are assimilated; and,
- Other subject matter understood as rights protecting not works but investments made by other agents than authors (publishers, producers, etc.) helping them to make their works available to the public (books, films, music records, etc.); it includes rights granted to audiovisual producers for the investment made on audio-visual recordings of works but also of any succession of images with or without sound (which are considered as films[4]).

For InVID, this means that a UGV is always qualified for copyright protection: UGV will be a work if sufficiently creative or a subject matter of copyright if not. Why does this matter? The difference is important because (1) only works benefit from moral rights; (2) copyright protection for works is longer than for other subject matters of copyright.

The survey presented in Sect. 8.2.2 shows that most UGVs are 'simple recording of facts' so they should be treated as other subject-matters of copyright, where moral rights will not apply per se. However, those UGVs constituting video reports/stories or documentaries qualify as works as a creative effort has been made by the author, so moral rights will apply.

8.1.1.2 Ownership

Copyright on works or other subject matter is exclusively owned by

- The author that created the work, from the sole fact of the creation.
- The person (natural or legal) that made an investment in any of the other subject matters of copyright (for videos, the person recording it).

---

[3] Art. 2 Berne Convention: (1) The expression 'literary and artistic works' shall include every production in the literary, scientific and artistic domain, whatever may be the mode or form of its expression, such as books, pamphlets and other writings; lectures, addresses, sermons and other works of the same nature; dramatic or dramatic-musical works; choreographic works and entertainments in dumb show; musical compositions with or without words; cinematographic works to which are assimilated works expressed by a process analogous to cinematography; works of drawing, painting, architecture, sculpture, engraving and lithography; photographic works to which are assimilated works expressed by a process analogous to photography; works of applied art; illustrations, maps, plans, sketches and three-dimensional works relative to geography, topography, architecture or science.

[4] Art. 3 Directive 2006/116/EC '(...) The term "film" shall designate a cinematographic or audiovisual work or moving images, whether or not accompanied by sound'.

This ownership Copyright Ownership is exclusive and vests on the original owner all rights that the copyright law grants (economic rights and moral rights if applicable). This means that UGV creator (whether the author or producer) has the monopoly of copyright in it. It is important to stress that the person who shot the video, by pressing the record button of the device (mobile phone or camera), is the creator of the UGV. This should be taken into account when contacting the user that uploaded the video because he might not be the content owner if he did not shoot it. This is, even so, when the owner of a device lends it to someone who then shoots a video, as described by Dubberley in his journalist's guide to copyright law and eyewitness media [2]. The guide illustrates this fact in p. 13 with the case of a photograph of Ben Innes with the hijacker of his flight shot by a member of the cabin crew. 'The reality is, the copyright of the image of Innes with Seif Eldin Mustafa belongs to the cabin crew member who took the shot, not Innes'.

The creator will be the only person/entity allowed to directly exploit, on an exclusive basis, the video. One mean of exploitation is by transferring or licensing economic rights on the video to third parties. Such transfer or license will allow the third party benefiting from it to exploit the video within the limits of the transfer or license: the third-party's rights on the video will have the exact scope of the transferred or licensed rights.

The main conditions that will determine such scope are: exclusivity or non-exclusivity; economic rights included; duration; authorised modalities and means of exploitation; territories. A legal use of a video under a license will be the use that complies with all and each of its conditions.

The survey in Sect. 8.2.2 shows that some UGVs are commissioned videos Commissioned Content. The commission of a video means it has been recorded under a contractual agreement (including also verbal agreements) that may include a transfer or license of rights (the extent of which will depend on the agreement with the recorder of the video). In these cases, it may be that the creator of the video (the person pressing the button) is not the owner of its economic rights because the creator has worked for a media company under an agreement that directly assigns copyright to the media organisation (such assignment being as wide as the scope of the agreement).

Videos uploaded to any platform under a Creative Commons Creative Commons (CC) license are videos that already carry a license. This means the creator is uploading the video under some very particular conditions for third parties to reuse it: the specific conditions of the Creative Commons license s/he has chosen for it. A legal use of a UGV under a CC license is the use that respects all and each of the conditions of the CC license.

8.1.1.3   Extent of Rights

Copyright is a set of rights that include, mainly:

- Moral rights Moral Rights[5]: when a human creation qualifies as a work, the author has a set of personal rights s/he cannot waive such as paternity (the right to be mentioned as the author) and integrity (the right to oppose to modifications prejudicial to the author's honour or reputation). Such rights cannot be waived, are perpetual in some jurisdictions and remain with the author even if s/he transfers his economic rights to a third party. This means s/he can enforce moral rights on his works (that is, issue proceedings if s/he detects any violation of such) even though s/he may not have any economic right on them.
- Economic rights Economic Rights: benefit both authors and other rights holders (they are then generically referred to as 'neighbouring' or 'related' rights). They cover acts of exploitation of works and other subject matters of copyright. Relevant rights for the digital market, according to the InfoSoc Directive (art. 2 and 3) are:

  - The reproduction right as: 'the right to authorise or prohibit direct or indirect, temporary or permanent reproduction of a work or other subject-matter by any means and in any form, in whole or in part: (a) for authors, of their works; (...) (d) for the producers of the first fixations of films, in respect of the original and copies of their films'.
  - The communication to the public right (including, for authors, the right to make the work available to the public) as: '1. (...) the exclusive right to authorise or prohibit any communication to the public of their works, by wire or wireless means, including the making available to the public of their works in such a way that members of the public may access them from a place and at a time individually chosen by them. (...)
  2. (...) the exclusive right to authorise or prohibit the making available to the public, by wire or wireless means, in such a way that members of the public may access them from a place and at a time individually chosen by them: (...)

---

[5]Moral rights are not harmonised at the EU level but have a minimum common definition under art. 6bis of WIPO Rome Treaty:

'(1) Independently of the author's economic rights, and even after the transfer of the said rights, the author shall have the right to claim authorship of the work and to object to any distortion, mutilation or other modification of, or other derogatory action in relation to, the said work, which would be prejudicial to his honour or reputation.

(2) The rights granted to the author in accordance with the preceding paragraph shall, after his death, be maintained, at least until the expiry of the economic rights, and shall be exercisable by the persons or institutions authorised by the legislation of the country where protection is claimed. However, those countries whose legislation, at the moment of their ratification of or accession to this Act, does not provide for the protection after the death of the author of all the rights set out in the preceding paragraph may provide that some of these rights may, after his death, cease to be maintained.

(3) The means of redress for safeguarding the rights granted by this Article shall be governed by the legislation of the country where protection is claimed.'

(c) for the producers of the first fixations of films, of the original and copies of their films'.

- Other Directives set compensation rights (when uses by third parties are made under legal exceptions or when exploitation cannot be individually authorised by the author). Primary rights will be managed by the rights holder directly or through his agents; compensation rights will mostly be managed by collective copyright societies.

For InVID, and considering that (1) eyewitness recordings of facts may not always qualify as a work but will always qualify as an audiovisual recording with neighbouring rights and (2) the acts of exploitation involve reproduction and public communication of the work or audiovisual recording, this means that UGV will always need copyright clearance with the author or rights holder.

8.1.1.4 Duration

Copyright is limited in time; although terms have been harmonised under the Directive 93/98/EEC, later replaced by Directive 2006/116/EC of the European Parliament and of the Council of 12 December 2006 on the term of protection of copyright and certain related rights, national legislations may still apply in their territories longer term for some works because of transitional provision periods in the adoption of the Directive.

- For works: copyright protection lasts for the lifetime of the author plus 70 years, though there are some special provisions such as with co-authorship works. In this case, the period starts running upon the death of the last of the co-authors.[6] After this period, works enter the public domain and can be freely exploited provided moral rights on the work are respected.
- For audiovisual recordings: related rights protection lasts for 50 years from the moment the recording was made or was first published.[7] After this period, recordings enter the public domain and can be freely exploited.

Considering the reuse of eyewitness recordings of current facts for breaking news, they will rarely exceed the above mentioned periods and will not be in the public domain. Consequently, reuses of UGVs from the duration perspective will always require authorisation from the copyright holder.

---

[6]Art. 1 Directive 2006/116/EC: "1. The rights of an author of a literary or artistic work within the meaning of Article 2 of the Berne Convention shall run for the life of the author and for 70 years after his death, irrespective of the date when the work is lawfully made available to the public".

[7]Art. 3 Directive 2006/116/EC: 'The rights of producers of the first fixation of a film shall expire 50 years after the fixation is made. However, if the film is lawfully published or lawfully communicated to the public during this period, the rights shall expire 50 years from the date of the first such publication or the first such communication to the public, whichever is the earlier'.

8.1.1.5 Exceptions

There is not any 'fair use' Fair Use provision in the EU that would give users the possibility to copy any copyright protected works or other subject-matters of copyright for limited and transformative purposes such as comment upon, criticism or parody as a defence for copyright infringement claims as it does exist in the United States.

Instead of that, the EU copyright framework works with limits and exceptions to copyright Copyright Exceptions. Such limits and exceptions search a balance between the exclusive rights of authors and rights holders and other fundamental rights vested in other individuals that enter into conflict with copyright when these individuals are users of copyright-protected works or other subject matters of copyright. Because authors' rights are also human rights, any exception or limit to them is of strict interpretation.

The Directive on the harmonisation of certain aspects of copyright and related rights in the information society (the so-called InfoSoc Directive), of 22 May 2001 harmonised the right of reproduction, the right of communication to the public, the right of making available to the public and the distribution right [3], with the effort to provide the rights holders with a high level of protection: the scope of exclusive rights were very broadly defined and adapted to the online environment. The Directive also introduced, in Article 5,[8] an exhaustive list of exceptions to copyright protection to allow for certain, specific activities that pertain to scientific research, the activities of libraries, and to disabled people. This list includes one mandatory exception, Exception 5.1, and twenty optional exceptions, Exceptions 5.2(a-o), as shown in Fig. 8.1. Member States' ability to introduce exceptions or extend the scope of any existing ones in their legislations is limited by the Directive's list.

According to paragraph 5 of Art. 5, all of these exceptions and limitations 'shall only be applied in certain special cases which do not conflict with a normal exploitation of the work or other subject-matter and do not unreasonably prejudice the legitimate interests of the rights holder' introducing here the Berne Convention 'three steps test'.[9]

8.1.1.6 Linking

The act of linking (including hyperlinking, deep linking, framing and embedding) refers to the act where no reproduction of works is made but the access to a work originally posted anywhere in the net is provided through an own page or site. According

---

[8]Directive 2001/29/EC of the European Parliament and of the Council of 22 May 2001 on the harmonisation of certain aspects of copyright and related rights in the information society http://eur-lex.europa.eu/legal-content/en/ALL/?uri=CELEX%3A32001L0029.

[9]Art. 9 Berne Convention: '(2) It shall be a matter for legislation in the countries of the Union to permit the reproduction of such works in certain special cases, provided that such reproduction does not conflict with a normal exploitation of the work and does not unreasonably prejudice the legitimate interests of the author. (3) Any sound or visual recording shall be considered as a reproduction for the purposes of this Convention'.

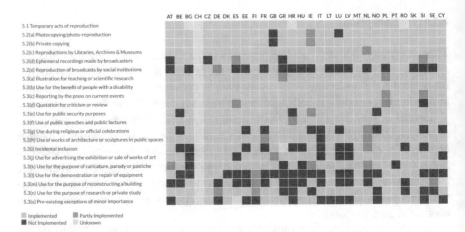

Fig. 8.1 Copyright exceptions in the European Union and their implementation status in the corresponding countries (*Source* http://copyrightexceptions.eu)

to a recent Court of Justice of the European Union ruling,[10] linking does not infringe copyright provided several conditions are met:

1. The linked work has legally been made available online with the consent of the rights holder.
2. No protection measures are circumvented, so the work is not communicated to any new public.
3. Persons acting for profit when publishing links should carry out the necessary checks to ensure that the work linked to is not illegally published.
4. Persons acting not for profit and publishing links to works made available cannot reasonably know that the work has been published without consent.

8.1.1.7 Orphan Works

These are works or phonograms protected by copyright in which no rights holders are identified or, even if one or more of them is identified, none is located despite a diligent search for them has been carried out (according to article 2.1 of the Directive 2012/28/EU). In this cases, this regulation authorises certain reuses of the content without requiring prior authorisation, as detailed in Annex A. However, InVID cannot benefit from this special permission because it is not one of the kinds of organisations enjoying it: public libraries, museums, educational establishments, archives, film or audio heritage institutions or public service broadcasters.

---

[10]See: Svensson case (C466/12); BestWater case (C-348/13); Sanoma case (C-160/15).

8.1.2   Relevant e-Commerce Legislation

Since InVID is an online service, it also needs to take into account e-Commerce legislation: The overall goal of the EU harmonisation efforts is to enable copyright-protected goods (e.g. films, software etc.) and services (e.g. services offering access to these goods and or providing verification of these works) to move freely within the internal market.

Directive 2000/31/EC on electronic commerce created the basic legal framework for online services, including electronic commerce in the Internal Market. The Directive removes obstacles to cross-border online services in the European Union and provides legal certainty to business and citizens alike. It establishes harmonised rules on issues such as the transparency and information requirements for online service providers, commercial communications, electronic contracts and limitations of liability of intermediary service providers.

The proper functioning of the Internal Market in electronic commerce is ensured by the Internal Market clause, which means that information society services are, in principle, subject to the law of the Member State in which the service provider is established. In turn, the Member State in which the information society service is received cannot restrict incoming services.

An intermediary service provider is an organisation that provides services for accessing, using or participating in the Internet; they may be organised in various forms, such as commercial, non-profit; privately owned, community owned. These services include also services provided free of charge to the recipient and funded, for example, by advertising or sponsorship.

In what may be of interest for the InVID project, it shall be pointed out that intermediary service providers storing information provided by the recipient of the service shall not be held responsible for contents uploaded by users in their platforms as long as:

1. It does not have knowledge of illegal activity or information and is not aware of facts or circumstances from which illegality is apparent;
2. Upon obtaining such knowledge or awareness, it acts expeditiously to remove or disable access to the information.

Therefore, if InVID provides tools for users to verify and license this content but does not upload content itself, it might be in a safer position regarding responsibility for possible infringing material uploaded by its users.

8.1.3   Future EU-Copyright Developments

At present, the proposed Directive on Copyright in the Digital Single Market 2016/0280 (COD) has been approved by the EU Parliament and the trilogue negotiations have begun, their conclusion being expected for early 2019. Recital 3 of the proposed Directive clearly points out that '*legal uncertainty remains, for both rights holders and users, as regards certain uses, including cross-border uses, of works and other subject-matter in the digital environment (...) there is a need to adapt and supplement the current EU copyright framework. This Directive provides for rules to adapt certain exceptions and limitations to digital and cross-border environments, as well as measures to facilitate certain licensing practices as regards the dissemination of out-of-commerce works and the online availability of audiovisual works on video-on-demand platforms with a view to ensuring wider access to content. In order to achieve a well functioning and fair marketplace for copyright, there should also be rules on the exercise and enforcement of the use of works and other subject-matter on online service providers platforms and on the transparency of authors' and performers' contracts and of the accounting linked with the exploitation of protected works in accordance with those contracts*'.[11]

In what may be of interest for the InVID project, the Directive addresses the liability of platforms (ISP) storing and giving access to large amounts of works uploaded by users for copyright infringements arising from such UGC (art. 13); therefore, it imposes new obligations for these ISP, such as the obligation to conclude agreements with rights holders in order to use their works and the obligation to cooperate in good faith with right holders to ensure unlawful content is not made available in the platforms. Some platforms have been excluded from this obligation such as those providing non-commercial services, small-sized enterprises (less than 50 employees, and a turnover below 10 million euros) and microenterprises (less than 10 employees and a turnover below 2 million euros).

The Directive also includes a text and data mining mandatory exception in the field of scientific research (art. 3), thus allowing scientists to analyse big corpora of text and data of materials that are lawfully accessible with the legal certainty that this activity does not amount to copyright infringement. The exception only benefits a limited group of beneficiaries ('research organisations': universities, research institutes or organisations conducting scientific research as their primary goal, on a non-profit basis or pursuant to a public interest mission recognised by a Member State) which entails that those that do not fall into the group will require rights holders' authorisation before they engage in text and data mining activities.

The changes introduced by the Directive will not significantly change the way InVID deals with copyright. In any case, their evolution will be monitored as stated in the conclusions and future work section, Sect. 8.4.

---

[11] https://eur-lex.europa.eu/legal-content/EN/TXT/PDF/?uri=CELEX:52016PC0593.

8.2 State of the Art

8.2.1 Review of Current Practices in the Media Industry

In April 2014, the Tow Center for Digital Journalism published a report on amateur footage[12] showing that, while 'UGC is used by news organisations daily', mainly 'when another imagery is not available', 'news organisations are poor at acknowledging when they are using UGC and worse at crediting the individuals responsible for capturing it'.

The key findings of the content analysis undertaken in 2013 for that report showed that as much as '72% of UGC was not labelled or described as UGC' and 'just 16% of UGC on TV had an onscreen credit'. The same report outlined that these 'troubling practices exist across both television and web platforms'.

The authors, Claire Wardle, Sam Dubberley and Pete Brown, wrote that many of the 64 interviews conducted for their research with news managers, editors, and journalists from 38 news organisations based in 24 countries around the world, 'used the term "Wild West" to describe the current landscape'.

'Most journalists, however, now know that copyrights exist with uploaders even after they share it on a social network and understand the need to seek specific permission to use someone's content. Still, there's a difference between what people know and what people do', this report explains.

'Certainly the pressure of rolling news means that there are more situations on 24-h news channels where a senior editor will make the decision to run with pictures without securing permission (knowing they will "sort it out" retrospectively if necessary) than on daily bulletin programmes. Broadcasters working outside the pressures of rolling news explained that obtaining permission from an uploader was mandatory before using the content'.

In InVID, we have been constantly analysing breaking news events (and their corresponding videos) to update our use cases and requirements as well as to keep up with new developments in online video usage.

During the Brussels bombings of March 22 2016, the video[13] corresponding to the frame shown in Fig. 8.2 was taken by a witness from the airport parking lot. This video was then shared with the Flemish publication Joods Actueel and through the WhatsApp mobile app where Anna Aronheim, then a defence correspondent for the Israeli 24 h news television channel i24news.tv, picked it up and shared it via her Twitter user channel. The video was retweeted more than 27,000 times and ended up very quickly on almost every news website and every news television worldwide, both in Web and broadcast.

It's only 6 hours after that Mrs. Aronheim acknowledged, in response to inquiries, that she was not in Brussels and that she had picked up the video from WhatsApp,

---

[12]https://academiccommons.columbia.edu/doi/10.7916/D88S526V.

[13]https://www.youtube.com/watch?v=Khb8DaXVXRI (first video posted on YouTube on 22 March 2016).

Fig. 8.2 Screenshot of Brussels airport bombing video from parking lot, March 22 2016. Video captured by Pinchas Kopferstein

without identifying the source of the footage. A couple of hours later, the Storyful 'social news agency' as it defines itself claimed they had got the diffusion rights on this video from the owner and issued a copyright.

Two days later, David Clinch, global news editor at Storyful, was interviewed by the WAN-IFRA World Editors Forum, and complained against 'the mass misattribution of a viral video'.[14]

In the study summarised in Table 8.1, conducted in November 2016, 8 months after the Brussels bombings, we initially used the same panel of media as in the Tow Center report on amateur footage, listed in Table 8.2, and looked at copyright and credit mentions of the Brussels video.

Then, we completed our study incorporating more media brands, as summarised in Table 8.3.

The above is just an illustrative example but shows the same results as the more systematic study conducted by the Tow Center about amateur footage and it also supports David Clinch's claim of 'mass misattribution'. Like Tow Center report's findings, channels do not properly mention the copyright holder or give proper credit to the owner. We find the same evidence with the viral video of the Brussels airport bombing.

Several reasons explain these findings:

- First, the urgency to report on breaking news events, especially when the only available eyewitness media comes from social networks. The cross-publishing of videos from mobile networks to web platforms render even more difficult the task to confirm the content ownership and to secure proper attribution.

---

[14]http://blog.wan-ifra.org/2016/03/24/mass-misattribution-of-viral-brussels-video.

Table 8.1 Copyright and credit mentions for the Brussels bombings viral video

Media and video link	Credit	Copyright	Mention (soundtrack/text)
Euronews English[a]	No	No	No
Euronews Hungarian[b]	No	No	No
CNN[c]	news_executive	@news_executive	No
BBC[d]	BBC	BBC	BBC TV coverage from Brussels as a series of explosions hit the city[e]
France 24[f]	@AAronheim	No	Aronheim tweet[g]
France 24 Arabic YT channel[h]	No	No	No
Telesur[i]	No	No	No
Al Jazeera English[j]	No	No	No
NHK World	N/A	N/A	N/A
Al Jazeera Arabic[k]	No	No	No

[a]http://www.euronews.com/2016/03/22/panic-and-chaos-follows-brussels-airport-blasts
[b]http://hu.euronews.com/2016/03/22/magara-vallalta-az-iszlam-allam-a-brusszeli-merenyleteket
[c]http://edition.cnn.com/videos/world/2016/03/22/brussels-airport-blast-explosions-elbagir-lklv.
cnn/video/playlists/deadly-explosions-rock-brussels/www.cnn.com
[d]http://www.bbc.com/news/world-35869074
[e]According to sources from the European Broadcasting Union, it seems that the BBC was among the media who managed to get in touch with the content owner and to reuse the video, although no proper credit is displayed
[f]http://mashable.france24.com/monde/20160322-les-images-amateurs-des-attentats-de-bruxelles?page=24
[g]The video was not retrieved on two of the three France 24 channels (French, English) but it was present on the French version of the Mashable publication, which is partially owned by France 24
[h]https://www.youtube.com/watch?v=5fO7huMnRgI
[i]http://videos.telesurtv.net/video/523613/belgicaelevan-alerta-maxima-en-bruselas-tras-atentados-con-explosivos
[j]http://video.aljazeera.com/channels/eng/videos/brussels-attacks:-explosions-hit-airport-and-metro/4811922768001
[k]http://www.aljazeera.net/news/international/2016/3/22/

Table 8.2 List of media outlets analysed in the Tow Center report on amateur footage

News organisation	Location of headquarters	Language
Al Jazeera Arabic	Doha, Qatar	Arabic
Al Jazeera English	Doha, Qatar	English
BBC World	London, United Kingdom	English
CNN International	Atlanta, United States	English
Euronews	Lyon, France	English
France 24	Paris, France	French
NHK World	Tokyo, Japan	English
Telesur	Caracas, Venezuela	Spanish

Table 8.3 Copyright and credit mentions by media brands beyond those in the Tow Center report

Media and video link	Credit	Copyright	Mention (soundtrack/text)
Deutsche Welle[a]	@AAronheim	No	Aronheim tweet
BFMTV[b]	@AAronheim	No	Aronheim tweet and several screenshots with BFMTV logo
Sky news[c]	Pictures Anna Aronheim	No	No
N24 Deutschland[d]	@AAronheim	No	No
i24news English[e]	No	No	No
i24news French[f]	No	No	No
Russia Today English[g]	@tar791	No	No
Russia Today English[h]	Courtesy @exen	No	No
Russia Today English[i]	@AAronheim	No	Aronheim tweet
RTVE[j]	No	No	Twitter images
Fox News[k]	Fox News	No	No
ABC News Australia[l]	ABC News	No	No

[a]http://www.dw.com/en/blasts-in-brussels-live-updates/a-19132784
[b]http://www.bfmtv.com/international/explosions-a-l-aeroport-de-bruxelles-961016.html
[c]http://news.sky.com/video/video-passengers-flee-after-blasts-at-brussels-airport-10215814
[d]http://www.n24.de/n24/Nachrichten/Politik/d/8260954/internationale-reaktionen-auf-die-anschlaege.html
[e]http://www.i24news.tv/en/tv/replay/news/x3zbfrl
[f]http://www.i24news.tv/fr/tv/revoir/no-playlist/x3zbnot
[g]https://www.rt.com/news/336593-explosions-brussels-video-inside/
[h]https://www.rt.com/news/336519-explosions-hit-brussels-airport/
[i]https://www.rt.com/news/336523-brussels-zaventem-visitors-flee/
[j]http://www.rtve.es/alacarta/videos/los-desayunos-de-tve/desayunos-bruselas-220316/3533764/
[k]http://video.foxnews.com/v/4812990754001/?#sp=show-clips
[l]http://www.abc.net.au/news/2016-03-22/brussels-airport-metro-rocked-by-explosions/7268106

- Second, the pressure of rolling news is very strong in breaking news situations and sometimes produces a ripple effect that eases the spread of hoaxes. If some big brand publishes a breaking news UGC video, other media are likely to follow, sometimes at the expense of being less rigorous in the verification process (and/or assuming that the big trustable brands have verified it and cleared the right to use it), taken for granted that the right of the public to be informed in a breaking news situation will overpass other rights.
- Third, the profusion of social networks, mobile instant messaging applications, microblogging platforms and new web sources is increasing competition (for media), complexity (for journalists and verifiers) and spreading speed.

8.2.2   Survey of Copyright Management News Industry Practices

This section includes the questions and responses from an online survey conducted to gather information about current practices in the news industry when dealing with UGV content and copyright. During the requirements collection phase of the InVID project, seven responses were collected to the survey available online as a Google Form.[15]

The survey includes questions about:

- The origin of UGVs, like WhatsApp, Reddit, 4chan, Go-Pro community channel, Snapchat, Instagram, Bambuser, Vine, Vimeo, Daily Motion, Meerkat, Periscope online, Twitter, Facebook or YouTube.
- The nature of UGVs, ranging among simple recordings of facts, video reports/stories, documentaries or other types identified by the responder. Additionally, it was also requested the amount of reused UGVs that were commissioned, if any.
- The current UGV rights management process, including how copyright owner are identified, contacted to get permission for the reuse and if records of such authorisations are kept.
- The relationships with content generators, like content providers proactively offering UGVs or the existence of an internal register of productive UGV providers that are contacted or encouraged to provide content.
- The experience with litigations about UGV, including litigation experiences and arrangements regarding those litigations.
- The requirements for an automated user-generated video rights management system that might support them during the process of clearing the rights of UGVs.

The full results for the survey are available [4] and this chapter just includes a summary of the main outcomes. Regarding the origin of UGV reused by the news industry, responses to the questionnaire place the focus on three social networks as the main sources of social media for news reporting: YouTube, Facebook and Twitter.

From the point of view of the nature of these videos, they are mainly recordings of facts, thus constituting subject-matter, not works, consequently not having associated moral rights as detailed in Sect. 8.1.1.1

When dealing with UGV rights, the main source to identify the owner is via social media user profiles, according to the survey results, and via direct conversation on the phone (or Skype and such like). Contributors are contacted mainly through social media messages. However, the most common way to get the authorisation to reuse is via e-mail.

Usually, the respondents keep record of these authorisations and include specific terms or conditions, which are related to specific territories, restricted time periods, exclusivity conditions or compensation requests.

Regarding the relationship with UGV creators, respondents only occasionally have content sent to them proactively. Respondents said they do keep track of users

---

[15] https://goo.gl/forms/DoyEpLzCkBdph9J23.

generating interesting content, but do not encourage them to generate and supply content actively. Most respondents have not been involved in litigations about UGV.

Finally, regarding what they would like to see in a UGV rights management system, they are interested in support through the whole process, from identifying and contacting the owner to obtaining a reuse authorisation the system keeps track of. They also want the system to be able to quickly reach the owner and clearly communicate the intended reuse so an agreement can be reached in a timely manner.

8.2.3 Social Networks Policies Regarding User-Generated Content

The focus of this section is on the social networks' policies regarding the social media made available through them. This is a key issue to explore in how InVID and its users can reuse social media. As the survey results show, the main sources of social media are YouTube, Facebook and Twitter. This is also supported by the experience of the InVID partners part from the news industry. The following sections summarise the relevant parts of social networks' Terms and Conditions (T&C) regarding content Terms and Conditions.

8.2.3.1 YouTube

Regarding content, YouTube's Terms of Service,[16] they state that content should not be directly downloaded and that the content owner retains all rights. Consequently, the owner should be contacted to seek authorisation for uses beyond consuming the content through YouTube services. It is assumed that the content owner is the person who has uploaded the content since s/he has claimed so when uploading the content by accepting YouTube terms for uploaded content: but this assumption may not always be true since many users are uploading third-parties content to social media platforms.

In this regard, YouTube makes the recommendations presented next when re-broadcasting YouTube content.[17] This also applies when republishing content outside the context of YouTube, for instance making the video available through a newspaper website without using YouTube features for video embedding:

- 'Credit the content owner. Though YouTube has a license to distribute the video, it's the YouTube user who owns the content. We encourage you to reach out to users directly when you find video you'd like to use, and to provide attribution by displaying the username or the real name of the individual, if you've obtained it'.

---

[16]https://developers.google.com/youtube/terms.
[17]https://www.youtube.com/yt/press/media.html.

- 'Credit YouTube in your re-broadcast of the video. When you show a YouTube video on television, please include on-screen and verbal attribution'.
- 'Contacting a YouTube user. Clicking on a YouTube username will take you to the user's channel, where you can see what personal information s/he has shared (name, website, location, etc.). From here, you can use YouTube's on-site messaging system to contact the user. First, you must be logged into your own YouTube account. Then, click on the username of the individual you'd like to reach out to and select "Send Message"'.

The previous guidelines apply to any video available under YouTube's terms. Alternatively, YouTube contemplates that uploaders make their content available using a Creative Commons license, concretely the CC-BY license: 'by marking an original video of your property with a Creative Commons license, you grant the YouTube community the right to reuse and edit this video'.[18] UGV licensed under this terms can be edited using the YouTube Video Editor and then downloaded from there.

With videos licensed under a CC-BY license, you are free to copy and redistribute the material in any medium or format and remix, transform, and build upon the material for any purpose, even commercially. The licensor cannot revoke these freedoms as long as license terms are followed. The only requirement is attribution while the derived videos do not need to be made available under the same CC-BY license.

This is the only Creative Commons license currently supported by YouTube, the least restrictive of all Creative Commons options. It is mainly intended to facilitate video remixing with artistic and creative purposes and not likely to be used by uploaders of eyewitness media. In any case, the InVID platform should make this information available to journalists to facilitate the process of UGV reuse. This information is available through YouTube's API.

8.2.3.2 Twitter

Like YouTube, Twitter also clarifies in its Terms of Service that the uploader retains all rights. Consequently, it is possible to contact the uploader to get permission for reuses outside the scope of this social network. However, as noted for YouTube, the assumption that the uploader is the author/creator of the content is to be cautiously taken: s/he may be uploading third-parties' content. In any case, the range of rights granted by the uploader is very wide,[19] as detailed next:

- 'You retain your rights to any Content you submit, post or display on or through the Services. What's yours is yours—you own your Content (and your photos and videos are part of the Content)'.
- 'By submitting, posting or displaying Content on or through the Services, you grant us a worldwide, non-exclusive, royalty-free license (with the right to sublicense)

---

[18]https://support.google.com/youtube/answer/2797468?hl=en.

[19]https://twitter.com/tos?lang=en.

to use, copy, reproduce, process, adapt, modify, publish, transmit, display and distribute such Content in any and all media or distribution methods (now known or later developed). This license authorises us to make your Content available to the rest of the world and to let others do the same. You agree that this license includes the right for Twitter to provide, promote, and improve the Services and to make Content submitted to or through the Services available to other companies, organisations or individuals for the syndication, broadcast, distribution, promotion or publication of such Content on other media and services, subject to our terms and conditions for such Content use. Such additional uses by Twitter, or other companies, organisations or individuals, may be made with no compensation paid to you with respect to the Content that you submit, post, transmit or otherwise make available through the Services'.

- 'Twitter has an evolving set of rules for how ecosystem partners can interact with your Content on the Services. These rules exist to enable an open ecosystem with your rights in mind. You understand that we may modify or adapt your Content as it is distributed, syndicated, published, or broadcast by us and our partners and/or make changes to your Content in order to adapt the Content to different media. You represent and warrant that you have all the rights, power and authority necessary to grant the rights granted herein to any Content that you submit'.

To sum up, the user grants to Twitter a worldwide, non-exclusive, royalty-free license (with the right to sublicense) to use, copy, reproduce, process, adapt, modify, publish, transmit, display and distribute such content in any and all media or distribution methods (now known or later developed). This license includes the right for Twitter to provide, promote, and improve the Services and to make content submitted to or through Twitter available to other companies, organisations or individuals for the syndication, broadcast, distribution, promotion or publication of such content on other media and services, subject to their terms and conditions for such content use. Such additional uses by Twitter, or other companies, organisations or individuals, may be made with no compensation paid to its owner with respect to the content that s/he submits, posts, transmits or otherwise make available through the Services. In addition, the user should represent and warrant that s/he has all the rights, power and authority necessary to grant the rights granted herein to any content that s/he submits.

For all of these reasons, and like in the case of YouTube, it might be also considered beyond the end of the project, and when commercial exploitation of InVID starts, to establish agreements with Twitter as a way of getting access to the content to be verified, as this kind of use can be granted by Twitter under the Terms of Service accepted by the uploader.

8.2.3.3   Facebook

Like for the rest of analysed social networks, Facebook's terms[20] also state that the user retains ownership of the content posted to Facebook, assuming s/he is not uploading third-parties' content:

- 'You own all of the content and information you post on Facebook, and you can control how it is shared through your privacy and application settings'.
- 'For content that is covered by intellectual property rights, like photos and videos (IP content), you specifically give us the following permission, subject to your privacy and application settings: you grant us a non-exclusive, transferable, sub-licensable, royalty-free, worldwide license to use any IP content that you post on or in connection with Facebook (IP License). This IP License ends when you delete your IP content or your account unless your content has been shared with others, and they have not deleted it'.
- 'When you delete IP content, it is deleted in a manner similar to emptying the recycle bin on a computer. However, you understand that removed content may persist in backup copies for a reasonable period of time (but will not be available to others)'.
- 'When you use an application, the application may ask for your permission to access your content and information as well as content and information that others have shared with you. We require applications to respect your privacy, and your agreement with that application will control how the application can use, store, and transfer that content and information. (To learn more about Platform, including how you can control what information other people may share with applications, read our Data Policy and Platform Page.)'
- 'When you publish content or information using the Public setting, it means that you are allowing everyone, including people off of Facebook, to access and use that information, and to associate it with you (i.e. your name and profile picture)'.
- 'We always appreciate your feedback or other suggestions about Facebook, but you understand that we may use your feedback or suggestions without any obligation to compensate you for them (just as you have no obligation to offer them)'.

In the case of Facebook, the user can also control how it is shared with using the privacy settings. For instance, the user can restrict content sharing to just his friends, so content is not publicly available or available through Facebook's API for data processing. Consequently, the legitimate interest exception mentioned before.

On the contrary, if content is shared publicly, Facebook's terms state: 'When you publish content or information using the Public setting, it means that you are allowing everyone, including people off of Facebook, to access and use that information, and to associate it with you (i.e. your name and profile picture)'. Consequently, in this case, the legitimate interest exception will apply and user data can be processed like in the cases of YouTube and Twitter.

---

[20]https://www.facebook.com/terms.php.

In addition, a Facebook user grants Facebook a non-exclusive, transferable, sublicensable, royalty-free, worldwide license to use any Intellectual Property content that s/he posts on or in connection with Facebook (IP License). This IP License ends when s/he deletes her/his IP content or her/his account.

8.3 InVID Rights Management Design

From the user perspective, the InVID technologies that exploit the functionality of the InVID Rights Management are the following:

- **InVID Dashboard**: it allows journalists to explore news events from social networks and identify social media posts and videos that they might use for news reporting. From the dashboard, they can also check the verification and rights status of the selected media items.[21] If verification is required, journalists can get support through the InVID Verification Application.
- **InVID Verification Application**: supports journalists during the video verification workflow.[22] This verification process also includes retrieving available information about the copyright status of the media item. If the journalist decides to reuse it, the application also supports the process of contacting the content owner and negotiating a reuse agreement.
- **InVID Verification Plugin**: it helps journalists to save time and be more efficient in their fact-checking and debunking tasks on social networks especially when verifying videos and images. Among others[23] the use is able to get a summary of the reuse conditions about a UGV, as defined by the social network the video is published in. If other reuses are intended, the user is recommended to contact the content uploader, a process that can be done directly or under the guidance of the InVID Rights Management Tool.

The aforementioned description of the functionality of the main integrated InVID technologies determines the life cycle of UGV from a copyright perspective. This life cycle is applied to InVID but is generalisable to any process involving the clearance of UGC for journalistic purposes. The steps of this life cycle are summarised in Fig. 8.3.

From Fig. 8.3 it is possible to analyse the legal implications, focusing on copyright law, of each of the identified steps:

1. The InVID Dashboard collects items as links from social networks using the APIs they provide. These items correspond to content uploaded by users, shown as step 0 in Fig. 8.3.
   Legal Perspective: the InVID components using these API should comply with their terms of service, as described in Sect. 8.2.2.

---

[21]Further details about this technology are provided in Chap. 10.

[22]Further details about this technology are provided in Chap. 11.

[23]Further details about this technology are provided in Chap. 9.

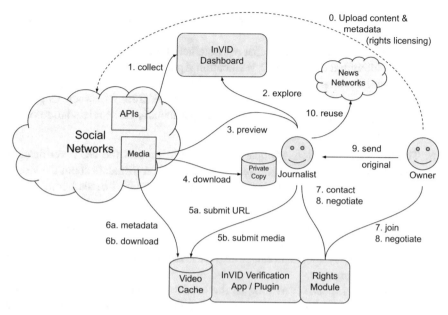

Fig. 8.3 UGV life cycle from a copyright perspective

2. The user consumes the social network items through links from the InVID Dashboard.
3. When media from the social networks is available, it is embedded or linked back to the social network so it is consumed from its source.
   Legal Perspective: the terms of service of social networks and copyright law allow linking or embedding practices. On the other hand, they forbid downloading or require getting permission from the content owner for content reproduction
4. In practice, when the user identifies an interesting piece of content, the journalist might directly download media from the social network for preservation purposes only, as recommended in different verification guidelines like Amnesty International's[24]
   Legal Perspective: downloading is not permitted by most social networks' terms of service, for instance, YouTube as detailed in Sect. 8.2.2. This chapter explores exceptions that might allow journalists to download media for verification purposes. Section 8.3.3 analyses alternatives like private copy or exceptions for 'press and reporting' purposes.
5. If the journalist is interested in the UGV but wants to check the accuracy or has doubts about its authenticity, the verification process can be triggered using the InVID Verification Application or Plugin.

---

[24]Amnesty International Citizen Evidence Lab, https://citizenevidence.org/2014/04/10/how-to-downloading-and-preserving-videos/.

a. The journalist submits the URL of the UGV in the corresponding social network.
b. Alternatively, if the journalist has obtained the video by other means, it can be submitted to the InVID Verification Application.
Legal Perspective: storing the submitted video is an act of reproduction that would require getting reproduction rights from its owner. Copyright exceptions are explored in Sect. 8.3.3, particularly those related to research purposes.

6. The InVID Verification Application and Plugin support the UGV verification process. Most of these verification steps are based on metadata about the video, other steps are content-based and thus require a temporal cached copy of the video binary file.

   a. For verification based on video metadata, it can be usually retrieved from the social network using the video URL and the corresponding metadata API. Alternatively, metadata can be also retrieved from the video file if submitted by the journalist.
   Legal Perspective: as long as the available metadata APIs are used and content is not involved, their corresponding terms of service are the only limitations to take into account. If the journalist submitted a content file, then the same considerations as for the previous point 5b apply.
   b. For verification based on video content, if the video file was not submitted by the journalist, it is necessary to retrieve the content from the social network or from alternative sources like the content owner.
   Legal Perspective: the terms of service of the social networks forbid downloading videos as detailed in Sect. 8.2.2. Moreover, copyright law requires reproduction permission from the content owner. In jurisdictions where press exceptions could allow reproduction of copyright protected material, the person sheltered by the press exception will presumably be the journalist, but not the InVID Verification Application or Plugin. Section 8.3.3 explores the applicability of other exceptions like research purposes.

7. If the journalist wants to reuse the UGV, the InVID Rights Management module can be used to contact the alleged content owner and establish reuse conditions. The journalist should first check, using InVID Verification Application or Plugin, if this is the first share of the video. Moreover, the invite sent to the social network user requests confirmation s/he is the person who shot the video and includes a disclaimer about this being assumed if the user accepts the invite. The owner should accept the invite in order to log in the Rights Management module and use the credentials of the social network where the content was posted in order to facilitate ownership verification.

8. When the alleged content owner joins the InVID Rights Management module, InVID first checks ownership of the UGV: this verification is based on the identity of credentials from the content owner accessing the platform with the credentials of the social network where UGV was posted. If the check is successful, then

the owner is invited to review the conditions of the reuse request, accept them or adjust them until s/he reaches an agreement with the journalist.

9. If a reuse agreement is reached, the content owner can then send the video file to the journalist. This might be a better quality version than the one available from social networks.

Legal Perspective: the agreement should include copyright license terms that allow reuse including rights licensed, scope (exclusivity, duration, territory, channels, etc.), economic reward if any,... It is also recommended that the agreement involves the content owner providing a copy of the original content to the journalist. This will be a legal reproduction that can then be reused under the agreed conditions.

10. After an agreement has been established with the content owner, it would then be possible to reuse the UGV under the terms established in that agreement. However, it is also anticipated that under pressing conditions about current events it might be impossible to get a response from the content owner in due time. Consequently, the journalist should be capable of overriding the InVID Rights Module and proceed to reuse under this particular conditions.

Legal Perspective: as long as an agreement with the content owner has been reached, it will enable the agreed reuses, for instance, to republish the video. However, in the situation of UGV about current events for which it has not been possible to contact or reach an agreement with the content owner, the journalist might also proceed to reuse it under copyright law exceptions like current events reporting, which are explored in Sect. 8.3.3. In this situation, the journalist should be made aware of possible risks and/or possible implications that s/he should check for her/his particular jurisdiction.

8.3.1   Rights Management Components

The rights management components that implement most of the legal requirements are part of the overall InVID Platform architecture. A detailed view of these components is provided in Fig. 8.4. In the sequel, further details about all the components related to rights management are provided. In particular, for the client side:

- **Rights Management App**: Web application initially conceived as the Content Owner App because it was intended to serve them. It provides them the landing page for invites, the registration mechanisms for content owners and the means to inspect reuse requests, define reuse policies and negotiate reuse terms. However, as it finally also provided functionality for journalists, it was finally named the Rights Management App. It helps journalist prepare reuse request and participate in the negotiation process.

- **uPort App**: mobile application developed by uPort and available for Android and iOS that helps users manage their identities if they intend to use the blockchain capabilities of InVID, as detailed next.

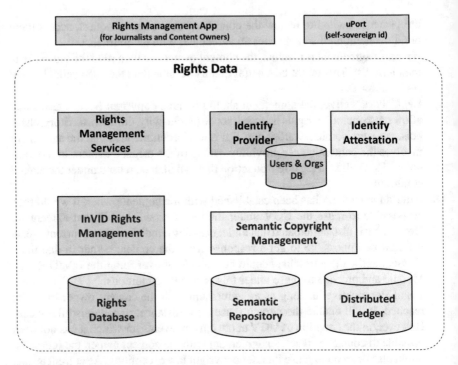

Fig. 8.4 Detailed architecture of the rights management components

And for the server side:

- **Rights Management Services**: this component provides the RESTful API that facilitates the integration of the Rights Management module with the rest of the InVID Platform.
- **Identity Provider**: centralises authentication of InVID users (journalists) at a platform level and provides the authentication tokens required for secure consumptions of the available services.
- **Identity Attestation**: Web service that provides attestations compatible with the uPort application about platforms users identity. Concretely, it provides attestations for users' e-mail and social network membership (Google, Facebook and Twitter). These attestations are stored in the users' devices thanks to the uPort application, so they can be managed by them in a self-sovereign way.
- **Users and Organisations Database**: this is the central store of InVID users' credentials and profile information, e.g. which organisation they belong to.
- **InVID Rights Management**: this component implements the Rights Management Services available through the API and coordinates the rest of the Rights Management module components.
- **Rights Database**: this is the main repository used by the module to store the entities that are part of the Copyright Model, which is detailed in Sect. 8.3.2.

- **Semantic Copyright Management**: this component complements the InVID Rights Management one and is responsible for dealing with the copyright management aspects that require the Copyright Ontology, the use of semantic technologies and reasoning about rights.
- **Semantic Repository**: this repository stores the representations of Rights Terms, Rights Policies or Rights Agreements using the Copyright Ontology. It also provides the reasoning capabilities that facilitate checking if an intended reuse is supported by existing policies or agreements, as detailed in Sect. 8.3.2.
- **Distributed Ledger**: once an agreement between a reuser (usually a journalist) and a content owner is reached, it is represented using the Reuse Agreement defined in the Copyright Model. To immutably store the agreement and when it was reached, so it can be used later for auditing purposes, a distributed ledger based on blockchain systems like Bitcoin will be used [5].

8.3.2 Copyright Model

This copyright model constitutes the core of the Rights Management module domain model. These are the entities and relationships capturing the static aspects of the legal domain analysed in Sect. 8.1.1. It is based on the Copyright Ontology Copyright Ontology [3] which facilitates implementing automated checking of reuse terms against existing reuse policies or agreements.

Copyright law is a very complex domain, so aiming to provide computerised support for rights management, InVID proposes to use semantic technologies and ontologies. Thanks to the reasoning capabilities these technologies provide, these semantic models can be then used to support intelligent decision support at the scale and level of detail required by UGV reuse. This approach has been previously tested in different research and development projects, with promising results in domains like music licensing, UGC monetisation or rights expression languages standardisation [6–8].

The main building blocks of the Copyright Ontology, which goes beyond an access control language and models the core concepts in the copyright domain, are the different rights that compose Copyright. From Economic Rights like Reproduction Right to related rights like Performers Rights, even considering Moral Rights.

However, this is not enough and computers require an understanding of copyright beyond the list of copyright rights to assist users during copyright management. The issue is to understand, for instance, what does it imply to hold the Making Available Right. To this end, at the core of the Copyright Ontology, there is the action model that represents the different 'states' a creation might go through during its life cycle, and the actions that copyright value chain participants can perform to move creations along that value chain, as shown in Fig. 8.5.

Each of these actions is connected to the corresponding right. For instance, the communicate action is governed by the Communication Right. Therefore, to hold the Communication Right on a creation like a video means that it is possible to perform

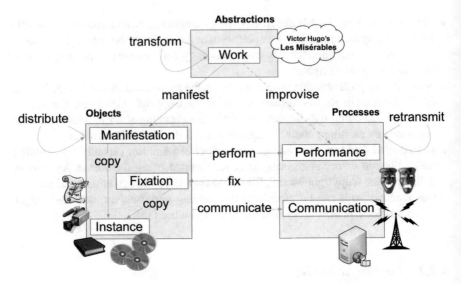

Fig. 8.5 The Copyright Ontology creation life cycle

the communication action on it and, depending on the medium, broadcast it or make it available from a Web page.

The Copyright Ontology provides a shared understanding of copyright terms and a reference framework for tools that guide users willing to state under what conditions they are making their content available. This framework will be used by rights management tools in InVID to assist UGV consumers and producers during the rights negotiation process. Additionally, the resulting formal rights statements can be used to keep track of previous decisions, to clarify liability issues and even to completely automate further interactions. To this end, agreements are stored in a distributed ledger repository, so they can be later audited in a secure way. The distributed ledger is presented in the detailed architecture diagram depicted by Fig. 8.4.

For instance, UGV producers can define their preferences in relation to how they want their content to be reused and the different compensations they require depending on the kind of reuse, the reuser, the territories where reuses take place, etc. Semantic technologies and the Copyright Ontology make it possible to very accurately and unambiguously define all these terms, so they can then be made machine actionable.

Existing tools, such as reasoners or rule engines, can be fed with the semantic versions of these rights expressions and define patterns of actions that are allowed by some previous agreement or prohibited by user-specific policies. Reasoners and rule engines can then check if a particular action that some reuser is trying to perform, like trying to broadcast a YouTube video about a current news event, is allowed or not by checking it against all semantic models created for digital rights expressions, policies or contract about that asset. The reasoner does the hard work of checking all possibilities, minimising implementation cost while maintaining the flexibility and

Table 8.4 Facets provided by the Copyright Ontology to model copyright actions details

Facet	Main role	Other roles
Who	Agent	Participant (indirect co-agent), recipient
When	PointInTime	Start, completion, duration
Where	Location	Origin, destination, path
What	Object	Patient (changed), theme (unchanged), result (new)
With	Instrument	Medium
Why	Aim	Reason
How	Manner	
If	Condition	
Then	Consequence	

scalability of the proposed solution. These features are supported by the Semantic Repository component depicted in Fig. 8.4.

The last building block of the copyright model provided by the Copyright Ontology are the roles that model the links between the previous copyright actions and the 'facets' of these actions, which include who can perform it, when or where. The full set of facets under consideration is presented in Table 8.4.

8.3.2.1   Modelling Example

This subsection presents a modelling exercise that uses the building blocks provided by the Copyright Ontology, presented in the previous section, to model part of real social media reuse agreement. It is the Storyful Agreement,[25] from which the following fragments are highlighted:

- 'The Storyful news agency finds newsworthy content and gets permission from owners to use it on TV, print, radio and websites'.
- 'By agreeing that your content may be used, you grant Storyful and its news partners permission to broadcast or republish your content. This permits Storyful and its partners to use your content in whole or in part in TV packages, in online players and/or on their YouTube channels. You retain all ownership rights'.
- 'Storyful always asks that partners credit any source when content is used'.
- '3. You hereby grant Storyful a worldwide, non-exclusive, royalty-free, perpetual, sub-licensable and transferable license to use, reproduce, distribute, prepare derivative works of, display, and perform the Content in any media formats and through any media channels'.

Using the Copyright Ontology, and focusing on just one of these terms, republish, the corresponding model based on copyright actions and facets will be:

---

[25] Storyful Content Agreement, http://www.storyful.com/clearance.

- **Action**: republish (governed by the Communication Right, concretely the Making Available Right)
- **Who**: Storyful
- **What**: uGVs/0Hu1cY
- **When**: from 2017-06-30
- **How**: non-exclusive
- **If (condition)**: attribute (recipient: UGV owner, what: 'attribution message').

The previous copyright term representation will be linked to a Reuse Agreement, which marks the pattern defined by the term as 'agreed'. Any action the reasoner detects as matching it will be authorised, taking into account that unrestricted facets are interpreted as any value is permitted. For instance, the 'where' facet is not restricted by the agreed term so it is interpreted as worldwide applicable. For instance, if later someone at Storyful requests the following reuse, it will be authorised because it matches the previously agreed term:

- **Action**: republish
- **Who**: Storyful
- **What**: uGVs/0Hu1cY
- **When**: 2017-07-10
- **Where**: USA

However, to be matched, the condition should be also satisfied so there should be a registered attribution action like:

- **Action**: attribute
- **Who**: Storyful
- **What**: 'Video from YouTube user "elrubius" '
- **Recipient**: elrubius

On the other hand, it is also possible to block actions from happening by using disagreements, instead of agreements. This can be done from a Reuse Policy, for instance. Then, even if the indented action matches an agreed reuse term, the disagreed pattern takes precedence and it will be disallowed, as shown in Fig. 8.6.

8.3.3 Copyright Exceptions Guidelines

These guidelines provide a review of the copyright exceptions identified in Sect. 8.1.1.5 and relevant for journalists and social media verification, and the InVID platform in particular. The guidelines for each copyright exceptions are presented in the next subsections.

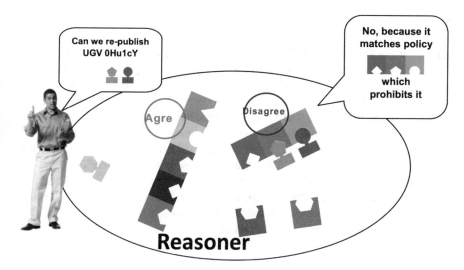

Fig. 8.6 Copyright reasoning based on action patterns defined using the Copyright Ontology

8.3.3.1   Scientific Research Exception

Text from the Directive 2001/29/EC[26]: Scientific research (5.3.a): 'use for the sole purpose of illustration for teaching or scientific research, as long as the source, including the author's name, is indicated, unless this turns out to be impossible and to the extent justified by the non-commercial purpose to be achieved'.

This exception is mainly relevant for InVID as a platform and as long as it is a scientific research project.

8.3.3.2   Ephemeral Recordings of Works by Broadcasting Organisations

Text from the Directive 2001/29/EC: Ephemeral recordings of works by broadcasting organisations (5.2.d): 'in respect of ephemeral recordings of works made by broadcasting organisations by means of their own facilities and for their own broadcasts; the preservation of these recordings in official archives may, on the grounds of their exceptional documentary character, be permitted'.

InVID is not a broadcasting organisation, therefore, it cannot benefit from this exception, where available. Only journalistic organisations that are also broadcasters might benefit, and, in any case, the intent of this exception is basically technical, for archiving and retransmission purposes.

---

[26]Directive 2001/29/EC of the European Parliament and of the Council of 22 May 2001 on the harmonisation of certain aspects of copyright and related rights in the information society. http://eur-lex.europa.eu/legal-content/en/ALL/?uri=CELEX%3A32001L0029.

8.3.3.3 Use by the Press

Text from the Directive 2001/29/EC: Use by the press Use by the Press Copyright Exception (5.3.c): 'communication to the public or making available of published articles on current economic, political or religious topics or of broadcast works or other subject-matter of the same character, in cases where such use is not expressly reserved, and as long as the source, including the author's name, is indicated, or use of works or other subject-matter in connection with the reporting of current events, to the extent justified by the informatory purpose and as long as the source, including the author's name, is indicated, unless this turns out to be impossible'.

Though InVID as a platform cannot benefit from this exception because it is not a press organisation, this is the fundamental exception to be used by the InVID users that are journalists when they are not able to get a reuse authorisation. However, they should take into account that it is only when reporting about current events.

8.3.3.4 Private Use

Text from the Directive 2001/29/EC: Private copy (5.2.b): 'in respect of reproductions on any medium made by a natural person for private use and for ends that are neither directly nor indirectly commercial, on condition that the rights holders receive fair compensation which takes account of the application or non-application of technological measures referred to in Article 6 to the work or subject-matter concerned'.

This exception is just for natural persons for private use and non-commercial purposes. Consequently, InVID cannot benefit from it neither the journalist acting on behalf of their organisations or with a commercial purpose.

8.3.3.5 Quotation for Criticism or Review

Text from the Directive 2001/29/EC: Quotation for criticism or review Quotation for Criticism or Review Copyright Exception (5.3.d): 'provided that they relate to a work or other subject-matter which has already been lawfully made available to the public, that, unless this turns out to be impossible, the source, including the author's name, is indicated, and that their use is in accordance with fair practice, and to the extent required by the specific purpose'.

This exception, which allows quotations as long as the relevant conditions are met, is meant to make Member States fulfil International Treaties obligations such as the one included in Article 10(1) of the Berne Convention, which reads 'it shall be permissible to make quotations from a work which has already been lawfully made available to the public, provided that their making is compatible with fair practice, and their extent does not exceed that justified by the purpose, including quotations from newspaper articles and periodicals in the form of press summaries'.

Consequently, this exception is relevant when trying to keep track of fake videos that quite likely will disappear. As per the Terms of Use of the social networks from where these videos come from, if the content disappears from the social network it should be also removed from InVID, even the associated metadata.

However, it is possible to benefit from this exception, in jurisdictions where it is available, when the aim is to create a new work that is a review or critic of the original UGV. For instance, to illustrate the evidence pointing out the modifications or facts that make the video a fake. To do so, several conditions should be met:

1. A new derived work should be published (it could be a report or a derived video);
2. The UGV should have been previously lawfully made available to the public: if not flagrantly illegal, it can be understood that content uploaded by users who accept terms and conditions where they warrant to be the creators and copyright holders of the uploaded content presumably entails a lawful publication;
3. The source and author name of the original UGV shall be indicated (unless impossible) when releasing the own work where the UGV is reviewed;
4. The use shall be accordant to fair practice and made to the extent required by the specific purpose of its own review work: this seems to be within the limits of the verification process.

8.3.3.6   Fair Use and Fair Dealing

Fair Use Fair Use is a United States judicially created doctrine that is codified, today, in section 107 of the US Copyright Act (USCA), which reads:

'The fair use of a copyrighted work... for purposes such as criticism, comment, news reporting, teaching (including multiple copies for classroom use), scholarship, or research, is not an infringement of copyright'.

This provision is a defence to a lawsuit, not a safe harbour. This means that an allegedly infringing use that would otherwise constitute a copyright infringement, may be considered 'fair' (non-infringing) by a Court upon verification, on a case-by-case basis, that (a) the use is made for criticism, comment, news reporting, teaching, or scholarship and research and (b) that it meets each and all of the four specific conditions listed in section 107 USCA, that reads:

'In determining whether the use made of a work in any particular case is a fair use the factors to be considered shall include:

1. the purpose and character of the use, including whether such use is of a commercial nature or is for non-profit educational purposes;
2. the nature of the copyrighted work;
3. the amount and substantiality of the portion used in relation to the copyrighted work as a whole; and
4. the effect of the use upon the potential market for or value of the copyrighted work'.

Fair use can apply to unpublished works (section 107 USCA in its last paragraph, reads: 'The fact that a work is unpublished shall not itself bar a finding of fair use if such finding is made upon consideration of all the above factors'.)

Since fair use is an analysis by a Court, there is no checklist that can determine, prior to any use, which uses can fall under the fair use doctrine.

EU Common Law jurisdictions such as the United Kingdom, Ireland and Cyprus include the concept of 'fair dealing' Fair Dealing in their copyright legislations. As the UK Copyright Office acknowledges[27]:

'Certain [copyright] exceptions only apply if the use of the work is a "fair dealing". For example, the exceptions relating to research and private study, criticism or review, or news reporting. 'Fair dealing' is a legal term used to establish whether a use of copyright material is lawful or whether it infringes copyright. There is no statutory definition of fair dealing—it will always be a matter of fact, degree and impression in each case. The question to be asked is: how would a fair-minded and honest person have dealt with the work?

Factors that have been identified by the courts as relevant in determining whether a particular dealing with a work is fair include:

- Does using the work affect the market for the original work? If a use of a work acts as a substitute for it, causing the owner to lose revenue, then it is not likely to be fair.
- Is the amount of the work taken reasonable and appropriate? Was it necessary to use the amount that was taken? Usually, only part of a work may be used.

The relative importance of any one factor will vary according to the case in hand and the type of dealing in question'.

In the UK, fair dealing for criticism, review or quotation is allowed for any type of copyright work, whereas fair dealing for the purpose of reporting current events is allowed for any type of copyright work other than a photograph.

Journalists based on jurisdictions where Fair User or Fair Dealing applies may rely on this special provisions when reusing content basically to report about current events. However, though its practical use might be similar to the presented for the Use by the Press copyright exception, journalists should check how it is actually regulated in the particular territory, shown in Fig. 8.7, where they are going to conduct the reuse. Summaries of the legislation about Fair Use and Fair Dealing worldwide are provided in the 'The Fair Use/Fair Dealing Handbook' [9].

8.4   Conclusions and Future Work

From a legal perspective and according to the current EU copyright framework, our recommendations regarding the legal scope of a platform for social media verification, like the InVID platform, are the following:

---

[27] https://www.gov.uk/guidance/exceptions-to-copyright.

Fig. 8.7   Countries where Fair Use of Fair Dealing applies as reported by Band and Gerafi [9]

- Legal coverage for verification operations involving content reproduction might be based on the research project exception, presented in Sect. 8.3.3. This includes content reproduction for UGV verification, plus public communication when fake content is detected. If the platform has a commercial purpose and cannot benefit from the research exception, the recommendation is to explore agreements with social media platforms in order to get permission for media reproduction for verification purposes as part of the terms and conditions agreed by the social network users. Alternatively, content can be downloaded directly by the platform users as natural persons based on the private use exception and then submitted by them to the platform for verification.
- Regarding the reproduction and making available fake content, especially for preservation, the verification platform could benefit from the quotation for criticism or review exception presented in Sect. 8.3.3 if it delivers a final review work of its own where the previous work (i.e. the UGV) is reviewed or criticised. The platform may rely upon this exception especially regarding the construction of a reference social media fakes database.
- Platform users, either journalists or media/press companies, shall ensure legal broadcasting through licensing of the UGV or the use by the press exception where available just for current events, as detailed in Sect. 8.3.3. If the use by the press exception is not possible, licensing for end users (media/press companies) reuse requires obtaining express authorisation. This can be achieved through a system requiring UGV creators to explicitly authorise such reuse, as facilitated by the InVID platform. However, first, content ownership should be checked or at least confirmed with the content uploader, as also facilitated by InVID. Ownership

is based on who shot the video and not on who uploaded it or who is the recording device owner, as detailed in Sect. 8.1.1.

- Finally, and just for platform users, not the platform itself, operating in countries where Fair User or Fair Dealing applies, they can rely on this special provision when reusing content basically to report about current events. A guideline for the particular territory where they are going to conduct the reuse can be obtained from 'The Fair Use/Fair Dealing Handbook' [9].

These recommendations have been implemented as part of the internal operations of the InVID platform but also as part of the InVID Rights Management module which facilitates journalists and content owners following them when social media reuse is intended.

This functionality allows the InVID users (journalists) to authenticate, to check UGVs (from YouTube, Twitter and Facebook) and to retrieve relevant copyright and contact information including a default attribution message. Moreover, journalists can generate reuse requests for the content they are interested in, which specify the scope of the reuse through one or more reuse terms. Finally, when the UGV content owner is not yet registered in InVID, journalists can also obtain a sample invite message that can be sent to the content owner.

On the other hand, content owners get mechanisms for authentication and social network credentials management. Content owners can also retrieve reuse request, including an invitation when they are not registered in InVID yet. Finally, they can accept, reject or negotiate these reuse requests. In case of negotiation, InVID users can also respond to the counterproposals about reuse conditions received from content owners in the same way, by accepting, rejecting or continuing the negotiation.

Additionally, InVID users are also capable of cancelling previous agreements, for instance, if there is a substantial change that makes the agreement unfair like a very successful UGV. In this case, the content owner might contact the journalist using the contact details that are provided with reuse request and also included in the agreement.

In addition to negotiation support, the project features functionality enabling semantic copyright management. This has facilitated the implementation, in a very flexible and extensible way, of and additional functionality for journalists: to check if there are previous agreements for a particular UGV that enable the kind of reuse they are interested in.

Forward-looking, the Rights Management module started to experiment with blockchain technologies for the storage of these agreements, so it is possible to get proof their existence and even non-repudiation. These experiences set the foundations for the generation of legally binding agreements among journalists and content owners, which will be explored as part of future work.

Acknowledgements We would like to thank Ramon Arnó for his guidance and support while addressing the privacy issues we have encountered along the development of the InVID project, ranging from project data management to GDPR compliance.

References

1. Wadhwa V (2014) Laws and ethics can't keep pace with technology. Technol Rev 15 (Massachusetts Institute of Technology)
2. Dubberley S (2016) A journalist's guide to copyright law and eyewitness media. Technical report, First Draft New. https://firstdraftnews.com/wp-content/uploads/2016/11/1stdraft_copyright.pdf
3. García R (2010) A semantic web approach to digital rights management. VDM Verlag, Saarbrücken. http://www.amazon.com/Semantic-Approach-Digital-Rights-Management/dp/3639157400
4. Garcáa R, Teixidor M, de Barrón P, Arnó R, Teyssou D (2016) Overview of UGC copyright management industry practices. Deliverable D4.1, InVID project (H2020- 687786). https://www.invid-project.eu/wp-content/uploads/2016/01/InVID_D4.1.pdf
5. Walport M (2016) Distributed ledger technology: beyond blockchain. Report 19, UK Government Office for Science. https://www.gov.uk/government/publications/distributed-ledger-technology-blackett-review
6. García R, Gil R, Delgado J (2007) A web ontologies framework for digital rights management. J Artif Intell Law 15(2):137–154. https://doi.org/10.1007/s10506-007-9032-6, http://www.springerlink.com/content/03732x05200u7h27/
7. García R, Gil R (2010) Content value chains modelling using a copyright ontology. Inf Syst 35(4):483–495. https://doi.org/10.1016/j.is.2008.12.001
8. García R, Sincaglia N (2014) Semantic web technologies for user generated content and digital distribution copyright management. In: Proceedings of the industry track at the international semantic web conference 2014 co-located with the 13th international semantic web conference (ISWC 2014), Riva del Garda, Italy, 19–23 October 2014. http://ceur-ws.org/Vol-1383/paper14.pdf
9. Band J, Gerafi J (2015) The fair use/fair dealing handbook. Technical report, Policybanwith. http://infojustice.org/wp-content/uploads/2015/03/fair-use-handbook-march-2015.pdf

Part III
Applications

Chapter 9
Applying Design Thinking Methodology: The InVID Verification Plugin

Denis Teyssou

Abstract This chapter describes the methodology used to develop and release a browser extension which has become one of the major tools to debunk disinformation and verify videos and images, in a period of less than 18 months. It has attracted more than 12,000 users from media newsrooms, fact-checkers, the media literacy community, human rights defenders, and emergency response workers dealing with false rumors and content.

9.1 Design Thinking Methodology: An Overview

There are several definitions of design thinking among the different schools teaching this concept and enterprises applying it in their innovation process. In a nutshell, design thinking is according to the US-based company IDEO that pioneered the methodology, a process for creative problem-solving.

The Hasso Plattner Institute (HPI), in Postdam, Germany, defines design thinking as "a systematic, human-centered approach to solving complex problems within all aspects of life. The approach goes far beyond traditional concerns such as shape and layout. Unlike traditional scientific and engineering approaches, which address a task from the view of technical solvability, user needs and requirements as well as user-oriented invention are central to the process."

The HPI precises: "This approach calls for continuous feedback between the developer of a solution and the target users. Design Thinkers step into the end users' shoes not only interviewing them, but also carefully observing their behaviors. Solutions and ideas are concretized and communicated in the form of prototypes as early as possible, so that potential users can test them and provide feedback long before the completion or launch. In this way, design thinking generates practical results."

According to the same source, the design thinking process is performed through six phases: **Understand** (the problem), **Observation** (of the users need and empathy to their needfinding), **Define** the point of view (reframing the challenge through the

D. Teyssou (✉)
Agence France-Presse, Paris, France
e-mail: denis.teyssou@afp.com

gained knowledge), **Ideation** (generating possible solutions), **Prototyping** (development of concrete solutions), and **Testing** (the designed solutions on the appropriate target group).

Some other schools like Paris Design School consider three major phases:

1. **Inspiration**: The strong initial focus is on user needs but rather than merely asking users to write down what they need, it is about observing users performing their daily work, talking to them and identifying problems, inefficiencies, bottlenecks, repetitive tasks, and time losses. In this regard, it is using anthropological or ethnographical methods to observe and analyze the users' needs.
2. **Ideation**: Bringing ideas to solve concrete problems, rapidly launching prototypes to test and check with the users if the envisioned solution does the job. Through iterative cycles, prototypes are refined to really meet the users' feedbacks.
3. **Implementation**: Phase when the optimized prototype comes to life through a pilot and reaches the market as a "real product", with business models options and storytelling.

In summary, we can say that design thinking is a transdisciplinary toolbox (or philosophy for some advocates) which aims to foster collaboration, brainstorming, ideation, invention, creation, and ultimately innovation in project management, through iterative short cycles. It helps to make the team converge toward a common understanding of the problems while encouraging divergent "thinking out of the box" and creative and innovative ideas. It also helps to mitigate risks of developing inappropriate solutions and to speed up the innovation process.

9.2 The Building of the InVID Verification Plugin

After one first year of the InVID project, the spread of disinformation online (often referred to as "fake news") became a global issue in December 2016, mainly due to the US presidential election.

As InVID technical partners had already developed several media analysis components presenting a significant improvement over the state of the art of verification techniques used by journalists, the author of these lines came up with the idea of building a browser extension, in order to quickly provide those tools to end users and benefit from their feedback.

This plugin, available initially for the Chrome browser and then also for Firefox, was designed as a verification "Swiss army knife" helping journalists to save time and to be more efficient in their fact-checking tasks, either for debunking online disinformation or to verify user-generated videos and images, especially in breaking news situations (Fig. 9.1).

Fig. 9.1 Screenshot of the InVID verification plugin after processing a video with one of its features

9.2.1   Why a Browser Plugin?

The pressure of real-time breaking news has always been important in journalism. Being the first to report on major issues has always been considered as a key achievement in the profession.

The never-ending race to deliver ever faster breaking news accelerated dramatically with the rise of the 24/7 news TV broadcasting. Then the Internet and social networks increased even more the time pressure in our high-speed societies.

In nineteenth-century empires, it took months or weeks to get international news until the telegraph submarine cables reduced that delay to a few hours. In the twenty-first century, news now spreads in milliseconds on social media and major events are broadcasted live on connected screens and devices.

Time to react, understand, and verify has shrunk dramatically while complexity of events, interactions, strategies, and technology is increasing endlessly. Using new tools is often difficult for journalists. In major newsrooms, they usually do not have administration rights on their computers to install new software, among security concerns.

Then, if the tool does not give satisfaction very quickly not to say immediately, it is rapidly considered useless and will not be used again. If it comes from a web platform, the URL tends to be buried, after a few days, into inboxes, below a continuous flow of emails as abundant as news items…never at hand when you need it in a hurry.

From there stemmed the idea of making a toolbox always at hand when you need it, directly embedded into your favorite browser: a toolbox where end users could access many different features and resources to facilitate their verification process.

The idea of making a verification plugin was also in line with the availability of several technical components and compatible with a freemium business model to provide free tools to end users while keeping commercial opportunities for more integrated products like the InVID Verification Application (see Chap. 11).

9.2.2 The CrossCheck Campaign

At the beginning of 2017, AFP Social Media team and AFP Medialab had the opportunity to join the CrossCheck[1] operation launched under the umbrella of First Draft News[2] around the French Presidential election (February–May 2017).

Funded by Google News Lab, CrossCheck was a collaborative journalism endeavor involving more than 30 French and International media organizations, with some academics and technology companies, bringing together newsrooms across France and beyond to accurately report false, misleading, and confusing claims circulating online, such as fact-checking rumors and debunking disinformation.

Questions from the audience were answered by the collaborative newsrooms: the focus was to investigate stories, comments, images, and videos about candidates, political parties, and all other election-related issues.

Participating in such a collaborative effort was key to observe and understand the daily journalistic work on debunking videos and pictures, to identify bottlenecks, cumbersome tasks, too "sophisticated" manipulations (for end users), and to ideate possible solutions accordingly. One of the goals was precisely to automate repetitive tasks, ease workflows, and avoid complexities.

A couple of tools, a YouTube thumbnail viewer similar to the Amnesty International Metadata Viewer[3] and a Twitter advanced search application were already developed as prototypes, before participating in CrossCheck, using the Python language and a web server internally within AFP.

The former was an attempt to enhance the Amnesty tool by querying more search engines. The latter was a try to automate a Twitter trick allowing a user to perform a query by interval of time using the operators "since" and "until" with a Unix timestamp. When Twitter evangelists give conferences within newsrooms, they often show this trick to journalists, using an Epoch converter[4] website to manually convert the current date, hour, and second into a numerical string understandable by Twitter search.

---

[1] https://crosscheck.firstdraftnews.org/france-en/.

[2] https://firstdraftnews.org/about/.

[3] https://citizenevidence.amnestyusa.org/.

[4] https://www.epochconverter.com/.

In journalism practice, the Twitter advanced search allows, for example, to query tweets with videos (including Periscope[5] live videos) within short intervals of time during a breaking news event.

Those two early developments were more dictated by a user innovation[6] approach than through a meticulous design thinking observation.

The design thinking study and observations made day after day during CrossCheck have highlighted the difficulties and cumbersome tasks undertaken by journalists during their verification process.

Those include taking manually several screenshots of video footage to later perform similarity search queries, most of the time only on Google images, or digging into multiple pages on YouTube, Twitter, or Facebook to find contextual information about the footage they would like to verify.

Those findings helped us to better define services such as the context aggregation and analysis or the automated video fragmentation to bring to the user all contextual information we can gather through APIs or the most representative keyframes. The latter allows the user to query keyframes by similarity on different and potentially complementary image search engines, such as Google images but also Yandex, Tineye, and Bing among others.

The findings were not only technical but also ethical: facing racist and xenophobic propaganda and massive campaign of disinformation spreading on social networks encouraged us to build and share our tools with the verification community.

The first alpha versions of the plugin were tested and refined by AFP's Social Media and Medialab teams during the campaign, ahead of launching the browser extension publicly, on July 3, 2017, during a First Draft News network event at the Council of Europe in Strasbourg, France.

9.2.3 An Open Platform

Since the very beginning, the InVID browser extension was conceived as an open platform welcoming third parties open-source tools (like the use of the mp4box.js BSD3-licensed library from Telecom-Paris Tech to read video metadata) or previous EU project developments like the Image Verification Assistant (Forensic analysis) created by partners CERTH-ITI and Deutsche Welle during the REVEAL[7] FP7 project.

The overall code of the extension was initially released under an MIT license (although some of the underlying services called through web services are not open source) as many open-source components used in the making were also under the same license. Without presuming the adoption of the toolbox, we also wanted to make sure that some components could be reused by the fact-checking community

---

[5]https://www.pscp.tv/.

[6]https://en.wikipedia.org/wiki/User_innovation.

[7]https://revealproject.eu/.

as a public good. We therefore followed an open innovation approach, "bridging internal and external resources to make innovation happen" [1].

And last but not least, "verification tools must be verifiable themselves"[8] as French mediologist Louise Merzeau[9] pointed out. Open-source tools or methods often referred online as Open-Source Intelligence (OSINT) facilitate such a meta-verification process. At the time of writing, more contacts have been made with companies or public research labs to include more verification tools in the plugin.

9.3   InVID Verification Plugin Toolkit Services

At the end of the InVID Horizon 2020 project, eight individual tools can be accessed through the browser extension plus a contextual menu and a launcher to detect video (and image) URLs in the webpages code.

1. The Analysis tab allows the user to query the InVID context aggregation and analysis service developed by CERTH-ITI.

   In a nutshell, this service (Fig. 9.2) is an enhanced metadata viewer for YouTube, Twitter, and Facebook videos that allows the user to retrieve contextual information, location (if detected), comments, and also the most interesting verification comments.

   It also allows the user to apply a reverse image search and check for the tweets talking about that video (on YouTube). This service is accessed through an API with an option to reprocess and refresh the analysis (to be able to update the analysis of a video).

2. The Keyframe tab (Fig. 9.3) allows the user to access to the video fragmentation service of CERTH-ITI. It allows the user to copy a video URL (from YouTube, Twitter, Facebook, Daily Motion, or Dropbox, as well as an mp4 file url) in order to segment it into visually and temporally coherent fragments and extract a set of representative keyframes for each fragment. Those keyframes can then be used for reverse search on the Web, either directly (left click on Google images) or through the contextual menu (with a right-click) that links to Google, Yandex, Tineye, Bing, Baidu, or Karma Decay (for Reddit) image indexes.

   There is also the option to upload a video file (in mp4, webm, avi, mov, wmv, ogv, mpg, flv, and mkv format). In that case, an iframe of a CERTH-ITI web application for video fragmentation and reverse image search (discussed also in Chap. 3) is displayed. The latest version of the service allows the user to extract more keyframes and therefore gives the opportunity to enhance the video reverse search. Those are the real keyframes of the video, not the thumbnails served by YouTube, Twitter, or Facebook.

---

[8]Merzeau, L. Les fake news, miroir grossissant de luttes d'influences. INAGlobal, May 2017. https://larevuedesmedias.ina.fr/les-fake-news-miroir-grossissant-de-luttes-dinfluences.

[9]https://en.wikipedia.org/wiki/Louise_Merzeau.

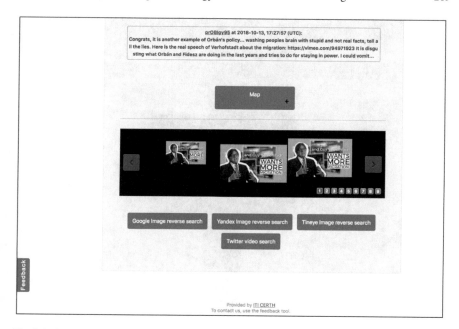

Fig. 9.2 Screenshot of the contextual analysis feature

Fig. 9.3 Screenshot of the keyframes extraction feature

Fig. 9.4 Screenshot of the YouTube thumbnails feature

3. The YouTube Thumbnails tab (Fig. 9.4) allows to quickly trigger a reverse image search on Google, Bing, Tineye, or Yandex Images with the four thumbnails extracted from a YouTube video.

   Up to four tabs (according to the number of thumbnails available) are opened automatically in the browser with the results of the reverse search while the four thumbnails are also displayed in the extension page. This feature is an enhancement to the Amnesty International Metadata Viewer tool. The Chinese search engine Baidu is not implemented here because it is filtering out YouTube content.

4. The Twitter search tab (Fig. 9.5) allows to enhance the Twitter advanced search for keywords or hashtag using the "since" and "until" operators, either separately or together to query within a time interval, up to the minute.

   It automatically translates the calendar date, hour, and minutes into a UNIX timestamp to make the query by interval of time, e.g., searching for first eye-witness pictures or videos just after a breaking news event. We have also added other features from Twitter advanced search such as "geocode", "near", "from", "language", and various filter operators. The feature goes beyond Twitter's available APIs, as it allows users to query any event from the past, through a selected time interval.

Fig. 9.5 Screenshot of the Twitter advanced search feature

Fig. 9.6 Screenshot of the magnifier feature

Fig. 9.7 Screenshot of the metadata reader feature

5. The Magnifier lens tab (Fig. 9.6) allows the user to display an image via its URL, to zoom or apply a magnifying lens on the image, or/and to enhance it through a bicubic algorithm to help discover implicit knowledge, such as written words, signs, banners …etc.

   The user can either enter the image url, upload an image from his/her local drive with the local file button, or drag and drop an image in another tab within the browser and copy and paste the local URL.

   Once the image is displayed from a URL, it is possible to perform a Google, Yandex, and Baidu reverse image search on it, or use the Image forensic service designed by CERTH-ITI and Deutsche Welle in the REVEAL project.

   If the user is processing a local image or has modified any image (via the provided sharp, flip, crop, or bicubic operations), s/he can either download the modified image or send it to a Google images tab which opens next in the browser.

   The flip feature was implemented as a response to the fake war photographer Eduardo Martins affair,[10] with the main finding being that reverse image search engines do not recognize mirrored images.

   The Magnifier lens tab also supports links of stored images in Dropbox and Google drive. A crop function asked by end users has been implemented in the 0.67 version of the browser extension.

6. The Metadata tab (Fig. 9.7) allows the user to check the Exif metadata of a picture in JPEG format or metadata of a video in MP4/M4V format, either through a link or through a local file.

---

[10]https://www.bbc.com/news/world-latin-america-41174069.

If geocoordinates are present in the metadata of a picture, a button link to Google maps is provided at the bottom of the metadata table.

As most metadata are erased on social networks, we recommend that journalists always ask for the original picture or video when they have obtained permission to use some user-generated material. On original footage, this metadata extraction service will be more useful in order to help determine the date of creation or the location.

7. The Video Rights tab (Fig. 9.8) provides access to the InVID Rights Management application. This service provided by partner Universitat de Lleida (Catalonia, Spain) gets a link from a YouTube, Facebook, or Twitter video and retrieves metadata about its rights, unless access is restricted by the content uploader or the social network.

It first provides the user with a summary of the reuse conditions, as defined by the social network hosting the video. If further reuse is intended, it is recommended to contact the content uploader. This can be done directly or under the guidance of the InVID Rights Management Tool.

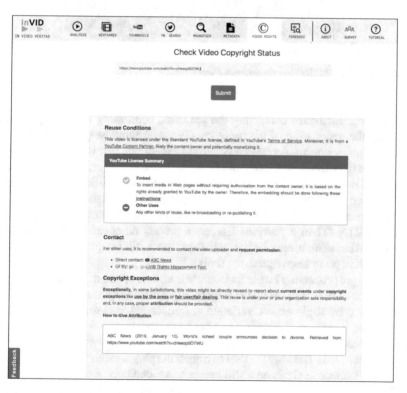

Fig. 9.8 Screenshot of the video rights feature

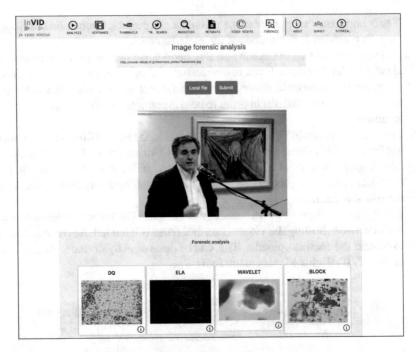

Fig. 9.9 Screenshot of the forensic analysis feature

The latter facilitates contacting the uploader, confirming authorship, or managing the negotiation of the reuse conditions. Alternatively, the Video Rights tab includes information about copyright exceptions if it is not possible to get consent from the author, as the use by the press exception or fair use/fair dealing. A final recommendation is made to the journalists regarding the attribution of the video authorship according to the platform requirements.

8. The Forensic tab (Fig. 9.9) provides the image forensic service developed by CERTH-ITI in a previous European project on social media verification, REVEAL. Being useful for journalists to detect still images manipulations, we added it in order to complete the toolkit.

   Apart from processing image links, there is also an option of uploading an image file from an iframe of the above service. Eight different filters analyzing residual traces left by compression, variation of frequencies, and wavelets help the user to assess if the image under review has been tampered.

9. The Contextual menu (Fig. 9.10) is reachable through a right-click on an image or a video URL. It allows the user to trigger the plugin services like the Magnifier or the Forensic analysis on a still image or a video keyframe.

   The user can also perform reverse image search by querying several engines with any image displayed on the Web (providing that the image link is available).

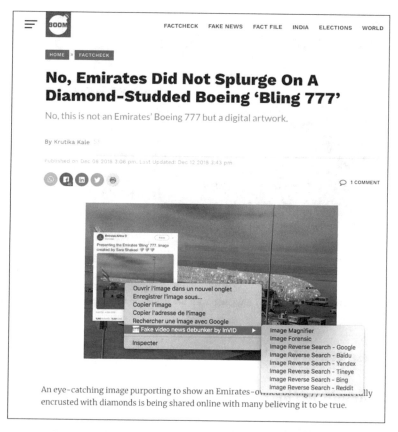

Fig. 9.10 Screenshot of the contextual menu applied on a picture displayed by Indian fact-checking website Boomlive

10. The launcher (Fig. 9.11), visible when clicking on the plugin icon in the browser, allows the user to find the video URL (direct link to the mp4 link) or images URL within a webpage, on several platforms like Liveleak or Instagram. The concept here is to facilitate the discovery of those links without digging into the webpage code.

    This feature was implemented following exchanges with the France 24 Observers, a team dedicated to verify user-generated content for the French external public broadcaster.

    The launcher helps users to find and grab video and image links (URLs) to later process them, notably in the keyframes fragmentation tool. This enhancement allowed the Verification Plugin to process videos from other platforms than initially expected.

Fig. 9.11 Screenshot of the InVID launcher with the detection of a mp4 video link on Liveleak platform

9.4 Results and Further Perspectives

9.4.1 Results so Far

The launch of the InVID browser extension in July 2017 triggered very positive feedback with articles published in The Next Web, Mediashift, Wired Italia, and praise on social media from Claire Wardle (First Draft managing director and a European Commission High Level Expert Group member on fake news who said the Verification Plugin was a "must-download"[11]) or Mark Frankel (then Head of BBC Social Media team, who qualified the plugin as "REALLY USEFUL") (Fig. 9.12).[12]

At the end of 2017, the plugin, available for both Chrome and Firefox browsers, attracted some 1,600 users. Feedback sessions with our lead users[13] from AFP, Deutsche Welle, BBC Social Media ("UGC hub") or France 24 observers journalists allowed us to enhance it with more reverse image search engines and with the above-described launcher.

In 2018, the plugin was demoed in news organizations (BBC, FranceTV, France Info, ARD, ZDF, BR, and many others), at several journalism schools (in France, Switzerland, Greece, Germany), in seminars or conferences on disinformation (Moscow, Roma at IFCN Global Fact V), in professional gatherings like WAN-

---

[11] https://twitter.com/cward1e/status/883343377022025732.

[12] https://twitter.com/markfrankel29/status/884791044566650881.

[13] https://en.wikipedia.org/wiki/Lead_user.

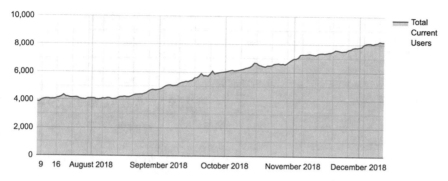

Fig. 9.12 Screenshot of the evolution of the total current users of the verification plugin according to Chrome store statistics

Fig. 9.13 Screenshot of a world map of verification plugin users according to Google analytics

IFRA World Editors Forum or Global Media. Adoption grew rather quickly all over the world, during and outside elections campaigns, reaching 4,000 users in May, 6,000 in August and 8,000 in December 2018 (Fig. 9.13).

Month after month, we got more recommendations from verification lead users, such as Craig Silverman,[14] Buzzfeed media expert and the editor of the Verification Handbook[15] (European Journalism Center) and also New York Times senior story producer Malachy Browne.[16] Some of our lead users even published videos about the

---

[14]https://twitter.com/CraigSilverman/status/956993823816781825.

[15]http://verificationhandbook.com/.

[16]https://twitter.com/malachybrowne/status/997947451175825408.

Country	Acquisition		
	Users ↓	New Users	Sessions
	8,239 % of Total: 100.00% (8,239)	**8,422** % of Total: 100.25% (8,401)	**29,601** % of Total: 100.00% (29,601)
1.　France	**2,289** (26.13%)	**2,286** (27.14%)	**7,659** (25.87%)
2.　India	**914** (10.43%)	**868** (10.31%)	**3,935** (13.29%)
3.　United States	**682** (7.79%)	**655** (7.78%)	**2,154** (7.28%)
4.　Germany	**546** (6.23%)	**533** (6.33%)	**1,552** (5.24%)
5.　United Kingdom	**520** (5.94%)	**476** (5.65%)	**1,915** (6.47%)
6.　Spain	**272** (3.11%)	**264** (3.13%)	**622** (2.10%)
7.　Netherlands	**189** (2.16%)	**172** (2.04%)	**1,680** (5.68%)
8.　Switzerland	**164** (1.87%)	**147** (1.75%)	**467** (1.58%)
9.　Belgium	**157** (1.79%)	**147** (1.75%)	**487** (1.65%)
10.　Brazil	**148** (1.69%)	**143** (1.70%)	**420** (1.42%)
11.　Canada	**143** (1.63%)	**139** (1.65%)	**283** (0.96%)
12.　Ukraine	**142** (1.62%)	**140** (1.66%)	**467** (1.58%)
13.　Italy	**141** (1.61%)	**127** (1.51%)	**391** (1.32%)
14.　Greece	**127** (1.45%)	**130** (1.54%)	**461** (1.56%)
15.　Iraq	**115** (1.31%)	**105** (1.25%)	**382** (1.29%)

Fig. 9.14 Screenshot of the top countries by users of the verification plugin according to Google analytics

plugin to showcase to their audiences how they verify videos with it, like Alexandre Capron from France 24 observers (Fig. 9.14).[17]

---

[17]https://twitter.com/Observateurs/status/1056829241663225856.

The number of monthly active users reached almost 2,000 in early 2019, booming in countries where fact-checking is becoming popular like India, Brasil (within the Presidential election period), and even Russia.

The plugin has attracted at least four communities of users in 18 months:

1. Journalists and fact-checkers.
2. Human rights defenders.
3. Media information literacy teachers and scholars.
4. Emergency response workers and law and enforcement administration (around EU 112 emergency number).

9.4.2 Further Perspectives

For the immediate future, the browser extension will be maintained and enhanced in a new Horizon 2020 project, WeVerify, where partners AFP, CERTH-ITI, and Deutsche Welle are again members of the consortium. New tools in imageboard and underground networks monitoring, social networks analysis, deep fakes recognition, and known fake news database with blockchain are expected to be developed in this new project and some of them will be included in the following releases of the browser extension.

We also plan to pursue the adaptation of the toolbox for the media education sector, notably by including pedagogical scenarios and more tutorial entries as well as finding ways to simplify the handling of the toolbox by teachers and students.

At the end of InVID, the Verification Plugin appears as a multi-sided platform where we create value for our end users, but also for platforms[18] providing the means for quicker and more efficient verification, and for tool providers willing to contribute and get their tools tested by a worldwide community of fact-checkers. The browser extension also helps to collect valuable data about what videos and pictures are being verified worldwide everyday by our users[19] and we plan to use this unique dataset for further improvements.

Reference

1. Lindegaard S (2010) Why open innovation matters

---

[18]AFP is participating in the Facebook Third-Party fact-checkers in more than a dozen of countries.
[19]Only anonymous data from users who have given us permission to do so under the EU GDPR policy are collected.

Chapter 10
Multimodal Analytics Dashboard for Story Detection and Visualization

Arno Scharl, Alexander Hubmann-Haidvogel, Max Göbel, Tobi Schäfer, Daniel Fischl and Lyndon Nixon

Abstract The InVID *Multimodal Analytics Dashboard* is a visual content exploration and retrieval system to analyze user-generated video content from social media platforms including YouTube, Twitter, Facebook, Reddit, Vimeo, and Dailymotion. It uses automated knowledge extraction methods to analyze each of the collected postings and stores the extracted metadata for later analyses. The real-time synchronization mechanisms of the dashboard help to track information flows within the resulting information space. Cluster analysis is used to group related postings and detect evolving stories, to be analyzed along multiple semantic dimensions such as sentiment and geographic location. Data journalists can not only visualize the latest trends across communication channels, but also identify opinion leaders (persons or organizations) as well as the relations among these opinion leaders.

A. Scharl (✉) · A. Hubmann-Haidvogel · M. Göbel · T. Schäfer
webLyzard technology gmbh, Vienna, Austria
e-mail: scharl@weblyzard.com

A. Hubmann-Haidvogel
e-mail: hubmann@weblyzard.com

M. Göbel
e-mail: goebel@weblyzard.com

T. Schäfer
e-mail: schaefer@weblyzard.com

D. Fischl · L. Nixon
MODUL Technology GmbH, Vienna, Austria
e-mail: fischl@modultech.eu

L. Nixon
e-mail: nixon@modultech.eu

© Springer Nature Switzerland AG 2019
V. Mezaris et al. (eds.), *Video Verification in the Fake News Era*,
https://doi.org/10.1007/978-3-030-26752-0_10

10.1 Introduction

The InVID *Multimodal Analytics Dashboard* helps to identify, track, and analyze topics and emerging stories across user-generated video sources. It is a Web-based *Single Page Application* (SPA; see Sect. 10.3) to navigate and analyze large repositories of digital content, following a multiple coordinated view approach [1]. Powered by the webLyzard Web intelligence platform, the dashboard extends previous work and applications in diverse domains such as sustainability [2], tourism [3], politics [4], and works of fiction [5].[1]

The dashboard has been developed as part of In Video Veritas (InVID), a 3-year Innovation Action funded by the *Horizon 2020 Programme* of the European Union that developed technologies to assess the veracity of emerging stories across social media channels.[2] The versatility of the platform enables a wide range of use cases. Journalists and communication professionals can identify trending topics, for example, or opinion leaders who have a strong impact on the public debate. The ability of the system to perform real-time analyses across channels makes sure that important aspects of a story are not overlooked. Data journalism can make use of the various data visualizations provided by the dashboard to illustrate developments in and across news stories along various dimensions visually.

The dashboard provides actionable knowledge by serving as a single access point to large collections of annotated online content that is heterogeneous in terms of authorship, update frequency, and contained type of knowledge (factual versus affective). Rather than relying on simple statistical representations, it conveys context information along various semantic dimensions. When properly disambiguated, such context information helps to track the origin and evolution of emerging stories in the public debate especially when trying to understand the impact of effective knowledge on the perception of an emerging story [6, 7]. For this purpose, three types of context information are of particular relevance:

- *Lexical context*: Specific vocabulary and sequence of words that precede or follow a statement [8, 9].
- *Geospatial context*: The author's location and the geospatial references contained in a document [10, 11].
- *Relational context*: Frequency distribution of named entities in the content repository, and co-occurrence patterns among these entities [12, 13].

The remainder of this chapter will present the user interface and its various analytic features including story detection, keywords-in-context, and geographic projections. It will also describe the data export capabilities of the dashboard, with a special focus on the automated report generator. The overview of the system architecture and underlying data services is followed by the result of a user evaluation. The concluding section summarizes the results and provides an outlook on possible future research avenues.

---

[1] www.weblyzard.com/showcases.

[2] www.weblyzard.com/invid.

10.2   User Interface Representation and Analytic Features

To select the most relevant subsets of the information space and visualize the extracted information in a modular manner, the dashboard offers four different access modes[3]:

- *Desktop mode*. Multiple coordinated view technology [1] to represent the various context dimensions in the desktop version.
- *Mobile mode*. A more linear user experience provided by a cross-platform HTML5 application to access analytic function through smartphones and other mobile devices.
- *Embedded mode*. Widgets to enrich third-party applications with data visualizations following a Visualization-as-a-Service (VaaS) approach.
- *Report mode*. A report generator for on-the-fly summaries independent of the dashboard's interactive features, as described in Sect. 10.2.6.

Figure 10.1 shows a screenshot of the desktop mode. The default view of the user interface includes a visual representation of emerging stories (story graph) as well as a table (story view) including thumbnail, header with keyword labels to summarize the story, information on the size and temporal extent of the story, and a list of four related documents.

In the upper left corner, there is a text input field to define search queries on the fly. Once the search has been triggered, the ASSOCIATIONS widget below shows co-occurring terms extracted automatically. The sequence of these terms reflects the degree of semantic association, while the values indicate the number of times those terms co-occurred with the search query in the chosen time interval. In the default view of the dashboard, this time interval is 7 days.

The BOOKMARKS section below the associations contains predefined queries and allows registered users to define and permanently store advanced search queries. Clicking on the bookmark labels triggers the search, while the rectangular markers on the left select them to be included in trend charts that will be shown later in this presentation. The default bookmarks in InVID categorize the news stories and their related documents based on the top-level subjects in the IPTC NewsCodes vocabulary.[4]

10.2.1   Story Detection and Visualization

Story detection identifies and describes groups of related documents (= stories) from digital content streams (see Chap. 2). A rich set of metadata is extracted for each identified story, including the origin of the story in terms of publication time and author, its impact on the public debate, the temporal distribution of related

---

[3] www.weblyzard.com/interface.

[4] www.iptc.org/standards/newscodes.

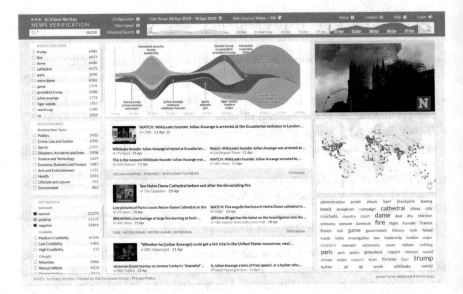

Fig. 10.1 Screenshot of the InVID dashboard showing the top stories extracted from 48,000 user-generated videos published between 08 and 18 April 2019

publications, and the best keywords to summarize the story's content. The results are shown as an interactive Story Graph (Fig. 10.2) together with a list of top stories each including a headline with the keywords and size of the cluster, a characteristic lead article, and a list of related documents.

Tooltips shown when hovering individual stories indicate their duration, the number of documents that belong to a particular story, and the associated keywords. A synchronization mechanism automatically highlights the corresponding story in the Story View as well. On click, users can use the tooltip to either focus on this particular story or to exclude its content from the query. Labels can be deactivated via the settings icon in the upper right corner, which also provides various graph rendering options.

Below the Story Graph, the stories are shown in more detail in the Story View—including a lead article and a selection of related documents. On hover, a playback button appears to watch this video in the right sidebar. Below the related documents, the top three keywords are shown to summarize the story, together with the total number of postings that belong to this story. An arrow down on mouseover allows expanding the set of related documents.

Clicking on any of the shown posting opens the document detail view (see Fig. 10.3). This displays the entire posting, together with extracted metadata such as location, social media metrics, and sentiment. Also visible for video documents are the concepts detected in visual analysis of the video (e.g., "Explosion Fire") and the fragmentation of the video into shots. The visual concepts are a news-relevant

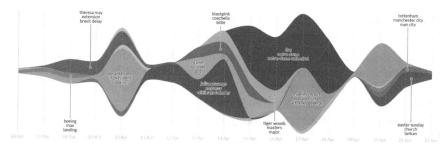

Fig. 10.2   Interactive story graph visualization of the InVID dashboard

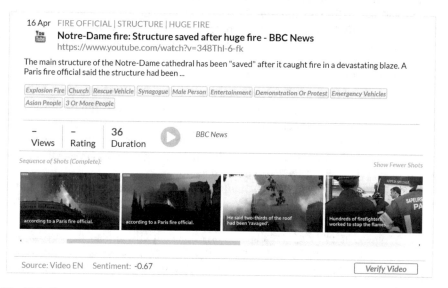

Fig. 10.3   Screenshot of the document detail view with concept labels and keyframe thumbnails

subset of the TRECVID SIN 2015 concepts list[5] (see Sect. 5.2 for more details). For each shot, a representative keyframe has been identified and is shown in temporal sequence. The keyframe integration allows dashboard users to obtain a quick overview of a selected video without having to play it in its entirety.

The "Verify Video" button in the lower right corner opens the InVID Verification Application, another key component of the InVID project (see also Sect. 11.4).

---

[5]https://trecvid.nist.gov/past.data.table.html.

10.2.2 Video Discovery and Browsing

Multiple video formats are supported by the dashboard both in the video detail panel as well as the video preview player (YouTube, Twitter, Facebook, Reddit, Vimeo, and Dailymotion). Where available, transcripts allow the text-based InVID dashboard to better access the semantic embeddings of video content in terms of its term associations and entity correlations. All these added source channels have been fully integrated into the dashboard, with their video content being playable with our video player, and their metadata content being searchable.

Unlike other news media discovery tools which require the user to make an active search and manually sort through the media content in the response, the InVID *Multimodal Analytics Dashboard* not only actively detects automatically current news stories but also pre-retrieves the relevant UGV and allows advanced browsing of the video material.

The collected video content can be browsed at different levels of granularity— i.e., the story level (groups of videos related to a story), the document level (a single video about a story), and the fragment level (a particular video fragment showing an event of interest)—through textual queries or by matching visual attributes with the visual concepts annotated to the documents. In the latter case, the user is able to browse a summary of a video document that includes only the fragments that relate to a selected set of (event-related) visual concepts.

In [14], we have shown that this multimodal video annotation and search in the dashboard enable journalists to find more relevant video material more quickly. The dashboard interface showing video fragments matching a visual concept search (via their keyframes) helped the journalists quickly establish if the content of the video was what they were searching for, discount obvious click-bait and select relevant content at the fragment level for verification through the InVID Verification Application before use.

10.2.3 Alternative Representations of Search Results

The floating menu on the left side opens automatically whenever the mouse pointer hovers over the main content area (which initially contains the list of stories). It offers various types of analyses and drill down operations. In addition to the default story view, for example, users can display a list of documents similar to the ranked set of results of a typical search engine.

The SENTENCE VIEW lists all sentences containing the search query, centering the search term and color-coding it to reflect positive versus negative sentiment.

The WORD TREE aggregates all these sentences in visual form. With the search term at its center, it allows users to quickly grasp the major threads in the public debate. Different font sizes indicate the frequency of phrases, while the connecting

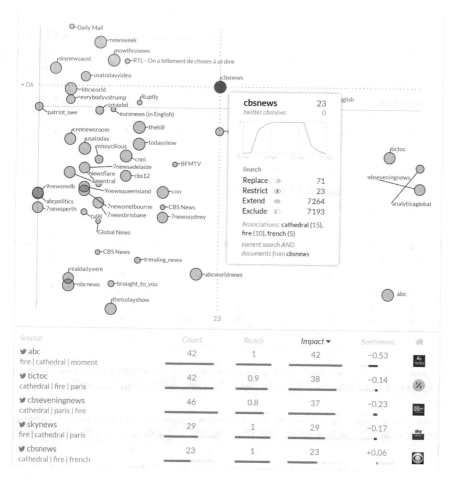

Fig. 10.4 Scatterplot showing the distribution of sources by frequency (horizontal axis) and sentiment (vertical axis), together with a list of sources ranked by impact, computed by multiplying the number of mentions with the reach of a source

lines highlight typical sentence structures. On mouseover, one can inspect a particular phrase and show related keywords.

The ENTITY LIST shows a table of persons, organizations, and locations that co-occur with the search term. Underneath the name of each entity, three keywords indicated what is being associated with this entity. The columns on the right show the frequency of references, the average sentiment expressed in these references, and the type of entity.

The SOURCE LIST (Fig. 10.4) adopts a similar format to indicate major content sources that influence the public debate regarding the search query. The keywords reflect what a particular source associates with the query. The columns on the right show number of mentions and potential reach of the source, calculated based on, e.g., number of followers (Twitter) or average traffic statistics (Websites). *Impact* multiplies the number of mentions with this reach indicator. The next column shows the average sentiment of all sentences that contain the query term. The visual version of this cross-channel analysis is the SOURCE MAP, a scatterplot where the horizontal axis represents the frequency of mentions, and the vertical axis positive versus negative sentiment. By hovering over a specific source, one can show the temporal distribution of its coverage, and what it associates with the search term. Whenever a new search is triggered, an animated transition highlights changes in the data point distribution.

10.2.4 Visual Sidebar Tools

The right sidebar not only contains the video playback functionality but also additional interactive visualizations that help to better understand the online coverage.

The GEOGRAPHIC MAP, for example, shows the regional distribution of this coverage. It does not show where the information originates, but rather which locations are being discussed in conjunction with the search term. The size of the circles shows the number of postings that refer to this specific position. Hovering over a circle activates the standard tooltip with a line chart and the top keywords associated with this particular location.

The TAG CLOUD also shows associated terms, but without the focus on a specific location. It is color-coded by sentiment. The saturation depends on the degree of polarity—vivid colors hint at emotionally charged issues, less saturated ones at a more neutral coverage. The tag cloud is a good example to show that the tooltips are not only a good way to analyze the coverage but also to refine the initial query. The first option "REPLACE" triggers a completely new search for the shown term. "RESTRICT" allows users to drill down to a specific aspect of the coverage by searching for all postings that contain both the original query term AND the tag cloud term. "EXTEND" yields all postings that contain either of the two terms, while "EXCLUDE" removes certain aspects from the analysis.

As mentioned above, the dashboard not only includes the default Story Graph but also line charts to shed light on recent trends. This function can be accessed via a floating menu on the left, whenever a user hovers over the Story Graph. The datasets to be compared in the trend chart are selected via the rectangular markers in the left sidebar and this can include any combination of associations, bookmarks, or metadata attributes.

The TREND CHART offers four different time series: Share of Voice is a relative measure of attention based on weekly frequency data. Sentiment shows the average positive or negative perception of a certain topic. Polarization is the standard deviation of sentiment, reflecting how contested a topic is. The term "oil spill", for example, has a low standard deviation since everyone agrees on its negative connotation. On mouseover, a tooltip shows the number of mentions and associated keywords in a given week.

The KEYWORD GRAPH is the visual representation of the associations shown on the left. It is a hierarchical display to summarize how a topic is perceived in the public debate, providing interactive features to expand the graph by either activating the tooltip via one of the nodes, or by clicking on the little "+" symbol in the upper right corner to search for additional associations with all child nodes. Similar to all other visualizations, the keyword graph can also be maximized to show additional details.

10.2.5 Configuration and Data Export

The overall setup and configuration of the dashboard is managed via the various menus embedded into the header. The most important of these menus is "Configuration", which allows switching between "Drill Down" and "Comparison" mode. In drill down mode, the numbers shown in the left sidebar represent the number of mentions in the context of the current search. Therefore, by definition, the sidebar counts in this mode can never exceed the total number of search results. In comparison mode, by contrast, the total number of mentions are shown, independent of the search query.

The configuration menu can also be used to select the interface language, and to activate or deactivate specific sidebar widgets. For example, one can show a keyword graph instead of the default tag cloud.

DATA EXPORT is the second menu of the header. It opens an overlay to download fully formatted PDF reports (see Sect. 10.2.6), the complete set of search results, or various types of datasets and visualizations in different formats. The PDF summaries reveal the impact of a story and keep others informed about the latest trends both within an organization, but also as an information service for partners and clients.

The third header menu, ADVANCED SEARCH, allows experienced users to specify complex queries, making use of all the metadata attributes automatically extracted from the online coverage. This includes not only text-based attributes such as keywords, entity references, and sentiment but also concepts and objects identified in the video itself (a fire truck, for example).

A list of these extracted concepts is also shown in the lower left "METADATA" sidebar, together with a classification of the search results into neutral, negative, and positive postings.

The time interval for the analysis can be chosen by either clicking on the "Data Range" setting or by using the interactive timeline. The Date Range menu opens an overlay with two interactive calendar elements, as well as a quick selector for the past few days, weeks, or months. The timeline provides a visual overview of the long-term temporal distribution of search results. The selected area can be expanded or moved, for example, to focus on a specific event a couple of weeks ago.

10.2.6   Report Generator

The report generator creates automated summaries of analytic results based on a search query or topic definition.[6] It makes use of webLyzard's portfolio of high-quality visualizations to produce professionally designed PDF reports. Optimized for print, such reports widen the platform's target group beyond the users of the interactive dashboard and unlock new application scenarios. Automated reports can serve as weekly management updates, for example, or as comprehensive on-the-fly briefings on recent events or the social perceptions of an issue.

The report generator offers a selection of five different report types, which are outlined in the following (the header always contains the search term, the date range as well as the chosen sources and languages):

- Trends and associations. Two line charts on the left show recent trends in daily coverage per sentiment category and source complemented by a third chart on the right to compare sentiment across sources. Colored indicators represent average values, small numbers next to the arrows the change between the first and last day. Two donut charts depict the overall distribution by sentiment and source. Underneath, a tag cloud and keyword graph summarize the most important semantic associations with the search term.
- Cross-media analysis. A scatterplot and frequency-sorted table present the top sources reporting about the search term. The size of the bubbles shows the overall reach of a source, their color ranges from red (negative) to gray (neutral) and green (positive). The table includes the top three keywords that a given source associates with the search term, the number of mentions, the reach of the source, the impact of the coverage (multiplying reach and the number of mentions), and the average sentiment expressed by each source.
- Opinion leadership. Similar to the cross-media analysis, the scatterplot shows how often persons were mentioned together with the search term, and whether this was done in a positive or negative context. The size of the bubbles indicates a person's overall number of mentions in the chosen time interval, independent of the search query. The table lists the identified opinion leaders together with associated keywords, the number of co-occurrences with the search term, and the average sentiment of these co-occurrences.
- Geographic distribution. The regional distribution of search results shown on a geographic map is followed by a corresponding list of locations (countries, states, or cities) that are most frequently mentioned together with the search term including top keywords to highlight regional differences in the coverage, the number of times a specific location is mentioned together with the search term, and the average sentiment of these mentions.
- Sentence analysis. Three tables show the most recent, the most positive, and the most negative sentences that contain the search term within the chosen time interval (filtering out redundant or very short sentences). The tables are followed by a word

---

[6]www.weblyzard.com/report-generator.

tree, which is a graph-based tool to quickly grasp the major threads in a public debate. The branches on both sides help to spot important expressions that often precede or follow the search term. The sentence analysis report is not available for asterisk (*) wildcard searches.

The Export drop-down of the dashboard's header menu provides access to the PDF reports. Users can create individual reports or convert them into a single multi-page document that includes all the available reports.

10.3 System Architecture

This section outlines the system architecture including the front-end and back-end processing tasks required to collect, annotate, and retrieve user-generated content assets. It then describes the microservice architecture used to host and operate InVID's own applications, as well as the REST API framework that enables third-party applications to access the InVID knowledge repository.

10.3.1 Front-End Processing

The Single Page Application (SPA) approach of the InVID Multimodal Analytics Dashboard has the advantage that the interaction with the Website provides a fluid user experience, allowing for multiple coordinated views and seamless updates of currently shown data, for example, animations in the case of new or refined queries. It also avoids multiple page reloads for sub-parts of the page whenever state changes occur.

The bulk of client-side JavaScript computations concerns state handling, checks when updates for specific components are necessary, triggering these updates, partial post-processing, inter-component interactions, and—most importantly—the rendering of visualizations. While complex visualizations as part of an interactive, seamless user experience cannot be pre-rendered, the computationally most expensive operations such as data aggregations and post-processing still take place on the server side by means of Elasticsearch queries.

10.3.2 Back-End Processing

The overall back-end processing workflow is reflected in the layered system architecture shown in Fig. 10.5. After emerging topics have been identified by means of cluster analysis, the content of videos that are relevant in conjunction with these topics are analyzed, annotated, and indexed. Based on the annotated metadata

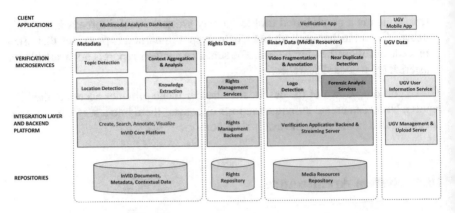

Fig. 10.5 InVID system architecture

elements an initial ranking is compiled. The automatic verification process then checks whether the video was already published in a different context and whether there are any traces of image manipulations. For videos that successfully pass this verification process, the system clarifies legal issues regarding the use of this video by identifying the producer and the contractual regulation of associated rights. Following this workflow, InVID provides an authenticity label for user-generated videos, using data services in conjunction with visual analytics tools to help broadcasters, news agencies, magazine editors, and bloggers to assess the trustworthiness of online content.

To implement this workflow, the system architecture shown in Fig. 10.5 consists of four tiers including the *client applications* in form of the InVID Dashboard, the InVID Verification Application, and the UGV Mobile App, the *verification microservices*, an *integration and backend layer*, and a persistence layer referred to as *repositories*. The architecture reflects the following design decisions:

1. A central metadata repository acts as a data exchange platform to all partners.
2. Three data producer applications are feeding the metadata repository, two of which are consumer oriented (Verification App and UGC).
3. Individual multimedia analysis services for content verification and integrity assessment are provided as RESTful Web services hosted by the respective project partners.

10.3.3   Microservice Architecture

The overall architecture was designed as a set of *microservices*, to be integrated by the three InVID applications via their respective application workflows. Microservice architectures have the advantage that services can be developed isolated at various speeds since they are only loosely coupled via their APIs. The actual service logic can be treated as a black-box system by the applications, ensuring high flexibility in development and release planning. This architecture also provides high modularity since the interfaces are strongly enforced and well documented. Most microservices developed as part of the InVID architecture offer basic Web interfaces for demonstration and debugging purposes. The design of distributed data flow control has been chosen to reduce the overall dependency on a single point of failure and thereby to guarantee the success of the individual partners' use cases—without compromising on the overall integration of all components into a singular, coherent architecture.

InVID's core architecture is the subset of services within the project that constitutes (i) the metadata model, (ii) the metadata repository as the central InVID metadata persistence layer, and (iii) the webLyzard Document and Search APIs[7] to efficiently ingest and retrieve metadata documents from the metadata repository. The Dashboard and other applications are then built on top of this core architecture.

In addition to the user evaluation summarized in the next section, ongoing technical evaluations and optimizations improved performance in terms of speed and throughput while increasing the overall uptime of the platform. This was largely achieved by container-based virtualization of all microservices, the migration to CockroachDB as distributed storage solution, fine-grained system monitoring services, and a continuous integration (CI) workflow.

10.3.4   Application Programming Interface (API) Framework

The APIs of the InVID core services expose functions to ingest, retrieve, and annotate content in the metadata repository to third parties. The API layer integrates input data (user-generated videos from social media platforms) and extracted metadata. The *Document API* is used for uploading unstructured content regardless of its provenance, and for annotating this content with sentiment, named entities, etc. The *Search API* has been integrated in the InVID Verification Application to provide access to metadata documents via JSON-based search queries. The *Image Service* is a data buffer for binary image files that can be reached via a RESTful API. It supports the addition of arbitrary image URL, downloading the images locally and making a permanent self-hosted version of the requested image available via a new URL. The service allows organizing images into partitions (i.e., thumbnails or keyframes), with cache invalidation possible by partition. The *Task API* is an internal API to manage and synchronize tasks between the dashboard and the content and metadata repository.

---

[7] api.weblyzard.com.

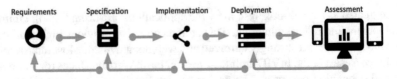

Fig. 10.6 Development process including iterative validation and optimization

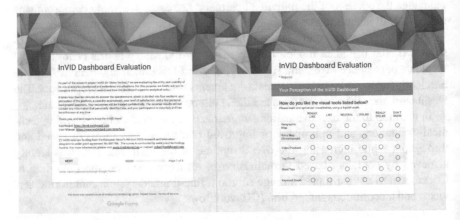

Fig. 10.7 Screenshot of the online questionnaire to conduct the InVID dashboard evaluation

10.4 Evaluation

The development process followed a series of iterative deployments, followed by feedback cycles after each deployment. This user-centered iterative process, shown in Fig. 10.6, promotes usability throughout the whole development life cycle [15].

As part of the final evaluation of the InVID *Multimodal Analytics Dashboard*, participants were invited to (1) watch a short video tutorial[8] introducing the main dashboard features, (2) formulate and run several test queries using the public dashboard prototype, and (3) complete an online survey shown in Fig. 10.7 that had been implemented using Google Forms. The participants were informed that their responses would be treated strictly confidential, and that reported results would not contain any personal information.

In total, 18 individuals from Austria, France, Germany, and Switzerland completed the survey—see Fig. 10.8 for the specific gender and age distribution. The respondents include employees of the media partners participating in the InVID project, as well as professional contacts from third-party organizations. The respondents had a variety of professional backgrounds (journalism, media production, law, economics, communications, information systems, and computer science) and current positions (managing directors, project and innovation managers, scientists, and consultants).

---

[8] go.weblyzard.com/invid-video-tutorial.

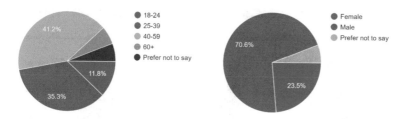

Fig. 10.8   Gender and age distribution of survey respondents

A known limitation of the survey is the fact that a video tutorial of 10 minutes does not suffice to train potential users of the platform. Training workshops that provide a complete overview of the functionality, by contrast, last between 3 and 5 h. But based on earlier discussions within the consortium it was concluded that participants should be able to complete the entire evaluation in about 45 min and choose their own time slot, given the rather limited time resources of our target group especially in the fourth quarter of the year. Therefore, this rather compact format was chosen to shed light on the perceptions of first-time users from media and communication organizations.

Figure 10.9 summarizes the perceptions of individual widgets of the InVID Dashboard, including features specifically developed for InVID as well as improved versions of existing components. Most widgets received a favorable assessment. The streamgraph-based Story Map visualization as well as the video playback functionality received particular good evaluations. We interpret the "dislikes" of widgets such as the tag cloud as a statement that reflects the comparably low degree of innovation, as compared to more advanced visualizations such as the Story Map or the Word Tree.

In terms of the integrated dashboard experience and the synchronization of its multiple coordinated views, the results were mixed. In the "Satisfaction" section of the survey, users liked the dashboard's navigation and particularly its visualizations, and considered the content reliable. In the "Usability" section, users commended the consistency and integration of the dashboard, but also found it complex and difficult to use. This can be partially explained by the survey's known limitation as stated above, a 10-min video tutorial can give a good first impression of the system's capabilities and features, but not replace a comprehensive training workshop. According to the respondents, the main application scenarios of the integrated dashboard, as shown in Fig. 10.10, are the analysis of emerging trends (88.9%), story detection and visualization (66.7%), and exploratory search (44.4%).

When asked about ways to improve the dashboard, the survey respondents made the following observations and suggestions (most of them already addressed in the latest dashboard release as of April 2019):

- Keyword extraction. Test users noticed co-reference variations such as "trump", "donald trump", and "president trump", and suggested to merge them. This represents a rather fundamental challenge best addressed with improved named entity

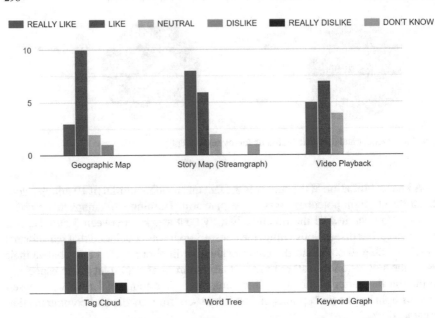

Fig. 10.9 Assessment of the individual widgets offered by the InVID dashboard

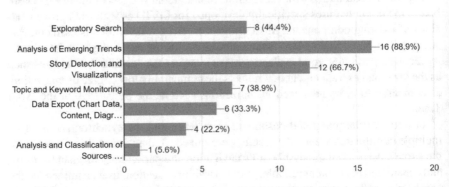

Fig. 10.10 Usage scenarios of the InVID dashboard

recognition and resolution techniques to relate various surface forms encountered in the text to a specific entity (person, organization, location), including disambiguation algorithms to distinguish among multiple entities with the same name. Steps taken were to normalize keyword n-grams against named entities indexed in a Semantic Knowledge Base (see Chap. 2), e.g., an n-gram "President Donald" gets normalized to "President Donald Trump", and n-gram "People's Republic" gets normalized to "People's Republic of China". The keyword detection component was rewritten to better cope with compound terms such as "denial of service" or "state of affairs" via the introduction of part-of-speech patterns that avoid the wrongful splitting of such common compound terms. Finally, switching the base

Linked Open Data repository underlying the named entities indexed in the Semantic Knowledge Base from DBPedia to Wikidata allowed for entities that have been added to Wikipedia only recently to become available to the InVID knowledge extraction pipeline more quickly, with impact on keyword quality. Therefore, as a step toward mitigation of this problem, a significantly improved version of the InVID knowledge extraction pipeline implementing these steps was deployed in May 2019.

- Source management. It was suggested to segment the social media sources into the accounts of official news sources, and actual user-generated content. While it is not feasible to implement this feature until the end of InVID, we will consider this feedback in the exploitation phase and in follow-up projects and have already started with the required classification process.
- Faceted search. Another suggestion related to the use of "facets" to refine queries. The InVID dashboard uses tooltips and an advanced search (not presented in the tutorial) to cover this functionality, as the number and heterogeneity of metadata attributes make it difficult to summarize them in the left sidebar. There is also limited space left, given that the left sidebar already contains associations, bookmarks, metadata attributes, and the search history. We aim to incorporate this feature in future releases of the advanced search, making it easier to define thresholds and value ranges.
- Simplification. Several comments referred to the complexity of multiple coordinated views and recommended to split up the dashboard or omit certain elements. This is already feasible using the embeddable versions of the various widgets, for example, to integrate the streamgraph in a third-party application. There is also a mobile version of the dashboard (mentioned but not shown in the tutorial), which provides a more linear user interface with one visualization per screen. Currently, the mobile version is a separate application, but in future projects we plan to build responsive design capabilities into the main dashboard as well, which will increase flexibility and allow to easily switch between various interface representations and widget combinations.
- Documentation. Requests included more guidance, additional explanations of individual functions, as well as a more detailed communication of the dashboard's use cases. We are currently implementing an extension of the dashboard header that will provide a compact, context-dependent help text to be updated on mouseover. For advanced users, this help feature will also offer a drop-down to show additional metadata, for example, a list of social media accounts most frequently mentioning a topic.

In addition to the issues listed above, user comments also referred to features that already exist within the InVID dashboard but were omitted due to time constraints (e.g., the analysis of search results over long time intervals), or features that would be almost impossible to implement without a complete redesign of the platform (e.g., the distinction of dashboard features by color, which would conflict with the current design principle of mainly using colors to compare topics or metadata attributes). Similarly, a general "back" function would be challenging to implement given browser-based limitations, but the dashboard's "Search History" (not shown in the tutorial) addresses this requirement by allowing users to repeat previous interactions.

10.5 Conclusions and Future Work

This chapter presented the InVID *Multimodal Analytics Dashboard* and its portfolio of visual tools to explore evolving stories and content clusters from various social media platforms. Currently supported platforms include Twitter, Facebook, YouTube, Reddit, Vimeo, and Dailymotion. User-generated videos published via such platforms influence opinion building at the local, regional, and international levels. The dashboard allows journalists, editors, and other professional stakeholders to explore the lexical, geospatial, and relational context of information flows across channels.

The Horizon 2020 research project ReTV ("Enhancing and Re-Purposing TV Content for Trans-Vector Engagement")[9] will advance the presented knowledge extraction and visualization methods, with a special focus on predictive capabilities and the seamless integration of content and audience metrics.

Acknowledgements The multimodal analytics dashboard presented in this chapter has received funding from the European Union's Horizon 2020 Research and Innovation Programme under Grant Agreement No 687786. The authors would like to thank the researchers and software engineers of webLyzard technology gmbh, MODUL Technology GmbH, the Department of New Media Technology at MODUL University Vienna, and the Swiss Institute for Information Science at HTW Chur for their continued efforts to improve and extend the platform, as well as for their feedback on earlier versions of this article.

References

1. Hubmann-Haidvogel A, Scharl A, Weichselbraun A (2009) Multiple coordinated views for searching and navigating web content repositories. Inf Sci 179(12):1813–1821
2. Scharl A, Herring D, Rafelsberger W, Hubmann-Haidvogel A, Kamolov R, Fischl D, Fls M, Weichselbraun A (2017) Semantic systems and visual tools to support environmental communication. IEEE Syst J 11(2):762–771
3. Scharl A, Lalicic L, Oender I (2016) Tourism intelligence and visual media analytics for destination management organizations. Springer, Cham, pp 165–178
4. Scharl A, Weichselbraun A (2008) An automated approach to investigating the online media coverage of us presidential elections. J Inf Technol Polit 5(1):121–132
5. Scharl A, Hubmann-Haidvogel A, Jones A, Fischl D, Kamolov R, Weichselbraun A, Rafelsberger W (2016) Analyzing the public discourse on works of fiction automatic emotion detection in online media coverage about HBO's game of thrones. Inf Process Manag 52(1):129–138. (Best Paper Award – Honorable Mention)

---

[9]www.retv-project.eu.

6. Weichselbraun A, Gindl S, Fischer F, Vakulenko S, Scharl A (2017) Aspect-based extraction and analysis of affective knowledge from social media streams. IEEE Intell Syst 32(3):80–88. https://doi.org/10.1109/MIS.2017.57
7. Cambria E (2016) Affective computing and sentiment analysis. IEEE Intell Syst 31(2):102–107. https://doi.org/10.1109/MIS.2016.31
8. Fischl D, Scharl A (2014) Metadata enriched visualization of keywords in context. In: Proceedings of the 2014 ACM SIGCHI symposium on engineering interactive computing systems, EICS '14. ACM, New York, pp 193–196. https://doi.org/10.1145/2607023.2611451
9. Wattenberg M, Vis FB (2008) The word tree, an interactive visual concordance. IEEE Trans Vis Comput Gr 14(6):1221–1228
10. Scharl A, Tochtermann K (2007) The geospatial web - how geo-browsers, social software and the web 2.0 are shaping the network society. Springer, London
11. Middleton SE, Kordopatis-Zilos G, Papadopoulos S, Kompatsiaris Y (2018) Location extraction from social media: geoparsing, location disambiguation, and geotagging. ACM Trans Inf Syst 36(4):40:1–40:27. https://doi.org/10.1145/3202662
12. Pujara J, Singh S (2018) Mining knowledge graphs from text. In: Proceedings of the eleventh ACM international conference on web search and data mining, WSDM '18. ACM, New York, pp 789–790. https://doi.org/10.1145/3159652.3162011
13. Weichselbraun A, Kuntschik P, Braşoveanu AM (2018) Mining and leveraging background knowledge for improving named entity linking. In: Proceedings of the 8th international conference on web intelligence, mining and semantics, WIMS '18. ACM, New York, pp 27:1–27:11. https://doi.org/10.1145/3227609.3227670
14. Nixon L, Apostolidis E, Markatopoulou F, Patras I, Mezaris V (2019) Multimodal video annotation for retrieval and discovery of newsworthy video in a news verification scenario. In: Kompatsiaris I, Huet B, Mezaris V, Gurrin C, Cheng WH, Vrochidis S (eds) MultiMedia modeling. Springer International Publishing, Cham, pp 143–155
15. Matera M, Rizzo F, Carughi GT (2006) Web usability: principles and evaluation methods. Springer, Berlin, pp 143–180

Chapter 11
Video Verification in the Newsroom

Rolf Fricke and Jan Thomsen

Abstract This chapter describes the integration of a video verification process into newsrooms of TV broadcasters or news agencies, which enables journalists to analyze and assess user-generated videos (UGV) from platforms such as YouTube, Facebook, or Twitter. We regard the organizational integration concerning the workflow, responsibility, and preparations as well as the inclusion of innovative verification tools and services into an existing IT environment. This includes the technical prerequisites required to connect the newsroom to video verification services in the cloud with the combined employment of third-party Web services for retrieval, analysis, or geolocation. We describe the different features to verify source, time, place, content, and rights of the video offered for journalists by the *InVID Video Verification Application* or *Verification App* for short, which can serve as a blueprint for realizing a video verification process for professional newsroom systems. In the outlook, we discuss further potential to improve the current verification process through additional services, such as speech-to-text, OCR, translation, or deep fake detection.

11.1 Introduction

Many news providers such as broadcasters, news agencies, websites, or publishers increasingly have to face the need to include more user-generated content (UGC) in their reporting. For many stories, there is hardly an alternative to utilize UGC, since for many incidents only a few images and videos from eyewitnesses are available. When catastrophes, accidents, attacks, or assassinations are over it is only possible to use the materials that have been shot by private persons, which were on place at the right time. As already shown in Chap. 1, the UGC may come from any source, so that the author, place, time, and content have to be verified. In case of breaking news, this verification process has often to be done in one day or even faster, since the story

R. Fricke (✉) · J. Thomsen
Condat AG, Berlin, Germany
e-mail: rolf.fricke@condat.de

J. Thomsen
e-mail: jan.thomsen@condat.de

© Springer Nature Switzerland AG 2019
V. Mezaris et al. (eds.), *Video Verification in the Fake News Era*,
https://doi.org/10.1007/978-3-030-26752-0_11

301

should be published as early as possible; otherwise, competitors have already issued their article. In addition, the verification is needed 24/7, since events from all over the world have to be reported via the Web. A video of interest should be verified as fast as possible, but nevertheless its correctness must be proven, especially if the publication could cause serious harm for some involved persons, in particular, if they are well known. The publishing organization should always consider that the trust of their readers in the disseminated information is an important value and builds the basis for its reputation.

There are some agencies and services which provide already verified UGC such as Storyful (https://storyful.com/), Reported.ly (https://reported.ly/), or Verifeye Media (https://www.verifeyemedia.com/) but they cannot cover the provision of materials from all domains and regions. Therefore, many news providers have engaged their own UGC verification experts for their newsrooms, which need to be equipped with powerful tools and extensive skills for the retrieval and verification of UGC.

While there are already several tools for the verification of general social media content such as SAMdesk (www.samdesk.io), Check (https://meedan.com/en/check), or Truly Media (www.truly.media), which support, for example, the fact-checking or verification of images,[1] there are hardly tools available for the verification of videos. The "best practice" published by First Draft News,[2] the Verification Handbook[3] as well as the Citizen Evidence Lab[4] only provide guidelines for manual video verification, which refers to tools for the analysis of certain aspects, but they do not support a seamless analysis process. The InVID project contributes with its outcomes to fill this gap by offering a toolset for the UGV retrieval, analysis, and verification regarding near duplicates, source, place, time, logos, and context. The InVID partners have gathered the requirements for video verification[5] of the main target groups from TV, news agencies, verification initiatives (e.g., First Draft News, CrossCheck[6]), and NGOs (e.g., Amnesty or Red Cross/Red Crescent) for the design of the Verification App on the basis of the services described in earlier chapters. A free subset of the commercial Verification App has already been provided since 2017 with the Verification Plugin (see Chap. 9). In the following part, we show the organizational and technical measures together with preparations and training measures needed for the inclusion of a tool-supported video verification in the newsroom.

---

[1] https://revealproject.eu/.

[2] https://firstdraftnews.org/.

[3] http://verificationhandbook.com.

[4] https://citizenevidence.org/.

[5] cf. Chap. 1.

[6] https://firstdraftnews.org/project/crosscheck/.

11.2 Video Verification in the Newsroom

11.2.1 Organizational Integration

The verification process according to First Draft News and the Verification Handbook covers several steps to check and validate the provenance, source, date, location, and motivation of videos. The establishment of this process in a concrete organization should consider its specific mission, structure, and workflow. The verification process usually extends the daily news production process, where mostly multilateral teams create stories in collaborative workflows toward the envisaged publication date. Both for long-term productions and breaking news this process begins with the idea of the topic and plot, which is step-by-step refined and furnished with pictures and videos toward the publication deadline. In many organizations, this process has become cross-department oriented to accelerate the production process,[7] since the formerly often practised delegation of productions to distinct departments has become too slow for the short publication cycles especially in case of breaking news.

When journalists find newsworthy videos[8] in their input stream from external channels or directly in social media networks, they can only uptake and reuse them after a validation. The detailed verification workflow including the responsibilities and communication mechanisms will be different for hierarchical-, flat-, or matrix-oriented organizations. However, they all have to assign similar roles of the verification process to certain persons who are in charge for

1. declaring that there is an emergency case,
2. the overall verification process,
3. selecting the persons to be involved, possibly also to include external experts or organizations,
4. receiving informed consent from eyewitnesses, and finally
5. the assessment of the UGV and decision for or against a publication.

The last role includes the final decision-making, which requires to summarize the verification results and assess the indicated source, facts, place, and time. This covers the weighting of different aspects with comments from different views, and ultimately accept the publishing of the video. The final assessment before reusing UGV needs the combination of several competences: to assess the trustworthiness of the video, estimate its relevance for the intended publication, and calculate the risk that the published content is completely or partly false. The different roles can be covered for smaller organizations by fewer or even one person, for larger ones they can be distributed over several groups such as editorial, legal, and finance departments.

Each organization should have guidelines regarding the workflow for the different distribution channels (TV, social media, print, or Web) and the communication

---

[7] www.businessnewsdaily.com/8179-cross-department-collaboration.html.

[8] Criteria for newsworthiness are, e.g., timing, significance or proximity, see https://www.mediacollege.com/journalism/news/newsworthy.html.

mechanisms between the involved departments, such as Mail, SMS, chat, or phone. It should be clarified which internal and external persons, departments, and organizations should be informed about decisions, and which analysis results should be provided for fact-checking organizations. All involved corporate personnel needs training for the procedures and tools based on best practice since in case of an emergency the processes should run smoothly and there will be no time for several attempts.

11.2.2 Preparations

As already shown in the introduction of this chapter, the verification is often needed very fast but nonetheless the correctness should be proved comprehensively. Despite the problem that the analysis of many facts and circumstances sometimes requires a lot of detective work, the needed time and quality of the verification could be profoundly improved through a good preparation.[9] One main measure to increase the efficiency is the extension of the collaborative process to external reliable trustworthy persons and networks. Each publishing organization should establish a trusted network of experts and organizations that could be utilized in case of emergencies. This network should be built up in advance since it is not possible to begin with its creation when an unexpected event occurs. In critical situations, the concerned persons are usually under pressure and they will only talk to you or even give you confidential information if you have established a trustful relation before. If their organization has a legal department, it could be helpful to agree on procedures to receive their consent.

Depending on the mission, domains, and location of the organization, the best practice recommends to weave different networks that can enrich and accelerate the information flow in case of critical events. For each type of these events, the news organization could create a contact list with the most relevant addresses and the responsible persons from official organizations (e.g., police, Red Cross, fire brigade), NGOs (Amnesty, Medicines Sans Frontiers, etc.), and private persons with good networks. It is also recommended to set up checklists with measures, best practice, tasks, tools, and fact-checking sources including an assessment of their trustworthiness. In addition, it makes sense to define which reports, forms, and checklists should be used as well as the places where they are stored. To remain in conformance with legal regularities it is helpful to have conventions what is needed from the UGV source before a publication, such as informed consent and possibly financial agreements at least via telephone or mail.

---

[9]See also: http://verificationhandbook.com/book/chapter8.php, "Chapter 8: Preparing for Disaster Coverage".

11.2.3   Newsroom Computer Systems

Since the main target groups of TV/Media organizations use Newsroom Computer Systems (NCSs) to process incoming news items, we will concentrate on the integration of a verification process into NCSs such as Scisys OpenMedia,[10] Avid iNews,[11] AP ENPS,[12] Octopus 8,[13] News Asset,[14] Ross Video,[15] AQ Broadcast,[16] Dalet,[17], or Superdesk.[18] Nevertheless, the inclusion of a verification process into related systems such as content management or program-planning systems will be very similar. The NCS receives a stream of news items from several channels of news agencies and other sources and offers them topic oriented within an appropriate time window to the news production teams. The amount of incoming news items for typical European broadcasters or news agencies often exceeds 5000 news items per day,[19] depending on the subscribed international and regional news channels. The number of shown news items can be reduced by filters according to the needs of a group (e.g., sports or finance) and the relevant time window. The NCSs usually support a collaborative story-centric news production with editing, commenting, version management, retrieval, and linking to external content.

11.2.4   Integration of a Verification Workflow into the IT Environment

The integration of a tool-supported verification workflow into an available IT environment should be planned according to the structure of the organization, its content production workflow, verification constraints, responsibilities, and signing procedures. The design of a flexible ecosystem which employs several verification services should follow their specific news production workflow. One input channel for the news production is the stream of daily news items gathered by the NCS, which could be used by journalists to identify relevant topics and to find interesting videos for reuse. Before a video can be included in a new production, it has to be assessed and validated. This verification should follow the leading best practice with the support of tools to analyze certain aspects such as the source, time, places, persons, or content

---

[10]https://www.scisys.de/.

[11]https://www.avid.com/.

[12]https://www.ap.org/enps/.

[13]https://www.octopus-news.com/.

[14]http://www.newsasset.com/.

[15]www.rossvideo.com.

[16]http://www.aq-broadcast.com/.

[17]https://www.dalet.com/.

[18]https://www.superdesk.org/.

[19]AFP, for example, dispatches ca. 5000 news stories daily https://www.afp.com/en/agency/about/afp-numbers.

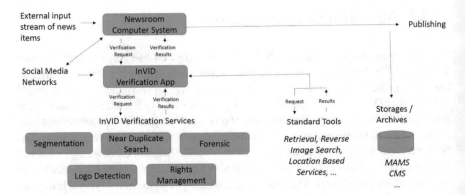

Fig. 11.1 Integration of the Verification App from InVID into a newsroom environment

of the video. Figure 11.1 below shows, as one example, the workflow with the use of the Verification App developed in the InVID project. The user invokes this application, which employs services for segmentation, near-duplicate search, forensic, and rights management to analyze the focused video. During this process, the journalist can also use standard tools such as for retrieval or reverse image search.

The results of the validation from the journalist and the verification tools, such as the assessment value returned by a near-duplicate search,[20] should be stored in the newsroom system and offered to all persons involved in the news production. The final decision about a publication should always be made by humans since it requires a careful consideration of circumstances and risks. For example, there can be the favorable situation that trustworthy eyewitnesses are available, but a high risk that the reputation of important persons could be damaged. In case of a clear positive assessment, the video can be passed to all defined distribution channels and permanently saved in a storage, which can be a CMS, Media Asset Management System (MAMS), or archive. If the assessment has left doubts and open questions, a further validation loop is needed. During the whole workflow we have to consider the security and privacy constraints, especially if confidential data should be provided for internal or even external user groups. Depending on the GDPR[21] as well as further national and corporate guidelines, it must be decided, whether the analysis results should be stored in the cloud or a private data space, which can also be a private cloud.

---

[20]The assessment value delivered by a near-duplicate search characterizes the degree of matching between the query video and the compared video.

[21]General Data Protection Regulation (GDPR), https://gdpr-info.eu/.

11.3   Video Verification as a Service

In this section, we describe the integrated approach of the video verification process in the newsroom from a technical point of view with the overall aim to provide video verification as a service. Here the overall vision could be a fully automatic process calculating some single or multidimensional value based on the main verification dimensions, i.e., the originality of the video, the trustworthiness of the conditions under which the video claims to have been recorded, the trustworthiness of the source or author, or the possible grade of tampering and the evaluation of social comments.

However, technically this has not been solved yet and it is still unclear if this could be achieved even with the application of more advanced AI techniques involving deep learning and large data sets. Hence, video verification is an interactive multi-step process, which aims at providing as much automatically generated data as possible, but also requires to enable the journalist to explore this data manually and have the final word. This process triggers further examinations and assessments of the results to finally make a decision on the status of the video or share this with other colleagues and experts. This means that video verification as a service cannot be a completely automated process in the background but rather requires the journalist to step in at different points of the process. This is exactly what the Verification App from InVID and the underlying integration of automated verification services are designed for. Generally, such a system needs to cover the following four main steps:

1. **Ingest the video**. This might be by uploading a single video, by importing it from own sources or by triggering a search function.
2. **Process the video**. This is a purely automated process which includes subsequent steps as well as parallel processes. The aim of this step is to collect as much data concerning the video as possible.
3. **Evaluate the video**. Currently, this is still a mainly manual process which involves a journalist to explore the collected data in order to decide whether the video might actually be false. This can also include to get in touch with the owner of the video him- or herself.
4. **Export the results** to the newsroom system for further use.

11.3.1   Requirements

There are several general software requirements like scalability, reliability, or specific user requirements concerning the front end that we will not regard in detail in this context. We have identified the following functional requirements which should be considered for the provision of a video verification as a service for newsroom systems (and partially for pure web-based systems, too):

- **A microservice-based open and extensible architecture**: Video verification is based on a collection of web services, which are partially dependent on each other but generally function as individual services. They produce some output which is added to the collected metadata of a given video or specific parts of it (such as keyframes). It must be possible to extend this collection with new services without interference with existing ones, and also to upgrade and replace existing ones. This is best achieved by employing an open architecture based on containerized microservices.

- **An integrated workflow management**: It must be possible to define a flexible workflow for the different verification services allowing to configure whether a specific service is triggered either automatically or manually, if it is executed subsequently or in parallel and in which particular order.
- **A common data model**: Results from the different services as well as video sources should be stored in a common format which is as far as possible compliant to existing standards such as the W3C Ontology for Media Resources[22] or https://schema.org/. Different video platforms label the various metadata such as channel, user, or place differently which requires a respective matching.
- **Import and export interfaces**: For embedding the processing into existing media environments, in particular, to export the results into a newsroom system by using a standard such as the MOS Protocol.[23]
- **A standard API** is preferably based on the common REST standard or the more recent GraphQL standard.[24] Additionally, a Linked Data endpoint could be provided.

Of course, for a productive service provision there are many more requirements covering also user and client management, usage statistics, or business-related requirements which are not covered here.

11.3.2 The Workflow Process

In this subsection, we discuss the overall workflow process as outlined above in more detail.

11.3.2.1 Ingestion of Videos

In the environment of newsroom systems, the ingestion of videos occurs either manually, triggered through a web search from a journalist or because she or he has received a specific video which needs to be analyzed. Another case can be that an automatic web search service has found videos in a general import stream from the Internet which are fed into the verification services. Videos which are generated

---

[22]https://www.w3.org/TR/mediaont-10/.

[23]http://mosprotocol.com/.

[24]https://graphql.org/.

within the production workflow of the own organization could be ingested as well, but in this case there should be no need for a verification. In the InVID solution both ways are supported, for the automatic ingestion a REST API interface is provided, and the manual ingestion can be done through the Verification App Web GUI (graphical user interface) as described below or else through a GUI attached to the newsroom system which is linked to the video ingestion service.

The ingestion of a video consists of mainly three steps: (a) registering the video in the system which also assigns a unique verification ID to the video, (b) collecting the already accessible metadata through the available APIs such as the YouTube Data API,[25] and (c) triggering the subsequent automatic steps of processing.

11.3.2.2   Processing the Video

The processing of the video is mainly a preparation for the later exploration and assessment, aiming at analyzing the video and collecting as much additional data as possible. Thus, this is not a real verification process itself but rather a prearrangement for the later (manual) verification. Generally, there are many possible processes for extraction, accumulation, transformation, and analysis of metadata. Within the InVID solution we concentrated on five basic analysis and detection services which have been identified as the most important video verification services and provide the basis for the addition of more services later on. In the outlook of this chapter, we will indicate some further possible extensions. These five basic services are described in detail in other chapters of this book, so we just recapitulate them shortly here:

- **Video analysis and segmentation** divides the video into segments and generates keyframes for each of them; this is a very important prerequisite for the later exploration. Optionally, some basic concept detection can be applied here.
- **Logo detection** is based on the video segmentation step and is aiming at easily identifying unknown channels and reuses in different postings.
- **Near-duplicate detection** is based on a local index of videos, which is constantly enhanced.
- **Context aggregation and analysis** is used for collecting additional metadata about the video and the channel or user who published it, and social reactions like comments, views, or shares.
- **Rights management** is for checking the licensing conditions for later reuse in the production process.

All these processes add information to the metadata about the video as described in the InVID Common Data Model (see below in Sect. 11.3.3). This metadata is the foundation for the next step, the exploration, evaluation, and assessment, which has to be performed manually by a journalist, either through the Verification App, or else through the newsroom system into which the resulting metadata has been imported.

---

[25]https://developers.google.com/youtube/v3/.

11.3.2.3   Evaluation of the Video

As stated before, until now an automatic evaluation of a given video which is able
to compute whether the video is false is still not in reach, apart from the fact that
the journalist should always make the final decision. Therefore, the evaluation and
assessment is a predominantly manual task. It cannot be performed automatically in
the background, but it can be supported by further tools and services which the journalist can trigger manually. The Verification App as described above is an example
of this verification toolbox. However, the same or adapted functionality can be easily
embedded and integrated into an existing newsroom system (see Sect. 11.2.3).

The manual journalistic tasks will be described in detail in Sect. 11.4 about the
Verification App, so we only mention those services which are also part of the back-
end service platform as the ones in the previous step with the difference that these
have to be triggered manually. These services include the following:

- **Forensic analysis** on whole videos as well as segments; via the forensic analysis
  a couple of filters can be applied to the video for enhancement or detection of
  irregularities. The forensic analysis generates derived videos which have to be
  compared manually with the focused video.
- **Near-duplicate analysis** on segments in order to detect whether parts of the video
  have been reused in other videos or vice versa.

The common feature of these services is that they are part of the back-end workflow
management. As such they are part of the service platform as opposed to purely
interactive tools which are added to the user interface and perform individual web-
based searches (e.g., searches with Google, Bing, or YouTube invoke a reverse image
search on various platforms). The latter ones are provided to the respective newsroom
client, while the former ones add information to the underlying InVID Common Data
Model. This also means that the results of the latter ones are displayed only ad hoc,
whereas the former ones are stored as well and hence are part of the export to the
newsroom system.

Other features, like the manual verification assessment, comments, and sharing
options, are also part of the user interface and have to be reimplemented in the
respective newsroom client as well, by making use of the underlying Common Data
Model.

11.3.2.4   Reuse and Export of Results

For an ad hoc examination of a given video, a lightweight tool[26] such as the InVID
Verification Plugin is probably sufficient. Within an extended newsroom workflow,
however, video metadata needs to be stored, extended, and made accessible to other

---

[26]Lightweight means in this context it is running only on the client and not requiring any server-side
or cloud-based installation.

related systems as well, such as Media Object Servers, CMS, or Content Delivery Networks. The licensing and reuse conditions need to be recorded as well as interactions with the owner or publishing channel.

Hence, all collected and asserted metadata need to be exported. Apart from proprietary interfaces, the most relevant standards here are as follows:

- MPEG-7 standard for content description.[27]
- MPEG-21 Multimedia framework with the main part for Digital Rights Management.[28]
- Material Exchange Format (MXF) which is basically a set of SMPTE specifications for the exchange of audiovisual data together with metadata.[29]
- The Core Open Annotation Framework from the W3C Open Annotation Community Group.[30]
- The W3C Ontology for Media Resources.
- Media Object Server Protocol for the interaction with Media Object Servers.

Generally, and unsurprising, the export of the metadata collected through the verification process requires the matching of the InVID Common Data Model to the target format which again might also require a change of the modeling language (InVID uses JSON, whereas, e.g., MOS and MPEG-7/21 use XML). For applications based on Semantic Web and Linked Open Data, the export format should be an RDF serialization format like N3 or JSON-LD.

11.3.3   The Common Data Model

In this section, we give an overview over the Common Data Model of InVID. The data is organized in different layers addressing several dimensions of related metadata. All these layers can be used to analyze different aspects during the video verification process (see Fig. 11.2):

1. The **video**: The basic video object consists of the media resource itself (the file or stream which can be addressed through a unique locator) and the associated metadata covering descriptive metadata, such as author, description, or language, and technical metadata, such as resolution or duration.
2. The **physical resource** (i.e., the mp4 file, etc.) is the basis for these types of analysis:

   a. **Results of the video segmentation** into shots, sub-shots, and keyframes.

---

[27]https://mpeg.chiariglione.org/standards/mpeg-7/mpeg-7.htm.

[28]https://mpeg.chiariglione.org/standards/mpeg-21.

[29]http://mxf.irt.de/information/specification/index.php.

[30]https://www.w3.org/community/openannotation/.

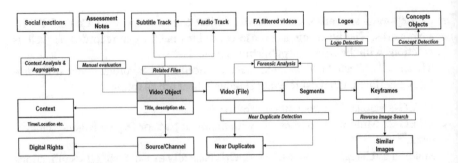

Fig. 11.2 A graphical representation of the Common Data Model showing the relations to the central video object

    b. The keyframes are the basis to invoke further analysis functions which deliver results such as **images** from a reverse image search, **detected concepts**, **recognized objects**, **detected logos**, **recognized faces**, or **text** recognized through Optical Character Recognition (OCR).

    c. **Near-duplicate videos** and **forensic videos** generated through the application of filters for a forensic analysis.

3. **Related files**, such as **audio track**, **subtitle tracks**, perhaps in different languages.
4. The video metadata includes data which gives rise to further examinations based on

    a. **Location** and **time** of recording, if available.

    b. The **source** (author, publisher, channel), which can be again used to perform searches on the Internet.

    c. **Social reactions** like sharing, view counts, and comments.

5. During the verification process further data is generated, or added manually, respectively. This is mainly:

    a. **Assessment**: whether the video evaluated as false, verified, in progress, etc.

    b. **General notes** added by journalists or other experts.

    c. Automatically added **verification data** based on AI/ML techniques would be in this category also once available.

6. For reuse in the newsroom production process digital rights information consists mainly of:

    a. **License and reuse conditions**.

    b. **Contact information** to get in touch with the author or owner, both for the verification as well as the conditions in case of a planned reuse.

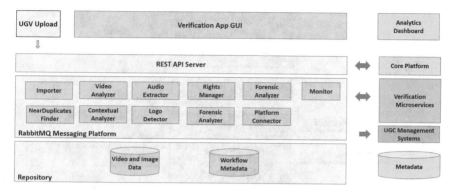

Fig. 11.3 The Verification App architecture with the different InVID layers and components

11.3.4   The InVID Solution

In this section, we give a short overview about how video verification as a service has been realized in InVID. The video verification platform in InVID is based on the Linked Media Management System [1] and the Verification App as the main user interface which gives access to all verification services and manages the interaction with the back-end platform.

The video verification service platform system consists of the following main components (Fig. 11.3):

1. A message broker system based on RabbitMQ,[31] providing the infrastructure for the asynchronous handling of events and communication with external REST services.
2. A NoSQL, document-oriented database (MongoDB[32]).
3. Individual verification service agent components, which independently handle each of the services and act as consumers or producers of the underlying Rabbit-MQ message broker. Additionally, a monitor agent communicates with each of these services to check the health state. Technically, these agents are implemented in Python.
4. A REST API which provides access to all verification services and data. Based on this REST API client applications are realized, most notably the Verification App GUI itself, but also an administration GUI as well as programmatic interfaces to other systems, such as newsroom systems.

The underlying RabbitMQ messaging broker allows for the following main features:

- Reliability: Even when a single agent crashes for some reasons, messages will be sent until they have been successfully processed. Even a failure of an individual

---

[31]https://rabbitmq.com.
[32]https://www.mongodb.com/.

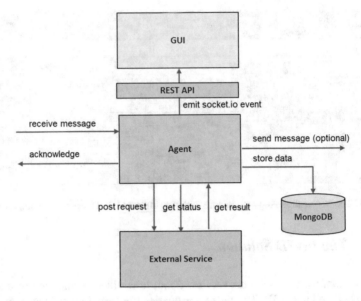

Fig. 11.4 The service agent design pattern showing the communication flows between the main agent component and the related components

agent has no effect on the system as a whole, except for the subsequent dependent services, which could then not continue to process that video.

- Scalability: Each agent can be instantiated multiple times and distributed among different services, so that highly parallel processing is possible.
- Configuration and adaptability: The workflow can be easily adapted to different configurations, which makes it easy to add new agents, replace agents, or bypass agents. While this is currently done through individual configuration, for future releases the usage of a specific framework like Apache Camel[33] is planned.
- Simplicity and maintainability: Although the overall system is quite complex and involves a lot of parallel communication, the general structure is quite simple, thus allowing for easy maintenance.

Each individual verification service agent follows the same design pattern (Fig. 11.4):

1. It receives a message which includes the InVID ID, the video URL, the source (YouTube, Facebook, etc.), and the video ID as provided by the platform.
2. It posts a request to the respective service.
3. It checks if the analysis results are available.
4. If the results are available it gets/downloads the needed files.
5. It stores necessary data in the local database.
6. If another service depends on this service, it again sends a message to that service.

---

[33]https://camel.apache.org/.

7. It acknowledges the original message at the producer of it.
8. Additionally, on every status change it updates the database with the current status and emits a socket.io event to the connected clients via the REST server, so they can update their status, too.

Each component and agent is deployed as a container based on Docker[34] and managed through Docker Swarm (for the future a migration to Kubernetes[35] is considered in order to take advantage of more advanced features).

11.3.5 Summarizing Video Verification as a Service

The Verification-as-a-Service approach enables the integration of video verification into different environments and business models, from low-profile ad hoc video verification as the InVID Verification Plugin demonstrates, to high-end clients such as the Verification App and external applications such as the InVID Dashboard, the UGC Management System, or newsroom systems from broadcasters and news agencies. It also allows for a fine-grained customization and selection of individual services, and can be hosted by cloud service providers as well as on-site. The Condat *Video Verification Server* is an actual implementation of the video verification-as-a-service approach which can be either hosted on-site or run in a cloud environment.

11.3.6 Technical Aspects of Video Verification Service Integration

Within this part, we describe how to integrate video verification in the newsroom from a purely technical point of view; for the organizational aspects cf. Sect. 11.2.3.

Figure 11.5 illustrates the general setting of the integration on a very high level. The newsroom system includes an NCS and a Media Object Server (MOS) which again features a MOS-Gateway to communicate with any type of external systems that generate or enhance so-called Media Objects.

Triggered by a process within the newsroom workflow, videos which need to be verified are imported into the Video Verification Server, processed through a staged verification process as described in Sect. 11.3.2. They are exported into an MOS-compliant format, imported again by this newsroom system and the results are displayed at the user interface in the target system. Additionally, the MOS-Gateway may interact with the Video Verification Service Platform via the REST Interface. This cycle describes a complete integration. Also, a partial integration is possible, which consists of importing the video into the Verification App and then just sending

---

[34]www.docker.com.

[35]https://kubernetes.io/.

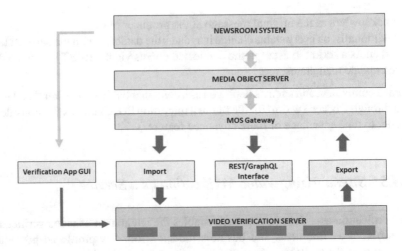

Fig. 11.5 General newsroom computer system scenario

back the link to the results in the Verification App and uses the Verification App Web GUI itself for further inspection and assessment. Both approaches have been realized within InVID: the integration with the WebLyzard Core Platform and Multimodal Analytics Dashboard (cf. Chap. 10 is an example of a full integration (however, in this case not in an MOS-compliant way) whereas the integration with the APA-IT UGC OnlineManager is an example of a partial integration (although these are not newsroom systems per se).

11.3.6.1   The MOS Standard

The MOS protocol consists of two main elements: exchange data formats and messages to handle the communication. Originated in the late 1990s the MOS protocol is still based on XML and either socket-based communication (version 2.8.5) or web services using SOAP/WSDL as the exchange format (version 3.8.4). This means by now there is yet no version available that supports a REST/JSON API interface which is the current de facto standard for web-based communication and also the interface supported by the Video Verification Server. However, most commercial NCS provides interfaces or gateways between the native MOS protocol and JSON/REST format, e.g., the Norwegian broadcaster NRK provides an open-source MOS-JSON gateway to their own news automation system called *Sofie*.

Generally, MOS enables the exchange of three types of messages:

(a) Descriptive data for media objects: The MOS "pushes" descriptive information and pointers to the NCS as objects are created, modified, or deleted in the MOS. This allows the NCS to be "aware" of the contents of the MOS and enables the NCS to perform searches on and manipulate the data from the MOS.

(b) Playlist exchange: The NCS can build and transfer playlist information to the MOS. This allows the NCS to control the sequence that media objects are played or presented by the MOS.
(c) Status exchange: The MOS can inform the NCS about the status of specific clips or the MOS system in general. The NCS can notify the MOS about the status of specific playlist items or running orders.

In the communication between the NCS/MOS and the Video Verification Server, the message types (a) and (c) are the most relevant. Type (a) is used to communicate results and type (c) to communicate begin and end of either the whole verification process, single steps, or error messages. Generally, the MOS protocol and thus the MOS-Gateway handles primarily the communication between the NCS and the Media Object Server, and in this respect the Video Verification Server is an external third-party component. Thus, a lot of messages which are part of the MOS protocol, such as CREATE or DELETE a media object in the Media Object Server, are irrelevant with respect to the Video Verification Server; messages triggering a video verification and importing results should always be UPDATE messages. Single media objects are called items in the MOS specification, which then again are included into stories.

We do not want to dive into the details of the MOS specification here, but rather focus on the most important part on how to transport results of the verification process. For this, the MOS <item> element provides a child element <mosExternalMetadata> which again has a child element <mosPayload> that can be used to encode the results. However, instead of transferring the whole set of data collected during the verification process in a single complex XML structure, we prefer to provide just a link to the results accessible via the REST API of the Video Verification Server, as in this example (vvs:5011 being the address of the Video Verification Server):

```
<item>
  [...]
  <objID>
  urn:openmedia:29752f1973e546f98e3172001752fe9f:00000001002E5AC1
  </objID>
  <mosExternalMetadata>
  [...]
    <mosPayload>
      <verificationResult>
        \url{https://vvs:5011/videos/5c08fd5345667d4acf1c9fb1}
      </verificationResult>
    </mosPayload>
  </mosExternalMetadata>
</item>
```

Via HTTP content negotiation the result could be either transmitted as JSON or else again in XML format. Of course, this is part of the integration with the specific NCS/MOS system and needs to be adapted to the respective environment.

The communication workflow looks like this:

1. Verification request from the MOS-Gateway, initiated by the newsroom computer system. This is done via a REST call which must include the ObjectID known to the Media Object Server; as a curl command this call looks as in this example:

```
curl -i -H ''Content-Type: application/json'' -X
    POST -d
    '{''url'':''\url{https://www.youtube.com/watch?v=
        FvIjkW43HxE}'',
    ''server'':''SP-TSZ-TOMFBP01'',
    ''objD'':''urn:openmedia:29752f19.[.....]''}'
    \url{https://vvs:5011/verify}
```

For a specific integration more parameters might be added such as specific service levels, e.g., whether to apply certain forensic filters for enhancing the video quality.

2. Processing of the video according to the verification workflow within the Video Verification Service Platform as described above.

3. Sending the result back to the MOS-Gateway which again updates the newsroom computer system. This is done via a SOAP message containing the above link to the verification result and object ID reference; the exact message may differ among proprietary systems.

With this we finish the description of the technical aspects of providing a video verification service platform and integrating this into a newsroom system environment.

11.4 The InVID Video Verification App

In the following, we will show the InVID Video Verification App that supports journalists through a graphical user interface during the whole validation workflow from the video analysis until the assessment of the results. The Verification App addresses individuals and groups of users from the TV/Media sector such as journalists, who want to analyze and verify videos from social networks for reuse in new media productions. The Verification App has been realized based on the underlying Video Verification Service Platform as described above. Being a stand-alone application the Verification App serves as an example for the general integration of video verification services into one of the professional newsroom environments.

11.4.1 Verification Services for the Journalistic Workflow

Usually, there are two journalistic workflow variants to receive and include user-generated videos. In the first variant, the journalist detects a video on a social media platform or any other source and transfers the video (i.e., its URL) to the Verification App for validation. When the analysis of the specific video has been finished, the video is returned together with the assessment result to the newsroom. In the second variant, the video is transferred from an external source into the newsroom system; when a journalist selects it for a possible reuse in a news production, the item is passed to the Verification App. When the verification of the video has been finished, it is returned to the newsroom and the state is updated according to the assessment result. The verification process itself employs the combined usage of verification tools, third-party tools, connection to social networks, and communication between involved journalists and experts (see Chap. 1).

11.4.2   Administration and User Tools

The verification process needs at least tools for an administrator of the organization to configure the Verification App according to the organization structure, i.e., to manage users, define permissions, configure storage, connect to external services, and generate usage statistics. The end users such as journalists or editors need at least a list of all analyzed videos with the core metadata, assessment results and functions to delete, forward, or reprocess videos.

11.4.3   Public and Private Data Spaces

During the verification process the videos and analysis results should be stored permanently in a database, so that the work can be interrupted and resumed. We have to decide, whether this database should be shared within a group, an organization, or even the public that can collaboratively view, analyze, and comment the same video. If we open up this data space, we should consider that users can see that somebody, or even who, is working on a specific video. TV/Media organizations, especially private ones, will usually collaborate in closed user groups possibly with a partner network who will need all together their private data space.

11.4.4   Third-Party Tools and Services

The verification process may include the automatic or semi-automatic[36] processing of tools and services to retrieve, analyze, or validate certain aspects of a video (see, e.g., Verification Handbook). They can be used to support time and location checking, rights management, or search by social media tools which do not offer a programming

---

[36]Semi-automatic means that the user controls the processing of a tool by selections and inputs.

interface. This includes, for example, a connection to fact-checking organizations and to establish a communication to external partners or social networks.

11.4.5 Parallel Processing of Verification Services

During the analysis of new videos the Verification App calls several remote services as described in the previous section. Most of the services can be executed in parallel in order to minimize the overall processing time. As a general estimate, the processing time of applying these services equals approximately the length of the video submitted.[37] Some services such as the application of forensic filters may take longer and should hence be triggered only on demand.

When the journalist has finished the analysis of the video via the user interface of the Verification App, the validation results are transferred through the back end to the NCS. The communication takes place in two phases: (a) the initial results of the automatically triggered services are sent to the NCS interface and (b) each intermediate update such as assessments by the journalist are directly sent to the NCS.

11.4.6 The Features of the Verification App

The Verification App shares a lot of features with its smaller brother, the InVID Verification Plugin (see Chap. 9), but offers more features on top of that. The main additional features are the visualization of the video tracks enabling a deeper examination of relevant shots and sub-shots down to frame level. In addition, the Verification App stores analysis results, metadata, and assessments in a database thus allowing a collaborative verification and integration into an overall news production workflow.

11.5 The User Interface

The Verification App can be accessed at https://invid.condat.de. It offers a graphical user interface consisting of three main components:

- A **video player** is used to analyze new videos and play them with several options to start and stop including a frame-by-frame navigation.
- Access to specific **verification services** on the right side to analyze and assess the whole video regarding near duplicates, video source, location, date, rights, and related social media traffic.

---

[37] Figure 11.6 "Progress Monitoring" shows an example for processing times of a video.

- The **video tracks** below the player, which visualize the video in more detail on several hierarchical levels: shots, sub-shots, and keyframes enabling a deeper analysis of video parts.

Figure 11.6 gives an overview of the features offered by the user interface of the Verification App,[38] which are described in more detail on the subsequent pages.

A. **Video Player**

1. *Verify video* starts the analysis of the video.
2. *Monitor progress* of the currently analyzed video.
3. *Play, Stop, Single Step* and further player features (mute, subtitles, full screen, etc.).
4. *Metadata* are shown right to the video.
5. *Adjust Brightness and Contrast* of the video.

B. **Verification Services** for the whole video

1. *Assessment/Notes* from users for the video.
2. *Near-duplicate search* with filters (similarity, date, resolution).
3. *Forensic analysis* of the whole video with function to compare query video and filtered video.
4. *Social media search* for further near duplicates by keywords.
5. *Source* information about the video provider derived from the metadata.
6. *Location/time* information extracted from the video metadata.
7. *Rights information* extracted from the video metadata and further rights databases.
8. *Comments/Tweets* related to the video from several social media channels.

C. **Video Tracks** analysis on shot, sub-shot, and frame level

1. *Play* slider.
2. *Shots and sub-shots* divide the video in logical units.
3. *Video forensic* for sub-shots analysis using specific filters.
4. *Keyframes* per sub-shot to activate reverse image search or image forensic analysis.
5. *Logos* detected in the video with reference to the original logo definition.
6. *Video forensic* results from already processed forensic analysis for sub-shots.
7. *Near duplicates* for segments of the video are shown in a list.
8. *User notes* can be inserted (by clicking on the upper right corner of the tracks card).

---

[38]Using a video shown in the US-based The Ellen Show: https://youtu.be/1KFj6b1Xfe8 fabricated from the original: https://youtu.be/ABy_1sL\discretionary-R3s.

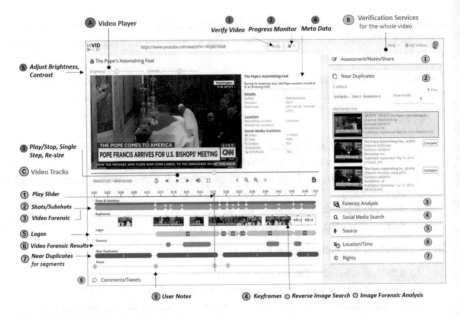

Fig. 11.6 The Verification App GUI—overview

11.5.1 Verification App Detailed Feature Description

11.5.1.1 Video Player

The user can analyze a new video for a URL from Twitter, Facebook, or YouTube by clicking the *Verify* button.[39] For some videos, an analysis is not possible (no shots, keyframes, or logos are shown and error messages are displayed) if the URL is not publicly accessible (in particular for Facebook), they need a log-in, their resolution is too low, or the video file is somehow corrupted.

The analysis of new videos usually needs less time than the video length until all results are available. Therefore, it is recommended to analyze videos above 3 min only if necessary. If the analysis needs more time than expected you can click on the green cogwheel to open the *Progress monitor*, which shows the execution of the different services running in parallel until they are finished. The following Fig. 11.7 shows an example of the progress monitoring for a video with a duration below 1 minute. If several videos are launched at the same time, the requests are queued and the position of the current video in the queue is indicated in the text below the progress bar for *Video analysis*.

---

[39] In order to get acquainted with the Verification App, we recommend to start with a preprocessed video. Examples are (1) The Popes magic trick removing a table cloth: https://www.youtube.com/watch?v=h-AkAF2Tc1k, (2) Paris attacks: https://www.youtube.com/watch?v=4XnGKJAarhA.

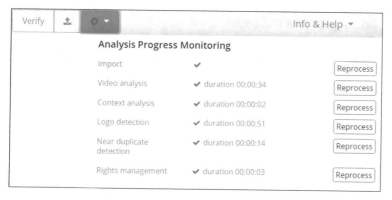

Fig. 11.7 Progress monitoring

Fig. 11.8 The video player

The Player shown in Fig. 11.8 provides several buttons and bars similar to common video players to *stop, play, single step, mute* the video or switch to full screen.

Initially, the basic video metadata, such as title, duration, and author, are shown right to the video player. In addition, the user can display the complete set of available metadata, which are as follows:

(i)   Retrieved metadata via the API,
(ii) Enriched data coming from the InVID contextual analysis, such as the videos long description,
(iii) Comments that contain keywords related to verification,
(iv) Locations mentioned in the metadata,
(v)   Tweets that share the input video, and
(vi) The publishing date and time of the video file in UTC.

The current version of the contextual verification service extracts context from YouTube, Twitter, and Facebook and maps them on the indicated metadata fields. Moreover, all available information about the channel and the contributor of the video

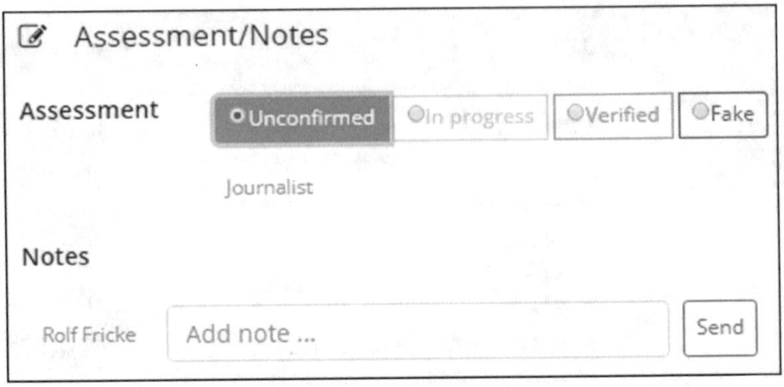

Fig. 11.9 Assessment and notes from users

are displayed, such as whether the channel belongs to a verified YouTube account. Additional useful information is derived, e.g., from the extraction and display of geographical locations found in the video description. The player also offers two sliders above the video to adjust *Brightness* and *Contrast*, which can also be used when playing the video.

11.5.2 Verification Services for the Whole Video

The right side of the Verification App offers verification services related to the whole video. This begins with a card for the assessment of the video by the users. The InVID approach does not provide an automatic assessment of the probability, whether the video is correct, there is instead a choice box shown in Fig. 11.9 where the users should manually indicate their assessment of the verification state from *unconfirmed'* up to *verified* or *fake*. The users may add explanations or notes which are stored and shared with other users verifying this video.

11.5.2.1 Near Duplicates

This service retrieves near duplicates of the selected video by querying the index of pre-analyzed videos of the InVID platform. This component aims to identify whether the selected video shot or sub-shot is part of another video, giving the journalists a clue about its originality. The retrieved near duplicates are presented in a card on the right side of the application. As illustrated in Fig. 11.10, they are initially shown in descending order based on their similarity with the query video.

The user can optionally rearrange the list based on the filters *similarity*, *date*, or *resolution*, and toggle the ascending and descending order. The number of shown results can be adjusted to improve the clarity. The video currently under examination

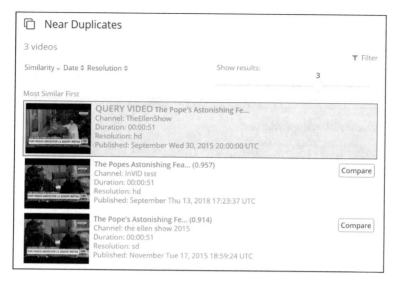

Fig. 11.10 Near-duplicate results and filters

Fig. 11.11 Compare query video and near-duplicate video

is marked with gray background to ease the verification. For example, when *date* and *earliest first* are selected, the user can directly see which videos were uploaded earlier than the focused video. If one of them already contains parts of the focused video, the latter one can apparently not be an original.

The near-duplicate service provides a *Compare* function that enables the user to visually examine the query video and a potential near-duplicate video in parallel. Both videos are displayed side by side and can be started and stopped synchronously by a single button. This allows to go manually stepwise through the videos and detect differences (Fig. 11.11).

While the near duplicates retrieval is based on visual similarity, the Verification App also offers a *Social Media Search* function to find further near duplicates based

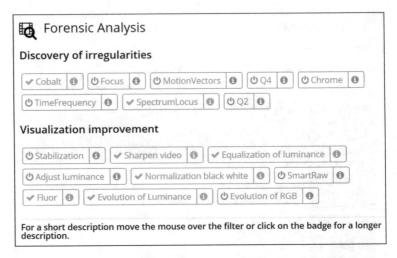

Fig. 11.12 Invocation of functions for the forensic analysis and visual improvement

on keywords. This search command line proposes keywords from the title and author, which can be eliminated by the user as well as new keywords can be added.

11.5.2.2 Forensic Analysis of the Whole Video Using Different Filters

This service comprises two groups of filters applied to the whole video: the tools (1) for discovery of irregular or abnormal patterns in the video and (2) for visual improvement (see Fig. 11.12). The first group identifies irregular patterns in videos, which were possibly caused by changes or manipulations and thus should be further analyzed by the user. The different filters mainly examine the video regarding different aspects, such as color, luminance, contrast, sound, or distribution of information. The second group allows the user to adjust the different aspects in order to improve the visual recognition of details in the video. A more detailed description for each filter is offered by clicking on the "i" field. Since these tools need some time for analysis, often longer than the duration of the video, they are all offered on demand. This allows the users to invoke only the most promising tools according to the current analysis objective in order to reduce the waiting time. The forensic services are provided by the InVID partner ExoMakina (www.exomakina.fr).

For each filter, the Verification App returns an output video with additional information that assists the user to identify suspicious areas, thus supporting the detection of manipulated parts of the video (Fig. 11.13).

The user is offered a *Compare* function, which shows the query video on the left and the version with marks from the selected filter on the right side. Both videos can be played and stopped synchronously, which helps the user to detect irregular parts of the video.

Fig. 11.13 Compare query video and filtered video

11.5.2.3 Source Information About the Video Provider

In the *Source* card, all available information about the publishing source is displayed. This information is aggregated from the contextual analysis, as well as the rights management service. In some cases, a mapping of metadata is required, e.g., for YouTube videos, if only channel information is available, it will be mapped onto the source (Fig. 11.14).

When present publishing time and locations mentioned in the description of a video are shown, as well as recording time and recording location, which are unfortunately very rarely available.

11.5.2.4 Rights Information Extracted from Video Metadata and Other Rights Sources

The rights and license management information as shown in Fig. 11.15 is retrieved from the rights management component. The current version of the Verification App returns the license for YouTube and Facebook videos. For YouTube, the App shows that a video uses, for example, the Creative Commons CC-BY license or the Standard YouTube license based on the Terms of Service.

In addition, the rights management provides a default attribution information that is also available through the Verification App. The rights management component also facilitates with the *Request Reuse* button to contact the content uploader and assists negotiations of reuse conditions, if the uploader is also the content owner. In upcoming versions of the Rights module, it will also deliver detailed information about reuse terms if an agreement has been reached, and the user logged into the Verification App can benefit from it.

11.5.2.5 Comments/Tweets Related to the Video from Different Social Media Channels

Information from several social media channels related to the focused video is shown in Fig. 11.16 in three groups: all comments, only verification-related comments and tweets.

Fig. 11.14 Information about the source

11.5.3 Video Tracks for Shots, Sub-shots, Keyframes, Notes

The video tracks card shown in Fig. 11.17 visualizes different types of timeline-based information of the video and enables to invoke further analysis and forensic services for shots, sub-shots, and frames.

The first track in dark- and lighter gray shows the shots and sub-shots of the video. The shots are automatically split on visual criteria in smaller sub-shots, which are displayed in light gray. The video can be played by (i) the play button "▶" below the video, (ii) positioning the slider in the timeline or (iii) click on particular shots or sub-shots of the video. Additionally, a frame-by-frame navigation is available by using the two arrows left and right of the play button. The timeline can be zoomed in and out by the buttons "+" and "−" (in the upper bar on the right of the card) and the visible segment can be shifted by the buttons "<" and ">".

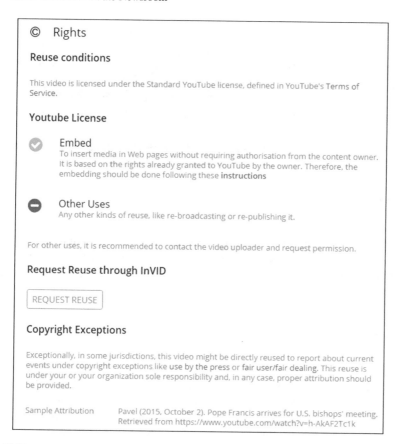

Fig. 11.15 Retrieved rights information about a YouTube video

Fig. 11.16 Comments/Tweets related to the video

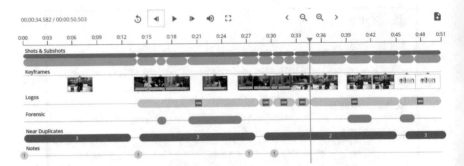

Fig. 11.17 Visualization of video tracks

Users can insert notes by clicking the symbol in the upper right corner of the video tracks card. Each note is associated with the current position of the video player timeline enabling several users to collaboratively discuss aspects related to certain shots, sub-shots, or frames.

11.5.3.1 Video Forensic for Sub-shots

For each sub-shot, the user can invoke a forensic analysis with a specific filter. Explanations about the use of each filter are provided to the journalists in the tooltips, enabling them to select the most promising filter(s) according to the current use case. Since the forensic analysis is a heavily computational-intensive process that may cause significant waiting times, the focus on smaller parts of the video and concentration on few filters could significantly reduce the time needed and allow the user to get the analysis results in a reasonable time. The results of the video forensic analysis for sub-shots are displayed in a separate track below the logos. The user can play the resulting video which contains the derived marks or information of the selected filter that should help to find manipulations in the video (Fig. 11.18).

11.5.3.2 Reverse Image Search and Image Forensic Analysis for Keyframes During a Single Step

The App offers representative keyframes for the sub-shots which were predetermined by the video fragmentation and annotation service. They enable the user to get a fast overview over the content. For the keyframes and each frame shown in the single-step mode, the user can invoke the functions reverse image search and image forensic offered in a separate window (see Fig. 11.19):

(i) **Reverse image search** to find other already existing similar images on the Web by selecting one of the available search engines (Google, Bing, Yandex, Baidu, and more).

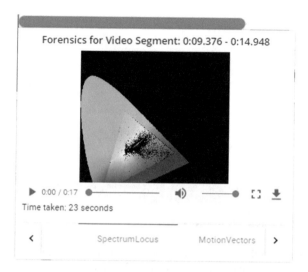

Fig. 11.18 A forensic filter

Fig. 11.19 Launch reverse image search and image forensic for keyframes and each frame during single step

(ii) **Image forensic analysis** using the services from the EU project Reveal. The user can select one of the available forensic filters, based on guidelines about the use and the findings of each filter. The image forensic analysis component requires some time for processing and then presents the resulting filtered image with the outcomes of the analysis in a separate track below.

The use of the single step enables a journalist to choose always the most appropriate frame to invoke a function, e.g., when a person or object is displayed in the optimum angle for a reverse image search.

Fig. 11.20 The detected
logos are presented in a
separate track

11.5.3.3 Logos Detected in the Video

All logos detected in the video using a logo database will be indicated in a separate
track. The logos can be of particular organizations or groups of interest (e.g., military
organizations or non-governmental organizations). The search is based on a list of
manually indexed logos, which can be extended by the user due to the need to
recognize newly appearing organizations in crisis zones or other areas of interest.
The logo-focusing track displays for each detected logo the officially registered one
in large format and a reference to the Wikipedia entry for the associated organization
(Fig. 11.20).

11.5.3.4 Near Duplicates for Segments of the Video

The Verification App also identifies near duplicates for smaller segments of the video.
The segmentation, which is different from the shot/sub-shot division, was calculated
during the initial video analysis. The near duplicates for each segment are shown in
a list, which allows the user to examine and play them in order to verify whether one
of them is a near duplicate of the focused video. The near-duplicate search on the
video-segment-level is an important feature due to the fact that often only particular
parts of a video are being reused in other videos. A near-duplicate search for the
entire video in such cases could return a low level of similarity and not indicate that
a small but very relevant part of the video was copied and reused in the query video
(Fig. 11.21).

11.5.4 Details About the Parallel Processing of Verification Services

When pushing the *Verify* button the analysis process is performed automatically in
the background. After the import and local caching of the video, the player will be

Near-Duplicates for 0:29 - 0:45 (2 out of 2 results)

1. Start: 29 End: 45

2. Start: 35 End: 45

Fig. 11.21 Near duplicates for segments

available after some seconds and all analysis processes, except Logo detection, are started in parallel. The Progress monitor, which can be activated by clicking on the green cogwheel, shows the analysis state of the following processes:

- The **Video analysis** covers the generation of shots/sub-shots and keyframes. This step is performed sequentially for all users working with the Verification App at the same time. If several videos are analyzed in parallel by different users, they are enqueued. Each user can identify its current queue position in the Progress Monitor.
- The **Logo detection** is always performed after successful completion of the video analysis.
- The **Contextual analysis** begins with getting metadata and then gathers related social media comments. If a video has a lot of tweets and retweets the processing can take quite long, independently of the video length (sometimes up to 30 min).

- The **Near-duplicate detection** is processed for the whole video as well as on parts in a three-step process: first near duplicates are searched with a similarity factor or 0.8. If no or only one video is found, the search is repeated with a factor of 0.7, and then with 0.6 if still no video is found. After that, no more near-duplicate search is triggered and in that case it might happen that the near-duplicate search does not return any results.
- The **Rights checking** of the information about the source and copyright conditions.

The results of the verification services are displayed already during the analysis process and can be utilized immediately by the user.

11.5.5 Discussion of Strengths and Limitations of the InVID Tools

The structured visualization of shots, sub-shots, and keyframes gives the user a good overview about the content of the video. It enables to identify and focus exactly on a video segment of interest, which is in our example the sub-shot where the pope makes the trick. The analysis features NDS, reverse image search, and forensic of the Verification App are designed for an employment on sub-shots and frames, which allows to generate exactly the needed analysis results as fast and resource preserving as possible. The NDS is a real innovation of the InVID project, since none of the available search engines can offer an NDS for videos. The validation during the project has shown that the NDS algorithms already work very well. However, at present the quality of the results can be limited, since the search space only includes videos gathered by searches based on textual terms derived from the focused video.

Our experience has shown strong results from the reverse image search of the established search engines, which have been improved during the last years, also for the search with cutouts or mirrored images. In many cases, it is helpful to try different search engines since, e.g., for videos from Asia or Africa the reverse image search results from Yandex (Russia) or Baidu (China) are often better than from Google or Bing. The image forensic needs training for the users according to the Reveal Tutorial,[40] which contains several examples of how the Reveal tool enables to recognize critical manipulations. The forensic for videos is still in an experimental stage. Based on the explanations of the tooltips from the InVID consortium partner ExoMakina, the video forensic can give hints about irregularities that the user can follow. However, a clear methodology for the detection of patterns that indicate possible manipulations has still to be worked out. And finally, the provision of notes along the video timeline about analysis results enables a collaborative verification by distributed user groups.

---

[40]http://reveal-mklab.iti.gr/reveal/index.html?tour=start.

11.6   Conclusions and Future Work

The current state of the InVID Video Verification Service Platform including the Verification App provides a good foundation for the semi-automatic validation of videos, as has been testified through several user evaluations.[41] To further improve the InVID toolchain, we have identified the following potential:

- Further verification services: Additional analysis features could be integrated, such as extraction and analysis of the audio track, including a speech-to-text recognition and translation, or an OCR analysis of keyframes which contains text, or named-entity recognition based on the video description as well as on the audio analysis. Furthermore, it would also be interesting to include tools for audio forensic, face detection, and identification of deep fakes.
- Very interesting would be the addition of automatic or semi-automatic services which calculate a grade or range of falseness based on each aspect, whether it is the supposed time and location, the content, the source, or further aspects about the video. However, this will be subject to future research and development of AI-based approaches.
- Addition of tools: At the user interface, a lot of more tools can be integrated that could provide geographical data, weather data for the supposed time and location, or statistical and sociological data.

Reference

1. Thomsen J, Sarioglu A, Fricke R (2016) The linkedtv platform -towards a reactive linked media management system. In: Joint Proceedings of the 4th international workshop on linked media and the 3rd developers Hackshop co-located with the 13th extended semantic web conference ESWC 2016, Heraklion, Crete, Greece, 30 May 2016. http://ceur-ws.org/Vol-1615/limePaper2.pdf

---

[41] https://www.invid-project.eu/wp-content/uploads/2016/01016/01/InVID, D7.2.

Part IV
Concluding Remarks

Chapter 12
Disinformation: The Force of Falsity

Denis Teyssou

Abstract This final chapter borrows the concept of *force of falsity* from the famous Italian semiotician and novelist Umberto Eco to describe how manipulated information remains visible and accessible despite efforts to debunk it. In particular, search engine indexes are getting confused by *disinformation* and they too often fail to retrieve the authentic piece of content, the one which is neither manipulated nor decontextualized.

12.1 The Force of Falsity

In a lecture given at the University of Bologna in the mid-nineties, entitled "The force of falsity" and included later in his book "Serendipities",[1] Italian semiotician Umberto Eco argued that false tales, "as narratives, seemed plausible, more than everyday or historical reality, which is far more complex and less credible. The (false, Ed.) stories seemed to explain something that was otherwise hard to understand".

And he added: "False tales are, first of all, tales, and tales, like myths, are always persuasive". A quarter of century after, the famous novelist could have added—if he had not passed away in February 2016—that digital tales are digital and therefore as such can be crawled, indexed, stored, modified, cut, sliced, copied, pasted, remixed, tampered, decontextualized, and reused for any purpose.

During the *CrossCheck*[2] operation on the 2017 French presidential election, one of the debunked stories was a viral video of a man presented on social networks as a migrant assaulting nurses in a French hospital (Fig. 12.1).

---

[1]Eco, U. Serendipities, Language and Lunacy. New York, Columbia University Press. 1998.
[2]https://crosscheck.firstdraftnews.org/france-en/faq/.

D. Teyssou (✉)
Agence France-Presse, Paris, France
e-mail: denis.teyssou@afp.com

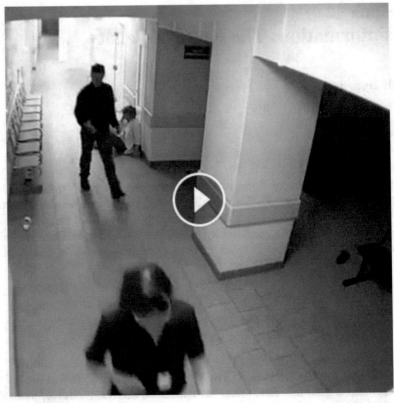

15,272,095 Views

Sos Racisme- anti-blanc   👍 Like Page
18 March at 19:34 · 🌐

on les soigne et ils en sont reconnaissant , la preuve ....mais
voila ce que les médias vous cachent !!! --------> une autre vidéo pour vous faire
découvrir la france cliquez sur ce lien suivant,---->
https://www.facebook.com/176360929501068/videos/246385459165281/

See Translation

Fig. 12.1 Screenshot of the fake migrant video shared on Facebook on March 18, 2017

The video was disgusting, producing emotional repulsion. "Here is what the media is hiding from you" could be read in the first caption. Later copies took the opportunity to launch a campaign against universal medical care.

But that so-called migrant was in fact a Russian citizen in a Novgorod (Russia) hospital, drunk according to the local press and caught 1 month before by a monitoring camera. The story was reported by several Russian media outlets.

An image similarity search on keyframes was enough to understand that this violent act was used out of context to spread an insidious xenophobic campaign, with millions of views on Facebook. The original video was only slightly cropped and its resolution was downgraded, as often, to make it more difficult to authenticate.

Copies of the same video were used again and again in the following days and weeks at least in Italy, Spain, South America, Belgium, Turkey, then France again, always alleging it was a migrant attacking local hospital staff members, triggering several millions views again and more debunks.

> *CrossCheck* was the first of a series of collaborative journalism projects bringing together newsrooms across France and beyond to accurately report false, misleading and confusing claims (stories, comments, images and videos about candidates, political parties and all other election-related issues) that circulated online during the French presidential election campaign in 2017.
>
> Organized under the umbrella of US nonprofit First Draft News and funded by Google News Lab to provide technical, administrative, and education support, CrossCheck aimed to provide the public with the necessary information to form their own conclusions.
>
> The author of this text participated in the CrossCheck France operation both as AFP staff member and as InVID project partner. This experience was crucial for InVID consortium to decide to release publicly the InVID Verification Plugin (see Chap. 9).

12.2 The Persistence of Falsity

Although the previous fake migrant video example has only reached the first of the five stages of election meddling proposed in 2017 by Finnish political science researcher Mika Aaltola,[3] it shows the level of insidious manipulation that circulates with impunity on social networks, fostering racism and extremism, during and beyond election campaigns.

---

[3]"Using disinformation to amplify suspicions and divisions" in Aaltola, M. Democracys Eleventh Hour: Safeguarding Democratic Elections Against Cyber-Enabled Autocratic Meddling, FIIA Briefing Paper 226, November 2017. Available at https://www.fiia.fi/sv/publikation/democracys-eleventh-hour?read (retrieved on 10/30/2018).

As French researcher in international and strategic affairs François-Bernard Huyghes[4] pointed out about micro-targeting of voters following the Cambridge Analytica scandal: "the goal is to make (the voter's) political choice appear to be spontaneous: I believe A, therefore I receive a message telling me that candidate Y thinks so as well. According to this model, we have gone from a strategy of mass political persuasion dumped by the media, to targeted soliciting tailored to our deepest wishes."

This is the goal of xenophobic online information manipulation: create a climate of fear, suspicion, distrust to prepare the voters' minds to pay attention, consider, and finally choose extremist or populist political offers promising to "solve" the migration crisis.

The above example is far from being isolated. A lot of information manipulation is linked to the world migration crisis caused by poverty, mass unemployment, wars, and global warming consequences.

In August 2018, another fake migrant video went viral in the Czech Republic, then in Western Europe and North America. It purported to show a television crew staging migrants drowning on a beach in Crete, Greece. AFP Factcheck debunked that disinformation and found two members of the incriminated crew: they were actually shooting a documentary about the 1922 Greek exodus from Asia Minor (Fig. 12.2).

Fig. 12.2 Screenshot of AFP Factcheck blog available at https://factcheck.afp.com/no-not-video-journalists-staging-migrants-drowning

---

[4]Huyghes, F-B, "Que changent les fake news?" La Revue internationale et stratégique, 110, 2018/2, pp. 83-84. Translated into English in Jeangène Vilmer, J. B. Escorcia, A. Guillaume, M. Herrera, J. Information Manipulation: A Challenge for Our Democracies, report by the Policy Planning Staff (CAPS) of the Ministry for Europe and Foreign Affairs and the Institute for Strategic Research (IRSEM) of the Ministry for the Armed Forces, Paris, August 2018. Available at https://www.diplomatie.gouv.fr/IMG/pdf/information_manipulation_rvb_cle838736.pdf (last retrieved on 11/3/2018).

The filming of the documentary was recorded with a smartphone by a Czech tourist on scene and that footage was reused to invent a conspiracy theory accusing the media of manipulating public opinion about the arrival of migrants' on the European coastline. Across YouTube, Facebook, and Twitter that video was watched by 1.2 millions viewers, according to an AFP count, before the real context could be established.

Other recent examples include the use of a video micro-fragment taken out of context, saying "we need migration" to target European parliamentarian and former Belgium Prime minister Guy Verhofstadt in an anti-migration video shared by the Hungarian government spokesman Zoltan Kovacs[5] and a 2017 video of an incident in a veterinary clinic in Kuwait being reused 1 year later and shared 40,000 times on Facebook in less than a month to allegedly depicts a Saudi man spitting on and hitting a woman presented as a London hospital receptionist.[6]

12.3   The Search Engines Confusion

The proliferation of those information disorders has an impact on search engines indexes as the original piece of information, often decontextualized, becomes more difficult to find and authenticate. Even the top world search engine, Google, is getting confused by the so-called "fake news". Searching for image similarity on a keyframe of the Russian video given as first example in this chapter, often triggers a wrong assumption on Google images such as: "French nurse assaulted by a migrant" (see Fig. 12.3) although the search engine also retrieves several websites presenting the debunking.

Such results on images contribute to the persistence of disinformation even if the list of results also presents several websites with the correct information to the reader. Nevertheless, even debunked, fake images, and videos can always be brought back to the surface on social networks. Previous and decontextualized videos of earthquakes, storms, floods, hurricanes, accidents, tsunamis, assaults, blasts, and terror attacks usually come back to light during new corresponding breaking news events, damaging the reputation of the media companies which are broadcasting those fakes without verification. Even video keyframes are also used to create fake images. A famous example is the so-called green picture of Osama bin Laden's death on May 2, 2011 (Fig. 12.4).

---

[5]https://factcheck.afp.com/clip-guy-verhofstadt-saying-europe-needs-migration-has-been-taken-out-context-hungarian-government (last retrieved on 10/30/2018).

[6]https://factcheck.afp.com/no-it-not-video-saudi-assaulting-london-hospital-receptionist   (last retrieved on 10/30/2018).

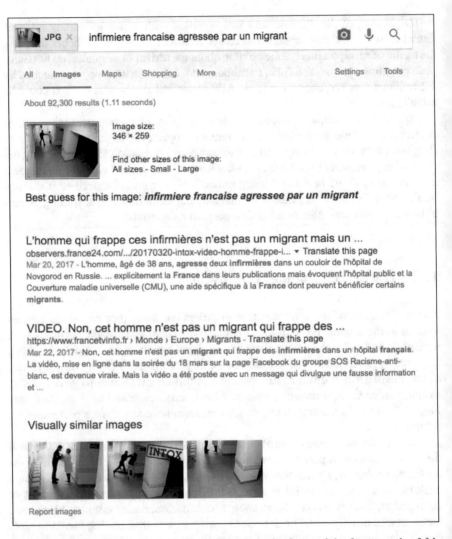

Fig. 12.3 Screenshot of an image similarity search on a keyframe of the first example of fake migrant video

An experiment undertaken during the InVID project showed that this particular image has a 89, 29% similarity with the following keyframe of Ridley Scott's movie Black Hawk Down (Fig. 12.5).

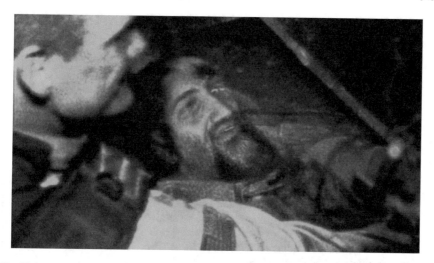

Fig. 12.4 Screenshot of the "green picture" of Osama bin Laden's death: a well-known tampered keyframe

Fig. 12.5 Screenshot of a keyframe of Ridley Scott's movie Black Hawk Down most similar to Osama bin Laden's "green picture"

   Despite this being known since 2011, searching for this keyframe in Google still triggers again a wrong assumption: dead bin Laden, bin Laden corpse, or bin Laden death photo real (Fig. 12.6).

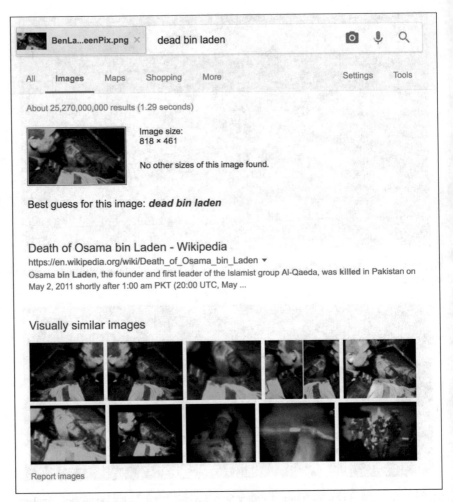

Fig. 12.6 Screenshot of a similarity search on Google images of Osama bin Laden's "green picture" (last retrieved on 11/15/2018)

12.4 A Provisional Conclusion

How can we avoid the proliferation of fake videos and stop them spreading over and over again despite being debunked? As Umberto Eco outlined in his "force of falsity" chapter: "although instruments, whether empirical or conjectural, exist to prove that some object is false, every decision in the matter presupposes the existence of an original, authentic and true, to which the fake is compared. The truly genuine problem thus does not consist of proving something false but in proving that the authentic object is authentic."

Building an authoritative database of known fakes proving the similarity with authentic videos or keyframes could help to enable faster debunking. It would help journalists and fact-checkers save time and avoid debunking the same content over and again, from one country to another, or from one language to another. It could also prevent search engines from adding to the confusion by relentlessly repeating information disorders, ruining their attempt to extract meaningful knowledge from video files and keyframes, through machine learning techniques.

Index

© Springer Nature Switzerland AG 2019
V. Mezaris et al. (eds.), *Video Verification in the Fake News Era*,
https://doi.org/10.1007/978-3-030-26752-0